Judgment and Salvation

"The Scriptures often refer to the Genesis flood as a great catastrophe and a great act of judgment. But in this book Dustin Burlet offers his readers hope by looking at the other side of the story. God didn't totally destroy the world. He preserved it and set his creation purpose going again. And the story is shaped so as to persuade its readers to accept such a hopeful worldview. So readers of Genesis and readers of Burlet's book, be encouraged!"

—**JOHN GOLDINGAY**, Fuller Theological Seminary

"The notion of divine judgment in the Old Testament is getting a lot of bad press these days. The flood narrative, which describes God as nearly destroying all of humanity is often viewed as incompatible with the revelation of God in Jesus Christ. But as Dustin Burlet skillfully demonstrates, the flood story was in fact written to teach the wonderful and surprising truth that the God of the Bible loves humanity and is constantly at work to redeem it."

—**PIERRE GILBERT**, Canadian Mennonite University

"Interpreting biblical narratives is always challenging for often popular perceptions are misleading. Dr. Burlet's detailed and informed analysis of the flood narrative in Genesis offers a helpful corrective, highlighting how the theme of divine salvation has not received sufficient attention. His analysis of the story using 'rhetoric as persuasion' casts fresh light on this important biblical narrative, revealing how it is a story about salvation as much as judgment."

—**T. DESMOND ALEXANDER**, Union Theological College

"In my judgment, Dustin Burlet has succeeded admirably in demonstrating beyond question that the intent of the author(s) in this passage is not primarily on God's annihilating judgment of humanity and the rest of his creation; rather, the primary emphasis is on everything Yahweh did to preserve the life of lost humanity and his spoiled creation, humanity's addiction to violent living notwithstanding. Thank you, Dustin."

—**VICTOR P. HAMILTON**, Asbury University, emeritus

"A superficial reading of the Noahic flood narrative in Genesis 6–9 too often results in the reader coming away from the text with an overwhelming sense of doom and gloom. However, by examining the narrative with some of the tools of rhetorical analysis, Dustin Burlet identifies the dominance of the theme of salvation. The text represents an aspect of the Hebrew worldview, and the lessons learned from it can contribute significant elements to a Christian worldview in our own day."

—**WILLIAM D. BARRICK**, The Master's Seminary, emeritus

"Dustin Burlet's study makes an interesting and significant contribution to scholarship and to the church. Burlet finds that the judgment motif is not the dominant concern of the author, as it often portrayed. It is encircled by the deliverance message with its focus on God as the all-powerful, just, and loving God whose creation purposes for humanity and creatures will not be thwarted by any human travail or moral failure."

—**KENNETH MATTHEWS**, Beeson Divinity School

"What is the biblical flood story there to *do* to us and for us? In this work, Dustin Burlet has advanced our ability to think about the question—both in developing a sound methodology and in carefully examining the biblical text itself. Even in those places I might judge differently, I found myself learning and enriched. I happily commend this book to you, and I am sure you will find it worth your time and thought."

—**C. JOHN COLLINS**, Covenant Theological Seminary

Judgment and Salvation

A Rhetorical-Critical Reading of
Noah's Flood in Genesis

DUSTIN G. BURLET

Foreword by August H. Konkel

☙PICKWICK *Publications* · Eugene, Oregon

JUDGMENT AND SALVATION
A Rhetorical-Critical Reading of Noah's Flood in Genesis

Copyright © 2022 Dustin G. Burlet. All rights reserved. Except for brief quotations in critical publications or reviews, no part of this book may be reproduced in any manner without prior written permission from the publisher. Write: Permissions, Wipf and Stock Publishers, 199 W. 8th Ave., Suite 3, Eugene, OR 97401.

Pickwick Publications
An Imprint of Wipf and Stock Publishers
199 W. 8th Ave., Suite 3
Eugene, OR 97401

www.wipfandstock.com

PAPERBACK ISBN: 978-1-6667-3672-4
HARDCOVER ISBN: 978-1-6667-9546-2
EBOOK ISBN: 978-1-6667-9547-9

Cataloguing-in-Publication data:

Names: Burlet, Dustin G., author. | Konkel, August H., foreword.

Title: Judgment and salvation : a rhetorical-critical reading of Noah's flood in Genesis / Dustin G. Burlet.

Description: Eugene, OR: Pickwick Publications, 2022. | Includes bibliographical references and indexes.

Identifiers: ISBN: 978-1-6667-3672-4 (paperback). | ISBN: 978-1-6667-9546-2 (hardcover). | ISBN: 978-1-6667-9547-9 (ebook).

Subjects: LSCH: Bible. Genesis VI–IX—Criticism, interpretation, etc. | Noah (Biblical figure). | Noah's ark. | Deluge. | Rhetoric in the Bible.

Classification: BS658 B96 2022 (print). | BS658 (ebook).

10/20/22

Permissions

Figure 1 "Communication Situation of a Narrative Text" reprinted from *Story and Discourse: Narrative Structure in Fiction and Film*, by Seymour Chatman. Copyright © 1978 by Cornell University. Used by permission of the publisher, Cornell University Press.

Figure 2 "The Structure of Narrative" published with revisions in *Old Testament Narrative: A Guide to Interpretation*. © 2009 Jerome T. Walsh. Used by permission.

Diagram from *Interpreting the Bible: A Popular Introduction to Biblical Hermeneutics*, by Terence J. Keegan, OP, copyright ©1985, published by Paulist Press, Inc., New York/Mahwah, NJ. www.paulistpress.com. Used with permission.

Figure 3 "Layers of Audience" reprinted from *The Persuasive Portrayal of David and Solomon in Chronicles: A Rhetorical Analysis of the Speeches and Prayers in the David-Solomon Narrative*, by Suk-il Ahn. Used by permission of Wipf and Stock Publishers.

Figure 4 "The Structure of Plot in Biblical Narrative" taken from *An Introduction to the Old Testament* by Tremper Longman III and Raymond B. Dillard. Copyright © 1994, 2006 by Tremper Longman III and Raymond B. Dillard. Used by permission of Zondervan.

Figure 5 "Assyrian Lamassu" by Rebecca H. Burlet. Permission granted to reproduce from artist.

Figure 6 "The Hebrew Conception of the World" copyright Denis O. Lamoureux. Permission granted to reproduce.

The Common English Bible (CEB) © Copyright 2011 COMMON ENGLISH BIBLE. All rights reserved. Used by permission. (www.CommonEnglishBible.com).

Christian Standard Bible®, Copyright © 2017 by Holman Bible Publishers. Used by permission. Christian Standard Bible® and CSB® are federally registered trademarks of Holman Bible Publishers.

The Holy Bible, English Standard Version®, copyright © 2001 by Crossway, a publishing ministry of Good News Publishers. Used by permission. All rights reserved.

GOOD NEWS BIBLE © 1994 published by the Bible Societies/HarperCollins Publishers Ltd UK, Good News Bible© American Bible Society 1966, 1971, 1976, 1992. Used with permission.

Holman Christian Standard Bible®, Used by Permission HCSB ©1999, 2000, 2002, 2003, 2009 Holman Bible Publishers.

Tanakh: The New JPS Translation according to the Traditional Hebrew Text. Copyright © 1985, 1999 by The Jewish Publication Society with the permission of the publisher.

The Lexham English Septuagint. Bellingham, Washington: Lexham, 2019. Used by permission of the publisher.

New American Bible, revised edition © 2010, 1991, 1986, 1970 Confraternity of Christian Doctrine, Washington, D.C. and are used by permission of the copyright owner.

(NASB®) New American Standard Bible®, Copyright © 1960, 1971, 1977, 1995, 2020 by The Lockman Foundation. Used by permission. All rights reserved. www.lockman.org/.

New Century Version®. Copyright © 2005 by Thomas Nelson. Used by permission. All rights reserved.

New English Bible, copyright © Cambridge University Press and Oxford University Press, 1961, 1970. All rights reserved.

Pietersma, Albert, and Benjamin G. Wright III, eds. *A New English Translation of the Septuagint: And the Other Greek Translations Traditionally Included under That Title.* New York: Oxford University Press, 2007. Online: http://ccat.sas.upenn.edu/nets/edition/.

New International Version (1984) HOLY BIBLE, NEW INTERNATIONAL VERSION®. NIV®. Copyright © 1973, 1978, 1984 by International Bible Society. Used by permission of Zondervan. All rights reserved worldwide.

New International Version Holy Bible, NEW INTERNATIONAL VERSION®, NIV® Copyright © 1973, 1978, 1984, 2011 by Biblica, Inc.® Used by permission. All rights reserved worldwide.

New Jerusalem Bible. Copyright © 1985 by Darton, Longman & Todd and Doubleday, a division of Random House. All rights reserved.

New King James Version®. Copyright © 1982 by Thomas Nelson. Used by permission. All rights reserved.

Holy Bible, New Living Translation, copyright ©1996, 2004, 2015 by Tyndale House Foundation. Used by permission of Tyndale House Publishers, Carol Stream, Illinois 60188. All rights reserved.

New Revised Standard Version copyright © 1989 National Council of the Churches of Christ in the United States of America. Used by permission. All rights reserved worldwide.

Revised English Bible Revised English Bible, copyright © Cambridge University Press and Oxford University Press, 1989. All rights reserved.

Revised Standard Version © 1946, 1952, and 1971 National Council of the Churches of Christ in the United States of America. Used by permission. All rights reserved worldwide.

Today's New International Version Copyright © 2001, 2005 by International Bible Society. Used by permission of Zondervan. All rights reserved worldwide.

I dedicate this volume to Bernie and Bernice Doan
in memory of Eugene Dziubek
Psalm 16:6

"The Lord sat enthroned at the Flood;
The Lord sits enthroned, king forever."

—Psalm 29:10 (JPS)

Contents

List of Illustrations | xv
Foreword by August H. Konkel | xvii
Preface | xxi
Acknowledgments | xxv
Introduction | xxvii
Abbreviations | xxxi

1 **Genesis and Noah's Flood** | 1
   The Genesis Flood Narrative: General Orientation | 1
   The Genesis Flood Narrative: Judgment and Salvation | 2
   The Genesis Flood Narrative: Cosmic
      Order through Covenant | 4
   Rhetorical Criticism: General Orientation | 7
   Rhetorical Criticism: Contemporary Scholarship | 8
   General Orientation to Presenting Issue(s) about
      the Genesis Flood Narrative | 11
   Diachronic (Source-Critical) Approaches—
      Concluding Thoughts | 25
   Synchronic Approaches—Concluding Thoughts | 26
   Conclusion | 28

2   **Methodology: Rhetorical Criticism** | 30
    Rhetorical Criticism—Introduction | 30
    Rhetoric as "The Art of Composition" | 32
    Rhetoric as "The Art of Persuasion" | 33
    A Rhetorical-Critical Model For Studying
        Hebrew Narrative | 36
    Conclusion | 82

3   **The Corruption of Humanity: Hope and
    Covenant** (Gen 6:5–8 // 9–22) | 84
    Introduction | 84
    Step One: Determining the Rhetorical Units | 85
    Step Two: Determining the Rhetorical Situation | 92
    Step Three: Determining the Rhetorical Strategy | 95
    Step Four: Determining the Rhetorical Effectiveness | 124
    Conclusion | 125

4   **It Cometh!** (Genesis 7:1–24) | 128
    Introduction | 128
    Step One: Determining the Rhetorical Units | 128
    Step Two: Determining the Rhetorical Situation | 135
    Step Three: Determining the Rhetorical Strategy | 138
    Step Four: Determining the Rhetorical Effectiveness | 155
    Conclusion | 156

5   **After the Rain: The Flood Subsides** (Gen 8:1–22) | 159
    Introduction | 159
    Step One: Determining the Rhetorical Units | 160
    Step Two: Determining the Rhetorical Situation | 164
    Step Three: Determining the Rhetorical Strategy | 167
    Step Four: Determining the Rhetorical Effectiveness | 184
    Conclusion | 186

6   **The Covenant: Conditions and Assurance** (Genesis 9:1–17) | 188
    Introduction | 188
    Step One: Determining the Rhetorical Units | 189
    Step Two: Determining the Rhetorical Situation | 195
    Step Three: Determining the Rhetorical Strategy | 197
    Step Four: Determining the Rhetorical Effectiveness | 209

7   **Conclusion** | 212
    Introduction | 212
    The Rhetorical-Critical Model | 213
    Elements of Persuasion in the Noachian Deluge Narrative | 214
    Summary of Results: Universalistic Language
        (Judgment and Salvation) | 215
    Further Work | 216

Bibliography | 219
Subject Index | 249
Author Index | 251
Ancient Document Index | 259

List of Illustrations

TABLES

1. The Covenant of the Noachian Deluge Narrative | 5
2. The Palistrophe of Genesis 6:5–8 | 12
3. Genesis 6:5b and Genesis 8:21b | 13
4. The Toledoth Structure of Genesis | 28
5. Major Features of Classical Rhetoric | 35
6. Beginning and Ending Markers | 41
7. Exigence and Audience | 47

FIGURES

1. Communication Situation of a Narrative Text | 51
2. The Structure of Narrative | 53
3. Layers of Audience | 55
4. Ancient Hebrew Conception of The Universe | 69
5. The Structure of Biblical Narrative | 74
6. Assyrian Lamassu | 77

Foreword

CREATION AND FLOOD NARRATIVES were foundational to the function and order of ancient societies. Lambert has reconstructed "The Babylonian Epic of Creation" from 86 tablets and fragments in the Assyrian script alone, along with numerous other texts relating to the chief god Marduk, 17 other related stories, plus other related materials.[1] This tome shows not only the supreme importance of the creation account in Mesopotamian ideology, but provides a literary context for understanding the Hebrew account of Genesis, which by contrast was preserved through continuous transcription as a living document. Related texts like that of the Gilgamesh Epic include an account of a flood that nearly destroys the human race, which is parallel in all its main features to the biblical narrative of Noah. The Mesopotamian stories evolved in the reality of society they intended to establish. The literary similarities of the Hebrew narrative are a cultural necessity, but the *Weltanschauung* is of an entirely different order.

The function of cosmology in ancient societies like that of Israel and Mesopotamia was to address fundamental questions that also grip all advanced societies. As expressed by Speiser in his analysis of biblical history, there are two main issues: "One is the relation of the individual to society. The other is the alignment of both individual and society to nature and

---

1. Lambert, *Babylonian Creation Myths*.

the universe."² The theology of the Scriptures is that earth and humans are the creation of one designated as holy, a fundamental declaration that this creator is outside the boundaries of space and time. Such a creator could never be discovered by those bounded by space and time. Their declarations of cosmology were known through revelation, the creator making himself known to the created person. Humans therefore have a unique relation to the world around them and within their communities.

Humans, designated as 'adam in the Hebrew Bible, are dependent on the holy, the source of all life. Rebellion against the holy took place in claiming a particular knowledge, described by the merism of "good and evil." This could be either a claim to all knowledge or the power to know what is good, which also requires omniscience. This rebellion led not only to alienation from the source of life, but to an unrelenting violence, in which Lamech declares vengeance was to be achieved seventy and seven times (Gen 4:24). The creation account then begins again with God creating 'adam as male and female, who now beget children in their image. Lamech seeks consolation from the pain (`itstsabon) that has resulted from the rebellion (Gen. 3:16, 17; 5:29) and names his son Noah. While Noah finds grace in the eyes of the Lord, the rest of humanity can only be described as "every thought and intent being evil continually" (Gen 6:5). At this point Yahweh engages his plan to begin again with Noah and his three sons. However, humanity after the flood remains unchanged from what it was before the flood (Gen 8:21). What then is the function of the flood in the ideology concerning the human race? Burlet's 2019 dissertation (McMaster Divinity College) titled "Cosmos to Chaos-Chaos to Covenant," revised for publication as *Judgment and Salvation*, probes the narrative for the answer to this fundamental question, asserting that the flood has a *redemptive* function in the biblical account of origins.

Argument in narrative is developed by means of rhetoric. This thorough study of the flood narrative employs a rhetorical analysis to each unit of the flood story to show how each part of the story contributes to the argument of the whole in addressing an altered relationship of humans under life giving power of Yahweh. 'adam continues to represent Yahweh and they do not self destruct in hostile relationships, though their lack of knowledge of the good remains unaltered. The flood story is a critical part of the answer of the Hebrew Bible to the two fundamental issues that grip modern societies just as much as the ancient ones.

---

2. Speiser, "The Biblical Idea of History in Its Common Near Eastern Setting," 2.

Moderns may think that they have a superior understanding of humanity and its relationship to the universe, so therefore a premise on which to be able to learn to live with each other. These achievements are indeed sophisticated and impressive, especially to those that have developed them, but the reality of the results is meagre. Such fundamental elements as time, space, and gravity can only be described in relative terms. The situation remains the way Hawking described it over three decades ago: "We already know the laws that govern the behavior of matter under all but the most extreme conditions . . . laws that underlie all of chemistry and biology. Yet we have certainly not reduced these subjects to the status of solved problems; we have, as yet, had little success in predicting human behavior from mathematical equations!"[3] In his sober review, Hawking rightly questions whether such an achievement can be conceived as possible. The current search for black holes may add another piece of evidence to the theory of relativity, but that really does not bring humanity any closer to knowing their role in the universe, nor to avoiding their tendency to self-destruction.

The research of this book should be of interest to anyone seriously wishing to understand the two fundamental questions of human life. The Hebrew claim to another kind of knowledge should not be simply dismissed, as there is plenty of evidence to support their concepts of the universe and human life. Understanding the rhetoric of the flood story as shown in this study will provide a sober re-evaluation of the real human condition. It was not perpetuated to describe a history of the past but to describe a reality of the present. It cannot be denied that present reality conforms precisely to the *Weltanschauung* of this ancient narrative.

August H. Konkel
McMaster Divinity College
Hamilton, Ontario, 2022

---

3. Hawking, *A Brief History of Time*, 168.

Preface

THE ORIGINS OF THIS book stem from my first teaching post located at Peace River Bible Institute (Sexsmith, AB, Canada). In the providence of God, the academic dean offered me the chance to teach an elective course engaging the topic of science, creation, and the Bible (history, literature, and theology) with respect to the first eleven chapters of the book of Genesis. I was intrigued. Unbeknownst to me at the time, a number of my students already had some exposure to the topic through the teaching of Denis O. Lamoureux. Lamaouruex became one of my primary academic conversation partners via his books, online media presence, and students. I also found the works of C. John Collins, Tremper Longman III, and John H. Walton to be extremely profitable to me.

These esteemed individuals, however, did not constitute my first exposure to the topic. For most of my life, I have been involved in the ministry of Christian camping, primarily through Circle Square Ranch (Halkirk, AB, Canada). Located in a world of multi-hued coulees and wind-sculpted hoodoos, spanning east from Drumheller to the Saskatchewan border and south to the United States, this region is known as the Canadian Badlands. It is also home to the largest deposits of dinosaur bones in the world.[1] Interestingly, numerous fossilized clams may be

---

1. See https://www.albertaparks.ca/albertaparksca/visit-our-parks/road-trips/canadian-badlands/. For a unique perspective on the Royal Tyrrell Museum, written by a Christian educator whose specialization concerns the intersection of science, faith, and culture, see Ray, *Baby Dinosaurs on the Ark*, 31–33.

found on the home quarter section of the ranch embedded in ironstone material; in every instance, the valves of the clams are closed, seemingly indicating that the process of fossilization must have occurred in a very short period of time through a catastrophic burial process.[2] Needless to say, these personal experiences were highly formative to my faith and understanding of Scripture.

As my instructing journey evolved it became clear to me the topic of Noah's Flood would not let me go. After my fourth year of full-time teaching at PRBI, my family and I left the Peace region of AB for me to pursue my PhD (Old Testament) at McMaster Divinity College (Hamilton, ON, Canada). Naturally, the focus of my dissertation was going to be the Noachian deluge narrative but I was uncertain what method I should leverage to study it. Nijay K. Gupta relates, "The magic is [often] in the method."[3] I soon found my love of rhetorical criticism (rhetoric as persuasion) through the influence and teaching of Stanley E. Porter and Cynthia Long Westfall. Explained below, Gupta's insight how "commentaries can be very stimulating . . . not so much for what they say, but what is left unsaid" also helped to cement that choice.[4]

At one time during my PhD, I had the privilege of being a Graduate Assistant for Paul S. Evans. Through his course "From the Beginning: Reading the Book of Genesis" my paths crossed with Luke J. Janssen whose passion and expertise intersected a great deal with my own study. Janssen became another key conversation partner in my critical thinking on these topics.

The Canadian American Theological Association and the Evangelical Theological Society both provided me the forum for continued dialogue and engagement on Noah's Flood.

Prior to earning my terminal degree, I was invited on the Christian Leaders Trip (Canyon Ministries).[5] William D. Barrick, Jeremy Lyon, Terry Mortenson, Clayton Schultz, and John Whitmore were excellent hosts and stimulating conversation partners throughout the seven day, two-hundred mile journey traversing roughly two-thirds of the Grand

---

2. See McLean, et al., *Evidence for Creation*, 167.
3. Gupta, *Prepare, Succeed, Advance*, 52.
4. Gupta, *Prepare, Succeed, Advance*, 65–66. Italics removed.
5. https://www.canyonministries.org/clt/

Canyon. Scintillating cuisine, scenic beauty, and iconic activities and learning adventures made for a first-class trip.[6]

Having lectured now at a wide variety of educational facilities in the western Canadian provinces including Peace River Bible Institute (Sexsmith, AB), Eston College (Eston, SK), Providence Theological Seminary (Otterburne, MB), Canadian Mennonite University (Winnipeg, MB), and Millar Bible College (Winnipeg, MB), I have often wished and desired for less of a wedge between academia/scholarship and the Church—especially in evangelicalism.[7] Kenton L. Sparks maintains, "Christians of many persuasions will agree that critical scholarship has often had destructive effects when it is brought into the pulpits and classrooms."[8] In addition, "theological reflection and intellectual inquiry" are sometimes permitted to "go no deeper than the capacities of the average person in the church pew."[9] Regrettably, this can often mean "uncomfortable complexity is flattened out," some "issues are resolved by a simple choice of alternatives," and, at times, "fine distinctions are lost in the ideological battle. In these camps there is little fear that further reduction of content for popular consumption could at times involve downright falsification."[10] Lastly, "breadth of audience" can sometimes be "substituted for depth of insight, and the pursuit of truth" can "become hostage to theological viewpoints that would fit nicely into child's Sunday school curriculum."[11] Of this I wish to have no part!

We must also avoid theological tribalism. Tremper Longman III puts it well.

> As pastors and scholars who want to understand the Bible's message as best we can, we have to work hard to address difficult biblical issues. As we do, we should expose ourselves to a broad range of opinions, not just reading or listening to those who

---

6. Details about these aspects of my academic journey are available through the GREAT Conversations Podcast, hosted by Calvin Smith titled "Genesis—From Every Angle." https://www.youtube.com/watch?v=TuV2DV8pBgM

7. A thorough, up-to-date exposé of the evangelical movement may be found in Bebbington, *The Evangelical Quadrilateral*. See also Bebbington, *Evangelicalism in Modern Britain*; Noll, *Scandal of the Evangelical Mind*.

8. Sparks, *God's Word in Human Words*, 359. See too Enns, "Reflections," 46. Cf. Vanhoozer, *First Theology*, 18.

9. Sparks, *God's Word in Human Words*, 366.

10. Hatch, "Christian Thinking," 91, quoted in Sparks, *God's Word in Human Words*, 366.

11. Sparks, *God's Word in Human Words*, 366.

are like us or who already agree with us... We can easily fall into a dangerous tribalism [in our work]. We write for, read, listen to, study only or predominantly with those who are in our [particular] 'tribe...'. The bottom line is that we need to avoid tribalism as well as the demonization of those with whom we disagree. Our research should be characterized by graceful and knowledgeable interaction with others.[12]

It is my hope and prayer this volume might serve to help bridge some of the above stated matters while also furthering the academic disciplines of rhetorical criticism and Genesis.

---

12. Longman, "Avoid Theological Tribalism—Read Broadly," 42. Cf. Walton, *Genesis*, 189. To belabor the point, "I believe some scholars work with the following, possibly subconscious, presupposition: God will forgive us if we are mean because the opposition is so obviously wrong and, after all, we are only defending the truth of the gospel. We often demonize the opposition and rationalize our lack of love because those on the other side are, of course, the enemies and are undermining God's truth and opposing his kingdom. Our defense of the truth, however, must never leave love behind. It is not an either-or dichotomy but a both-and proposition. It is possible both to stand firmly for the truth of God's Word and to have genuine love for those with whom we differ." Köstenberger, *Excellence*, 229.

Acknowledgments

STANLEY E. PORTER ASSERTS: "Academic publishing is at the heart of the advancement of learning in the intellectual world. Academic publishing provides the venue where the newest ideas are proposed and developed, and where scholars intellectually expose themselves to the scrutiny of their peers to see if their ideas can pass muster."[1] I am thankful I do not walk this path alone!

There are many who have assisted me in this publishing adventure. I would like to thank the students and team members of each of the academic institutions where I have had the privilege of sharing different aspects of this book in the classroom. I would also like to thank the fellows of the various theological associations I engage with for providing me the forum for continued dialogue and engagement on Noah's Flood. Their comments and feedback were much appreciated. August H. Konkel (my first advisor) and Mark J. Boda (my second advisor) are to be especially thanked for their effectual guidance and mentorship throughout my PhD endeavor and beyond. This book would never have seen the light of day apart from their continued support and encouragement. I would also like to extend my gratitude to Paul S. Evans (who chaired my defense) and Carol M. Kaminski for her comments and feedback as my PhD external examiner.

---

1. Porter, *Inking the Deal*, 1.

I also have immense gratitude for the many people who have read and engaged with the content of this manuscript (either in full or in part). These include Barry Bandstra, Rob Blazecka, Josh Chalmers, Brad Cowie, Mike Doerksen, David Fuller, Chris Loewen, Jason Pluim, Brett Surbey, and Rick Wadholm Jr. While I did not appropriate all of your comments this book is much the better for them. The sharp eyes of my primary editor, Joy Kaut, also kept me from many blunders. Thank you all very much!

Numerous pastors and various members of certain churches, such as the Paradise Valley Church of God, the Paradise Valley Gospel Hall, the Paradise Valley United Church, Sexsmith Grace Bible Fellowship, and People's Church Hamilton must go on record for their faithful financial and prayerful support as well as the opportunity to share different aspects of this book. Much thanks also to MacGregor EMC.

A special shout-out must also go to Josiah and Lisa Barton, the Brassington family, Les and Tina Derksen, Bernie and Bernice Doan, Brad and Barb Cowie, Oloyede Ade and Yemi Fatogun, Ryan Fenton, the Flint family, Andrew Gale, Jason Gayoway, Justin and Nicole Heslin, the Hoogstaad family, Yuya and Anna Inaba, Jacquie Lefebvre, Ben Mc-Gragh, Cory and Sierra Rotchford, Shawn Rotchford, Tony Sawler (and co.), Nicki Scott, Pat Shea, Alex Stewart, Brian Stothard, Bree and Leah Timmons, Juan Paulo Reyes Valderrama, Lyndon and Marlene Wall, Brad and Anita Wester, Will Whyte, and Justin and Hailey Worthington. One also acknowledges the many others who helped facilitate my success. While space forbids an exhaustive catalog you are by no means forgotten by me. Thank you all!

Immense gratitude must also be expressed to my extended family who came alongside me throughout this journey. Special mention here should also be made of Ron (and Shirley†) Craig as well as the Burlet, Deneschuk, Doerksen, Fehr, Friesen, Hagel, Klassen, Lorenz, Muñoz, Stirling, Tobin, and Viel families as well as some others not formally on record here. Of course, none of this would have been possible apart from the love and support of my in-laws, Jake and Emily Friesen, and my own mom and dad, Ray and Merle Burlet. Thank you very much!

I would also like to thank each member of my own family for their support. My children, Malachi (10), Ezra (8), and Daisha (6) warrant special mention as they deferred much fun time together so that their dad could work. Lastly, my beloved wife, Rebecca, deserves the highest praise and accolades for her unwavering support and unfailing, unconditional love. Thank you!

Introduction

WHAT FOLLOWS IS A brief orientation to *Judgment and Salvation: A Rhetorical-Critical Reading of Noah's Flood in Genesis*. The Flood of Genesis is often portrayed in the canon of Scripture as being an all-encompassing, catastrophic event which had the power to forever shape and change the world of that time (Matt 24:36–44; Luke 17:26–27; Heb 11:7; 1 Pet 3:20–21; 2 Pet 2:5, 3:6). By means of "violence" (חמס), humanity had the effect of "corrupting" (שחת) the "good" (טוב) earth God had created (see Gen 6:5–6, 12; cf. Gen 1:31). God thus proclaimed he would "destroy" (שחת) and "wipe" (מחה) it out along with "all life" (כל בשר) from the face of the earth (Gen 6:7, 11–13, 17; 7:4, 21–23). There is, however, both judgment and salvation in the Genesis Flood.

Noah found "favour" (חן) in the sight of the LORD (Gen 6:8). Covenanting with Noah, his sons, and all of creation, God preserved a remnant of humanity and all life on earth (Gen 6:18–21; 7:1–3, 7:7–9, 7:13–16; 8:16–22; 9:1–17). Given such, this book contends the text of the Noachian deluge narrative categorically underscores all God did to preserve life in spite of the disaster. That is to say, despite the picture of devastation the narrative depicts, the prominent emphasis of the text is on deliverance and redemption i.e., salvation, not judgment. The focus of the Genesis Flood is acutely bent towards God's salvific rather than punitive purposes.

The arc of salvation within the Flood narrative can be broken down into two main ideas. First, God's intention for creation is not thwarted and, secondly, God commits himself to his intentions of creation. His intention for creation can be stated as thus: the establishment of order via covenant showing the sanctity of human life and the upholding of all life. This involves, in particular, humanity as his image bearers, including the *lex talionis* (life for life) principle.

Though there is no shortage of scholarship about the book of Genesis (or Gen 1–11) in general, a lacuna exists concerning a methodologically rigorous analysis of the persuasive, rhetorical nature of the Noachian deluge narrative. This book seeks to remedy this short-coming through delineating the text's essential persuasive strategy—noting also its literary artistry—as it engages in a detailed reading of this specific portion of Scripture (Gen 6:5—9:17).

The book is divided into six chapters. Chapter 1 (introduction) provides a general orientation to the Genesis Flood account. This involves a summation of the prominent concerns relating to this study of Noah's Flood, namely the juxtaposition of humankind's inherent responsibility and the opportunity for a second chance. To be specific, this mostly involves the conciliatory disposition of the Deity (Post-Flood) and the inter-relationship of Gen 6:5–7 and Gen 8:20–22. These concerns are addressed through interaction with various diachronic and synchronic perspectives. Some engagement with ancient Near East flood myths is also present. Lastly, this chapter includes an introduction to rhetorical criticism.

Chapter 2 clarifies the primary method employed throughout the book; a modified form of George A. Kennedy's model of rhetorical criticism (rhetoric as persuasion). This particular rhetorical critical approach involves four main steps: (1) determining the rhetorical units, (2) determining the rhetorical situation, (3) determining the rhetorical strategy, and (4) determining the rhetorical effectiveness. A brief conclusion rounds off the analysis.

Using the above stated methodology, chapter 3 engages the text of Genesis 6. Chapters 4 through 6 work through the subsequent chapters of Gen 7–9. Chapter 7 (the conclusion) provides a summation of the book, clarifying comments concerning its distinctive contributions, and, lastly, some suggestions for further work that could also be done in the field.

To close, I wish to echo the words of Charles Halton, "May our God forgive us if this topic and even this book spur division in place of unity and strife instead of love."[1]

---

1. Halton, ed., *Genesis*, 163.

Abbreviations

AB	Anchor Bible
ABD	David Noel Freedman, ed. *Anchor Bible Dictionary*. 6 vols. New York: Doubleday, 1992
AT	author's translation
ASV	American Standard Version
AV	Authorized Version
BBE	Bible in Basic English
BBR	*Bulletin for Biblical Research*
BBRSup	Bulletin for Biblical Research, Supplements
BDB	Francis Brown, Samuel R. Driver, and Charles A. Briggs. *A Hebrew and English Lexicon of the Old Testament*. Oxford: Clarendon, 1907
BHRG	Christo H. J. Van der Merwe et al. *A Biblical Hebrew Reference Grammar*. 2nd ed. New York: Bloomsbury T. & T. Clark, 2017
BHS	Karl Elliger and Wilhelm Rudolph. *Biblia Hebraica Stuttgartensia*. Edited by A. Schenker. 5th rev. ed. Stuttgart: Deutsche Bibelgesellschaft, 1997

BHQ	Abraham Tal, ed. *Biblia Hebraica Quinta, Fascicle 1: Genesis*. BHQ 1. Stuttgart: Deutsche Bibelgesellschaft, 2015
BZAW	Beihefte zur Zeitschrift für die alttestamentliche Wissenschaft
CBQ	*Catholic Biblical Quarterly*
CEB	Common English Bible
CSB	Christian Standard Bible
COS	William W. Hallo, ed. *Context of Scripture*. 3 vols. Leiden: Brill, 1997–2002
DBI	Leland Ryken et al., eds. *Dictionary of Biblical Imagery*. Downers Grove, IL: IVP Academic, 1998
DCH	David J. A. Clines, ed. *The Dictionary of Classical Hebrew*. 9 vols. Sheffield: Sheffield Academic, 1993–2016
DG	J. C. L. Gibson. *Davidson's Introductory Hebrew Grammar: Syntax*. 4th ed. Edinburgh: T. & T. Clark, 1994
EncJud	C. Roth, C. and G. Wigoder, eds. *Encyclopedia Judaica*. 16 vols. Jerusalem: Keter, 1971–1972
ESV	English Standard Version
EVV	English Versions
GBHS	Bill T. Arnold and John H. Choi. *A Guide to Biblical Hebrew Syntax*. 2nd ed. New York: Cambridge University Press, 2018
GKC	Wilhelm Gesenius and E. Kautzsch. *Gesenius Hebrew Grammar*. 2nd ed. Translated by A. E. Cowley. Oxford: Clarendon, 1910
GNB	Good News Bible
HALOT	Ludwig Koehler et al. *The Hebrew and Aramaic Lexicon of the Old Testament*. Study Edition. Translated by M. E. J. Richardson. 2 vols. Leiden: Brill, 2001
HCSB	Holman Christian Standard Bible
HSM	Harvard Semitic Monographs
HUCA	*Hebrew Union College Annual*

IBHS	Bruce K. Waltke and M. O'Connor. *An Introduction to Biblical Hebrew Syntax*. Winona Lake, IN: Eisenbrauns, 1990
ISBE	Geoffrey W. Bromiley, ed. *The International Standard Bible Encyclopedia*. 4 vols. Rev. ed. Grand Rapids: Eerdmans, 1979–88.
JAOS	*Journal of the American Oriental Society*
JBL	*Journal of Biblical Literature*
JBQ	*Jewish Biblical Quarterly*
JETS	*Journal of the Evangelical Theological Society*
JM	Paul Joüon and Takamitsu Muraoka. *A Grammar of Biblical Hebrew*. Rev. ed. Subsidia Biblica 27. Rome: Pontifical Biblical Institute, 2006
Joüon	Paul Joüon and Takamitsu Muraoka. *A Grammar of Biblical Hebrew*. Rev. ed. Subsidia Biblica 27. Rome: Pontifical Biblical Institute, 2006
JPS	Jewish Publication Society
JSNTSup	Journal for the Study of the New Testament Supplement Series
JSOT	*Journal for the Study of the Old Testament*
JSOTSup	Journal for the Study of the Old Testament Supplement Series
KJV	King James Version
LES	Ken M. Penner, ed. *The Lexham English Septuagint*. Bellingham, WA: Lexham, 2019
LHBOTS	Library of Hebrew Bible / Old Testament Studies
LXX	The Septuagint/Old Greek (OG)
M	Masoretic Text as represented in *BHS* or *BHQ*
MSS	Manuscripts
MT	Masoretic Text as represented in *BHS* or *BHQ*
NAB	New American Bible
NASB	New American Standard Bible (1995 update)

NCV	New Century Version	
NEB	New English Bible	
NETS	Albert Pietersma and Benjamin G. Wright III, eds. *A New English Translation of the Septuagint: And the Other Greek Translations Traditionally Included under That Title.* New York: Oxford University Press, 2007. Online: http://ccat.sas.upenn.edu/nets/edition/	
NIB	Leander E. Keck, ed. *The New Interpreter's Bible*. 12 vols. Nashville, TN: Abingdon, 1994	
NICOT	The New International Commentary on the Old Testament	
NIDOTTE	William A. VanGemeren, ed. *New International Dictionary of Old Testament Theology and Exegesis.* 5 vols. Grand Rapids: Zondervan, 1997	
NIV 1984	New International Version (1984)	
NIV 2011	New International Version (2011)	
NJB	New Jerusalem Bible	
NJPS	New Jewish Publication Society	
NKJV	New King James Version	
NLT	New Living Translation	
NRSV	New Revised Standard Version	
OBT	Overtures to Biblical Theology	
OG	Old Greek/The Septuagint (LXX)	
OT	Old Testament	
REB	Revised English Bible	
RSV	Revised Standard Version	
SamPent	Samaritan Pentateuch	
SBL	Society of Biblical Literature	
SBLDS	Society of Biblical Literature Dissertations Series	
SBLSymS	Society of Biblical Literature Symposium Series	
Siphrut	Siphrut: Literature and Theology of the Hebrew Scriptures	

TDOT	G. Johannes Botterweck et al., eds. *Theological Dictionary of the Old Testament.* Translated by John T. Willis et al. 16 vols. Grand Rapids: Eerdmans, 1974–2018
TLOT	Ernest Jenni and Claus Westermann, eds. *Theological Lexicon of the Old Testament.* Translated by Mark E. Biddle. 3 vols. Peabody, MA: Hendrickson, 1997
TNIV	Today's New International Version
TWOT	R. L. Harris et al., eds., *Theological Wordbook of the Old Testament.* 2 vols. Chicago: IL: Moody, 1980
Vg	Vulgate
VT	*Vetus Testamentum*
VTSup	Vetus Testamentum Supplements
WTJ	*Westminster Theological Journal*
ZAW	*Zeitschrift für die alttestamentliche Wissenschafte*

In addition to those indicated above, abbreviations for biblical books and other ancient texts follow conventions set forth in Billie Jean Collins et al., eds., *The SBL Handbook of Style: For Biblical Studies and Related Disciplines*, 2nd ed. (Atlanta: SBL, 2014).

1

Genesis and Noah's Flood

THE GENESIS FLOOD NARRATIVE: GENERAL ORIENTATION

AS THE FIRST BOOK of the Pentateuch, Genesis is "the fountainhead from which the Bible's 'Torah' (its teaching) flows."[1] The controversies surrounding the book have lasted for millennia and show no signs of abating.[2] Few exegetical matters require as much pedagogical and pastoral sensitivity as dealing with those issues concerning the first eleven chapters of Genesis.[3] Given the challenging (and often complex) nature of these topics and the diversity of opinions, the subject of the Noachian deluge narrative, in particular, has aroused much interest.[4]

Canonically, the Noahide Flood is primarily recounted in chapters 6 through 9 of the book of Genesis.[5] The events themselves unfold in the

---

1. Goldingay, *Genesis*, ix.

2. Kidner once opined, "There can scarcely be another part of Scripture over which so many battles, theological, scientific, historical and literary, have been fought, or so many opinions cherished." Kidner, *Genesis*, 9. See too Davidson and Turner, *Manifold Beauty of Genesis One*, 1–13; Janssen, *Soul-Searching*, 65–70, 194–97.

3. Burlet "Heutagogy and Teaching Genesis 1–11," 30–33; Copan and Jacoby, *Origins*, 209–12. See too Lennox, *Seven Days*.

4. See Chen, *Primeval Flood Catastrophe*, 1–3; Stallings, *Genesis Cataclysm*, 1.

5. Cohn, *Noah's Flood*, 11. For detailed, analytic comparisons between the images of primeval history in Babylonia, canonical literature, and the parallel Enochic

"account" (תולדת) of the patriarch Noah (Gen 6:9—9:29).[6] The narrative begins with him (6:9) and ends with him (9:29).[7] The account is also situated in the milieu of the ancient Near East and the immediate context of Gen 1–11.[8]

THE GENESIS FLOOD NARRATIVE: JUDGMENT AND SALVATION

In the canon of Scripture, the Genesis Flood is often portrayed as being an all-encompassing, catastrophic event (Matt 24:36–44; Luke 17:26–27; Heb 11:7; 1 Pet 3:20–21) which had the power to forever shape and change the world at that time (2 Pet 2:5, 3:6).[9] The cause for this hydrologic disaster, though, unlike that of the ANE accounts, is moralistic.[10] Showcasing the morality of the biblical narrative, it is written "all life" (כל בשר) had "corrupted" (שחת) its way on the earth (Gen 6:12).[11] Some consider the *Nephilim* (see Gen 6:1–4) to be a trigger.[12] Scripture, however, explicates

---

tradition(s), see Kvangig, *Primeval History*. Further information on the Flood and intertestamental literature may be found in Yoshikawa, "Prototypical Use of the Noahic Flood," 268–350.

6. Boda notes, "Elsewhere in the Old Testament, the term refers to genealogical lists, that is, lists of people who were born within a family, clan, or tribal unit (Exod 6:16, 19; 28:10; Num 1:20–42; 3:1; Ruth 4:18; 1 Chr 1:29; 5:7; 7:2, 4, 9; 8:28; 9:9, 34; 26:31)." Boda, *Severe Mercy*, 17. Cf. Steinberg, "Genesis," 281–82; Ska, *Pentateuch*, 24–25.

7. Bauks, "Intratextual Exegesis," 184.

8. Not all scholars, however, agree with the schema of dividing Genesis between Gen 1:1—11:26 and Gen 11:27—50:26. For example, certain individuals wish to see the genealogy of Shem (Gen 11:10–26) included as part of the so-called ancestral period. See Sternberg, "The Genealogical Framework," 41–50. Other scholars, however, contend Gen 1–9 should be thought of as an individual unit. See Clark, "The Flood and the Structure of the Pre-Patriarchal History," 184–211. Still, others believe the Flood itself may have originally constituted the end of the primeval age. See Hiebert, *The Yahwist's Landscape*, 80–82. Cf. Rendtorff, "Gen 8:21," 69–78; von Rad, *Genesis*, 122.

9. France, *Matthew*, 943; Pao and Schnabel, "Luke," 348; Davids, *2 Peter and Jude*, 270–71.

10. See Longman and Walton, *Lost World of the Flood*, 66–69.

11. For a thorough grammatical analysis of the unique phrasing of this verse (cf. Ezek 16:47) see the NET Bible.

12. For a select overview on this topic, see Kaminski, "Beautiful Women or False Judgment?," 457–73; Gentry and Wellum, *Kingdom Through Covenant*, 181–83; Wright, *Origin*, 5–55; Clines, "Sons of God," 33–46; Keiser, "The 'Sons of God,'" 103–20; Spero, "Sons of God," 15–18; Feinman, "Sons of God," 73–100; Day, *Creation to Babel*, 77–97; Marrs, "Sons of God," 218–24; Huey Jr., "Yes," 210–29; Walton, "No,"

the Genesis Flood was directly related to "violence" (חמס).[13] That is, the sinful behavior of humanity (Gen 6:5–6). Human beings had the effect of "corrupting" (שחת) the "good" (טוב) earth GOD had created (Gen 1:31). As such, GOD proclaimed he would "destroy" (שחת) and "wipe" (מחה) it out, along with "every living thing" (כל בשר), so as to obliterate all life from the face of the earth (Gen 6:7, 11–13, 17; 7:4, 21–23, cf. 8:21; 9:11–16).[14]

Prior to the Flood in Genesis, GOD had set out his intention for his creation to "bless" (ברך) humanity and to see them flourish, abound, and reign in dominion over the earth as his image-bearers (Gen 1:26–31). The Flood becomes a pressing concern with this course of action, as it seems to be in direct contrast to GOD's purpose at creation. If humanity is altogether removed from the earth what happens next? The narrative shows Noah found "favour" (חן) in the eyes of the LORD (Gen 6:8).[15] Covenanting with Noah, his sons, and all of creation, GOD preserved a remnant of humanity and all life on earth (Gen 6:18–21; 7:1–3, 7:7–9, 7:13–16; 8:16–22; 9:1–17). As such, judgment and salvation are in the Genesis Flood account.

As will be demonstrated throughout this book: "GOD's mercy exceeds his wrath."[16] The text of the Genesis Flood categorically underscores what GOD did to "preserve" life in spite of the disaster.[17] GOD gave the world a second chance (Gen 8:21–22; cf. Gen 6:5–7) through a

---

210–229; Walton, "Sons of GOD," 793–98; Longman and Walton, *Lost World of the Flood*, 122–28; Collins, *Reading Genesis Well*, 187–90; VanGemeren, "Sons of GOD," 320–48; Stuckenbruck, *Rebellious Angels*. Cf. Okoye, *Genesis 1–11*, 91–95; Hendel, "Demigods," 13–26; Hendel, "Sons of GOD," 8–13, 37.

13. Swart and Van Dam state that this term expresses "cold-blooded and unscrupulous infringement of the physical rights of others, motivated by greed and hate and often making use of physical violence and brutality." Swart and Van Dam, *NIDOTTE* 2:178. Another scholar asserts that "this is virtually a technical term for the violation of the weak by the strong, a breach of a just order, an order provided for by GOD." Konkel, "Promise and Covenant," 20. For more information see Walker, "Noah and the Season of Violence," 380; Dundes, ed., *Flood Myth*, 71; *DCH* 3:256; *HALOT* 1:329; Haag, *TDOT* 4:482; Stoebe, *TLOT*, 1:437–39. Cf. Faro, *Evil in Genesis*.

14. Fretheim, *Creation Untamed*, 5, 37, 42; Walton, *Genesis*, 307–8.

15. See Kaminski, *Was Noah Good?*; Keiser, "Nuancing Kaminski's *Was Noah Good?*," 195–204.

16. Waltke and Yu, *Old Testament Theology*, 287.

17. Fretheim, *Creation Untamed*, 46. Cf. Kaminski, *Was Noah Good?*, 13; Clines, *Pentateuch*, 83.

"re-creation" event.[18] Noah's Flood can thus be seen as a "flood of grace."[19] Or, as John Goldingay eloquently puts it, "Floods of waters have not quenched love (Song 8:7)."[20]

To restate, despite the vivid picture of devastation the Genesis Flood account depicts, the emphasis of the narrative is deliverance and redemption, i.e., salvation, not judgment. Again, the focus of the text is acutely bent towards GOD's "salvific rather than punitive" purposes.[21] Thomas A. Keiser judiciously notes the difference between deliverance (i.e., redemption) and salvation in that "redemption is deliverance while salvation is entrance into blessing."[22]

The arc of salvation in the Flood narrative can be broken down into two main ideas. First, GOD's intention for creation is not thwarted and, secondly, GOD commits himself to his intentions of creation. His intention for creation can be stated as thus: the establishment of order via covenant showing the sanctity of human life and the upholding of all life.[23] This involves, in particular, humanity as his image bearers, including the *lex talionis* (life for life) principle.[24] The specifics of the *lex talionis* principle will be dealt with at length later on in this book.

THE GENESIS FLOOD NARRATIVE: COSMIC ORDER THROUGH COVENANT

The Noachian covenant is described as being "long-lasting" (ברית עולם) in Gen 9:16 (cf. Sir 44:17–18).[25] It is also notable that GOD "gives" or "establishes" his covenant (Gen 6:18; 9:9, 11, 12, 17) with Noah but the

---

18. See Waltke and Yu, *Old Testament Theology*, 292–302. Cf. Walton, *Genesis*, 337; Boda, *Heartbeat*, 98–99.

19. Keil and Delitzsch, *Pentateuch*, 141. Cf. Greenway, *Love of All Creatures*, xiv.

20. Goldingay, *Genesis*, 147.

21. Boyd, *Crucifixion*, 1140. Cf. Humphreys, *Character of God*, 64–72; Shaviv, "Flood," 531.

22. Keiser, *Genesis 1–11*, 128. One scholar states, "The objective of GOD's work in redemption is to free people to be who they were created to be the effect of which is named salvation. Fretheim, *God and World*, 10. Italics removed.

23. See Kaminski, *From Noah to Israel*, 1. Cf. Gentry and Wellum, *Kingdom Through Covenant*, 179–209.

24. Waltke and Yu, *Old Testament Theology*, 303; Konkel, "In Defense of Human Values," 32–35.

25. Walton, *Covenant*, 131–33; Boda, *Heartbeat*, 96.

standard language for "covenant initiation," that is, to "cut a covenant" (כרת ברית) with other biblical patriarchs (cf. Gen 15:18; 17:7, 9, 21) is absent.[26] See below:

Table One—The Covenant of the Noachian Deluge Narrative

English Gloss	Hebrew	Stem	Verse(s)
Establish	קוּם	Hiphil	6:18
Establish	קוּם	Hiphil	9:9
Establish	קוּם	Hiphil	9:11
Give	נתן	Qal	9:12
Establish	קוּם	Hiphil	9:17

Given the difference, some posit an "implicit covenant between Creator and creature."[27] With respect to Noah and the Flood (Gen 9:9, 11, 12, 17; cf. Gen 6:18), C. John Collins maintains: "this covenant goes beyond humankind and embraces the animal kingdom as well. This may look like an advance on the arrangement with Adam, but is more likely an explication of it. Even though the word 'covenant' is not used for GOD's relationship with Adam, it is a good and accurate word."[28] In a similar way, Peter J. Gentry and Stephen J. Wellum also assert:

> The construction *hēqîm běrît* in Genesis 6 and 9 indicates that GOD is not initiating a covenant with Noah but is rather affirming for Noah and his descendants a commitment initiated previously. This language clearly denotes a covenant established earlier between GOD and creation, or between GOD and humans at creation. When GOD says that he is affirming or upholding his covenant with Noah, he is saying that his commitment to his creation—the care of the Creator to preserve, provide for, and rule over all that he has made, including the blessings and

---

26. See Gentry and Wellum, *Kingdom Through Covenant*, 179–95; Martens, *NIDOTTE* 3:903–4.

27. Oswalt, *Isaiah 1–39*, 446. Cf. Williamson, *Oath*, 69–76.

28. Collins, *Reading Genesis Well*, 191. Cf. Davidson and Turner, *Manifold Beauty of Genesis One*, 82–98.

ordinances that he initiated through and with Adam and Eve and their family—are now to be with Noah and his descendants.²⁹

Though some may quibble, the idea of a preexisting covenant with either creation or humanity is erroneous. There was no need for covenants in the beginning. As Mark J. Boda states:

> A ברית (covenant) is not necessary within a family unit, that is, a parent does not need a covenant with a child, nor a sibling with another sibling. These are natural, trustworthy relationships. No covenant is necessary in the original creation since Yahweh GOD is identified as a parent producing child, as the 'image/likeness of GOD' language makes clear (see Gen 5:1–3). Once the human couple is banished from the garden in Gen. 3, this family status is annulled, and a covenant is now necessary to structure the relationship between humanity and GOD . . . this covenant makes possible a renewal of the kinship relationship. The Noachic covenant forms an important bridge between creation and redemption, as GOD reestablishes kinship relationship with humanity and all of creation. By placing the Noachic covenant in canonical position before Israel's redemptive story and its relational agreements . . . we are reminded that the redemptive agreements with Israel were part of a much larger story of redemption that would impact not just all nations (Gen. 10) but also all creation. The relational agreement with Noah is thus key to understanding humanity's function as vice-regents over all creation and GOD's desire through a redeemed humanity to see creation realize its full potential.³⁰

The significance of salvation is further highlighted by the text's reiteration that it was through Shem, Ham, and Japheth, the three sons of Noah (and the only other men who came off the ark), that the earth was "populated/scattered" (נפצה) after the Flood (Gen 9:18–19; 10:1–32).³¹

GOD also "speaks of an accounting for the blood of humanity in [Gen] 9:4–6; establishing the *lex talionis*, the retaliation law, applied

---

29. Gentry and Wellum, *Kingdom Through Covenant*, 188. See too Schreiner, *Covenant*, 19–29. Cf. Mason, *Covenant*, 47–87; Mason, "Another Flood," 177–98.

30. Boda, *Heartbeat*, 100. MT pointing for Hebrew characters removed. As one scholar puts it, "A covenant was a way of making kin out of non-kin." Richter, *The Epic of Eden*, 73. Cf. Block, *Covenant*, 15–16.

31. For a thorough grammatical analysis of the unique phrasing of this verse (cf. Gen 11) see the NET Bible.

here to murder."[32] This provision enables mortals to act for GOD—as his image bearers—to the extent of being able to take human life (cf. Exod 21:12–36; Josh 20:1–6). Consequently, humans have the capacity to mitigate "violence" (חמס), the very thing explicitly stated to be the root cause of the Flood itself (Gen 6:5–6, 11–13).

The assertion of the Flood emphasis being on salvation instead of judgment heavily draws on the well-known "Spread-of-Sin, Spread-of-Grace" rubric (a key heuristic device to account for the overarching content of Genesis).[33] In like manner, it also leverages the familiar "Creation–Uncreation–Re-Creation" theme.[34] That being said, this volume builds on these ideas through providing clear(er) data and more cumulative evidence(s), albeit with a much narrower focus, i.e., the Noachian deluge narrative, specifically. This will be done by means of a rigorous yet oft-under-utilized methodology, namely rhetorical criticism (rhetoric as persuasion).

RHETORICAL CRITICISM: GENERAL ORIENTATION

Within Hebrew Bible/Old Testament (hereafter HB/OT) studies, there are two different branches of "rhetorical criticism" with a "sharp distinction" that has developed between them: (1) "rhetoric as the art of composition" and (2) "rhetoric as persuasion."[35] This book takes the latter approach in its examination of the Genesis Flood account. Put simply, *"rhetoric is the art of effective communication."*[36] Rhetorical criticism thus "delves deeply

---

32. Boda, *Severe Mercy*, 22.

33. Clines, *Pentateuch*, 70–80; Waltke and Yu, *Old Testament Theology*, 308–111. Von Rad states, "We see, therefore (already in the primeval history!), that each time, in and after the judgment, GOD's preserving, forgiving will to save is revealed . . . What is described, therefore, is . . . the story of a continually new punishment and at the same time gracious preservation, the story . . . of a way that is distinguished by progressive divine judgment, but that, nevertheless, man [sic] could never have travelled without continued divine preservation." Von Rad, *Genesis*, 153. The schema of Reward, Punishment, and Forgiveness is also noted. See Boda, *Severe Mercy*, 12, 32–34.

34. See Clines, "Flood," 128–42; Clines, *Pentateuch*, 80–84; Waltke and Yu, *Old Testament Theology*, 307–8.

35. Barker, *From the Depths of Despair*, 28. See too Trible, *Rhetorical Criticism* 32. Most HB/OT studies do not put ideological, post-modern, and liberation criticisms under rhetorical criticism. Evans, *Invasion of Sennacherib*, 31; Walsh, *Old Testament Narrative*, 5; Stewart, "Ethos of the Cosmos," 43; Gorman, *Elements*, 12–13, 259–64.

36. Gorman, *Elements*, 5. Italics original. Cf. Barker, "Disputed Temple," 5.

into the heart of the text and considers its persuasive intent and effect."[37] Rhetorical criticism effectively "fills the void" between diachronic and synchronic approaches such as form, source, and literary criticism(s).[38]

Rhetorical criticism considers the text "as we have it," how such a text (like Genesis, for instance) would be received by an audience of "near contemporaries," and the persuasive strategy of the text.[39] In this respect, the text has "'power' that influences institutions, societies, and cultures with each reading."[40] This particular aspect of my methodology will be short-handedly labelled throughout the rest of the book as being world-view formative rhetoric.[41]

RHETORICAL CRITICISM: CONTEMPORARY SCHOLARSHIP

No shortage of scholarship exists concerning either Genesis *in toto* or Gen 1–11.[42] The same cannot be said about rhetorical criticism in HB/OT studies. Of the most relevant works published since 2015, only Barker's *Disputed Temple*,[43] Harper's *'I Will Walk Among You,'*[44] and Ahn's *Persuasive Portrayal*[45] make use of a rhetorical-critical, rhetoric as persuasion, method.[46]

---

37. Barker, *From the Depths of Despair*, 1.

38. Barker, *From the Depths of Despair*, 32. For further clarity concerning the authorship, text, and readership dialectic in synchronic and diachronic studies, see Schnittjer, *Old Testament Use of the Old Testament*, xxxiv–xxxv; Barton, *Reading the Old Testament*, 237–46.

39. Kennedy, *New Testament Interpretation*, 3–4. Definitions of key terms will be discussed later.

40. Donaldson, "New Rhetoric," 246.

41. For more details in this regard, see chapter 2. Cf. Scult, "Pentateuch," 13–14

42. A review of works published from 2015 to 2020 on Genesis are found in Schneider, "In the Beginning and Still Today," 142–59. On resources published prior to 2015 consult Evans, *Guide*, 67–78. Cf. Sparks, *Pentateuch*. For a fine (annotated) list of older suggestions for further reading about the Flood, see Dundes, ed., *Flood Myth*, 439–45.

43. Barker, *Disputed Temple: A Rhetorical Analysis of the Book of Haggai*.

44. Harper, "'I Will Walk Among You': The Rhetorical Function of Allusion to Genesis 1–3 in the Book of Leviticus."

45. Ahn, *The Persuasive Portrayal of David and Solomon in Chronicles*.

46. One notes that though Provan does discuss rhetorical criticism, his (obtuse?) assessment is that "narrative criticism," i.e., literary criticism, is better suited for

While Tremper Longman III and John H. Walton explicitly state in *The Lost World of the Flood* they are "seeking first and foremost the literary-theological interpretation offered by the text,"[47] they also devote an entire chapter to the proposition that "Genesis 1–11 Uses Rhetorical Devices."[48] Alongside this, they also provide two other chapters which contend: (1) "The Bible Uses Hyperbole to Describe Historical Events," and (2) "Genesis Appropriately Presents a Hyperbolic Account of the Flood."[49] As will be noted in chapter 2, hyperbole is a key aspect of my usage of rhetorical criticism. In brief, Longman and Walton maintain "real events," such as Noah's Flood, were "rhetorically shaped for theological reasons," often using hyperbole.[50] Regrettably, the authors do not provide technical definitions to many key terms (such as rhetoric, persuasion, or hyperbole, for example) in their esteemed work, nor do they offer a distinct rhetorical-critical method.[51] Much the same thing applies to Griffin's *Creation and the Flood*.[52]

Many of these infelicities, however, have been remedied by C. John Collins in *Reading Genesis Well*. Collins applies a special "Lewisian, critically intuitive approach" while also discussing "lexical semantics," "speech-act theory," and "sociolinguistics," alongside "rhetorical" and "literary" criticism.[53] While Collins himself admits many of the aforementioned disciplines can be "abstruse and sometimes counterintuitive, as well as contradictory between themselves . . . Lewis offers a model of someone who intuitively (albeit informally) steers a wise path through the difficulties."[54] To reiterate, Collins maintains that C. S. Lewis, by means of his varied academic work and writings, is able to "help us to

---

reading the book of Genesis since "rhetorical criticism is best suited for the study of poetic texts or perhaps NT letters." Provan, *Discovering Genesis*, 40–41, 43–44.

47. Longman and Walton, *Lost World of the Flood*, 15.

48. Longman and Walton, *Lost World of the Flood*, 21–29.

49. See Longman and Walton, *Lost World of the Flood*, 30–35, 36–41.

50. Longman and Walton, *Lost World of the Flood*, 29, 30–41.

51. See Lovett, Review of *Lost World of the Flood*, 149–51; Halley, Review of *Lost World of the Flood*, 36–39. Cf. Hiltz, Review of *Lost World of the Flood*, 616–17; Burlet, Review of *Lost World of the Flood*, R67–R72. Compare and contrast Longman, *Genesis*, 7–10; Longman, "Biblical Narrative," 69–79; Walton, *Genesis*, 21.

52. See Griffin, *Creation and the Flood*, 163–72.

53. Collins, *Reading Genesis Well*, 25–29.

54. Collins, *Reading Genesis Well*, 25.

formulate a critically rigorous reading strategy for Genesis 1–11."[55] Concerning the art of persuasion, in particular, Collins offers the text of Gen 1–11 should best be understood as "rhetorical history."[56] The author also states this text serves as "prehistory" and "protohistory," which, according to Collins, is a "*social function*, not a *literary form*. The main literary form . . . is prose narrative and that prose varies in its style and register and thus in its language level."[57]

Collins states the "purpose of the stories is to lay the foundation for a worldview . . . Thus, Genesis aims to tell the story of beginnings the right way, to counter the other stories; it professes to offer the divinely authorized way for its audience to picture the events."[58] As will be noted in chapter 2, this is a key component of the rhetorical-critical method I will employ. Though Collin's work is of superb quality and is highly recommended, the dearth of particulars concerning the text's specific rhetorical strategy and rhetorical technique(s) is bothersome.[59]

It is evident; therefore, a new rhetorical-critical study is needed that is not only sensitive to the persuasive nature of the Noachian deluge narrative, in general, but also provides a methodologically rigorous delineation of the text's persuasiveness in all of its facets.[60] As will be noted later on, a somewhat modified form of George A. Kennedy's model of rhetorical criticism is particularly conducive to this end. The basic steps of this model include: (1) determining the rhetorical units, (2) determining the rhetorical situation, (3) determining the rhetorical strategy, and (4) determining the rhetorical effectiveness. A brief conclusion rounds out the analysis. Further details concerning rhetorical criticism (as a discipline in biblical studies), the specifics of the Kennedy model itself, and my own nuances to this methodology are found in chapter 2

---

55. Collins, *Reading Genesis Well*, 18. Emphasis original.

56. Collins, *Reading Genesis Well*, 141.

57. Collins, *Reading Genesis Well*, 148. Italics original. Cf. Branson, "Paradigm," 141–56.

58. Collins, *Reading Genesis Well*, 153.

59. See Burlet, Review of *Reading Genesis Well*, 140–44. Cf. Markos, Review of *Reading Genesis Well*, 129–31; Moore, Review of *Reading Genesis Well*, 114–15; Cartledge, Review of *Reading Genesis Well*, 370–72; Noonan, Review of *Reading Genesis Well*, 551–53.

60. Cf. Griffin, *Creation and the Flood*; Stallings, *The Genesis Cataclysm*. See also Rogers, *The Biblical Flood*.

The remainder of chapter 1 orients readers to the most critical issues about the Genesis Flood that are pertinent to this specific study. It also describes various approaches that seek to elucidate these matters. Lastly, it argues why a rhetorical-critical approach is a necessity.

GENERAL ORIENTATION TO PRESENTING ISSUE(S) ABOUT THE GENESIS FLOOD NARRATIVE

Though the postdiluvian world found comfort at times from the Flood account (see Isa 54:9), many aspects of the Noachian deluge narrative are also something of a puzzle. The conciliatory disposition of the Deity towards his creation (post-Flood), in particular, is especially vexing given the paradox that exists between Gen 6:5–7 and Gen 8:20–22. See below:

> Now the LORD saw the wickedness of humanity on the earth–that every inclination of the thoughts of their mind was only evil continually. Then the LORD was remorseful that he had made human beings on the earth. The LORD was grieved within his innermost being. So, the LORD said: "I will remove humanity, whom I have created, from the face of the ground: human beings, beasts, creeping things, up to and including even the birds of the sky–for I am remorseful that I have made them." (Gen 6:5–7—AT).

> Then Noah built an altar to the LORD and he took of every clean animal and of every clean bird and he offered burnt offerings on the altar. Then the LORD smelled the pleasing odor and the LORD resolved within himself: "I will never again curse the ground, due to humanity; Though the inclination of humanity's mind is evil from youth. Nor will I ever again destroy all life as I have just done. All the days of the earth,
> Seedtime and Harvest, Cold and Heat, Summer and Winter, Day and Night, Shall not cease." (Gen 8:20–22—AT)

Given the remarkable damage GOD had just unleashed on the world—an unnerving depiction of the reversal of creation, i.e., the cosmos becoming chaos—one is not amiss to wonder why GOD's perspective towards the created order, the works of his hands (see Psalm 8:1–9; 19:1–6; 139:1–18), seemed to have changed so suddenly.[61] Exactly how does the kindness, goodness, and mercy of GOD correlate with his judgment,

---

61. See Clines, "Flood," 142; Noort, "Flood," 36. Cf. Mettinger, *Eden Narrative*, 75.

wrath, and justice in light of the Flood?[62] Regrettably, some have chosen to bracket out, ignore, or gloss over this problem.[63] The answer to this troublesome question is evident through the activities of God within the narrative. God constrains himself in executing his judgment and wrath because of the import of human life and his beloved creation.[64]

To restate, prior to the unfolding of the Flood (Gen 6:5–7), the language of Genesis suggests the downward spiral of sin, evil, and disorder had reached its climax.[65] Few passages are "so explicit and all-embracing as this in specifying the extent of human sinfulness and depravity."[66] This unsettling portrayal of events can be arranged in a rough chiasm:[67]

Table Two—The Palistrophe of Genesis 6:5–8

A The LORD "sees" humanity (Gen 6:5)

    B The LORD is "remorseful" (נחם) that he made humans (Gen 6:6a)

        C The LORD is "grieved" (עצב) within his innermost being (Gen 6:6b)

        C' The LORD says "I shall 'wipe out' (מחה) humanity" (Gen 6:7a)

    B' The LORD is "remorseful" (נחם) that he made humans (Gen 6:7b)

A' The LORD "sees" Noah (6:8)

Through the schematic above, it is evident human immorality is of grave consequence to God; in point of fact, it is explicitly noted as being the very reason for the Flood (Gen 6:5–7).[68]

---

62. Fretheim, "God and Violence," 22; Fretheim, "Wrath," 14–17. Cf. Goldingay, *Genesis*, 131.

63. Some examples of those who fail to specifically explicate the Noachian deluge narrative include Wilgus and Carroll, eds., *Violence of God*, Lamb; *God Behaving Badly*; Kissileff, ed., *Reading Genesis*.

64. See Tverbeg, "The Flood's Deeper Message of Mercy." No pages. Online.

65. See Burlet, "Impassible Yet Impassioned," 116.

66. Wenham, *Genesis 1–15*, 144. See too Jacobsen, "Eridu Genesis," 529; Wiesel, "Noah's Warning," 4.

67. The following diagram is a modified version of Wenham, *Genesis 1–15*, 136. For details on chiasms, in general, also known as a palistrophe (the function of which is to highlight the centre or fulcrum), see Watson, *Classical Hebrew Poetry*, 32; Gorman, *Elements*, 41, 100. Cf. Boda, "Chiasmus in Ubiquity," 55–70.

68. See Wenham, "Genesis, Book of," 249. Cf. Brasnett, *The Suffering of the Impassible God*, 11.

Given such, is it not strange that immediately after Noah offered his sacrifice(s) to GOD, GOD resolved within himself (ויאמר יהוה אל לבו) to never again "curse" (Piel קלל) the "ground" (אדמה) "because" (כי) of "humans" (האדם) "even though" (כי) the inclination of the human heart is evil from its youth (see Gen 8:20–22)?[69] A diagram to elucidate this matter is provided below:

Table Three—Genesis 6:5b and Genesis 8:21b

Gen 6:5b	Gen 8:21b
וכל יצר מחשבת לבו רק רע כל היום	כי יצר לב האדם רע מנעריו
Every inclination of the thoughts of their mind was only evil continually (AT)	Though the inclination of humanity's mind is evil from youth (AT)

While the omission of the terms "all, everyone" (כל), "thought, device, plan" (מחשבת), "only" (רק), and "all the day, continually" (כל היום), may be thought by some individuals to display GOD's "more lenient attitude after the flood, in view of his mercy," the insertion of "from his youth" (מנעריו) in Gen 8:21b functions as a clue to the "reapplication" of Gen 6:5b.[70] Alongside this, the LXX text of Gen 8:21, which reads ὅτι ἔγκειται ἡ διάνοια τοῦ ἀνθρώπου ἐπιμελῶς ἐπὶ τὰ πονηρὰ ἐκ νεότητος, also highlights humanity's responsibility for the evil inclination of their own mind(s) even more than the MT.[71] The NETS renders Gen 8:21 as "for the mind of humankind applies itself attentively to evil things from youth." The LES has "everyone was focused in his [sic] heart on evil things all their days." Another scholar translates: "(because) the mind of mankind [sic] is studiously involved in evil matters from childhood."[72] I prefer: "For human thought clings to wickedness–even from youth." Irrespective of the minutia, humanity appear to be just as depraved (worse?) after the Flood as before the devastation.

While the text does not linger over this turn of events, a multiplicity of arguments and analogies exist to account for it. Though each

---

69. For an up-to-date discussion of some of the issue(s), see Sollereder, *Animal Suffering*, 28–29. Cf. Oates, "The Curse," 32–33.

70. Kaminski, *Was Noah Good?*, 88. Cf. Greenberger, "Noah," 30–31.

71. See Peters, *Noah Traditions*, 16.

72. Wevers, *Genesis*, 111.

proposal has varying degrees of exegetical and methodological rigor, nuance, and theological consequence(s), resolving this tension is critical since much of the Genesis Flood narrative hinges on this "change in Yahweh's inclination."[73]

As David J. A. Clines incisively puts it, the theme here could be said to be either:

> a. Humankind tends to destroy what GOD has made good. Even when GOD forgives human sin and mitigates the punishment, sin continues to spread, to the point where the world suffers uncreation. And even when GOD makes a fresh start, turning his back on uncreation forever, the human tendency to sin becomes manifest. Or:
> b. No matter how drastic human sin becomes, destroying what GOD has made good and bringing the world to the brink of uncreation, GOD's grace never fails to deliver humankind from the consequences of their sin. Even when humanity responds to a fresh start with the old pattern of sin, GOD's commitment to his world stands firm, and sinful humans experience the favour of GOD as well as his righteous judgment.[74]

Clines claims Gen 1–11 is "utterly ambiguous" in helping one "opt decisively" between option 'a' or 'b;'[75] He thus states one must look to the rest of the Pentateuch for answers.[76] As will be made clear in the analysis portions of this book (chapters 3, 4, 5, and 6), the Noachian deluge narrative (in itself) necessitates option 'b.' The main point, again, is that Noah's Flood is not so much "focused on destruction, but . . . GOD's salvation."[77] The Flood is a "severe mercy."[78]

Syntax and Grammar

The "juxtaposition of humankind's inherent responsibility and the opportunity for a second chance" is both cryptic and "fascinating" (cf. Gen

---

73. Brueggemann, *Theology of the Old Testament*, 363. Cf. Boyd, *Crucifixion*, 1121–42.
74. Clines, *Theme of the Pentateuch*, 83.
75. Clines, *Theme of the Pentateuch*, 83.
76. Clines, *Theme of the Pentateuch*, 83.
77. Cf. Waltke and Yu, *Old Testament Theology*, 300.
78. See Boda, *Severe Mercy*, 11–13.

6:5–7 and Gen 8:20–22).⁷⁹ As briefly noted above, much depends on the function, sense, and rendering (translation) of the (כי) conjunction in Gen 8:21b: (1) causal, (2) empathic, or (3) concessive.⁸⁰ As Victor P. Hamilton states:

> If we translate the conjunction *kî* as 'for, because,' instead of 'however, even though,' we are faced with a conundrum. GOD will never again destroy the earth because of man [sic], because from the start man's [sic] heart is evil. But according to 6:5, this is precisely the reason GOD sends the Flood in the first place. Here is the paradox: GOD inundates the earth because of man's [sic] sinfulness, and subsequently promises never again to destroy the earth because of man's [sic] sinfulness. In more blunt terms, their interpretation is that GOD is frustrated because the Flood has not really worked. It has destroyed the human race, but it has not changed human nature. Post-flood man [sic] is also a reprobate. In retrospect GOD sees that he has acted unwisely and too simplistically. But happily he admits his mistake and is willing to learn from it. It is possible [though] to retain the causal nuance of *kî* and observe here not a contradiction but a vivid demonstration of GOD's grace. In spite of a justifiable motivation for continued judgment, GOD chooses not to exercise that option.⁸¹

Hamilton judiciously favors the "concessive" or "emphatic" nuance and rendering of the conjunction. He states: "The rule we follow is that *kî* be given its more usual causal force unless greater sense can be extracted by taking the conjunction as a concessive or an emphatic, as is the case here. Thus this verse functions as a ringing testimony to the mercy of GOD, who henceforth will not give man [sic] his just desserts. The punishable

---

79. This astute observation comes from an esteemed children's book author. Pinkney, *Noah's Ark*, no pages. For more information on the reception history of the Flood story in North America, see, Dalton, *Children's Bibles in America*.

80. See Hamilton, *Genesis 1–17*, 309–10. Cf. *BHRG* §40.29.

81. Hamilton, *Genesis 1–17*, 309. Cf. Kidner who states: "grammatically, the clause *for the imagination* . . . could be either an expression of *for man's* [sic] *sake* or else the reason for saying 'never again'. Theologically it must be the former: the LORD's resolve not to renew the judgment is based on the accepted sacrifice (*cf.* 1 Sa. 26:19; Col. 1:20), not on man's [sic] incorrigibility, which had been the very ground of the judgment (6:5–7) and still called for its renewal; it ever counts in the sinner's favour." Kidner, *Genesis*, 93. All italics and emphases original. For a different perspective, see Goldingay, *Genesis*, 135.

will not be punished."[82] In brief, GOD is not just the Great Destroyer but the Great Deliverer, Redeemer, and Sustainer.[83]

The Ancient Near East and Sacrifice

John H. Walton has popularized: "The Bible was written *for* us but not *to* us."[84] This stresses how the Bible is "high context" in nature.[85] With this emphasis, a precise consideration of the concept of "cognitive scope" is germane to an effective interpretation of Noah's Flood.[86] All matters pertaining to "divine accommodation" are also a necessity.[87] This involves an astute awareness of the "cognitive environment" of the ANE.[88] ANE literature, such as the Sumerian myth of Ziusudra,[89] the epic of Gilgamesh (Utnapishtim),[90] and Atrahasis is key.[91] Comparing certain aspects of the Flood with these myths increases the scope and nuance of the analysis.[92]

---

82. Hamilton, *Genesis 1–17*, 310.

83. Cf. Humphreys, *Character of God*, 64–72; Shaviv, "Flood," 531.

84. Walton, "Interpreting the Bible," 327. Emphasis original. See too Miglio et al., eds. *For Us, But Not to Us*.

85. Simkins, *Creator and Creation*, 41–42. Cf. Walton, *Genesis*, 24–25.

86. To be clear, "the term 'cognitive scope' depicts the mental or intellectual tools through which everyone sees and understands the natural world. An implication of the scope of cognition is that our perception and knowledge of nature have limits and boundaries. This is similar to the margins of a visual field when using the optical scope of a scientific instrument . . . Thanks to telescopes and microscopes our modern scope of cognitive competence is much wider and greater than that of ancient people." Lamoureux, *The Bible and Ancient Science*, 90.

87. The most recent (and notable) volume here is Hilber, *Old Testament Cosmology and Divine Accommodation*.

88. Walton, "Ancient Cognitive Environment," 333–39. With respect to "cognitive environment criticism," see Walton, *Ancient Near Eastern Thought*, 11, 18; Walton, *Old Testament Theology for Christians*, 16.

89. See Best, *Noah's Ark and the Ziusudra Epic*.

90. See George, ed., *The Babylonian Gilgamesh Epic*.

91. See Lambert and Millard, eds., *Atra-Ḫasīs*.

92. A (select) overview of resources involving comparative analysis include Hallo, "Introduction," *COS* 1: xxiii–xxviii; Hays, *Hidden Riches*, 3–38; Walton, *Ancient Near Eastern Thought*, 3–30; Walton, *Ancient Cosmology*, 1–6; Tsumura, "Genesis," 52–57; Goldingay, *Genesis*, 152–54; Steinmann, *Genesis*, 108–11; Provan, *Reading Genesis*, 49–58. For more information on this topic, in general, see Oswalt, *The Bible Among the Myths*.

Concerning the Genesis Flood, specifically, James K. Hoffmeier summarizes things well: "like various Mesopotamian flood heroes, Noah made an offering after disembarking and 'the LORD smelled the pleasing aroma' (8:21), but there is no comical depiction of GOD being hungry and thirsty, craving human sustenance or buzzing around the offering like a famished fly!"[93] Similarly, Longman and Walton also opine:

> The biblical account predictably correlates with what Israelites believed about Yahweh. He has no needs and has not become unaccountably angry such that he needs to be calmed down. The 'pleasing aroma' of Genesis 8:21 functions exactly as it does within the framework of the sacrificial system in the Torah. There is no sense that Noah is interacting with a needy GOD who easily loses his temper.[94]

It is important to note that the rhetoric used in the Noachian deluge narrative (as in all the book of Genesis, in fact) is "tacit."[95] Kenneth A. Mathews (rightly) asserts: "rather than true polemic . . . the Genesis accounts are inferentially undermining the philosophical basis for pagan myth. There are undertones of refutation in Genesis 1–11, but they are not disputations."[96]

Concerning GOD's conciliation more specifically, (Gen 8:20–22; cf. Gen 6:5–7), many scholars are persuaded GOD's anger is primarily cooled due to the sweet smell of the "bountiful barbeque of slaughtered animals."[97] The purpose of the sacrifice, however, is not explicitly stated within the Flood account itself. Walton explains:

> The text says he 'sacrificed burnt offerings,' which serve a broad function in the later sacrificial system of Israel. It is more important to note what the text does not call the sacrifice. It is not a sin offering, nor is it specifically designated a thank offering. The burnt offerings that Moses' audience were familiar with are usually associated with petitions or entreaties set before GOD.[98]

---

93. Hoffmeier, "Genesis 1–11," 53. Cf. Sarna, *Genesis*, 59, 356; Mathews, *Genesis 1—11:26*, 392–94.

94. Longman and Walton, *Lost World of the Flood*, 81.

95. Walton, *Lost World of Genesis One*, 103. Cf. Peterson, *Genesis*, 63–64; Wenham, *Rethinking Genesis*, 51.

96. Mathews, *Genesis 1—11:26*, 89. Cf. Davidson and Turner, *Manifold Beauty of Genesis One*, 55–75.

97. Whedbee, *Comic Vision*, 52. Cf. Wenham, "Genesis 1–11," 92.

98. Walton, *Genesis*, 315. See also Okoye, *Genesis 1–11*, 104–5. Cf. Hartley, *Leviticus*, 17–18.

To summarize, the LORD smelled the "soothing aroma" (ריח הניחח) of Noah's "offerings" (עלת) (Gen 8:20). GOD then avowed within himself to never again destroy the world as he had done and to never again "curse" (Piel קלל) the ground (Gen 8:21–22).[99] It seems clear, therefore, Noah's offering "assuages GOD's heart with regard to sin" and that "the biblical narrative is calculated to place all wisdom on GOD and promote human trust and obedience to him."[100] While Yahweh the Creator is distinctly unlike the gods of the ANE in that he does not need people to sustain him (nor is he a part of the created order of things and subject to nature), many still find it troubling how easily GOD's anger seems to have been placated after the Flood.[101]

The Character and Nature of GOD

One of the more provocative proposals to resolving the challenges that exist between Gen 6:5–7 and Gen 8:20–22 is the idea GOD is akin to a "mad scientist, trying to get things right in the laboratory, trying plan B after plan A fails."[102] Concerning such, Goldingay maintains:

> The Genesis flood story thus affirms that GOD has faced the monumental obstacle to the creation project constituted by the negative inclination of the human mind, has therefore thought of abandoning this creation project, but has determined not to do so . . . the significance of the Genesis flood story is to acknowledge that GOD could decide to destroy the whole world, for one reason or another, and to affirm that actually GOD will not do so. There is not such a balanced relationship between the capacity to give life and take it away. Yhwh . . . has equally the power to do either, but not the will. Giving life is natural to Yhwh, whereas killing is not.[103]

---

99. See Hamilton, *Genesis 1–17*, 307–8. I will return to this point again later on.

100. Waltke and Yu, *Old Testament Theology*, 291. The NET Bible elucidates: "The one who escaped the catastrophe could best express his gratitude and submission through sacrificial worship, acknowledging GOD as the sovereign of the universe." Cf. Hartley, *Leviticus*, 24–25.

101. Cf. Prescott, *Imagery from Genesis*, 54–58; Wiesel, "Noah's Warning," 3–20.

102. See Gentry and Wellum, *Kingdom Through Covenant*, 181 who characterize the work of Goldingay, *Theology*, 1:161–84. Cf. Hawk, *Violence of the Biblical God*, 118.

103. Goldingay, *Theology*, 1:178–79.

Related to this, some scholars also propose the Genesis text implies "second thoughts, reflections that suggest a change in GOD."[104] In light of this: "one might ask whether GOD in the aftermath of the flood considers the flood a mistake. After all, he realizes that the flood does not resolve the problem of human sin, but "even so" (v. 21) he will not replicate such a judgment."[105]

In response to this query, Longman understands, canonically speaking, "GOD's ultimate purpose was 'to provide an appropriate historical demonstration of the ultimate destiny of a world under sin.' But now ... GOD determines to maintain cosmic order until the end, thus creating room for his work of redemption as he seeks to reconcile wayward humanity with himself."[106] This is a reasonable and fair assessment.

Yet, the question remains as to whether or not GOD was "moved" by the Flood.[107] Walter Brueggemann asserts:

> The flood has effected no change in humankind. But it has effected an irreversible change in GOD, who now will approach his creation with an unlimited patience and forbearance. To be sure, GOD has been committed to his creation from the beginning. But this narrative traces a new decision on the part of GOD ... the GOD-world relation is not simply that of a strong GOD and needy world. Now it is a tortured relation between a grieved GOD and a resistant world. And of the two, the real changes are in GOD.[108]

---

104. Humphreys, *Character of God*, 69.

105. Longman, *Genesis*, 126.

106. Longman, *Genesis*, 126 (citing Robertson, *The Christ of the Covenants*, 114).

107. Weaver, *The Nonviolent God*, 107. Cf. Alexander, *Paradise*, 58–60; Brown, *Ethos*, 60.

108. Brueggemann, *Genesis*, 81. Italics original. Brueggemann also states: "It is popularly thought ... the crisis of the flood is to place the world in jeopardy. But a close reading indicates that it is the heart and person of GOD which are placed in crisis. The crisis is not the much water, which now has become only a dramatic setting. Rather, the crisis comes because of the resistant character of the world which evokes hurt and grief in the heart of GOD ... while GOD wills creation to be turned toward him, he does not commandeer it ... rather, it is done by the anguish and grief of GOD, who enters into the pain and fracture of the world. The world is brought to the rule of GOD but only by the pathos and vulnerability of the creator. The story is not about the world assaulted and a GOD who stands remote. It is about the hurt GOD endures because of and for the sake of his wayward creation." Brueggemann, *Genesis*, 78–79. See too Brueggemann, *Theology*, 362–63. Cf. Waltke and Yu, *Old Testament Theology*, 68–72; Maier, "Repent," 135–37.

Fretheim, however, assesses the Genesis Flood may be (metaphorically) understood as being the tears of God:

> That divine judgment and divine tears go together has considerable theological import. Without the references to divine tears, God would be much more removed and unmoved. Judgment accompanied by weeping, though still judgment, is different–in motivation and in the understanding of the relationship at stake . . . Although God may give the people up to the effects of their sinfulness, God does not finally give up on them. God's judgment is always in the service of the ultimate will of God to save. To that end, God can use judgmental *effects* for a variety of positive purposes, such as refining, cleansing, insight, and discipline.[109]

While the doctrine of divine impassibility is the source of much confusion, consternation, and debate, the sum total of Scripture clearly teaches God takes no pleasure in the death of the wicked (see Ezek 18:23; 33:11) for God is not willing that anyone should perish (2 Pet 3:8–10; cf. 1 Tim 2:4; Ps 30:5).[110] Of course, other passages may also be cited, many of which are often rooted in Yahweh's self-revelation (see Exod 34:6–7).[111] Even so, it is evident the Noachian deluge narrative, in itself, has antecedence and "sets a context for the story of redemption."[112]

Many posit Noah's Flood was some sort of "cosmic flop."[113] As W. Lee Humphreys declares: "for all God's apparent power and effectiveness in the story of the Great Flood, little is effected by God in the long haul. His authority, in contrast to his power, seems reduced or at least open to question. *The Great Flood is a demonstration of power and might, but in the end it is a wash.*"[114] In like manner, Fretheim, too, maintains if the purpose of the Flood "was to cleanse, it was in some basic sense a failure. Perhaps the purging of the negative *effects* of human sin on the created order is what is in mind."[115]

---

109. Fretheim, *Creation Untamed*, 60. O'Connor, *Genesis*, 110.

110. Vanhoozer, *Remythologizing Theology*, 387–468. Cf. Matz and Thornhill, eds., *Divine Impassibility*. For more details, see Walton, *Genesis*, 308; Block, *Ezekiel 1–24*, 581–83.

111. See Boda, *Heartbeat*, 35–51.

112. Boda, *Heartbeat*, 102.

113. See Borgman, *Genesis*, 35–36; Mann, *Book of the Torah*, 33.

114. Humphreys, *Character of God*, 73. Emphasis original.

115. Fretheim, *God and World*, 81. Emphasis original.

In contrast, Boda discerns that far from being a cosmic do-over, the Genesis Flood functions to make possible "a renewal of the kinship relationship" between humanity and GOD.[116] As Boda also states: "It is obvious from Gen. 8:21 and the narratives that follow the covenantal agreement (Gen. 9:20-27; 11:1-9) that sin is not eradicated by the flood. The focus then is on the establishment of this relationship after producing a new creation. As with the redemptive covenants, this creational covenant is identified as an 'everlasting covenant' (9:16)."[117]

To summarize, the Noachian deluge narrative is a stage for indescribable redemption, deliverance, and salvation, not a cosmic flop of inexpressible destruction and judgment.[118]

Competing Theologies?

It is well known within the academy that the Flood text of Genesis was often dissected by scholars throughout the late nineteenth and early twentieth centuries, as it was usually regarded to be the perfect specimen to test case the (source-critical) documentary hypothesis.[119] This approach (for the most part) is predicated on the belief that the traditionally accepted final form of the Flood was composed of two different versions which were spliced and interwoven with one another, namely "an older one 'J' (the

---

116. Boda, *Heartbeat*, 100.

117. Boda, *Heartbeat*, 96. Mathews states, "The mitigation of GOD's former policy is plain when read against his antediluvian changes (6:5-7). Both 6:5 and 8:21 have the words 'inclination,' 'his heart,' and 'evil,' but 6:5 has the inclusive "every,' 'only,' and 'all.' In 6:5 the emphasis is on the unprecedented pervasiveness of sin, which deserved divine retribution, and in 8:21 GOD acknowledges that sin is a given with humanity and has ruled the human heart from the outset (i.e. Adam's sin)." Mathews, *Genesis 1—11:26*, 392.

118. Kaminski asserts, "In spite of the divine judgment against humankind, GOD's intentions for his creation will not be thwarted." Kaminski, *From Noah to Israel*, 1. Cf. Walton, *Genesis*, 331; Boda, *Severe Mercy*, 22.

119. Wenham, "Pentateuch," 116-44; Alexander, *Paradise*, 229-330; Baker, "Source," 798-805. For recent trends, see Alexander, *Paradise*, 331-59; Baker Jr. et al., eds., *Composition of the Pentateuch*; Dozeman et al., eds., *Pentateuch*, 3-240; Gmirkin, *Genesis*, 22-33; Carr, *Genesis*, 41-98; Blenkinsopp, *Pentateuch*, 1-30; Campbell and O'Brien, *Pentateuch*, 1-10; Baden, *Pentateuch*, 13-33; Dozeman and Schmid, eds., *Farewell to the Yahwist?*, 1-27; Van Seters, *Yahwist*, 3-17; Blenkinsopp, "Genesis," 1-15. Cf. Garrett, *Rethinking Genesis*, 13-90; Garrett, "Hypothesis," 28-41; Steiner, "Literary Structure," 544-46.

Yahwistic account) and a later one, 'P' (the Priestly version), that adapted the story in the sixth-century BCE for a new audience of exiles."[120]

In this way, it was usually understood that the first task of the interpreter was to attempt to recreate the source material.[121] In point of fact, each of the major scholars of this time period, S. R. Driver (1904),[122] John Skinner (1910),[123] Hermann Gunkel (1910),[124] Gerhard von Rad (1961),[125] E. A. Speiser (1964),[126] and Claus Westermann (1974),[127] for example, in effect, wrote commentaries on the 'J' and 'P' versions of the Genesis Flood story rather than on the final form of the text itself.[128] Traditionally, the following verses from within the Noachian deluge narrative are accepted as being part of the 'J' (Yahwist) source, namely Gen 6:5–8; 7:1–5, 7–10, 12, 16b, 17b, 22–23; 8:2b–3a, 6–12, 13b, 20–22. The 'P' (Priestly) source is assumed to be comprised of Gen 6:9–22; 7:6, 11, 13–16a, 17a, 18–21, 24; 8:1–2a, 3b–5, 13a, 14–19; 9:1–17.[129]

This approach has often led many scholars to the conclusion there are actually two distinct (and often competing) "theologies of the Flood," one from the 'J' version and the other from the 'P' version.[130] For instance, the anthropomorphism of GOD smelling the pleasing odor (see Gen 8:21) is often taken as "a sure sign of the theological primitivism of the Yahwist, as opposed to the Priestly writer who is more like us."[131]

---

120. Clifford, "Inundation or Interpretation," 25. Cf. Kloppenborg, "Source Criticism," 342. More details on the dating of the book of Genesis and related matters are addressed in chapter 2.

121. Kaminski, *Was Noah Good?*, 22. See too Chisholm, "Source Criticism," 181–90. Cf. Dozeman et al., eds., *Pentateuch*.

122. Driver, *Genesis*, 82–108.

123. Skinner, *Genesis*, 150–58, 158–74.

124. Gunkel, *Genesis*, 60–84, 138–51.

125. Von Rad, *Genesis*, 118–25, 125–34.

126. Speiser, *Genesis*, 44–59.

127. Westermann, *Genesis 1–11*, 384–480.

128. Much of this sentence's wording has been derived from Evans, *Guide*, 78.

129. Skinner, *Genesis*, 148; Driver, *Genesis*, 85–86; Gunkel, *Genesis*, 60, 138–46; Westermann, *Genesis 1–11*, 397–98; Campbell and O'Brien, *Sources*, 214; Boadt et al., *Old Testament*, 101; Dozeman, *Pentateuch*, 106; Steinmann, *Genesis*, 113; Kawashima, "Sources," 51–70; Habel, "Two Flood Stories," 18–25; Galambush, *Reading Genesis*, 42. While this division is "fairly standard" some may still "dissent here or there." Hamilton, *Genesis 1–11*, 16.

130. Kaminski, *Was Noah Good?*, 9. See also Mann, *Book of the Torah*, 30.

131. Kikawada and Quinn, *Before Abraham Was*, 105.

Another scholar asserts: "the priestly narrative material tends to make GOD less human-like . . . than other narratives in Genesis."[132] Claus Westermann's statements about Noah are also representative:

> The abrupt mention of him in [Gen] 6:8 is meant to show that, in contrast to P's presentation, the motive for Noah's preservation lies with GOD and not in Noah's piety The *waw*-adversative at the beginning clearly refers this sentence to vv. 6–7 . . . there is an element of contradiction here. The corruption of humankind is portrayed in v. 5 as radical and all-embracing; in v. 8 however one among humankind can find favor with GOD. P on the contrary is rationalistic. He begins with Noah's righteousness in 6:9 so as to set in relief from the very beginning the reason for the exception. This is a typical difference between J and P.[133]

Though duly cognizant of what source-criticism brings to the academy at large, not all supporters of this approach wish to emphasize the potential discontinuity of the Noachian deluge narrative.[134] What, then, is one to do with 'J' and 'P'? Robert S. Kawashima offers: "To discern the complex meaning of the flood . . . begin with the two underlying sources, J and P. One can bring out their distinctive ideas most fully by comparing them on three key points: the motive for the flood, the function of the flood, and the conclusion of the flood."[135]

To be clear, according to 'J,' the source of the problem is the "violence" (חמס) of people (Gen 6:5), while for 'P,' the reason for the Genesis Flood is "the 'corruption' of the 'earth' itself, due to the 'corruption' and 'violence' of 'all life'—that is, both humans and animals" (Gen 6:11–13).[136] Given such, the problem (for 'P') is not directly related to that "moral agency peculiar to humans."[137] It is thereby deduced by many source-critical scholars that (for 'J') the Flood functions as a type of "universal punishment" for the sin(s) of humanity while, in contrast, "P's flood cleanses the earth from pollution, apparently caused by bloodguilt."[138]

---

132. Smith, *Priestly Vision*, 66.

133. Westermann, *Genesis 1–11*, 411–12. Cf. Collins, *Reading Genesis Well*, 111.

134. See, for example. Campbell and O'Brien, *Sources of the Pentateuch* and *Rethinking the Pentateuch*.

135. Kawashima, "Sources," 66. Cf. Van Seters, *Yahwist*, 24–28, 192–214.

136. Kawashima, "Sources," 66.

137. Kawashima, "Sources," 67.

138. Kawashima, "Sources," 67. See too Frymer-Kensky, "Atrahasis Epic," 147–55; Frymer-Kensky, "Pollution, Purification, and Purgation," 399–414.

It is also notable in this diachronic (source-critical) framework, the apex of the Genesis Flood is also contingent upon one's understanding of both the 'J' and 'P' sources that are claimed to lay behind the final form of the Genesis text. To this end, Lawrence Boadt opines:

> The climax for the J version comes in Genesis 8:20–22, in which GOD's forgiveness extends even to lifting the curse upon the earth for what human have done in their hearts. People may still choose to sin, but the goodness of GOD and his everlasting mercy will be seen in the bounty and the regularity of nature's seasons ... (Gen 8:22). P's climax comes in Genesis 9:1–17 where GOD renews the blessing of Genesis 1 on human beings. P even enlarges the covenant conditions so that now people may eat meat as well as plants, thus removing the last restrictions on their rule over the creatures of the world. But with it comes an increased obligation to respect human life ... (Gen 9:6).[139]

Antony F. Campbell and Mark A. O'Brien also assert:

> There are two stages to the ending of the story. In the first, Noah's sacrifice is followed by GOD's decision never again to destroy life because of human evil. What was intolerable before the flood (6:5) is now tolerated. While there is no reflection offered on this, the place of Gen 6:5 and 8:21b–22 in the same narrative can only imply that GOD has had a radical change of heart. In the second stage, much the same is said in different language. The world is blessed again, as at the start of creation. But it is a less-than-perfect world, a world in which there is to be fear and bloodshed. Yet GOD makes a covenant never again to destroy this world by flood, a covenant to which no condition is attached.[140]

To be specific, from a source-critical perspective, such phenomena have (traditionally) been explained through the differences between 'J' and 'P'; that is "while J tells a story of fratricide, P proclaims the law that forbids murder. The language of P stands apart from that of J both chronologically and in content by making use of a theological, conceptual vocabulary for the stories of the primeval event."[141] Gerhard von Rad likewise argues: "Going beyond the Yahwist's representation, the Priestly document now

---

139. Boadt et al., *Old Testament*, 100.
140. Campbell and O'Brien, *Pentateuch*, 215. Cf. Kawashima, "Sources," 68.
141. Westermann, *Introduction*, 104.

speaks of a covenant, which GOD made with Noah and his descendants."[142] The next section summarizes matters and offers conclusions.

DIACHRONIC (SOURCE-CRITICAL) APPROACHES—CONCLUDING THOUGHTS

Though there is, relatively speaking, rather broad agreement among diachronic (source-critical) scholars concerning the "demarcation of the sources in the flood story, there is much less unanimity about their relationship."[143] While many scholars agree 'J' and 'P' should not be thought of as independent sources, given the wide disparity that exists between them, many traditional source-critical explanations of the Genesis Flood tend to rely quite heavily upon the work of the final editor(s), that is, the *Redakteur*, in order to construct a "logically coherent narrative."[144] Even so, there is little to no agreement about how these two stories have been combined.[145] Has the 'J' source been worked into the "basic 'P' document"?[146]

If one assumes some type of 'J-type' redaction, that is, a "reworking" of 'P' by 'J,' how does one resolve the problem of 'J' antedating 'P'?[147] The situation becomes increasingly more complex when one begins to notice the not insignificant Mesopotamian parallels of the ANE myths—as one scholar astutely observes, "it is strange ... that both J and P versions should lack features of the common tradition, but when combined create an account which resembles it."[148]

One need not concur with the criteria upon which source-criticism is built in order to appreciate the "artistry of the Hebrew narrative."[149]

---

142. Von Rad, *Genesis*, 133. Cf. Driver, *Genesis*, 98; Batto, "Covenant of Peace," 187–211; Chisholm, "The 'Everlasting Covenant,'" 237–53; Gunn, "Deutero-Isaiah and the Flood," 493–508; Streett, "Day's of Noah," 33–51. Cf. Dumbrell, *Covenant and Creation*, 13, 22; Waltke, "The Phenomenon of Conditionality," 126, 131; Dearman, *Hosea*, 197–98; Stuart, *Hosea*, 98–99.

143. Wenham, *Genesis 1–15*, 168. Cf. Gertz, "Source Criticism," 169–80.

144. Kawashima, "Sources," 68. See too Halpern, "What they Don't Know," 16–34.

145. Kawashima, "Sources," 68.

146. Wenham, *Genesis 1–15*, 168.

147. Wenham, *Genesis 1–15*, 168.

148. Wenham, *Genesis 1–15*, 168–69. Cf. Buth, "Methodological Collision," 138–54.

149. Kaminski, *Was Noah Good?*, 21–22. Cf. Turner, *Plot-structure of Genesis*.

Admittedly, however, this is mostly because the literary structure of the Genesis Flood account is usually attributed to the work of a final redactor.[150] In summary, this study takes umbrage with most traditional diachronic (source-critical) explanations of the Genesis Flood as they tend to unnecessarily complicate issues of plot in their accounting of the final redactor and often fail to adequately explain how two such divergent and competing theologies would remain in the final redaction of the text.[151]

Kawashima asserts the "more complicated and therefore conjectural the composition of a passage is . . . the more complicated and therefore conjectural must be its interpretation."[152] Even so, this study argues a rhetorical-critical approach based upon the final form of the text offers more effective and more compelling evidence concerning the rhetoric of the Noachian deluge narrative since it chooses to engage with the text as it presently stands—not as it (perhaps) once stood. This is not a "false comfort" but a bold reality.[153]

SYNCHRONIC APPROACHES— CONCLUDING THOUGHTS

Unlike source-critical (diachronic) stances, a literary-critical approach argues for a synchronic reading of the Genesis text that is particularly aware of and especially sensitive to the final form of the Noachian deluge narrative.[154] In this way, singular phenomena which were commonly used by many source-critical scholars to bolster the so-called "patchwork quality" of the Genesis Flood text, such as variations of the divine name (Elohim/Yahweh) and certain twice repeated materials, for instance, are not perceived as being "doublets" in the "classic source-critical interpretation" but rather as part of the "careful construction" of the Flood narrative itself.[155]

150. See Walton, *Genesis*, 316; Longman and Walton, *Lost World of the Flood*, 136–42.

151. See Weeks, *Sources and Authors*, 53–64, 67–72. Cf. Fretheim, *Creation, Fall and Flood*, 109–11; Fretheim "Genesis," 322–23, 384–97.

152. Kawashima, "Sources," 69.

153. Kawashima, "Sources," 70. Cf. Kaminski, *Was Noah Good?*, 22–23; Boda, *Severe Mercy*, 4–5.

154. Kaminski, *Was Noah Good?*, 22–23; Hawk, "Literary," 536–44; Beal et al., "Literary," 159–67. Cf. Reno, *Genesis*, 33, 147, 192, 223.

155. Barton, "Literary Criticism," 527. See too Walton, *Genesis*, 315; Rooker, "Genesis," 59. This does not, however, necessarily entail a "highly schematic interpretation" of the account." Kaminski, *Was Noah Good?*, 23.

Genesis and Noah's Flood

To state things differently, rather than attempt to reconstruct the sources that lie behind Noah's Flood, the primary task of the literary-critical scholar is to engage the "signals which give a wide variety of directives to the reader as to how to actualize the text," discerning the text's literary and structural features.[156] In this way (a literary-critical framework), "the question of sources does not have to dominate the interpretation of the text."[157] Thomas Brodie reasons:

> The issue is not whether something can be divided in two (or three or four) but whether it is more intelligible when taken as a unit. When Genesis is taken as a unit it is indeed perplexing, but ultimately it is supremely intelligible—great literary art, with a magnificent vision of the struggle and richness of life and of a transcendent dimension surpassing human calculation . . . the text is complex, but it is orderly.[158]

Put otherwise, in this literary-critical, synchronic method, the received, final text, is not a

> [b]arrier beyond which one must—in order to do Biblical scholarship—necessarily press, nor an end product that should most properly be analyzed for evidences of its origins. True though it is that its literary history may at times encompass many centuries, several strata of tradition, and a variety of editorial influences, it is itself—the final text—susceptible of study as a system of meaningful and artistic wholes.[159]

For the purposes of this study, specifically, the fact that the Genesis Flood narrative is deeply embedded within the account of the patriarch Noah (Gen 6:9—9:29) is of great significance since it suggests "a different 'text' than the text(s) suggested by a source critical approach."[160] To be clear, the "superscriptions" in which "*toledoth*" (תולדת) appears "serve to divide the text into blocks."[161] The "shift to one family within humanity, Noah's, is accomplished through a . . . dramatic event—the Flood. After the flood,

---

156. Campbell and O'Brien, *Pentateuch*, 214.

157. Brodie, *Genesis as Dialogue*, xiv. See too Anderson, *Creation*, 73.

158. Brodie, *Genesis as Dialogue*, 500. See also Middleton, *Liberating Image*, 64–65. Cf. Harrison, *Introduction to the Old Testament*, 547.

159. Clines et al., eds., *Art and Meaning*, i.

160. Kaminski, *Was Noah Good?*, 21–22. Hamilton argues this feature of the book of Genesis is "so distinctly woven into one tapestry as to constitute an unassailable case for the unity of the section." Hamilton, *Genesis 1–17*, 29.

161. Turner, "Genesis," 350. See also Boda, *Severe Mercy*, 16.

Noah's family is all that is left of humanity. This is the second narrowing."[162] In Genesis, the end point is the family of Jacob.[163] See below.[164]

Table Four—The Toledoth Structure of Genesis

(Introduction) Gen 1:1—2:3	When God began to create . . . (or) In the beginning . . .
Gen 2:4—4:26	This is the *toledoth* of the Heavens and the Earth
Gen 5:1—6:8	This is the book of the *toledoth* of Adam
Gen 6:9—9:29	This is the *toledoth* of Noah
Gen 10:1—11:9	This is the *toledoth* of Shem, Ham, and Japheth (repeated in 10:32)
Gen 11:10-26	This is the *toledoth* of Shem
Gen 11:27—25:11	This is the *toledoth* of Terah
Gen 25:12-18	This is the *toledoth* of Ishmael
Gen 25:19—35:29	This is the *toledoth* of Isaac
Gen 36:1—37:1	This is the *toledoth* of Esau (repeated in 36:9)
Gen 37:2—50:26	This is the *toledoth* of Jacob

CONCLUSION

A synchronic, literary-critical methodology is immensely helpful in helping one to ascertain the overall focus and emphasis of the Genesis Flood

---

162. Thomas, *Generations*, 80. Cf. Waltke and Yu, *Old Testament Theology*, 285.

163. This focus becomes even more narrower by the *toledoth* of Num 3:1 "to the Aaronide priesthood and the civil leadership represented by Moses." Thomas, *Generations*, 2. See too Johnson, *Genealogies*, 22–23.

164. This chart has been constructed from the templates of Miller and Soden, *In the Beginning*, 60; Boda, *Severe Mercy*, 16; Hamilton, *Genesis 1–17*, 2; Halton, ed., *Genesis*, 29; Walton, *Genesis*, 35, 40.

account; it will, as such, be extensively leveraged throughout this study.[165] Yet, as noted above, rhetorical criticism captures the persuasive intent of the text far more effectively than the literary critical method. That is to say, a critical component generally absent from most synchronic analyses is a thorough description of the many facets (and function) of the text's rhetoric. Bruce K. Waltke and Charles Yu contend:

> To think critically about the Old Testament's theology first involves that the theologian exegete the texts . . . they must also think critically about the writer's rhetoric. Much of the Old Testament is artistic narrative . . . In other words, they use rhetoric to communicate their message. Consequently the theologian must reflect critically on their rhetoric in order to engage with their messages.[166]

Said otherwise, it is not a lack of exegetical care, theological acumen, or even an insufficiently rigorous methodological framework, *per se*, that makes literary-criticism unequal to the task at hand. Why, then, does this study of the Noahide Flood require rhetorical criticism? Two things necessitate this decision: First, rhetorical criticism offers a "new appreciation for the artistry of the greatest literature ever written."[167] As Boda asserts: "The book of Genesis functions as the introduction to the Torah, which in turn lays the foundation for the entire Old Testament, in terms of both its story and its theology."[168] Rhetorical criticism understands this great honor and leverages the *crème de crème* of the literary-critical discipline but also moves beyond it. Second, rhetoric is uniquely equipped to move arguments away from stasis and towards resolution. Given the acrimony surrounding Genesis can there be a better way to handle GOD's Word?[169]

---

165. See Keiser, *Genesis*, 126–27. Cf. Peterson, *Genesis*, 62.

166. Waltke and Yu, *Old Testament Theology*, 9–10. See too Longman, "Historical-Grammatical Exegesis," 149; Fox, "Rhetoric," 1. Cf. Fee, *New Testament Exegesis*, 183.

167. Waltke and Yu, *Old Testament Theology*, 10.

168. Boda, *Severe Mercy*, 16.

169. Cf. Davidson and Turner, *Manifold Beauty*, 12.

2

Methodology
Rhetorical Criticism

RHETORICAL CRITICISM—INTRODUCTION

IN HEBREW BIBLE/OLD TESTAMENT studies (HB/OT), specifically, the origin of rhetorical criticism is agreed upon by scholars to have stemmed from James Muilenburg's presidential address to the Society of Biblical Literature (December 18, 1968) entitled "Form Criticism and Beyond."[1] In this work, Muilenburg maintained the rhetorical critic should undertake a "responsible and proper articulation of the words in their linguistic patterns and in their precise formulations" so as to uncover "the texture and fabric of the writer's thought."[2] Alongside this, Muilenburg states:

> What I am interested in . . . is . . . understanding the nature of Hebrew literary composition, in exhibiting the structural patterns that are employed for the fashioning of a literary unit, whether in poetry or in prose, and in discerning the many and various devices by which the predications are formulated and

---

1. Donaldson, "New Rhetoric," 246; Barker, *From the Depths of Despair*, 26; Ahn, *Persuasive Portrayal*, 17–19; Trible, *Rhetorical Criticism*, 5; Soulen, *Biblical Criticism*, 183; Barton, *Reading the Old Testament*, 199; Black, "Rhetorical Criticism," 170; Anderson, "Rhetorical Criticism," ix. This lecture was later published by *JBL* in 1969. See Muilenburg, "Form Criticism," 1–18. For a list of other scholars doing work that was similar to Muilenburg (though not necessarily calling it rhetorical criticism) see Lundbom, *Jeremiah*, xxvii–xxviii.

2. Muilenburg, "Form Criticism," 7.

Methodology

ordered into a unified whole. Such an enterprise I should describe as rhetoric and the methodology as rhetorical criticism.³

Rhetorical criticism, at least as construed by Muilenburg, thus encourages what is traditionally understood to be a "close reading" of the text.⁴ In such a reading, one pays careful attention to those things which "constitute the artistry of the text."⁵ That is to say, one seeks to discern "structural patterns, verbal sequences, and stylistic devices that make a coherent whole."⁶ Although Muilenburg portrayed his methodology as being a supplement to form criticism, rhetorical criticism has since become "a full-fledged discipline practiced in different ways."⁷

Much to the chagrin of many scholars, there is no one model agreed upon by all adherents of rhetorical criticism.⁸ This is because much depends on how one defines the terms "rhetoric" and "rhetorical."⁹ Stanley E. Porter opines: "for some rhetoric means the categories used by the ancients, as reflected in the classical orators or in the handbooks on rhetoric, or in some combination of both. For others, rhetoric means rhetorical strategies developed in subsequent times and places."¹⁰ In sum, "rhetoric is not a single thing and neither can it be defined simply."¹¹ As noted above, within HB/OT studies, there are two different branches of "rhetorical criticism" now being practiced with a "sharp distinction" that

---

3. Muilenburg, "Form Criticism," 8.

4. Evans, *Invasion of Sennacherib*, 31; Fitzgerald, "Rhetorical Analysis," iv–vi. To be clear, this means a "deliberate . . . consideration of all the parts of a text in order to understand it as a whole." Gorman, *Elements*, 102

5. Barker, *From the Depths of Despair*, 26. See too Muilenburg, "Form Criticism," 12–13.

6. Trible, *Rhetorical Criticism*, 26. Cf. Muilenburg, "Form Criticism," 17.

7. Trible, *Rhetorical Criticism*, 32. Cf. Muilenburg, "Form Criticism," 4; Lundbom, *Jeremiah*, xxvi–xvii; Fitzgerald, "Rhetorical Analysis," 24.

8. Porter, "London Introduction," 20.

9. For an overview of rhetoric, including its origins and early history, see Herrick, *The History and Theory of Rhetoric*, 1–62; Walker, *Rhetoric and Poetics in Antiquity*, 3–138; Stamps, "Rhetoric," 953–55. For a list of studies on rhetorical criticism, in general, see Fitzgerald, "Rhetorical Analysis," 25. Cf. Collins, *Reading Genesis Well*, 43.

10. Porter, "Heidelberg Introduction," 21, 25. The key question here is "whether a great deal of the discourse is common to all human communication, and whether some modern aspects could not be more adequate in describing it," or, to put the matter another way, whether "ancient theories of argumentation are an ideal, or even the most adequate, way of studying argumentation." Thurén, *Argument and Theology*, 32.

11. Porter, "Heidelberg Introduction," 21. Cf. Hwang, *Rhetoric of Remembrance*, 9–11.

has developed between them: (1) rhetoric as "the art of composition" and (2) "rhetoric as persuasion."[12]

RHETORIC AS "THE ART OF COMPOSITION"

Of the two afore-mentioned branches of rhetorical criticism, "the art of composition" focuses on the literary and stylistic (aesthetic) features of the text.[13] This branch of rhetorical criticism generally follows Muilenburg's primary proposal that "rhetorical criticism should be the study of stylistics of composition in Hebrew prose and poetry, and that a study of stylistics will underscore the unity of biblical texts."[14] Though termed "rhetorical," this approach is much more "a form of literary criticism which uses our knowledge of the conventions of literary composition practiced in ancient Israel and its environment to discover and analyze the particular literary artistry found in a specific unit of Old Testament text."[15] In the words of Muilenburg:

> The basic contention of Gunkel is that the ancient men of Israel, like their Near Eastern neighbors, were influenced in their speech and their literary compositions by convention and custom. We therefore encounter in a particular genre or *Gattung* the same structural forms, the same terminology and style, and the same *Sitz im Leben*.[16]

"Poetics" also describes many elements of this specific branch of rhetorical criticism.[17] Adele Berlin defines poetics as "the science of literature," which inductively "seeks to abstract the general principles of literature from many different manifestations of those principles as they occur in actual literary texts."[18] To put the matter another way, "poetics helps us to

---

12. Barker, *From the Depths of Despair*, 28.

13. Trible, *Rhetorical Criticism*, 28, 32–40.

14. Dozeman, "Rhetorical Criticism," 714. Scholars in this camp consider the "primary task of rhetorical criticism as finding 'integrating devices' to determine the limits of the literary unit of the text . . . these devices 'bind the unit together and help set its boundaries.'" Ahn, *Persuasive Portrayal*, 19. Cf. Fitzgerald, "Rhetorical Analysis," 26–33.

15. Watson and Hauser, *Rhetorical Criticism*, 4. See too Wuellner, "Rhetorical Criticism," 453.

16. Muilenburg, "Form Criticism," 4.

17. See Evans, *Invasion of Sennacherib*, 29–31; Möller, *Prophet in Debate*, 29.

18. Berlin, *Poetics*, 15. See also Sternberg, *Poetics*. Cf. Waltke and Fredricks, *Genesis*, 33.

know *how* texts mean so that we can better understand *what* they mean."[19] Grant Osborne states: "interpretation of narrative has two aspects: poetics, which studies the artistic dimension or the way the text is constructed by the author; and meaning, which recreates the message that the author is communicating. The 'how' (poetics) leads to the 'what' (meaning)."[20]

The biblical authors were "artists of language. Through their verbal artistry—their rhetoric—they have created their meaning. So meaning is ultimately inseparable from art, and those who seek to understand the biblical literature must be sensitive to the writer's craft."[21] Many contemporary HB/OT studies continue to adhere to Muilenburg's principles apply and leverage this specific model of rhetorical criticism, i.e. "the art of composition."[22] As noted in chapter 1, this study employs certain aspects of both poetics and literary-criticism (as a whole).

RHETORIC AS "THE ART OF PERSUASION"

The same year Muilenburg's programmatic article was published, another lynch-pin work on the topic of rhetorical criticism also came to print, namely *The New Rhetoric: A Treatise on Argumentation* by Perelman and Olbrechts-Tyteca.[23] While Muilenburg and his "school" continued to focus on "stylistics," that is, "the art of composition," Perelman and Olbrechts-Tyteca (among others) were influential in shaping what would become the second main branch of rhetorical criticism, something Phyllis Trible calls "the art of persuasion."[24] Such scholars took a keen interest in "rhetoric as argumentation," i.e., analyzing texts in terms of their persuasive capacity, thus reverting to rhetoric's "classical Aristotelian conception."[25] This "alternative conception" of rhetoric came to be known

---

19. Lowery, *Towards a Poetics*, 2. Emphases original.

20. Osborne, *Spiral*, 203.

21. Clines et al., eds. *Art and Meaning*, i.

22. For a list of such scholars, see Trible, *Rhetorical Criticism*, 32–40; Hwang, *The Rhetoric of Remembrance*, 9–11; Ahn, *Persuasive Portrayal*, 21–22; Barker, *From the Depths of Despair*, 27.

23. Perelman and Olbrechts-Tyteca, *New Rhetoric*. Cf. Möller, *Prophet in Debate*, 23.

24. See Trible, *Rhetorical Criticism*, 32, 41–52. For more details, see Möller, *Prophet in Debate*, 24–25.

25. Möller, *Prophet in Debate*, 24.

as "rhetoric reinvented" or "rhetoric reevaluated."[26] As noted above, this model considers the text "as we have it'" and how such a text would be received by an audience of "near contemporaries."[27]

Many who adhere to this branch believe Muilenburg (and his followers) do not pay enough attention to "the suasive ... aspects of biblical literature."[28] Wilhelm Wuellner, for instance, famously wrote in 1987 of the "Babylonian captivity of rhetoric reduced to stylistics" and "the ghetto of an estheticizing preoccupation with biblical stylistics."[29] While united against the "rhetoric as composition" branch, a deep schism exists within this group that turns on whether or not to keep the categories of classical Greco-Roman rhetoric or appropriate something modern.[30] The following chart encapsulates the major features of classical Greco-Roman rhetoric.[31]

While there is much debate in academia concerning such, the lack of correspondence between the two languages, the differing function(s) of their literary (and oral texts), and the potential to inadvertently impose an "Occidental paradigm on an Oriental work,"[32] makes relying on Greco-Roman rhetorical theory an undesirable rubric for studying HB/OT narrative.[33] It still has its use as a "heuristic device for identifying and analyzing patterns of argumentation."[34]

---

26. Möller, *Prophet in Debate*, 25. See too Trible, *Rhetorical Criticism*, 55–56.

27. Kennedy, *New Testament Interpretation*, 3–4. Cf. Barker, *From the Depths of Despair*, 32, 37.

28. Howard, "Rhetorical Criticism," 102. See also Ahn, *Persuasive Portrayal*, 19.

29. Wuellner, "Rhetorical Criticism," 457, 462.

30. See Fee, *New Testament Exegesis*, 183.

31. See Trible, *Rhetorical Criticism*, 9. For more details, see Porter, ed., *Handbook of Classical Rhetoric*.

32. See Hwang, *Rhetoric of Remembrance*, 10. Cf. Sonnet, Review of *Choose Life!*, 93–98.

33. Hwang, *Rhetoric of Remembrance*, 10. See too Wuellner, "Jesus' Sermon," 97–99.

34. Stamps, "Rhetorical and Narratological Criticism," 233. Cf. Donaldson, "New Rhetoric," 246.

Table Five—Major Features of Classical Rhetoric

Three Elements of Communication			
• speaker or author			
• speech or text			
• audience or reader			
Three Types of Communication	Judicial (*forensic*)	Deliberative (*hortatory*)	Demonstrative (*epideictic*)
• Focus:	Justice	Expediency	Adulation/Denunciation
• Setting:	Law court	Public assembly	Public ceremony
• Purpose:	Persuasion	Persuasion	To please or to inspire
• Time:	Past	Future	Present
• Emphasis:	Speech	Audience	Speaker
Three Goals of Communication			
• intellectual goal of teaching			
• emotional goal of touching the feelings			
• aesthetic goal of pleasing so as to hold attention			
Five Parts of Rhetoric			
• Invention (*inventio*):	discovery	of material	suitable to the occasion
• Structure (*dispositio*):	arrangement	of material	in an organized whole
• Style (*elocutio*):	choice	of appropriate	words; use of tropes
• Memory (*memoria*):	formulation	of mnemonic	systems/preparations
• Delivery (*pronunciatio/actio*):	features	of oral	presentations

To summarize, rhetorical-critical scholars agree on the benefits of examining the literary nature of the biblical text and the unique qualities that lend it "esthetic power and appeal;" as such, rhetoric as "the art of persuasion" not only builds on rhetorical criticism as "the art of composition" but also, it may be said, surpasses it.[35] "Rhetoric as persuasion" HB/OT scholars argue the role of the "rhetorical critic is both to analyze

35. Barker, *From the Depths of Despair*, 33.

the literary features of the text but further to articulate the impact of the given unit upon its audience."[36] As Burton L. Mack states:

> By linking the persuasive power of a speech not only to its logic of argumentation, but to the manner in which it addresses the social and cultural history of its audience and speaker, Perelman and Olbrechts-Tyteca demonstrated the rhetorical coefficient that belongs to every human exchange involving speech, including common conversation and the daily discourse of a working society. This takes rhetoric out of the sphere of mere ornamentation, embellished literary style, and the extravagances of public oratory, and places it at the center of a social theory of language.[37]

Such assertions have implications for an effective rhetorical analysis of the Noahide Flood.

A RHETORICAL-CRITICAL MODEL FOR STUDYING HEBREW NARRATIVE

The plethora of literary strategies and poignant imagery of the Genesis Flood make it a worthy text to examine.[38] A rhetorical-critical approach is also appropriate as it allows the interpreter (exegete) to enter the world of the text and examine a discrete literary unit; issues surrounding the text's compositional unity also make it a valuable field of inquiry for flow of argumentation.

The Kennedy Style Rhetorical-Critical Model

The following section functions as a sort of road map to the specific type of rhetorical-critical model this study leverages; the particulars find their origins within George A. Kennedy's most prominent volume *New Testament Interpretation Through Rhetorical Criticism*. The broad contours of the model will be given first prior to offering the details of how this study will adapt Kennedy's approach so as to better handle the unique challenges that are inherent to studying Hebrew narrative—including the distinct features of divine speeches. The sum of these modifications has

---

36. Barker, *From the Depths of Despair*, 29. Cf. Watson and Hauser, *Rhetorical Criticism*, 14.

37. Mack, *Rhetoric*, 16. For more details, see Möller, *Prophet in Debate*, 23–27.

38. Cf. Barker, *From the Depths of Despair*, 33.

been derived from the judicious work of a number of HB/OT rhetorical-critical scholars.[39] The works of Joel Barker[40] and Suk-il Ahn,[41] in particular, stand out as exemplars due to the not insignificant modifications they made to the model for studying Hebrew texts.

It is worth noting "Kennedy's proposal incorporates an articulated procedure. His is truly a method, not merely an interpretive perspective."[42] The high degree of specificity Kennedy's method employs makes it particularly apt for doing accurate analyses of literary texts. According to Kennedy, the goal of rhetorical analysis is "the discovery of the author's intent and of how that is transmitted through a text to an audience."[43] In this way, rhetorical analysis focuses on the intention of the text is and how the text itself achieves its goal.[44] As noted, this involves a 'close' (but not atomistic) reading in order to discern and delineate how the text's form, structure, and use of imagery points towards its persuasive intent.[45] A rhetorical-critical approach also invites the interpreter to consider how the text's "literary artistry" shapes or affects the respondent and to discover the ways in which it seeks to effect, persuade, and influence its audience to respond in the manner it invites or to adopt a particular point of view.[46]

Aside from providing clear definitions of argumentation and rhetoric, the Kennedy model consists of five stages: the rhetorical critic must (1) identify the rhetorical unit(s) in the text, (2) clearly identify the rhetorical situation and determine the rhetorical problem (exigence) that precipitated or occasioned the need for a rhetorical response, (3) offer a thorough delineation of the rhetorical species of the discourse at hand, (4) examine the arrangement of material in the text, including devices of style; that is, the rhetorical strategy of the text must be examined, and, finally (5)

---

39. See Ahn, *Persuasive Portrayal*, 21–22 for a full listing of scholars who leverage Kennedy's model.

40. Barker, *From the Depths of Despair to the Promise of Presence: A Rhetorical Reading of the Book of Joel*.

41. Ahn, *The Persuasive Portrayal of David and Solomon in Chronicles: A Rhetorical Analysis of the Speeches and Prayers in the David-Solomon Narrative*.

42. Black, "Biblical Interpretation," 256. See too Black, "New Testament," 77–92.

43. Kennedy, *New Testament Interpretation*, 12.

44. Ahn *Persuasive Portrayal*, 21.

45. Walsh, *Old Testament Narrative*, 5; Barker, *From the Depths of Despair*, 25; Barker, "Rhetorical Criticism," 676.

46. See Barker, *From the Depths of Despair*, 1.

conduct a review as to what implications the discourse has for the audience and, whether the discourse fits the rhetorical exigence. To reiterate step five, the rhetorical critic must assess the rhetorical effectiveness of the text, that is, did it meet the demand to which it was first fashioned?[47] A brief conclusion rounds out the analysis and provides closure.

Black helpfully defends the broad utility of Kennedy's model for biblical studies, stating it represents "the most comprehensive understanding of rhetoric . . . into which the concerns of competing definitions may be fairly subsumed."[48] Witherington and Myers say much the same thing with respect to the constructive nature of Kennedy's model and the effectiveness of his overarching method of analysis (rhetorical criticism).[49] Even so, this approach is not one an interpreter should "slavishly" follow.[50] Certain modifications need to be made to the model.

Step One: Determining the Rhetorical Units

The first step of rhetorical analysis is to determine the boundaries of the rhetorical units which exist in the text. The goal is to divide the text into "discrete passages in order to see both how they communicate their message and how they fit into the broader shape" of the rest of the narrative.[51] A rhetorical unit must have within itself a "discernible beginning and ending, connected by some action or argument."[52]

According to Wuellner, these sub-units are "argumentative" because they contain attempts to persuade or to affect some sort of change in

---

47. These five steps are an amalgamation of the procedure outlined by Kennedy, *Rhetorical Criticism*, 33–38 and a somewhat different five-step system delineated by Mitchell, "Rhetorical Criticism," 622. See also Stamps, "Rhetorical and Narratological Criticism," 224–25; Ahn, *Persuasive Portrayal*, 22–23; Möller, *Prophet in Debate*, 37–43; Barker, *From the Depths of Despair*, 37–65.

48. Black, "Biblical Interpretation," 256.

49. See Witherington, "Almost Thou Persuadest Me," 63–88 alongside Myers and Witherington, "Response to Stanley Porter," 547–49. Cf. Porter and Dyer, "Oral Texts?" 323–41; Porter, "Unproven Claims," 533–45; Porter "Ben Witherington on Rhetoric," 551–52; Fee, *New Testament Exegesis*, 166.

50. Barker, "From the Depths of Despair," 50. See also Bovard, "Rhetorical Questions," 20; Walton, "Rhetorical Criticism," 6. Cf. Hwang, *Rhetoric of Remembrance*, 10–11.

51. Barker, *From the Depths of Despair*, 66.

52. Kennedy, *New Testament Interpretation*, 34. See too Ahn, *Persuasive Portrayal*, 23.

reasoning or imagination within the intended or implied audience.[53] The range of a rhetorical unit varies from a single verse (such as a *toledoth* notation or superscription), to an entire book (such as Genesis, Joel, Ruth, etc.), or a series of books (such as the Pentateuch or the Book of the Twelve).[54] One rhetorical unit may also be enclosed or embedded in another.[55] The interpreter must always seek to delineate the interrelationship of the different subunits "with an eye towards articulating their function in building the argument of the larger rhetorical unit."[56]

The primary difficulty of this step is properly identifying the units of text the narrative intends and designs as units rather than imposing an artificial scheme onto the narrative.[57] As Muilenburg asserts: "the first concern of the rhetorical critic . . . is to define the limits or scope of the literary unit, to recognize precisely where and how it begins and where and how it ends . . . [a]n examination of the commentaries will reveal that there is great disagreement on this matter, and . . . more often than not, no defense is offered for the isolation of the pericope."[58]

To this end, paraphrasing John Callow, the progression of the author's thought is best seen in the light of their own grouping of material(s), i.e., as the author moves towards their communicative goal, they do not do so in an undifferentiated string of clauses—the clauses will be grouped and the grouping will be controlled by the author's purpose.[59]

Three things must be done in order to establish a text as a distinct unit: (1) mark the unit's beginning, (2) mark the unit's end, and (3) understand the shape of the unit as a cohesive whole. This last step involves understanding how each of the specific parts of the rhetorical unit are bound together to form a self-contained "package" that has internal cohesion.[60] Coherence means "the constituents of a unit will be semantically

---

53. Wuellner, "Rhetorical Criticism," 455. The concerted focus on argumentation distinguishes the concept of a rhetorical unit from a literary unit. See Hester, "Rediscovering," 7; Barker, *From the Depths of Despair*, 38.

54. See Ahn, *Persuasive Portrayal*, 23; Wuellner, "Rhetorical Criticism," 455.

55. Kennedy, *New Testament Interpretation*, 34.

56. Barker, *From the Depths of Despair*, 31. See too Wuellner, "Rhetorical Criticism," 455.

57. See Dorsey, *Literary Structure*, 21.

58. For a rigorous attempt at increased precision on these matters, see Heller, *Narrative Structure*.

59. Callow, "Units and Flow," 464.

60. Dorsey, *Literary Structure*, 21–24; Wendland, *Discourse Analysis*, 24–70.

compatible with one another. Corresponding to the three subclasses of constituents of a unit, it is expected that a well-formed unit will have referential coherence, situational coherence, and structural (relational) coherence."[61]

Some examples of the techniques used to create this type of internal cohesion involve intrinsic correspondence.[62] By this is meant: (a) sameness in the number/person of participants, (b) related time length involved for an event, (c) no known shifts in the events locale/place, (d) same speed of action (rapid and/or spanning a long length of time or slow and/or covering a brief length of time, such as a single conversation or incident), (e) analogous genre and literary forms (such as prose or poetry), (f) frequent repetition of the same word throughout the unit (keyword) and other related grammatical and/or syntactic forms, including (g) repeated verbal form patterns, (h) patterned repetition of information, (i) arranging the material in an inclusio, (j) arranging the material using chiasmus, (k) employing a recurring motif, or (l) uniformity of topic and/or theme.[63] Some examples of different beginning and ending markers are seen below.[64]

---

61. Beekman et al., *Semantic Structure*, 21.

62. For details on delimitation criticism (a method I do not leverage here), see Tov, *Scribal Practices*, 145–64 and the Pericope series, which includes Korpel and Oesch eds., *Delimitation Criticism*. Cf. Lyon, *Reassessing Selah*, 17.

63. Dorsey, *Literary Structure*, 23–24. Porter, "Pericope Markers," 175–95, has seven general characteristics: (1) discourse markers, such as conjunctions and particles that mark the beginning and ends of sections, (2) cohesion and segmentation, (3) participant chains, (4) word order and referential distance, (5) topic and topic shifts, (6) thematic focus and thematization, and (7) text types. I am indebted to Doosuk Kim for this reference (private communiqué).

64. Most of the information in this chart comes from Dorsey, *Literary Structure*, 21–23; Ahn, *Persuasive Portrayal*, 65. For more details, see Muilenburg, "Linguistic and Rhetorical Usages," 135–60; Muilenburg, "Form Criticism," 1–18; Pickering, *Framework for Discourse Analysis*, 279–80; Bar-Efrat, "Some Observations," 154–73; Berlin, *Poetics*, 101–10; Fokkelman, *Biblical Narrative*, 208–9; Fitzgerald, "Rhetorical Analysis," 26–27; Longacre, *Grammar of Discourse*, 18–21; Gorman, *Elements*, 39–43.

Table Six: Beginning and Ending Markers

Beginning Markers (BM)	Ending Markers (EM)
Title or Superscription	Poetic Refrain
Introductory Formula e.g., "these are the generations of *x*" "there are three things ... four things"	Concluding Formula e.g., "and the land had peace for *x* years" "and it was evening ... the *n*th day"
Common Beginning Word or Phrases e.g., "behold!" "woe!" "therefore" "in that day/in these days" "the days are coming" "hear!" "for" "surely"	Conclusion (a) resolution of tension, (b) completion of action, (c) death of central character, (e) final outcome, (f) end of reign
Vocative	Summary
Rhetorical Question	Flashback
Imperative	Closing Prophetic Speech
Orientation (one or more clauses setting the stage for the upcoming narrative or instructions to a prophet about the delivery of the message that follows)	Association with Audience's Own Time (a concluding story with a statement about the significance or consequences of the story in the audience's own time, often including the phrase "to this day")
Abstract (one or more narrative clauses that summarize the whole upcoming story)	Poetic Climactic Lines or Concluding Exclamation
First Part of an *Inclusio*	Last Part of an *Inclusio*
First Part of a *Chiasmus* Various Shifts: (a) time, (b) place, (c) characters or speakers, (d) theme or topic, (e) genre, (f) narrative technique (speed of action/mood)	Last part of a *Chiasmus* Various Shifts: (a) time, (b) place, (c) characters or speakers, (d) theme or topic, (e) genre, (f) narrative technique (speed of action/mood)
Grammatical/Syntactical Signals (a) person of the verbs, (b) use of *waws* (conjunctive/disjunctive), (c) verbal forms (*wayyiqtol* verbs/non-*wayyiqtol* verbs)	Grammatical/Syntactical Signals (a) person of the verbs, (b) use of *waws* (conjunctive/disjunctive), (c) verbal forms (*wayyitqtol* verbs/non-*wayyiqtol* verbs)

Concerning grammatical and syntactical signals: "grammar is the architectural blueprint of communication."[65] More recent works on linguistics further suggest "the exegesis of any narrative depends not only on questions of grammar and syntax, but also on questions of textuality, and particularly on the identification of text structure and thematic net."[66] "Signals of aperture and closure"[67] may also be detected through shifts in the narrative about the person(s) of the verb(s), whether it is the main speaker or a primary or secondary character in the account.[68]

Unlike the rather straightforward shift of the person of the verb, the meaning of the clause-level *waw* is "nuanced" and requires more analysis.[69] Thomas Lambdin states:

> (1) conjunctive-sequential, in which the second clause is temporally or logically posterior or consequent to the first, and (2) disjunctive, in which the second clause may be in various relations, all non-sequential, with the first. The major device in Hebrew for signalling the difference between conjunctive and disjunctive clauses is the type of word which stands immediately after the wə-:wə- (or wa-) + verb is conjunctive [-sequential] wə- + non-verb is disjunctive.[70]

It is unnecessary to rehearse the defining characteristics of the function(s) of the *waw* except to say "disjunctive clauses are distinguished by function as contrastive and scene-shift disjunctive *waw* clauses."[71] As noted by Bruce K. Waltke and Michael O'Connor: "there are two common types of disjunction. One type involves a continuity of scene and participants, but

---

65. Osborne, *Hermeneutical Spiral*, 63. See too Noonan, *Advances in the Study of Biblical Hebrew*, 31–50.

66. Cotterell, "Linguistics," *NIDOTTE* 1:155. See too Cotterell and Turner, *Linguistics*, 11–36. Cf. Reed, *Philippians*, 88–122; Westfall, *Hebrews*, 28–56; Lee, *Romans*, 33–86. I am indebted to Doosuk Kim for these references pertaining to contemporary linguistics (private communiqué). See too Fuller, *Habakkuk*.

67. Barker, *From the Depths of Despair*, 38.

68. See Van Pelt, ed., *Basics of Hebrew Discourse*, 84, 108–12.

69. See Patty, "'Hebrew Narrative Technique,'" 3. See too *IBHS* §39.2.1c.

70. Lambdin, *Biblical Hebrew*, 162. Italics removed. Cf. *BHRG* §40.23; *IBHS* §39.2.1.d; *GBHS* §3.54.3.3; Joüon §176/177; Van Pelt, ed., *Basics of Hebrew Discourse*, 59–60.

71. Patty, "Hebrew Narrative Technique," 4. The most thorough delineation of the uses of the *waw* in HB/OT studies, as a whole, may be found in the Robert Chisholm's *A Commentary on Judges and Ruth*. For a clear discussion of his method, which I try to follow in this book, see Chisholm, *Workbook*, 263–64; Chisholm, *Exegesis*, 119–42.

a change of action, while the other is used where the scene or participants shift."[72] In this case:

> If the disjunctive *waw* is used in a situation with *continuity of setting*, the clause it introduces may *contrast* with the preceding ... specify contemporary *circumstances* ... or causes ... or provide a *comparison* ... [a] disjunctive-*waw* clause may also shift the scene ... refer to new participants [or] indicate 'either the completion of one episode or the beginning of another.'[73]

Given the above, it is understood that by paying close attention to the text's use of the *waw*, one is able to better discern various signals of aperture and closure, thus enabling one to more precisely demarcate the rhetorical units. Much the same thing also applies to verbal forms.[74]

It is also understood "the basic narrative story line of a [Hebrew prose] text is based upon chains of WAYYIQTOL clauses."[75] That is to say, the *wayyiqtol* "moves the narrative action forward. The two primary modes of progression with the *wayyitqol* are temporal and logical."[76] As such, whenever non-verbal clauses, such as participial, verbless, and incomplete or any other additional verbal clauses governed by *qatal, yiqtol,* or *wĕqatol* "appear in the *narrative story line of a text,* these verbal and non-verbal clauses provide either nonsequential, 'background' information or mark episode boundaries."[77]

In sum, this study maintains one can discern different rhetorical units through close attention to a text's internal structure: (1) persons of verbs, (2) *waws*, (3) and verbal forms.

Step Two: Determining the Rhetorical Situation

The second step of rhetorical criticism is to determine the rhetorical situation of the text at hand. It is important to note 'rhetorical situation' is to be distinguished from both the 'rhetorical act' and the 'persuasive

---

72. *IBHS* §39.2.3a.

73. *IBHS* §39.2.3b, c. Italics original. Cf. Patty, "Hebrew Narrative Technique," 4.

74. To be clear, "the seemingly endless functions of *waw* are actually not so much functions of *waw* alone but of the larger clausal and supra-clausal structures of which *waw* is a part" (Van Pelt, ed., *Basics of Hebrew Discourse*, 60).

75. Heller, *Narrative Structure*, 26.

76. See Patty, "'Hebrew Narrative Technique," 4. See too *IBHS* §33.2.1a.

77. Heller, *Narrative Structure*, 26. Emphasis original. See too *IBHS* §33.2.1c; Van Pelt ed., *Basics of Hebrew Discourse*, 68–83. Cf. Jouön §118.g.

situation.' That is to say, a persuasive situation exists "*whenever* an audience can be changed in belief or action by means of speech" while a rhetorical situation is "a specific situation that determines and controls the rhetorical utterance it occasions" and is characterized by an "'exigency which amount[s] to *an imperative stimulus*' and which the rhetorical discourse is designed to address with the aim of modifying it."[78] The use of this nomenclature requires some explanation since 'situation' is not standard nomenclature in the vocabulary of rhetorical theory. As Lloyd F. Bitzer opines: "'audience' is standard; so also are 'speaker,' 'subject,' 'occasion,' and 'speech.' If I were to ask, 'What is a rhetorical audience?' or 'What is a rhetorical subject?'—the reader would catch the meaning of my question."[79] Bitzer defines the term 'rhetorical situation' at length:

> [Rhetorical situation is] a complex of persons, events, objects, and relations presenting an actual or potential exigence which can be completely or partially removed if discourse, introduced into the situation, can so constrain human decision or action as to bring about the significant modification of the exigence ... Any *exigence* is an imperfection marked by an urgency; it is a defect, an obstacle, something waiting to be done, a thing which is other than it should be.[80]

Kennedy describes the rhetorical situation as roughly corresponding to the *Sitz im Leben* of form criticism.[81] In this way, the purpose of determining a text's rhetorical situation is to "look behind the text and examine the society, circumstances, and historical era that produced it."[82] Similarly, one of the great strengths of this particular model of rhetorical criticism is its "potential to examine the three primary foci of interpretation," namely "the author ('the world behind the text'), the discourse ('the world of the text'), and the reader ('the world in front of the text')."[83]

---

78. Möller, *Prophet in Debate*, 26, italics original. Möller cites Bitzer "Rhetorical Situation," 249–52. For details on "rhetorical act" and "rhetorical situation," see Brinton, "Situation," 234–36; Ahn, *Persuasive Portrayal*, 33.

79. Bitzer, "Rhetorical Situation," 1. Cf. Consigny, "Rhetoric," 182.

80. Bitzer, "Rhetorical Situation," 6. Italics original. See also Bitzer "Functional Communication," 21–38; VanOsdel, "Rhetorical Situation," 1–6.

81. Kennedy, *New Testament Interpretation*, 34. See too Muilenburg, "Form Criticism," 4. Cf. Gorman, *Elements*, 82.

82. Barker, *From the Depths of Despair*, 39.

83. Barker, "From the Depths of Despair," 44. Cf. Möller, "Rhetorical Criticism," 689.

Of course, "while not all rhetorical-critical studies will attempt a project of such ambition, the history of rhetorical-critical interpretation suggests that all of these levels of interpretation are appropriate to consider. A[n effective] rhetorical-critical study will need to establish its orientation towards these levels of interpretation when it studies particular texts."[84]

Regrettably, it is often nearly impossible to recognize the situation of an ancient text by "conventional historical analysis, since in most cases we do not know enough about the original circumstances of the author or the audience—and even if *we* knew, it is not certain the author shared our knowledge."[85] As such, it is more useful to look at the type of situation in which the text appears to be aimed to "function as appeal or argument, that is, its *rhetorical situation*."[86]

The rhetorical situation of a text thus functions as a sort of "backdrop" to explain "why and how the rhetor composed the text."[87] As one scholar notes, rhetorical situation consists of "the author's picture of the audience and ... the intended effects of the texts."[88] Both the *Sitz im Leben* and the historical situation of a text differ from the text's rhetorical situation in that the rhetorical critic looks "foremost for the premises of a text as appeal or argument."[89]

Kennedy generally employed Bitzer's understanding of rhetorical situation noting three main components: (1) exigence, (2), audience, and (3) constraints.[90] Bitzer indicates "the second and third are elements of the complex, namely the *audience* to be constrained in decision and action, and the *constraints* which influence the rhetor and can be brought to bear upon the audience."[91] Each of these three distinct elements are essential to the construction of a rhetorical situation and, thereby, require further analysis and explanation of how they interrelate and intersect with one another. Even though these criteria "provide the framework for rhetorical communication, Bitzer attempts to leave space for the creativity of the rhetor by asserting the situation does not predetermine the discourse."[92]

84. Barker, "From the Depths of Despair," 44.
85. Thurén, *Argument and Theology*, 32. Emphasis original.
86. Thurén, *Argument and Theology*, 32. Emphasis original.
87. Barker, *From the Depths of Despair*, 39. See too Möller, *Prophet in Debate*, 27.
88. Thurén, *Argument and Theology*, 32.
89. Wuellner, "Rhetorical Criticism," 456.
90. See Bitzer, "Rhetorical Situation," 8; Bitzer, "Functional Communication," 23.
91. Bitzer, "Rhetorical Situation," 6. Italics original.
92. Barker, *From the Depths of Despair*, 39.

Rhetorical Situation: Exigence

Exigence relates to any problem, obstacle, or conflict that requires a solution.[93] Exigencies are essential for all cogent rhetorical communication to occur for "if there are no problems in the present environment, no questions needing answers, no objects or ideas awaiting discovery, then there is no need for rhetorical tasks such as persuasion, advocacy, or mediation."[94]

According to Bitzer, every rhetorical situation has "at least one controlling exigence which functions as the organizing principle: it specifies the audience to be addressed and the change to be effected."[95] Likewise, another scholar contends: "the antecedent of every rhetorical situation is the exigence from which the situation derives its significance."[96] In this way, Bitzer ties the rhetorical situation to a specific problem that exists in a specific time and place (space) the rhetor believes requires addressing.[97]

Rhetorical Situation: Audience

Concerning Bitzer's second component, audience, it may be assumed every discourse presumes an audience; for if an audience does not exist, the speaker does not have to make discourse.[98] Persuasion, also, by its very nature, necessitates an audience since it is always "*addressed* discourse."[99] An audience thus becomes the "necessary condition" for performing any kind of argument.[100] Though this will be discussed below, Bitzer states the

---

93. Bitzer, "Rhetorical Situation," 6. Cf. Burlet, "Cosmos to Chaos," 46

94. Barker, *From the Depths of Despair*, 39. See also Bitzer, "Functional Communication," 25–26.

95. Bitzer, "Rhetorical Situation," 6.

96. Miller, "Rhetorical Exigence," 118.

97. See Ahn, *Persuasive Portrayal*, 26; Barker, *From the Depths of Despair*, 40. I will address this issue later on.

98. Ahn, *Persuasive Portrayal*, 27.

99. See Burke, *Rhetoric of Motives*, 38. Emphasis original.

100. Perelman and Olbrechts-Tyteca, *New Rhetoric*, 18. See too Ahn, *Persuasive Portrayal*, 27. Concerns about applying a particular type of rhetorical model that was originally intended for public discourse to texts are keenly addressed by Eagleton who maintains: "rhetoric . . . examined the way discourses are constructed in order to achieve certain effects . . . its horizon was nothing less than the field of discursive practices in society as a whole, and its particular interest lay in grasping such practices as forms of power and performance." Eagleton, *Literary Theory*, 179. For further information, see Möller, *Prophet in Debate*, 26–27.

Methodology

audience consists of those individuals "capable of being influenced by the discourse and of being mediators."[101] For Bitzer, "the audience is involved in a rhetorical situation only to the extent that it is 'capable of being constrained in thought or action in order to effect positive modification of the exigence.'"[102]

There are several factors that also come into play here. These include the facticity (or existence) of the exigence and the interest it may possibly generate among the audience. Bitzer proposes four scenarios concerning the interplay of these matters between the audience and the rhetor: (i) agreement about both the facticity of the exigence and the level of interest in the exigence, (ii) agreement about the facticity of the exigence but disagreement about the level of interest in it, (iii) disagreement about the facticity of the exigence but agreement concerning the level of interest in the exigence, and (iv) disagreement about both the facticity of the exigence and the level of interest it should generate.[103] The most optimal scenario is where the audience and the rhetor agree about both the facticity of the exigence and the level of interest in the exigence. A moderately optimal scenario is where disagreement arises concerning only the level of interest in the exigence *or* its facticity. Suboptimal scenarios involve disagreement on all sides.

Table Seven—Exigence and Audience

Suboptimal → Moderately Optimal → Most Optimal

Single Scenario	Scenario 'A'	Scenario 'B'	Single Scenario
Disagree FE	Disagree FE	Agree FE	Agree FE
Disagree IE	Agree IE	Disagree IE	Agree IE

Legend: FE = facticity of exigence; IE = interest of exigence

With respect to prophetic literature, alongside certain other biblical examples, the prophets tend to have a much more vested degree of interest in the topic than what the audience usually has.[104] As such "prophetic

---

101. Bitzer, "Rhetorical Situation," 8.

102. Ahn, *Persuasive Portrayal*, 27, quoting Bitzer, "Functional Communication," 23.

103. Bitzer, "Functional Communication," 29–30; Barker, *From the Depths of Despair*, 40.

104. See Kennedy, *Comparative Rhetoric*, 137.

literature often derives its exigence from the gap between the audience's understanding and the divinely mediated message that the prophet presents."[105] Given the numerous challenges inherent to situations where the audience and the rhetor disagree, either with respect to the facticity of the exigence or concerning the level of interest in the exigence itself, successful persuasive discourse usually requires at least some sort of "adaptation to the audience."[106] To illustrate; an effective rhetorical discourse may be compared to "a feast . . . at which the dishes are made to please the guests . . . and not the cooks."[107] Some go so far as to state the rhetor should depart from their premises only when they know they are "adequately accepted" and, if they are not, the rhetor's first concern is to reinforce them with "all the means" at their disposal.[108] At least one element, therefore, of the rhetorician's role should be to guide an audience towards recognizing the presence of an exigence and the proper response to it.[109] It is also reasonable to assert the rhetor customarily begins with certain premises that are already approved by the audience and often seeks to reinforce these premises through their rhetoric.[110]

With respect to situations where the audience and the rhetor strongly disagree on the exigence, either with respect to its facticity or the level of interest it should generate, such as prophetic literature, it becomes practically impossible to persuade one to respond.[111] This may be the only situation that could 'truly' be called 'persuasive' for only then do the audience and the speaker actually agree a given discourse could actually modify the situation.[112] In this way, "the creation of a shared interest in a given exigence is one of the first requirements of successful rhetorical communication."[113] This is one way to attempt to distinguish a "rhetorical situation" from a historical situation. James D. Hester contends:

---

105. Barker, *From the Depths of Despair*, 41. See too Sandy, *Plowshares*, 73.

106. Perelman, *New Rhetoric and Humanities*, 57. See also Perelman and Olbrechts-Tyteca, *New Rhetoric*, 23–26; Arnold, "Oral Rhetoric," 194.

107. Perelman and Olbrechts-Tyteca, *New Rhetoric*, 24.

108. Perelman and Olbrechts-Tyteca, *New Rhetoric*, 21.

109. See Barker, *From the Depths of Despair*, 40. Cf. Kotter, *Leading Change*.

110. Perelman and Olbrechts-Tyteca, *New Rhetoric*, 286; Booth, *Rhetoric of Fiction*, 124; Kennedy, *New Testament Interpretation*, 45; Ahn, *Persuasive Portrayal*, 27.

111. Garret and Xiao, "Rhetorical Situation Revisited," 38.

112. See Barker, *From the Depths of Despair*, 37–38.

113. Barker, *From the Depths of Despair*, 41.

Methodology

> It is important to maintain a clear distinction between an historical situation, or event, and the rhetorical situation, which may emerge as a pragmatic response to that event. The rhetorical situation is historically grounded and its constituents are 'real,' that is, the components of the situation can be examined by interested persons. However, the situation becomes rhetorical, not simply historical, when audience and speaker both perceive the exigence, that the interests of the speaker and audience are related, and that discourse can be pragmatic, in other words, that the audience is capable of modifying the exigence.[114]

It is worth noting Bitzer's formulations of the rhetorical situation only includes those persons who existed within the context of the original discourse. He does not take into account any individual(s) who may also be moved or stimulated by the persuasive appeal of the rhetor outside of the first exigence (which may or may not even exist or be "operational" in the world of the new audience).[115] As Barker states: "this merits consideration when one studies the biblical text since the text derives much of its significance from its ability to speak persuasively to audiences in situations far removed from its original exigence."[116]

Kennedy adeptly handled this anomaly by changing Bitzer's definition to include "both an immediate and a universal audience."[117] Given such, the term "audience" need not be limited to those persons or individuals to whom the speaker addressed initially but may also be extended to include the so-called "text world audience," i.e. a "universal audience."[118] In this way, the discourses' audience can extend beyond the initial "ensemble" of those whom the rhetor initially wished to influence (the immediate audience) to include anyone who comes into contact with the rhetorician's work in the future (universal audience).[119]

The "rhetorical" and "situational" audiences share a "common interest" in a given exigence and may act on the rhetor's appeals, even though

---

114. Hester, "Speaker, Audience, and Situations," 79.

115. See Barker, *From the Depths of Despair*, 40.

116. See Barker, *From the Depths of Despair*, 40. See too Ahn, *Persuasive Portrayal*, 33.

117. Kennedy, *New Testament Interpretation*, 35. Cf. Barker, *From the Depths of Despair*, 55–56.

118. See Ahn, *Persuasive Portrayal*, 28.

119. See Perelman and Olbrechts-Tyteca, *New Rhetoric*, 19, 31–34; Kennedy, *New Testament Interpretation*, 35; Ahn, *Persuasive Portrayal*, 28.

they were not a member of the "actual audience" of the discourse.[120] A "situational audience" is defined as a "*witness* to the rhetorical situation: knowledge of the rhetorical exigence is direct."[121] The "universal audience" is "the complex of readers or hearers upon whom the text may have persuasive appeal."[122]

Some rhetoricians consider the audience as the "active center" of the rhetorical situation and believe the audience, as the "pivotal element," links "the rhetorical exigency (the audience's unsolved questions), the constraints (the audience's expectations), and the rhetor (as a member of the audience)."[123] By placing emphasis upon the audience, "the debate over the facticity of the exigency loses much of its force since the important question becomes whether the audience accepts that an exigency exists."[124] Arthur B. Miller contends "the ultimate character of an exigence is a conclusion in the mind of its perceiver," i.e. the audience, developing "the proposition that within the limits specified by each exigence, the *ultimate* or *perceived* nature of the exigence depends upon the constraints *of the perceiver*."[125] This is one way Aristotle's maxim "no analysis of communication can be complete without a thorough study of the role of the receptors of a message" cannot be overstated.[126] Details concerning the relationship that can exist between the rhetor and the audience and how they can serve to demonstrate the subjective nature of determining exigence need not be given here.[127]

Since this study deals with biblical narrative as rhetoric, two literary concepts—implied author and implied reader—must be noted.[128] Narratologist Seymour Chatman explains:

120. See Barker, *From the Depths of Despair*, 58–59.

121. Hunsaker and Smith, "Issues," 148. Emphasis original.

122. Barker, *From the Depths of Despair*, 59. Cf. Patrick and Scult, "Rhetoric and Ideology," 80; Perelman and Olbrechts-Tyteca, *New Rhetoric*, 31; Ahn, *Persuasive Portrayal*, 31; Powell, *What is Narrative Criticism?*, 20; Gitay, "Rhetorical Criticism," 124.

123. Garret and Xiao, "Rhetorical Situation Revisited," 39.

124. Garret and Xiao, "Rhetorical Situation Revisited," 39.

125. Miller "Rhetorical Exigence," 111–12. Emphasis original.

126. Aristotle, *Rhetoric*, 1.9.1257b as mediated through Ahn, *Persuasive Portrayal*, 28.

127. For further information on this point, see Barker, *From the Depths of Despair*, 41.

128. See Ahn, *Persuasive Portrayal*, 16. See too Nelles, "Authors and Readers," 22–46.

Methodology

A narrative is a communication; hence, it presupposes two parties, a sender and a receiver. Each party entails three different personages. On the sending end are the real author, the implied author, and the narrator . . . ; on the receiving end, the real audience (listener, reader, viewer), the implied audience, and the narratee.[129]

The following diagram functions as a 'primer' to communicate the diverse elements of the communication situation of a narrative text that have just been noted.[130]

Figure One—Communication Situation of a Narrative Text

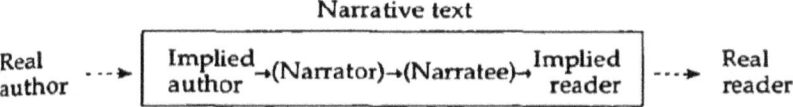

Chatman makes clear: "the box indicates that only the implied author and implied reader are immanent to a narrative, the narrator and narratee are optional (parentheses). The original 'real' author and original 'real' reader are outside the narrative transactions as such, though, of course, indispensable to it in an ultimate practical sense."[131] Both the implied author and the implied reader are separated from and distinguished from the original author and reader.[132] Notably, "the direction of the arrows gives a primacy to the sender in narrative communication."[133]

There are three levels of sender and receiver: (1) the narrator and the narrative audience (narratee), (2) the implied author and the implied

---

129. Chatman, *Story and Discourse*, 28.

130. The following image comes from Chatman, *Story and Discourse*, 151. Ahn has a similar diagram. Ahn, *Persuasive Portrayal*, 17. Regrettably, it is missing certain critical components (such as the box and parentheses). Cf. Phelan, *Somebody Telling Somebody*, 13, 18. For similar work which does not directly relate to Chatman, see Sailhamer, *Pentateuch*, 11; Longman, *Literary Approaches*, 145; Longman and Dillard, *Introduction*, 33.

131. Chatman, *Story and Discourse*, 151.

132. Booth, *Rhetoric of Fiction*, 73. Cf. Ahn, *Persuasive Portrayal*, 16; Nelles, "Authors and Readers," 22.

133. Ahn, *Persuasive Portrayal*, 17. Detractors of this approach tend to find meaning other than the sending end of the narrative translation. See Iser, "The Reading Process," 279–99; Walsh, *Old Testament Narrative*, 1–9.

audience, and (3) the original author and the original audience; alongside this, there are also two levels of rhetoric: (1) the implied author and the implied audience and (2) the narrator and the narrative audience.[134] Consequently, "the implied author conveys messages to the implied audience through the narrator and narrative audience as part of the narrative itself" and, "in general, the narrator delivers the messages of the implied author."[135] This means the implied author speaks through the narrator in a narrative and as the narrative advances, the narrative audience is extended to the implied audience.[136]

In contrast, some scholars maintain the narrator and narratee are actually "optional" and, as such, they choose to place the stress or emphasis upon the implied author and the implied reader.[137] Other scholars maintain the narrator and the narratee are "constitutive, not just optional, factors in narrative communication."[138] Jerome T. Walsh helpfully clears the air in his portrayal of the structure of narrative. See the diagram below:[139]

Figure Two—The Structure of Narrative

Real Author → | Implied Author → | Narrator → | characters, settings, events, etc. | → Narratee | Implied Reader → | Real Reader →

STORY

NARRATIVE

TEXT

On the outermost edge is the 'real [original] author' and the 'real [original] reader' which exist in the "primary world" while the innermost box (story) is a "secondary world" where "individuals live (characters) and

---

134. See Ahn, *Persuasive Portrayal*, 34 from whom much of this sentence's wording is derived.

135. Ahn, *Persuasive Portrayal*, 34. Cf. Rimmon-Kenan, *Narrative Fiction*, 90–92.

136. See Ahn, *Persuasive Portrayal*, 34.

137. Chatman, *Story and Discourse*, 151. See also Shen, "What is the Implied Author," 80–98; Stefanescu, "Revisiting the Implied Author Yet Again," 48–66.

138. Rimmon-Kenan, *Narrative Fiction*, 91.

139. This diagram has been reproduced from Walsh, *Old Testament Narrative*, 6 who credits its origins (with slight modifications) to Keegan, *Interpreting the Bible*, 94. Cf. Sailhamer, *Pentateuch*, 14.

things happen (events) in particular circumstances (settings)."[140] Of course, the narrator tells the story to the narratee via a particular form/genre (literature). Concerning those "two oddly named figures," namely the "implied author" and the "implied reader," Walsh states, with respect to the fact each of them occur within the box (narrative) that encompasses 'story,' "the implied author and implied reader are not entities like the narrator and narratee; they are essentially *constructs made by the (real) reader*. In other words they are the names for parts of the process by which the reader makes sense of the text."[141] Thus, the implied author relates to "the core of norms and choices" of the narrative itself.[142] The implied reader "designates the norms and values necessary for an interpretation of a narrative guided by the author."[143]

While most scholarship indicates the text's original author is a composite, in order to read biblical narrative as a "coherent unity, the reader must *posit* a single authorial mind to explain that coherence."[144] Walsh expounds:

> This author, presupposed by the reader's readiness to accept the narrative as coherent, and constructed by the reader out of clues selected as meaningful is the 'implied author.' The 'implied reader' (some critics speak of the 'ideal reader') is the reader who understands perfectly and precisely what the implied author is saying, and brings nothing extraneous to that understanding. Or, to put it another way, the implied reader has all and only those capacities that the implied author expects. This reader ... is constructed by the real reader out of clues implied in the text.[145]

Another scholar asserts that from the point of view of the original author, a "successful reading of his book must eliminate all distance between the essential norms of his implied author and the norms of the postulated [implied] reader."[146] Both the implied author and reader need to be distinguished from the original author and reader in the "primary" or

---

140. Walsh, *Old Testament Narrative*, 7. See too Clines, "Many Voices," 121.

141. Walsh, *Old Testament Narrative*, 8. See too Westfall, "Narrative Criticism," 238.

142. Booth, *Rhetoric of Fiction*, 74–75.

143. Ahn, *Persuasive Portrayal*, 16, drawing from Booth, *Rhetoric of Fiction*, 138.

144. Walsh, *Old Testament Narrative*, 8. Italics original.

145. Walsh, *Old Testament Narrative*, 8. See too Clines, "Many Voices," 121.

146. Booth, *Rhetoric of Fiction*, 157.

original world.¹⁴⁷ Notably, 'implied author' relates to "the core of norms and choices" of the narrative itself, while 'implied reader' "designates the norms and values necessary for an interpretation of a narrative guided by the author."¹⁴⁸ Walsh notes:

> This gap between the implied reader and us is why incorporating reader-response awareness into our interpretation is almost inescapable. Our differences *will* affect us. Attention to those differences gives us some limited control over the ways in which they individualize our interpretations and shape the meanings we realize; it will also enable us to celebrate the diversity of different readings of a text not as a contest to see who can find the 'right' meaning but as a measure of the rich potential inherent in any great text.¹⁴⁹

At this time, it behooves us to remember that much as discourse has two levels of rhetorical situation (the text-world rhetorical situation and the author's real world rhetorical situation), there are also "two layers of audience in relation to a narrative discourse," namely the implied audience and the narrative audience.¹⁵⁰

To restate, if one differentiates between the narrator and the implied author, i.e. the former relays what is going on (events), where it is taking place (settings), and to whom the events are happening (characters), while the latter "conveys its intention through the narrator's telling," the difference between the implied audience and the narrative audience is that "in a narrative, the implied audience is the addressee(s) of the implied author . . . and the narrative audience is the hearer(s) of the narrator. Both the implied audience and the narrative audience constitute two kinds of audiences within a narrative world."¹⁵¹ See below:¹⁵²

---

147. Booth, *Rhetoric of Fiction*, 73. Cf. Ahn, *Persuasive Portrayal*, 16.
148. Booth, *Rhetoric of Fiction*, 74–75, 138. Cf. Ahn, *Persuasive Portrayal*, 16.
149. Walsh, *Old Testament Narrative*, 9. Italics original.
150. See Ahn, *Persuasive Portrayal*, 33.
151. Ahn, *Persuasive Portrayal*, 34.
152. This diagram has been reproduced from Ahn, *Persuasive Portrayal*, 34.

Figure Three—Layers of Audience

```
the implied author ----------------------------------the implied audience

         the narrator----------the narrative audience
         (characters)          (characters' audience)
```

These two layers of audience relate to the study of the Noachian deluge narrative in that the actual text of Genesis conveys the message of the text to the implied audience through the narrative discourse (via the implied author) while the narrator "deploys the story through the character's speeches and acts."[153] The implied audience is thus the addressee of the implied author's retelling of the Flood while the narrative audience is the addressee(s) of the narrator (or characters).[154] In this way, "the implied audience cannot always be separated from the narrator because in some cases the implied author speaks as the narrator. One needs to recognize two levels of author, audience, and situation in the narrative discourse."[155] The implied audience remains the ideal audience for reception of the material presented by the implied author. The next section details the final component of Bitzer's rhetorical situation—constraints.

Rhetorical Situation: Constraints

The third component of Bitzer's rhetorical situation are the constraints that surround a rhetorical situation.[156] These constraints are made up of "persons, events, objects, and relations which are parts of the situation because they have the power to constrain decision and action needed to modify the exigence."[157] They involve such things as "beliefs, attitudes, documents, facts, traditions, images, interests, [and] motives."[158] Alongside this, constraints include "the degree of interest in the topic

---

153. Ahn, *Persuasive Portrayal*, 34. Cf. Schmid, *Narratology*, 118, 121. For more details on GOD as a 'character' within the book of Genesis, specifically, see Cotter, *Genesis*, 171–79. Cf. Humphreys, *Character of God*.

154. Cf. Ahn, *Persuasive Portrayal*, 34–35.

155. Ahn, *Persuasive Portrayal*, 35.

156. Bitzer, "Rhetorical Situation," 8.

157. Bitzer, "Rhetorical Situation," 8.

158. Bitzer, "Rhetorical Situation," 8; Bitzer, "Functional Communication," 31–33. Ahn, *Persuasive Portrayal*, 28, quoting Bitzer, "Rhetorical Situation," 8.

that the speaker and audience possess, the capacity for modification of the situation, the risk incurred in responding, the obligation and expectation of a response, the familiarity with a topic, and the immediacy of the situation."[159]

According to Bitzer, there are two classes of constraints: (1) those originated or managed by the rhetor and the rhetor's methods, something which Aristotle called "artistic proofs," and (2) other constraints which may be operative within the situation, i.e. Aristotle's "inartistic proofs."[160] Each of these classes must be taken into account by the rhetor in order to effectively determine the scope and nature of the rhetoric to be employed so as to persuade the audience in a judicious fashion. Given such, though rhetors may work hard to help establish a particular rhetorical situation, there remain limitations as to what they can actually construct.[161]

Rhetorical Situation: Critiques and Modifications

Since its inception, Bitzer's definition of rhetorical situation has been critiqued by other scholars—primarily Richard E. Vatz, Scott Consigny, and Alan Brinton.[162] To be specific, in contrast to Bitzer's concern for objectivity, Vatz argues for a thoroughly subjective understanding of situation. He maintains "meaning is not discovered in situations, but *created* by rhetors" and rhetoric is "a *cause* not an *effect* of meaning. It is antecedent, not subsequent to a situation's impact."[163] Consigny takes more of a "middle approach" between Bitzer and Vaz.

> Consigny deftly moves between the poles of situational particularities and rhetorical creativity, noting that the job of the rhetor includes both articulating specific problems out of indeterminate rhetorical situations, and being receptive and engaged in the given situation so that the problems that the rhetor address remain relevant. He finds a middle ground between Bitzer's assertion that the rhetorical situation governs the rhetor's choices

---

159. Barker, *From the Depths of Despair*, 41. See too Bitzer, "Functional Communication," 31–33.
160. Bitzer, "Rhetorical Situation," 8.
161. See Barker, *From the Depths of Despair*, 40–41.
162. The work of Stamps, "Rethinking," will be considered later on in this chapter.
163. Vatz, "The Myth of the Rhetorical Situation," 157, 160. All emphases original.

Methodology

and Vatz's understanding of the rhetor's freedom to create a variety of exigences out of a given situation.[164]

To summarize, Consigny believes the rhetorical situation to be "an indeterminate context marked by troublesome disorder which the rhetor must structure so as to disclose and formulate problems."[165] As such, Consigny claims Bitzer "errs in construing the situation as determinate and predetermining a 'fitting' response."[166] At the same time, Consigny opines the rhetorical situation is not created "solely through the imagination and discourse of the rhetor. It involves particularities of persons, actions, and agencies in a certain place and time; and the rhetor cannot ignore these constraints if he is to function effectively."[167] Consigny also maintains Vatz errs in "construing the rhetor as completely free to create his own exigences at will and select his subject matter in a manner of 'pure arbitration.'"[168]

To solve this quandary of "integrity" (Bitzer) and "receptivity" (Vatz), Consigny calls for rhetoric to be construed as "an art of topics or commonplaces."[169] In brief: "the art of using the topics allows the rhetor both the integrity that he sees missing in Bitzer's paradigm and the receptivity that he sees missing in Vatz's. Bitzer's rhetor enters problem; Vatz's rhetor invents problems; Consigny's rhetor solves problems."[170] Also of great import is Brinton's idea of the "objectivity of exigence."[171] Alan Brinton states:

> Rhetorical action aims at changing the facts, not simply at changing the relation between the facts and the rhetor's interests. The relation could be changed by changing either term. But from the rhetor's point of view the locus of deficiency is in the set of facts which Bitzer calls 'the factual component.' The deficiency is not the discrepancy between his interests and those facts. If the deficiency, the exigence, were the gap between facts and interests,

---

164. Barker, *From the Depths of Despair*, 42.
165. Consigny, "Rhetoric," 178.
166. Consigny, "Rhetoric," 178.
167. Consigny, "Rhetoric," 178.
168. Consigny, "Rhetoric," 178.
169. Consigny, "Rhetoric," 181. That is to say, the topic "functions both as instrument and situation; the instrument with which the rhetor thinks and the realm in and about which he thinks." Consigny, "Rhetoric," 182.
170. Gorrell, "Rhetorical Situation," 398.
171. Young, "Bitzer," 288.

modification of interests would count equally as removal of the exigence. It is the facts which the rhetor aims to change.[172]

In addition, Brinton maintains: "exigence is objective in the sense that it is composed of phenomena, some of which may be subjective, but all of which are objectively phenomena."[173] This argument is noteworthy for this particular study since it "entails the concept of definition from the perspective of the rhetor."[174] Alongside this, Brinton further states "as rhetors, Brutus and Mark Antony may confront the same factual circumstances, but each speaks to and attempts to modify (through his hearers) a different exigence."[175] The difference in exigence is "accounted for by the rhetor's interests; the factual component is the same for both."[176]

Rather than engaging in *reductio ad absurdum* here, as some suggest,[177] Brinton is astutely aware of Bitzer's distinctions between "the factual component" and "the interest component" of a rhetorical situation and judiciously modifies his approach.

RHETORICAL SITUATION: CONCLUDING THOUGHTS

Biblical scholars have much to consider in attempting to define the term "rhetorical situation." A significant factor for a rhetorical-critical study of the Genesis Flood, specifically, is "the chronological distance and paucity of supporting evidence" means it is difficult to "establish the 'world behind the text' with certainty. At the least, it is precarious to use this idea of rhetorical situation for texts in which theories about the date of composition may span centuries."[178]

Given Kennedy's goal is the "discovery of the author's intent and ... how that is transmitted through a text to an audience,"[179] something clearly "predicated on the assumption that it is possible to recover the original author and the historical-cultural situation about which he

---

172. Brinton, "Situation in the Theory of Rhetoric," 246.
173. Brinton, "Situation in the Theory of Rhetoric," 244.
174. Young, "Bitzer," 288.
175. Brinton, "Situation in the Theory of Rhetoric," 244.
176. Young, "Bitzer," 288.
177. See Barker, *From the Depths of Despair*, 41.
178. Barker, *From the Depths of Despair*, 50.
179. Kennedy, *New Testament Interpretation*, 12.

is writing," it is evident . . . some time must be spent in finding a way through this impasse.[180] Several ideas to this end have been posited.

One author posits "the close connection between the rhetorical situation and the discourse makes it inevitable that the major elements of the rhetorical situation are reflected in the discourse itself."[181] In response, while one may attempt to look for clues in the discourse, there is a "certain circularity to the process: the historical reality of the book's composition is derived from the text and the text is then interpreted in view of those conclusions."[182] The frustration(s) that would result from this process (given the range of rhetorical strategies that are found within the text itself, among other matters) precludes this as a suitable course of action.[183]

Another approach is to continue to concentrate on the "world-behind-the-text" and seek to determine the book of Genesis' composition and redactional history so one can find a *terminus ad quem* for the book's compilation.[184] This method remains somewhat hypothetical and is subject to challenge from those who have different theories regarding the text's transmission history.[185] Constructing a viable 'world-behind-the-text' understanding of the rhetorical situation of the Noachian deluge narrative turns on "whether it is possible to modify this concept so that it can work with a text . . . which effectively camouflages its historical situation."[186] This point will be addressed in more detail below after a discussion of an entextualized approach.

An alternative third position is to nuance the concept of rhetorical situation by using it "synchronically." Dennis L. Stamps defines a synchronic approach to rhetorical situation as "the situation embedded in the text and created by the text which contributes to the rhetorical effects of the text."[187] The "entextualization" process involves viewing the rhetorical situation as a "phenomenon that occurs on the level of the 'world of the text' and examining the situation or exigences that the text

---

180. Barker, *From the Depths of Despair*, 43.
181. See Shaw, *Speeches of Micah*, 25.
182. Linville, "Looking Glass," 286. Cf. Barker, *From the Depths of Despair*, 44–45.
183. See Barker, *From the Depths of Despair*, 44–45.
184. This was the approach of Möller in his analysis of Amos in *Prophet in Debate*.
185. See Barker, *From the Depths of Despair*, 46.
186. Barker, *From the Depths of Despair*, 47. See too Anderson, "Rhetorical Criticism," xv–xvi.
187. Stamps, "Rethinking," 199.

appears to create and to which it responds."[188] Regarding this approach, one notes that though Bitzer was predominantly concerned with historically locatable situations, he does acknowledge certain "persisting" situations that evoke texts which "exist as rhetorical responses *for us* precisely because they speak to situations which persist—which are in some measure universal."[189] Bitzer's concession of these "persisting situations" thus helps the rhetorical critic in considering rhetorical situation differently—namely synchronically.[190]

To restate, the synchronic, entextualized approach attempts to separate the "rhetorical situation" from a "historical situation" by means of a "narrative story world."[191] It is this "entextualized world" which gives rise to the persuasive capacity of the text with respect to its hearers and readers.[192] This attempts to justify, hermeneutically, some of the circular problems noted in the first approach above.[193] The predominant need for this approach is as follows: (1) it is often not possible to precisely recognize the actual situation of an ancient text by "conventional historical analysis, since in most cases we do not know enough about the original circumstances of the author or the audience—and even if *we* knew, it is not certain the author shared our knowledge"[194] and (2) "even if the interpreter can objectively determine the situation of the addressees, there is no guarantee the text's author understood their situation in the same way."[195] In brief, the synchronic, entextualized understanding of rhetorical situation is a particularly adept solution whenever it is inordinately difficult (or impossible) to firmly establish the "world behind the text" since this approach offers a way forward through the frustration of locking the text into a indeterminable historical context. As Joel Barker states:

> The persuasiveness of the argument is linked tightly to the literary presentation of the situation; if there is correspondence, then the text may be capable of eliciting a fitting response from

---

188. Barker, *From the Depths of Despair*, 47.

189. Bitzer, "Rhetorical Situation," 259. Emphasis original.

190. See Burlet, "Cosmos to Covenant," 62–63. Cf. Barker, *From the Depths of Despair*, 48. Cf.

191. Wuellner, "Jesus' Sermon," 92–118, esp. 99–100.

192. See Barker, *From the Depths of Despair*, 49–50. Cf. Gitay, "Jeremiah," 42.

193. I am indebted to Mark J. Boda for this insight via private communiqué.

194. Thurén, *Argument and Theology*, 32. Emphasis original.

195. Barker, *From the Depths of Despair*, 47, citing Thurén, *Rhetorical Strategy of 1 Peter*, 71.

its audience. The textual presentation of the situation becomes the basis for the argument of the whole communication and its individual rhetorical units. In positing its own rhetorical situation, the text conditions the speaker and the audience to accept a new reality in which the discourse operates. This new reality should provoke the audience to response.[196]

Given the number of favorable reviews Barker's handling of this specific step has received, it would seem an entextualized, synchronic approach to rhetorical situation offers rhetorical critics the best opportunity to leverage the text and permit its persuasive power to have influence beyond the time and place of its original utterance.[197] One reviewer goes so far as to state:

> Barker provides a sensitive and convincing rhetorical analysis of the book of Joel . . . His reworking of this particular rhetorical critical method may end up providing a valuable step away from the past circularity between scholarly rhetorical analysis and historical-critical arguments. The book is worth its price for that theoretical move alone.[198]

Another reviewer asserts this is "probably one of the most insightful gains of the book."[199] While I agree with this assessment, it is not above reproach. One individual, for example, asserts:

> Barker's methodology exhibits a certain subjectivity, especially as applied to Joel's prophecy with its uncertain date and provenance. Barker's rhetorical reading of Joel places everything within the 'world of the text.' The historicity of a real situation is replaced by the exigencies implied by the text. A real audience is replaced by an 'implied audience.' It would seem that to measure effectiveness, some interaction between the text and the real world would be necessary . . . [h]as this book persuaded real people in real time?[200]

---

196. Barker, *From the Depths of Despair*, 49. Cf. Stamps, "Rethinking," 199–200, 210.

197. See Knight, Review of *From the Depths of Despair*, 74; Jones, Review of *From the Depths of Despair*, 92–94; Kelle, Review of *From the Depths of Despair*, 188; Purcell, Review of *From the Depths of Despair*, 114–16.

198. Kelle, Review of *From the Depths of Despair*, 188.

199. Purcell, Review of *From the Depths of Despair*, 115.

200. Jungels, Review of *From the Depths of Despair*, 568.

In light of the above, the "world-behind-the-text" approach espoused by Möller seems to merit some further consideration. Since a good portion of this step pertains to and is interrelated with "determining rhetorical effectiveness," see step five below, further details will be offered there.

Step Three: Determining the Rhetorical Species

The third step of the model is to consider the rhetorical genre (or rhetorical species) of the text. Kennedy's method has three possible rhetorical genres: (1) judicial (or forensic) rhetoric, *genus iudiciale*, (2) deliberative (or hortatory) rhetoric, *genus deliberativum*, and (3) demonstrative (or epideictic), *genus demonstrativum*.[201] These three genres of rhetoric were originally formulated by Aristotle (and possibly derived from civic oratory).[202] They are most easily differentiated by the type of response demanded from the audience.[203] Kennedy notes "in a single discourse there is sometimes utilization of more than one species," and even though "the definition of the species as a whole can become very difficult" a discourse "usually has one dominant species which reflects the author's major purpose in speaking or writing."[204]

Judicial rhetoric requires one to render a decision about a past event; the basic argument here involves the question of "truth or justice"[205] or "guilt and innocence."[206] Deliberative rhetoric aims at effecting a decision about what would be the best course of action at a later time (whether it is in the immediate or long-term future). As such, it concerns itself with the question of "self-interest and future benefit."[207] Lastly, with respect to epideictic rhetoric, Kennedy offers it either celebrates or condemns someone (or something) and, therefore, seeks to either reinforce or undermine assent to some value or belief shared by both audience and

---

201. Kennedy, *New Testament Interpretation*, 19, 36; Möller, *Prophet in Debate*, 39.

202. Ahn, *Persuasive Portrayal*, 25. Cf. Collins, *Reading Genesis Well*, 43.

203. Black, "Biblical Interpretation," 254; Barker, *From the Depths of Despair*, 51. A fourth genre (the spiritual speech or sermon, *genus praedicandi*) appeared under the influence of Christianity. See Möller, *Prophet in Debate*, 39; Siegert, "Homily and Panegyrical Sermon," 421–43.

204. Kennedy, *New Testament Interpretation*, 19.

205. Kennedy, *New Testament Interpretation*, 19–20.

206. See Collins, *Reading Genesis Well*, 43.

207. Kennedy, *New Testament Interpretation*, 20.

speaker (with a specific view towards harmonization).[208] Perelman and Olbrechts-Tyteca view it as being "basically educational in nature."[209]

Each of these genres of rhetoric contains its own features and exists in both positive and negative forms: *prosecution* and *defense/apology* (judicial), *exhortation* and *dissuasion* (deliberative), and *encomium* and *invective* (demonstrative).[210] One notes "the selection of genre is itself an inventional choice and has to be set into the context of the interaction between and among speaker, audience, and situation."[211] Alongside this, "a text's dominant genre is indicative of its principal rhetorical strategy rather than its major purpose."[212]

Though a plethora of HB/OT rhetorical-critical scholars attempted to do so, there is no clear way to successfully define and delineate the rhetorical species of any given biblical text. Yet, given the historical precedent of including this step, it is imprudent to ignore this process altogether (passé Shaw's discussion of Micah).[213]

While a number of scholars have considered how rhetorical genre relates to the rhetorical situation of a text, many scholars, such as Möller (Amos)[214] and Renz (Ezekiel),[215] do not readily employ the categories of rhetorical genre in their discussion of specific texts or rhetorical units in the same methodologically precise way Kennedy's model typifies.[216] Similarly, Barker (Joel) is cautious (but open) to the benefits of leveraging Aristotelian schematics. After discussing these matters, Barker concludes it is "unclear" whether determining the rhetorical genre of the various subunits of the discourse will "definitively improve our understanding of

---

208. Kennedy, *New Testament Interpretation*, 20.

209. Ahn, *Persuasive Portrayal*, 25. See also Perelman and Olbrechts-Tyteca, *New Rhetoric*, 47–54; Barker, *From the Depths of Despair*, 51. Cf. Möller, *Prophet in Debate*, 39.

210. Kennedy, *New Testament Interpretation*, 20, 36. Cf. Walton, "Rhetorical Criticism," 4.

211. Hester, "Speaker, Audience, and Situations," 91–92.

212. Möller, *Prophet in Debate*, 40. With respect to this point, specifically, the author also states: "the distinction made here between the employment of a certain genre and the resultant effects, it should be noted, reflects the classic 'speech-act-theoretical differentiation' between illocution and perlocution." Möller *Prophet in Debate*, 40. For further information on this matter, see Stewart, "Ethos of the Cosmos," 44–45.

213. Shaw, *Speeches of Micah*, 23. Cf. Barker, "From the Depths of Despair," 73.

214. Möller, *Prophet in Debate*, 39–40, 104–53.

215. Renz, *Rhetorical Function*, 23–24, 57–61.

216. See Barker, "From the Depths of Despair," 73.

the text's persuasive strategies and effects."[217] Others are more forthright: "Such identification is often inconclusive and controverted and in the end not especially efficacious in providing new insights."[218]

The problem of discerning what precisely it is one should do in step three of Kennedy's rhetorical-critical method is not isolated to prophetic texts alone. While Duke (Chronicles) does an excellent job of surveying Aristotle's types of rhetorical speech, including an exhaustive delineation of his forms of proof, it is uncertain how helpful the genre classification of Chronicles as "deliberative rhetoric"[219] is in properly discerning the rhetorical import of the text.[220] Similarly, Ahn's work (Chronicles) seems to be equally unfruitful concerning this step.[221]

If one were to employ such terminology about the Flood, the text is dynamic in its nature. It seemingly employs a mix of epideictic rhetoric (laudatory), often with respect to the person of Noah (Gen 6:9b–10, 18–22; 7:1, 5, 7–9, 13–16, 23; 8:1, 18–19, 20, 21–22; 9:1–3, 9–17), judicial rhetoric, often with respect to the account of the Deluge itself (Gen 6:11–12; 7:4, 10–12, 17–24; 9:2, 4–6), and deliberative rhetoric, often concerning choices and a proper course of action (Gen 6:13–21; 7:1–4, 23; 8:6–12, 13, 21–22; 9:1–7, 9–11, 12–16). Even so, "one cannot make hard and fast distinctions since the text may contain features of multiple genres in a given passage."[222]

Given such, rather than follow Möller and Barker's lead (cf. Ahn) in subordinating this sort of discussion to the rhetorical strategies the text itself employs to make its persuasive appeal, this study proposes this specific step should be disposed of altogether and a discussion of 'worldview formative rhetoric' should take its place instead.[223]

217. Barker, "From the Depths of Despair," 73–74.
218. Olbricht, "Rhetorical Criticism," 326.
219. See Duke, *Persuasive Appeal*, 39–46 and 74–77.
220. As one reviewer states, "[h]is effort to read a biblical work in accordance with Aristotelian categories is suggestive, and his attempt to assess the Chronicler's purpose offers a useful contribution to the ongoing discussion of what the book is trying to say. In the end, however, his results, like those of many recent literary treatments, seem more convincing when presented than when one reads the biblical work they purport to describe. Duke makes a game try, but the Chronicler keeps getting in the way." Greenspahn, Review of *Persuasive Appeal*, 110. Cf. Throntveit, Review of *Persuasive Appeal*, 314.
221. See Quine, Review of *Persuasive Appeal*, 102–3.
222. Barker, *From the Depths of Despair*, 54.
223. See Burlet, "Cosmos to Chaos," 68. Cf. Faro, *Evil in Genesis*, 220.

Methodology

It seems prudent that rather than belabor the nuances of judicial, epideictic, deliberative rhetoric, one should instead re-classify the biblical text as worldview formative rhetoric.[224] One may abandon any further explanation and entirely eliminate 'step three' of the Kennedy model.

Hebrew Narrative as Worldview-Formative Rhetoric

Rhetoric may be broadly defined as "the process by which people influence others for good through the use of language, images, symbols, and metaphors."[225] Within this book, rhetoric shall be defined as "the means by which a text establishes and manages its relationship to its audience in order to achieve a particular effect."[226] Rhetoric "includes stylistic devices, but goes beyond style to encompass the whole range of linguistic instrumentalities by which a discourse constructs a particular relationship with an audience in order to communicate a message."[227] In other words, consideration of stylistics should not be undertaken "independently of the purpose they must achieve in the argumentation."[228]

Rhetoric takes seriously the idea all literature is "*social* discourse."[229] As Terry Eagleton notes, speech and writing are "largely unintelligible outside the social purposes and conditions in which they were embedded."[230] They should not be understood "merely as textual objects" to be "aesthetically contemplated or endlessly deconstructed" but taken as "forms of *activity* . . . inseparable from the wider social relations between writers and readers, orators, and audiences."[231] Establishing the context of a narrative (including varied audiences) is critical to a proper interpretation of its rhetoric (see step two).

"Authors cannot be exhaustive in their telling of the event . . . they choose what is important or, better stated, what they think is important

---

224. Further aspects of this will be addressed later on within this chapter.

225. Longman, ed., "Rhetoric," 1427–28.

226. Patrick, *Rhetoric of Revelation*, xvii, citing Patrick and Scult, *Rhetoric*, 12. Cf. Westfall, "Resurrection," 112; Mack, *Rhetoric*, 15–16; Thurén, *Argument and Theology*, 50–51; Stewart, "Ethos of the Cosmos," 44; Stamps, "Rhetorical Device," 25.

227. Patrick and Scult, *Rhetoric*, 12.

228. Perelman and Olbrechts-Tyteca, *New Rhetoric*, 142.

229. Wuellner, "Rhetorical Criticism," 462–63. Emphasis original.

230. Eagleton, *Literary Theory*, 179. Emphasis original.

231. Eagleton, *Literary Theory*, 179. Emphasis original. See too Alexiou, *Elixir of Democracy*.

about the event. Thus, authors provide the perspective through which we hear or read about the event."[232] With respect to narrative, in particular, "the reading of narrative has multiple dimensions in that when we read a narrative, we use our intellects, emotions, ideologies, and ethics."[233] In this sense, one of the key objectives of biblical Hebrew narrative (and prose), in general, is to "bring about changes in the readers, to create persons different from what they were before the reading took place."[234]

Narratives also help humanity to map reality.[235] They facilitate effectual, positive changes to one's values and behaviors alongside their perceptions of morality and ethics. Kevin J. Vanhoozer asserts: "a narrative displays a worldview, an interpreted world. In addition to relating a series of events, authors take up an attitude towards it ... narratives are powerful instruments for shaping the way we see, imagine and think about the world."[236] In this general sense, all narrative is "rhetorically shaped" and contains argumentation (rhetoric).[237] It is not a stretch to argue the Genesis Flood text, specifically, should ultimately be thought of as being a rhetorical (or persuasive) composition.[238] With respect to worldview, by this term is meant:

> The basic way of interpreting things and events that pervades a culture so thoroughly that it becomes a culture's concept of reality—what is good, what is important, what is sacred, what is real. Worldview is more than culture, even though the distinction between the two can sometimes be subtle. It extends to perception of time and space, of happiness and well-being. The beliefs, values, and behaviors of a culture stem directly from its worldview.[239]

---

232. Longman and Walton, *The Lost World of the Flood*, 21. See too Vogt, *Pentateuch*, 48–49.

233. Ahn *Persuasive Portrayal*, 16.

234. Fretheim, *Pentateuch*, 40. See too Wenham, *Story as Torah*, 17–43.

235. For clarity, a narrative is defined within this study as a "selective record of a series of events that uses shared conventions to convey the author's communicative intention in an engaging manner." Vogt, *Pentateuch*, 48. Cf. Ryken, *Words of Delight*, 515; Robinson, "Narrative," 236.

236. Vanhoozer, "Exegesis and Hermeneutics," 59.

237. Longman and Walton, *The Lost World of the Flood*, 21.

238. Mack, *Rhetoric*, 10; Kitchen, *Old Testament*, 17; Collins, *Reading Genesis Well*, 114–23; Vogt, *Pentateuch*, 52. Cf. Aaron, *Genesis Ideology*, 9–22, 89.

239. Hill, "Worldview Approach," 129. See too Hill, *Worldview Approach*, 3–15.

Another scholar states: "[a] worldview is a set of presuppositions (assumptions which may be true, partially true or entirely false) which we hold (consciously or subconsciously, consistently or inconsistently) about the basic make up of our world."[240] Worldview, however, is not to be confused with world-picture.[241] Davis A. Young and Ralph F. Stearley argue:

> The ancient world universally believed that the dome-like vault of the sky is a glassy, crystalline *solid*... Some commentators attempt to avoid the force of the statement by claiming that Scripture is using phenomenal language, the language of appearance. But that's our problem. The Israelites would not have seen it that way. The sky didn't just look solid to them; they believed it to be a solid.[242]

That being said, there is a marked "difference between how ancient people *depicted* the cosmos and what they truly believed about the structure of the cosmos."[243]

Othmar Keel and Silvia Schoroer explain:

> People in the ancient Near East did not conceive of the earth as a disk floating on water with the firmament inverted over it like a bell jar, with the stars hanging from it. They knew from observation and experience with handicrafts that the lifting capacity of water is limited and that gigantic vaults generate gigantic problems in terms of their ability to carry dead weight. The textbook images that keep being reprinted of the 'ancient Near Eastern world picture' are based on typical modern misunderstandings that fail to take into account the religious components of ancient Near Eastern conceptions and representations... Ancient Near Eastern images are conceptual, not photographic. They combine

---

240. Sire, *Naming the Elephant*, 19. Cf. Bartholomew, *Biblical Hermeneutics*, 477. For more details, see Bartholomew and Goheen, *Living at the Crossroads*; Sire, *The Universe Next Door*; Wolters, *Creation Regained*; Walsh and Middleton, *Transforming Vision*. Cf. Porter, "Lewis's Worldview," 3–50.

241. For a clear distinction between "worldview" and "world-picture" and its significance for the Bible, see Collins, *Reading Genesis Well*, 243–64; Chisholm "History or Story," 57–58.

242. Young and Stearley, *The Bible, Rocks and Time*, 206–7. Emphasis original. See too Greenwood, *Scripture and Cosmology*, 24–29; Enns, *Inspiration*, 41–45; Lamoureux, *The Bible and Ancient Science*, 108–36; Walton, *Genesis*, 110–13; Walton, *Job*, 371–73; Walton, *Ancient Cosmology*, 86–100; Walton, "Cosmology," 116–20; Soden, "Cosmology," 120–24; Simkins, *Creation*, 15–40. Cf. Mortenson, "The Firmament," 113–33.

243. Davidson and Turner, *Manifold Beauty*, 72. Emphasis original.

aspects of (empirical) experience of the world and worldly outlook, sometimes in a (to our mind) grotesquely mixed-up way.[244]

A traditional depiction of the ancient Hebrew conception of the world is seen below.[245]

It is almost indisputable biblical texts are predicated on "worldview formation" and are inculcated via a specific meta-narrative that stretches across the sum total of the canon.[246] It is also almost nearly impossible to refute one of the primary aims of Scripture is to positively shape, impact, and influence the sum total of a person's character and being, including the affective, cognitive, and volitional elements of what it means to be human.[247]

---

244. Keel and Schroer, *Creation*, 78–80. In addition, saying the ancients read Genesis through a so-called 'primitive cosmology concept of the universe' is different than saying that they got this concept from the text itself. I credit Brad Cowie for this judicious insight via private communiqué. For more details, see Faulkner, *Falling Flat*, 301–39. Cf. Hilber, *Old Testament Theology and Divine Accommodation*, 44–48

245. For comparable graphic illustrations, see Stanhope, *(Mis)interpreting Genesis*, 88; Hilber, *Old Testament Cosmology and Divine Accommodation*, 45; Copan and Jacoby, *Origins*, 215; Davids, *2 Peter and Jude*, 269; Greenwood, *Scripture and Cosmology*, 26; Presutta, *Biblical Cosmos*, 190; Enns, *Inspiration*, 43; House and Mitchell, *Old Testament Survey*, 21; Hill and Walton, *Survey of the Old Testament*, 385; Scott, *Evolution vs. Creationism*, 66; Anderson, *Creation*, 21; Miller and Soden, *In the Beginning*, 44; Walton, "Genesis," 8; Ross, *Job*, 77; Routledge, *Old Testament Theology*, 131; Lamoureux, *Evolutionary Creation*, 122; Lamoureux, "No Historical Adam," 48; Lamoureux, *The Bible and Ancient Science*, 109. Cf. Mortenson, "The Firmament," 127, 129, 130–32; Faulkner, *The Expanse of Heaven*, 310. See too Hill, *Worldview Approach*, 10 and Okoye, *Genesis 1–11*, 27 (who both modify Sarna, *Understanding Genesis*, 5); Glover, *Firmament*, 81 (who uses the work of Christian, *Philosophy*, 512); Keel and Schroer, *Creation*, 83 (who uses the figure in Keel, "Weltbild," 161); Dillow, *The Waters Above*, 9 (who uses the figure found in *The Interpreter's Dictionary of the Bible*, 1:703); Collins, *Reading Genesis Well*, 245 (who uses the image within the *UBS Handbook on Genesis*, 27). For a Babylonian conception of the world, see Horowitz, *Geography*, 20–42.

246. See Collins, *Reading Genesis Well*, 119–20, 134–38; Peterson, *Working the Angles*, 121.

247. See Combrink, "Rhetoric," 112–13, 115–18. One notes that some of these categories are somewhat anachronistic in an ancient Hebrew worldview. As such, these "distinctions are more heuristic than essential." Brown, ed., *Character and Scripture*, xii. I am indebted to Alex Stewart (private communiqué) for this insight and reference.

Figure Four—Ancient Hebrew Conception of The Universe

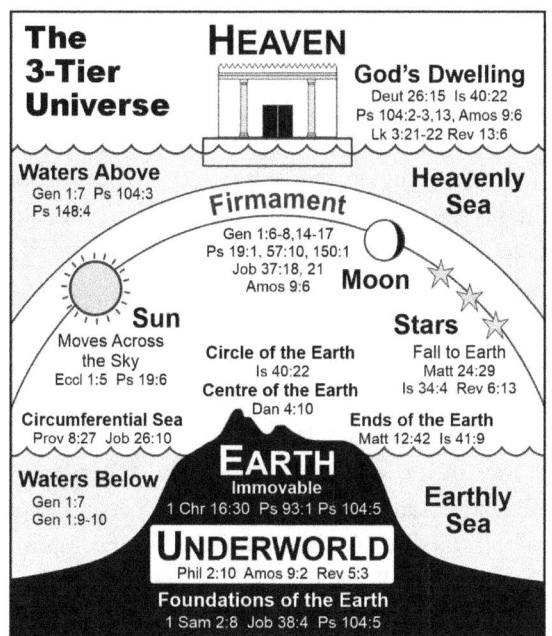

Concerning the Torah, specifically, one clear objective of this text was to "bring about changes in the readers, to create persons different from what they were before the reading took place."[248] The text functions to "shape the beliefs, practices, and dispositions of the target communities" so as to enable what C. S. Lewis has deemed "'the transition from thinking to doing.'"[249] The function of Genesis was to positively effect the Hebrew worldview or meta-narrative.[250] Genesis also facilitates the answers to some "big" questions, such as: "Where did we come from? What has gone wrong? What has been done about it? Where are we now in the whole process?"[251] As Hermann Gunkel maintains, Genesis is "the beginnings of theology and philosophy."[252] Genesis cultivates the principles which underlay an understanding of proper relationships: (1) GOD

---

248. Fretheim, *Pentateuch*, 40. Cf. Howard, "Rhetorical Criticism," 103.

249. Collins, *Reading Genesis Well*, 44. Cf. Barker, "From the Depths of Despair," 72.

250. Carlson and Longman, *Science, Creation and the Bible*, 14; Carson, "Genesis," 145–46.

251. See Collins, *Reading Genesis Well*, 89, 119, 135, and 243–64 from whom these questions have been derived.

252. Gunkel, "Legends," xiv

to the universe; (2) humanity to God; (3) humanity to God's creation; (4) humanity to humanity; and (5) humanity to self.[253]

Step Four: Assessing the Rhetorical Strategy

The fourth step of the Kennedy model is to assess the rhetorical strategy of the text. It is at this stage rhetorical criticism as "the art of persuasion" most resembles rhetorical criticism as "the art of composition."[254] In this step, the interpreter looks for literary (stylistic) devices, structural patterns, and such so as to better ascertain how the text itself was crafted so as to effectively communicate its message.[255] This study's approach differs from the Muilenburg "rhetoric as composition" school in that the goal of the analysis is to move beyond aesthetics and the literary quality of the text, to capturing the way the text's construction reveals its "persuasive force."[256] It is this concerted attention to describing the text's persuasive appeal which distinguishes "the art of persuasion" from "the art of composition."[257]

Consideration of stylistics should always be undertaken in view of the purpose it achieves in argumentation.[258] In other words, rhetoric as persuasion scholars view stylistic features as "instruments" of the rhetor used intentionally to affect and persuade the audience and not simply as "embellishments of discourse."[259] To re-state, a rhetoric as persuasion rhetorical critic does analyze certain literary features of the text, but also articulates their potential persuasive impact.[260] Consequently, any study

---

253. Carlson and Longman, *Science, Creation, and the Bible*, 14; Collins, *Reading Genesis Well*, 134–36; Simkins, *Creation*, 168–72. Cf. Lowery, *Toward a Poetics*, 1–2.

254. See Barker, *From the Depths of Despair*, 54, 75.

255. See Trible, *Rhetorical Criticism*, 26. Cf. Patrick and Scult, *Rhetoric*, 12.

256. Barker, *From the Depths of Despair*, 75.

257. With respect to this point, some scholars also argue that the ability to move from describing what the argument looks like to delineating and explaining why the text retains its persuasive appeal is actually what moves this approach from rhetorical *analysis* to rhetorical *criticism*, specifically. See Barker, *From the Depths*, 75; Hester, "Kennedy and the Reading of Paul," 154.

258. Perelman and Olbrechts-Tyteca, *New Rhetoric*, 142.

259. Ahn *Persuasive Portrayal*, 24–25; Barker, *From the Depths of Despair*, 54.

260. Barker, *From the Depths of Despair*, 29. See also Watson and Hauser, *Rhetorical Criticism*, 14; Howard, "Rhetorical Criticism," 103.

of a text's rhetorical strategies must keep its persuasive (rhetorical) potential at the center (versus the periphery) of the analysis.²⁶¹

Given their frequent use within HB/OT studies, one should also be aware of the five canons of classical Greco-Roman rhetoric: (1) invention (*inventio*), (2) arrangement (*dispositio*), (3) style (*elecutio*), (4) memory (*memoria*), and (5) delivery (*actio* or *pronuntiatio*). Both *memoria* and *actio/pronuntiatio* relate specifically to oral presentations.²⁶²

First, *inventio* involves seeking "potent arguments."²⁶³ This includes *materia*, "the discovery of material suitable to the occasion."²⁶⁴ It also entails *status*, the determination of the issue at stake, and *topoi*, the selection of techniques deemed suitable to supporting the position of the rhetorician.²⁶⁵ Rhetoricians are intentionally selective in their strategy. They consistently seek to leverage and employ that which will persuade their audience to their own point and dissuade them from alternative viewpoints.²⁶⁶

Aristotle also discusses certain "proofs," of which *ethos* (the moral character of the rhetorician), *pathos* (the ability to put the audience into a particular frame of mind via the text), and *logos* (the details of the text or the speech itself) are the most pertinent.²⁶⁷ Through noting and leveraging these three categories, in general, one becomes more astutely aware of the wide range and breadth of persuasive appeals—from the rational and cognitive types to the emotive and imaginative ones—thus garnering greater insight into the different ways a rhetor can construct a persuasive appeal within a text.²⁶⁸ One scholar notes "in Hebrew rhetoric, the driving force behind the assertive discourse of one speaking for GOD is authority, which substitutes for ethos in classical rhetoric."²⁶⁹ Each of

261. See Barker, *From the Depths of Despair*, 75 from whom much of this sentence's wording was derived. Cf. Fishbane, *Text and Texture*.

262. See Olbricht, "Delivery and Memory," 159–67; Möller, *Prophet in Debate*, 41; Trible, *Rhetorical Criticism*, 8; Ahn, *Persuasive Portrayal*, 23.

263. Ahn, *Persuasive Portrayal*, 23.

264. Trible, *Rhetorical Criticism*, 8.

265. Much of the phrasing of the above sentence comes from Möller, *Prophet in Debate*, 41.

266. See Lenchak, "Choose Life!" 57; Brandt, *Rhetoric of Argumentation*, 14.

267. See Möller, *Prophet in Debate*, 41; Barker, *From the Depths of Despair*, 55. Notably, some scholars actually schematize the majority of their work under these self-same rubrics. See Duke, *Persuasive Appeal*, 81–147.

268. Wuellner, "Rhetorical Criticisms," 461; Möller, *Prophet in Debate*, 42; Barker, *From the Depths of Despair*, 55.

269. Lundbom, *Hebrew Prophets*, 189.

the three work together: "intellect of itself 'moves nothing': the transition from thinking to doing, in nearly all men [sic] at nearly all moments, needs to be assisted by appropriate states of feeling."[270]

Second, *dispositio* attempts to "determine the rhetorically effective composition of the speech and mold its elements into a unified structure."[271] *Dispositio* usually involves line-by-line and verse-by-verse analysis of the argument (including assumptions, topics, and rhetorical features) in order to determine "what subdivisions it falls into, what the persuasive effect of these parts seems to be, and how they work together to some unified purpose in meeting the rhetorical situation."[272] Karl Möller defines *dispositio*, stating:

> [I]nterest in a text's dispositio, its structure or the organization of its argument, goes beyond the mere delineation of its rhetorical units referred to as the first step of rhetorical-critical enquiry. The focus at this point is on the persuasive effect of the textual units. To uncover this effect, the critic asks whether and how these units work together to achieve some unified purpose, or indeed fail to do so.[273]

Third, *elocutio* pertains to the style of a text.[274]

The rhetoric as persuasion branch of rhetorical criticism regards stylistic features not as mere "embellishments" but duly recognizes rhetoricians leverage such things so as to "amplify certain parts of his or her discourse."[275] Many rhetorical critics examine them so as to "elucidate their role for the argumentative development of the rhetorical discourse."[276] It is thus understood Hebrew narrative, in particular, provides the "implied audience with information about the past and forces it

---

270. Collins, *Reading Genesis Well*, quoting Lewis, *Preface to Paradise Lost*, 51–53.

271. Kennedy, *New Testament Interpretation*, 23.

272. Kennedy, *New Testament Interpretation*, 37.

273. Möller, *Prophet in Debate*, 42. For more details see Wuellner, "Arrangement," 31–87.

274. Möller, *Prophet in Debate*, 42. See also Ahn, *Persuasive Portrayal*, 24. "Style" is the "choice of proper language and figures of speech to best express the argument." Webb, "Petrine Epistles," 376. Cf. Kennedy, *Rhetorical Criticism*, 25–30. It is understood that stylistic devices "hook" and "grab" audience's attention alongside helping to facilitate information retention, thus aiding in the art of persuasion. Ryken, et al., eds., *DBI*, xiii–xxi.

275. Möller, *Prophet in Debate*, 42.

276. Möller, *Prophet in Debate*, 42.

to make decisions. The degree to which the implied audience accepts the story depends on the rhetorical effectiveness of the narrator."[277]

On a different note, though we lack an "ancient Hebrew manual on narratology," some key features of Hebrew narrative do include the following: (a) the narrator is reliable and omniscient, often serving as the voice and perspective of GOD if no divine speech occurs within the text itself, (b) the narration is scenic, that is, the emphasis is on direct action and interaction of the characters rather than on descriptive details of the environs, (c) narratives are sparsely written, focusing only on what is essential for the narrative, (d) scribes often use *Leitwortstil*, i.e. they will repeat key words or phrases so as to draw attention to thematic issues, (e) scribes often employ wordplays, generally for ironic contrasts, (f) scribes often used heighted speech using poetic diction: elevated diction of a speech is evidence of its significance; often oracular, it may even be divine speech, (g) scribes often use repetition, such as similar kinds of events and scenes in different circumstances, (h) scribes usually employ analogy and contrast, where the characters and scenes are like and unlike one another.[278]

In sum, biblical writers often communicate their point of view via "indirect and laconic means" with the emphasis on "*showing* (displaying the heart by action and speech) versus *telling* (explicitly stating what kind of person the character is)."[279] As Collins explicates: "the biblical material . . . is highly pictorial; this is not a weakness, it is a strength. It does not prevent the Bible writers from speaking truly; it actually enables them to achieve their rhetorical goals."[280]

Aside from assessing the physical, temporal, and cultural settings in a story, there are also a few basic factors of narrative technique which shape the rhetoric of the text.[281] These include: (a) variations in the narrative point of view, (b) norms of judgment (criteria of right and wrong as implied on the basis of the narrator's attitudes towards certain

---

277. Ahn, *Persuasive Portrayal*, 9.

278. This material (including generous amounts of exact phrasing and wording) has been derived from Collins, *Reading Genesis Well*, 45–47. See also Waltke and Fredricks, *Genesis*, 33–43; Ryken, *The Bible as Literature*, 68–69; Buchanan, "Literary Devices," 202–3.

279. Collins, *Reading Genesis Well*, 46. All emphases original. See too Long, *King Saul*, 31.

280. Collins, *Reading Genesis Well*, 76–77. See too Longman, *How to Read the Psalms*, 117. Cf. Huw, *In the Way of Story*.

281. On these specific elements, see Ryken, *Words of Delight*, 54–62.

characters and actions),²⁸² (c) dynamics of distance in the characterizations (the degree of sympathy or alienation, involvement or detachment between narrator, audience, and characters of the story), and (d) the plot (including conflict, suspense, resolution, and the establishment and reversal of expectations).²⁸³

The structure of a biblical narrative can be graphically depicted as follows:²⁸⁴

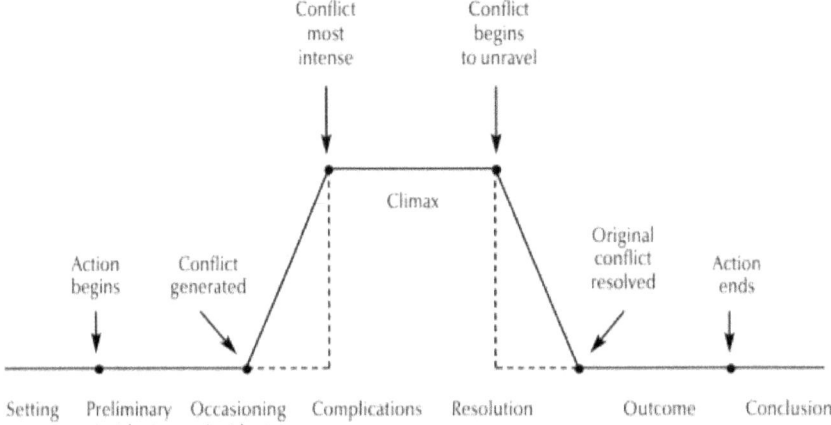

Figure Five—The Structure of Biblical Narrative

Plots can usually be traced by means of some type of conflict (occasioning or inciting incident) between characters in the story.²⁸⁵ As Leland Ryken notes: "the essence of plot is a central conflict or set of conflicts moving toward a resolution."²⁸⁶ In addition, dialogue and speech (whether indirect, direct, or inside a quotative frame) are also important elements of narrative plot.²⁸⁷ The narrator employs such to control "the pace of the

---

282. The narrator is always deemed as "reliable." See Phelan, *Somebody Telling Somebody*, 231–34.

283. Boomershine, "Narrative Rhetoric," 115; Ryken et al., eds., *DBI*, 720–27; Ryken, *The Bible As Literature*, 68–69; Longman, "Biblical Narrative," 71–78, Long, *King Saul*, 21–42.

284. Longman and Dillard, *Introduction*, 33. Cf. Gorman, *Elements*, 102; Vogt, *Pentateuch*, 55.

285. Longman, *Literary Approaches*, 159.

286. Ryken, *The Bible As Literature*, 40. See also Ryken, *Words of Delight*, 62–71. Cf. Thomas, *Story*, 30–60.

287. Miller, *Speech*, 1–2. "The preponderance of direct discourse [in Genesis]

plot, at times delaying the advancement of the action and/or focusing on a particular character to accentuate the narrative moment or character."[288] Dialogue and speech emphasizes the "core" of story, indicating "key turning points or climaxes in the structural framework of a narrative."[289] Robert Alter refers to Hebrew narrative as "narration-through-dialogue."[290] The narrator or implied author also utilizes dialogue and/or speeches to contribute to the "liveliness of the passage and to provide information in an artistic way"[291] In addition, "the representation of speech extends beyond dialogue to perform a variety of narrative functions. It may introduce characters, recount their inner character, index relationships, and provide background information for the narrative."[292] Speeches and dialogue can "legitimate the actions of a character by providing the reason for those actions," revealing "the ideological message of the narrator."[293] The narrator can convey "the inner psychology and ideology of a character" through someone's words.[294] As Ahn states, speeches "express thoughts, motives, desires and beliefs."[295]

Other particulars the interpreter must take account for in order to effectively assess a text's rhetorical strategy include ancient literary conventions, styles, and tropes. In some cases, this can include "theological geography."[296] It is understood that so-called "academic arithmetic" was also not uncommon. "The E-sangil Tablet, formerly understood as offering an accurate physical description of Babylon's ziggurat, has been

---

supports Robert Alter's and Adele Berlin's observations that narrative provides a supporting role to link and frame dialogue. Characters and the plot are brought to life through the polyphony of direct discourse, revealing inner thoughts and interpersonal conflicts dramatically, and actively engaging the reader/listener through the vehicle of dialogue and reported speech in a way that narrative alone fails to accomplish." Faro, *Evil in Genesis*, 37–38. Cf. Van Pelt, ed., *Basics of Hebrew Discourse*, 84.

288. Boda, "Prayer as Rhetoric," 286.

289. Boda, "Prayer as Rhetoric," 286. Cf. Sternberg, *Poetics*, 168.

290. Alter, *Art of Biblical Narrative*, 69. See too Vogt, *Pentateuch*, 57–58.

291. Boda, "Prayer as Rhetoric," 286.

292. Miller, *Speech*, 2. See also Bar-Efrat, *Narrative Art in the Bible*, 64–77; Hodge, *Days of Genesis*, 154–55.

293. Boda, "Prayer as Rhetoric," 286. See too Ryken et al., eds., *DBI*, 727.

294. Boda, "Prayer as Rhetoric," 286. On "biblical idioms of internal speech," see Schnittjer, *Old Testament Use of Old Testament*, xxxii. Cf. Carasik, *Theologies*, 104–24; Steiner, "He Said, He Said," 485–91.

295. Ahn *Persuasive Portrayal*, 10. Cf. Bitzer, "Rhetorical Situation," 5.

296. Duguid, *Ezekiel*, 471–72.

characterized as a document more interested in abstract ideas than real buildings, and in consequence the question has been raised as to whether a ziggurat like the one described by it was ever really built."[297]

Even when a particular medium allowed for more "realistic" depictions, "conventions and rhetorical objectives" have often determined the representation.[298] To underscore this point, some scholars compare narrative historiography writing to portraiture.[299] Other scholars use other forms of artistic expression. Note the following graphic of an Assyrian *Lamassu*.[300] Adele Berlin states:

> What appears ... is actually a representation of a representation. It is a picture (two-dimensional) of a statue (three-dimensional). The statue is a representation of an object that does not exist in real life, but that can nevertheless be represented as if it did. (We can represent and naturalize things that are imagery.) It is a creature with the legs and body of a lion, a human head, and wings. All three of its components exist independently in real life, but here are combined. But look again. Do lions have five legs? Was it the intent of the artist to represent a five legged lion? No! Five legs are there, but they represent only four legs. Ancient convention demanded that a side view contain four legs and a front view contain two legs. Even though the two views are combined, each must remain 'true' to itself, and so the sum

---

297. George, "The Tower of Babel," 92. See too Longman and Walton, *Lost World of the Flood*, 75–76.

298. Longman and Walton, *Lost World of the Flood*, 76.

299. "It perhaps cannot be overstated, however, that history writing/narrative, even biblical history, is more like painting, specifically portraiture, than videotaping: Portrait artists are in a sense 'constructionists,' they make creative choices in composing and rendering their historical subject. But they are far from simply imposing structure on an amorphous body of isolated 'facts' (an eye here, a nose there). Their task is to observe the contours and the character of their subject, the relationships between the various features, and to capture in a visual representational medium these essentials of their subject. No two portraits are exactly alike, of course, because no two portrait artists see the subject in just the same way or make the same creative choices in rendering it. But neither are competent portraits of the same subject utterly unlike, for they are constrained by the facts–the contours and structures of the subject. In their representational craft, portrait artists compose (i.e. construct) their painting, but they do not simply impose structure on their subject. Might it not be the same for narrative historians?" Provan et al., *Biblical History*, 111. See too Long, *Art of Biblical History*, 329–30.

300. For comparable images, see Berlin, *Poetics*, 14; Copan and Jacoby, *Origins*, 109; Greer et al. eds., *Behind the Scenes of the Old Testament*, 166; Keel and Schroer, *Creation*, 27.

of the legs of the parts is more than the sum of the legs of the real object. (One leg serves a double function, belonging to both the side and frontal view). Even though we are not ancient Assyrians, and no longer use this same artistic convention, we naturalize this statue without difficulty, scarcely noticing the number of legs until it is pointed out. But the legs of the lion should remind us that *representations of reality do not always correspond in every detail to reality*.[301]

In brief, strict "realism is not the objective."[302] Much depends on the persuasive stratagem.[303]

Figure Six—Assyrian Lamassu

Given the pervasiveness of "universalistic rhetoric" throughout the Noachian deluge narrative, the place of hyperbole must also be reckoned with.[304] Hyperbole was pervasive throughout the ANE in both art and culture, i.e., iconography, wall-paintings, reliefs, speech, and writing.[305] Hyperbole may be thought of as a "deliberate exaggeration for the sake of

301. Berlin, *Poetics*, 14. All emphases original.

302. Longman and Walton, *Lost World of The Flood*, 76.

303. See Collins, *Reading Genesis Well*, 57–58, 193; Longman and Walton, *Lost World of The Flood*, 36–41. One understands, of course, that an image "communicates differently than a text. It has its own codes and language that need to be read and interpreted properly." Bodi, "Mesopotamian and Anatolian Iconography," 166.

304. See Longman and Walton, *Lost World of the Flood*, 29–41.

305. Watson, *Classical Hebrew Poetry*, 316–20; Longman and Walton, *Lost World of the Flood*, 76; Collins, *Reading Genesis Well*, 57.

effect."[306] Wilfred G. E. Watson defines hyperbole as a "way of expressing exaggeration of some kind (regarding size, numbers, danger, prowess, fertility and the like) using common expression. By this means the idea stands out."[307] Hyperbole may also be understood as a "rhetorical trope which carries emotive and valuative meaning."[308]

Much hinges on the Hebrew word "all" (כל).[309] This indefinite pronoun has a quantifying function.[310] When the pronoun is used "in construct with a definite singular noun, it often carries the idea of 'the totality of the individual unit of the specific entity.'"[311] When combined with a plural definite noun, it "expresses the 'totality of the specific group and conveys the nuance of 'all.'"[312] While more nuance is possible, the term clearly "expresses the idea of 'totality.'"[313]

Esteemed Hebraist and biblical commentator Bruce K. Waltke and Cathi Fredricks observes that while many "evangelicals favor a local flood," the Genesis "narrator, even allowing for oriental hyperbole, seems to have in mind a universal flood."[314] Waltke lays out what have become, for some people, the fault lines of the debate over Noah's flood: "The geological arguments favoring a local flood assume that the history of the earth's geology is uniform, but the text represents a geological cataclysm and a re-creation of the earth."[315]

---

306. Cruise, "Detecting and Mitigating Hyperbole," 88. See also Burgers et al., "HIP," 163–78.

307. Watson, *Classical Hebrew Poetry*, 316–17. Cf. Ryken, *Words of Delight*, 515.

308. Silverman, "Yes We Can (Hyperbolize)!," 268.

309. According to one scholar, the term is used 72 times (!) within Gen 6:1—9:17 which is "an enormous amount considering the entire Flood narrative covers only 85 verses... The word כל only occurs 342 times in the entire book of Genesis (which is 50 chapters long). Thus, 21 per cent of all occurrences are found in these four chapters." See Kruger, "Does 'All' Always Mean All?," 216. Cf. Even-Shoshan, *A New Concordance of the Old Testament*.

310. See *BHRG* §36.5.1. See too Naudé, "Interpretation and Translation of *Kol*," 408–21.

311. Smith, "Whom, Where, or What," 136.

312. *BHRG* §36.5.4.

313. Smith, "Whom, Where, or What," 136 citing Sauer, *TLOT* 2:614. See also *DCH* 4:394–413; *HALOT* 2:474a; Ringgren, *TDOT* 7:135–43; Oswalt, *TWOT* 1:441; Nel, *NIDOTTE* 2:657–58. Cf. Schmidt, "Translating Kōl," 179–91.

314. Waltke and Fredricks, *Genesis*, 132–33.

315. Waltke and Fredricks, *Genesis*, 133. Of course, "By GOD's willful design, the *heilsgeschichte* (faith/theological history) is incarnationally embedded within and throughout the *historie* (natural/human history). The truth of the divine reality (which

Methodology

It is beyond the scope of this book to deal with the geological implications of the Genesis Flood.[316] This work seeks to focus on rhetoric and hyperbole (universalistic and totalic language) in the Genesis Flood as it pertains specifically to language concerning judgment and salvation.

Step Five: Determining the Rhetorical Effectiveness

The final step of the so-called Kennedy model is to determine the text's rhetorical effectiveness. Rhetorical effectiveness is intimately connected with and deeply related to both rhetorical situation and audience.[317] In Kennedy's words, rhetorical effectiveness reviews the text's "success in meeting the rhetorical exigence and what its implications may be for the speaker or audience."[318] Rhetorical effectiveness essentially allowed Kennedy the opportunity to summarize each of the previous steps of the model and to "expand its implications beyond the narrow boundaries of the text in question."[319] While this step could potentially be done by asking whether or not the rhetoric successfully modified the exigence, one often lacks the evidence to evaluate a discourse's historical effectiveness since we "rarely have a record of the response of the audience that heard the message."[320] Möller contends one's focus should be on whether or not the rhetorical utterance had the *potential* to successfully modify the exigence.[321] This involves evaluating the discourse's "internal logic"

---

is reality itself) is one" (Stallings, *Genesis Cataclysm*, 15). At the same time, however, it is important to note that in our "current fallen reality, Scripture and nature are not on an equal par. Despite having the same author, nature—as it exists now—pales in comparison with Scripture concerning stand-alone veridical value. Therefore, all of natural revelation (second-line evidence) must be viewed through the lens of Scripture (first-line evidence) and not the reverse" (Stallings, *Genesis Cataclysm*, 18).

316. More details on some of these aspects concerning Noah's flood may be found in the footnotes contained in Burlet, "Heutagogy and Teaching Genesis 1–11." See also Stallings, *Genesis Cataclysm*, 41–98; Griffin, *Creation and the Flood*, 146–49. Cf. Rogers, *The Biblical Flood* alongside Snelling, *Earth's Catastrophic Past*.

317. Ahn, *Persuasive Portrayal*, 31; Barker, *From the Depths of Despair*, 58.

318. Kennedy, *New Testament Interpretation*, 38. Cf. Barker, *From the Depths of Despair*, 55–56.

319. Barker, *From the Depths of Despair*, 56.

320. Barker, *From the Depths of Despair*, 56.

321. Möller, *Prophet in Debate*, 42–43. Cf. Ahn, *Persuasive Portrayal*, 31.

and "persuasive thrust."[322] Though it is not without its detractors, this approach is actually quite commendable.

Stamp's synchronic, entextualized rhetorical situation has much to offer. In Stamps' approach, rhetorical critics seek to answer the question of whether or not (or, more precisely, to what degree) the discourse or rhetorical unit "could function as effective persuasion within the situation to which it is being applied."[323] Barker states: "rhetorical effectiveness remains a nebulous concept . . . the need to develop a more nuanced approach . . . cuts to the core of rhetorical criticism as a discipline."[324]

This study will seek to leverage a "both/and" schema for determining rhetorical effectiveness.[325] That is to say, this study will initially examine each of the main units of the Noachian deluge narrative from within the text itself, i.e. a synchronic, entextualized rhetorical situation. Then, based upon the evidence provided by means of the final form of the text, it will comment on rhetorical effectiveness on the basis of that information.

The chronology of the final form of Genesis is disputed.[326] Still, it is evident the Torah was addressed to a people who were already living under covenant stipulations and failing miserably.[327] Scripture also shows signs the implied readers of the Pentateuch experienced the apostasy of Israel, the devastation of Jerusalem, and the deportation and exile to Babylon which began with Judah in 587 BC (Lev 26:27–44; Deut 4:25–31; 8:19–20; 28:36–37, 45–68; 29:20–28; 30:1–20; cf. 1 Kgs 8:46–53; 9:6–9; 2 Kgs 21:8–15).[328] The exilic nature of the Pentateuchal final form

322. Barker, *From the Depths of Despair*, 56.

323. Barker, *From the Depths of Despair*, 55.

324. Barker, *From the Depths of Despair*, 55–56. Cf. Anderson, "Rhetorical Criticism," xvii–xviii.

325. Cf. Ahn, *Persuasive Portrayal*, 31.

326. One scholar states, "The Mosaic era certainly accounts for many of the key features in Genesis" and none of the observations that would pertain to a date in the fifth-century post-exilic era "are problems for a date in the united monarchy period." Wenham, *Story as Torah*, 41–42. Others opine the "final version of Genesis was evidently written no earlier than 1000 BC, since the monarchy, to which the text refers, was established in the late eleventh century (cf. Gen 36:21)." Copan and Jacoby, *Origins*, 13. Still, others contend Genesis reached its final form in the Persian Period. Provan, *Discovering Genesis*, 49–58. Cf. Dozeman, *Pentateuch*, 525–45; Hess *Old Testament*, 32–36; Alexander, *Paradise*, 333–45; Longman and Dillard, *Introduction*, 40–51; Arnold, *Genesis*, 12–18; Kawashima, "Sources," 52. See too Hendel and Joosten, *Hebrew Bible*, 127–30.

327. Sailhamer, *Meaning of the Pentateuch*, 26. Cf. Fretheim, *Pentateuch*, 40–63.

328. The many parenthetical comments inserted in Deuteronomy (Deut 1:2, 7;

Methodology

is also demonstrated by the statement there was never again a prophet like Moses in Israel (see Deut 34:10–12).[329] In addition to this, as Copan and Jacobay offer, the "final version of Genesis was evidently written no earlier than 1000 BC, since the monarchy, to which the text refers, was established in the late eleventh century (cf. Gen 36:21)."[330]

To reiterate, Scripture insinuates the implied first audience of the Torah were those persons who survived the wilderness wanderings and crossed the Jordan River under Joshua's leadership (see Lev 14:34; Num 34:2; Deut 18:9; 19:1; 26:1; 27:2; 31:1–9). Due to the lack of historical specificity concerning the Genesis Flood account, it is difficult to determine the audience to whom it was originally addressed or what impact it could have had.[331] While it is clear the Torah would be pertinent to Israelites living before the exile, the shape of the final form of the Pentateuch does not speak as clearly to a preexilic life-setting.[332] This study will therefore seek to determine the rhetorical effectiveness of the Genesis Flood account based upon a late-exilic final form of the Pentateuch (cf. Deut 34:10–12).[333]

Lastly, rhetorical effectiveness involves "assessing the impact of the constituent parts as they work together to create the broader message of the whole discourse."[334] Once an interpreter has determined the rhetorical units of the texts (step one), constructed the rhetorical situation, including its exigencies, implied author(s), audience(s), etc. (step two), set aside the discussion of rhetorical species (step three) in favor of formative worldview-rhetoric, and delineated various rhetorical strategies employed in the text (step four), the last step is to assess in what manner

---

2:10–12, 20–23, 34; 3:4–7, 9, 11, 13–14, 16–17; 4:9, 20, 23, 44–49; 11:30; 30:1; 31:6–8; 34:3) also suggest not only a temporal distance from the events that transpired in the text but also some loss of memory, both geographical and historical, thus implying an audience spatially removed from Canaan. See Fretheim, *Pentateuch*, 41–42.

329. One scholar asserts: "Clearly, the author who made this statement knows about the entire line of prophets who followed Moses ... a huge jump is made here at the end of Pentateuch, taking us from the last days of Moses to the last days of the prophets." Sailhamer, *Meaning of the Pentateuch*, 31. See too Sailhamer, "Genesis 1–11," 89–106.

330. Copan and Jacoby, *Origins*, 13.

331. Cf. Collins, *Reading Genesis Well*, 125.

332. Cf. Collins, *Reading Genesis Well*, 125–30.

333. Sailhamer, *Meaning of the Pentateuch*, 26. See too Sailhamer, "Genesis 1–11," 89–106. Cf. Provan, *Discovering Genesis*, 53–55; Collins, *Reading Genesis Well*, 125–30.

334. Barker, *From the Depths of Despair*, 65.

the text achieves its objectives, i.e. to assess its rhetorical effectiveness (step five).

This final step is clearly dependent upon each of the steps that came before it. The results one offers here are often conditioned by the results of each of the previous steps. To put it differently, each of the steps of the Kennedy model work together, synergistically, and are interdependent on each other. Rather than ask "does the text 'hang together?,'" the rhetorical-critical critic demonstrates: (a) that it does and (b) how?[335] Step five is critical in that demonstration. Thus concludes our summation of the Kennedy model (with modifications).

CONCLUSION

This study of the Genesis Flood leverages the basic framework of Kennedy's step-by-step method of rhetorical criticism (with some not insignificant modifications). It joins other scholars by employing the "rhetoric-as-persuasion" branch of rhetorical criticism. Many of these individuals explicitly leverage Kennedy's method for analyzing HB/OT texts, such as Barker (Joel), Möller (Amos), and Ahn (Chronicles). The high degree of specificity Kennedy's method employs make it particularly apt for doing an effective analysis of Hebrew narrative.

Aside from providing a brief history of the discipline of rhetorical criticism (rhetoric as persuasion) and offering clear definitions of argumentation, rhetoric, hyperbole, and the like, this chapter also discussed Hebrew narrative as being persuasive, worldview formative rhetoric.

This process involved a discussion of the procedures involved in: (1) ascertaining the rhetorical unit(s) in the text, (2) identifying the rhetorical situation and discerning the rhetorical problem that precipitated or occasioned the need for a rhetorical response, (3) determining the rhetorical species of the discourse at hand—further discussion on this point revealed this step is not necessary to a study of suasive Hebrew narrative, (4) delineating the procedure for noting the specific arrangement of material in the text, including devices of style; that is, examining the particulars of how the rhetorical strategy of the text should be examined, and, finally, (5) underscoring the procedure for how one would conduct a review as to what implications the discourse has for the audience and

---

335. See Barton, *Reading the Old Testament*, 201. Cf. Boadt et al., *Old Testament*, 67.

whether or not the discourse fits the rhetorical exigence, i.e. did it meet the demand to which it was first fashioned?

3

The Corruption of Humanity
Hope and Covenant (Gen 6:5–8 // 9–22)

INTRODUCTION

SINCE THE GENESIS FLOOD narrative involves plot, sequence, and time (chronology and calendar), an effective rhetorical-critical study must be done in stages, with each of the shorter "scenes" of the main account receiving its own treatment prior to a final analysis of the narrative.[1] The study begins by analyzing Gen 6:5–8, a pericope which some have poignantly called "The Prelude to Disaster."[2] These verses make clear the occasioning incident of the narrative (human violence) and establish the main characters (Noah and GOD).[3] The analysis extends to Gen 6:9–22. This section involves the rising action component of the plot of the Noachian deluge narrative.

This chapter reveals how the text of the Flood communicates different aspects of GOD's character. Despite the prevalence of sin in the created order, GOD demonstrates his redemptive, merciful, and salvific nature alongside his justice and wrath. By covenanting with Noah and commanding him to build, victual, and enter an ark (along with

---

1. For a graphic depiction of the Deluge plot-line, see Mathews, *Genesis 1—11:26*, 354. See too Longacre, "Flood," 95. For a precedent on the use of 'scene' see Wenham, *Genesis 1–15*, 169; Waltke and Fredricks, *Genesis*, 133. Cf. Block, *Covenant*, 14–15.

2. Wenham, *Genesis 1–15*, 136 and 143; Wenham, *Rethinking Genesis*, 58.

3. Longman, *Literary Approaches*, 159; Ryken, *The Bible As Literature*, 40. Cf. Buchanan, "Literary Devices," 202.

The Corruption of Humanity 85

representatives of the animal kinds) GOD provides a way to preserve all life on earth and manifest his glory and goodness.

STEP ONE: DETERMINING THE RHETORICAL UNITS

The first step of this study involves determining the boundaries of the rhetorical units. For the sake of clarity, the rhetorical subunits (or sections) labeled "main" correspond to the first level of an outline and are schematized by upper-case Roman numerals (I, II, III). "Primary" rhetorical subunits correspond to the second level of an outline; schematized by Arabic numerals (1, 2, 3). "Secondary" rhetorical subunits correspond to the third level of an outline; schematized by lower-case Roman numerals (i, ii, iii). "Lower level" subunits correspond to the fourth level of an outlined; schematized by lower-case letters of the English alphabet (a, b, c). Anything below this level is rendered as being *marked* without the presence of any other forms of notation.

The cohesion (referential, situational, and structural) of the first main rhetorical subunit, entitled "Initial Divine Comments Concerning Humanity" (Gen 6:5–6), is evidenced by there being correspondence of: (a) participants, namely the LORD (Gen 6:5a, 6) and humanity (Gen 6:5b, 6), (b) topic, theme, orientation, and mood, i.e. the complete and utter depravity of humanity (Gen 6:5, cf. Gen 6:8) alongside GOD's sensitivity and awareness of such things (Gen 6:5–6), and, lastly, (c) comparableness of narratival time, place, and speed of action, note the *wayyiqtol* verbs (Gen 6:5–6). In addition to this, Yahweh is the main person of each of the *wayyiqtol* verbs of this pericope (Gen 6:5–6), including the Qal verb "to see" (ראה), the Niphal verb "to regret" (נחם), and the Hithpael verb "to cause pain" (עצב). Yahweh is also the subject of the Qal verb "to make" (עשה) in Gen 6:6. Lastly, each of GOD's thoughts are mediated by the narrator (Gen 6:5–6) as compared to direct speech (Gen 6:7).[4]

The next main rhetorical subunit, entitled "The Great Purge" (Gen 6:7), hangs together by virtue of it being a divine speech—its internal coherence is thus demonstrated through the introductory formula of Gen

---

4. Many commentators agree Gen 6:5–8 constitute a single unit of text. See McKeown, *Genesis*, 50; Waltke and Fredricks, *Genesis*, 118; Mathews, *Genesis 1:1—11:26*, 339; Wenham, *Genesis 1–15*, 136. Some scholars, however, consider Gen 6:5–10 to be a distinct unit. So Hamilton, *Genesis 1–17*, 272. Others propose Gen 6:5–12 to be a unit. See Sailhamer, *Genesis*, 116. These proposals fail to recognize the import of speech patterns as boundary markers.

6:7a, "then the LORD said."[5] This pericope has correspondence of: (a) participants, i.e., the LORD (Gen 6:7a, c) and his creation (Gen 6:7b, c), (b) topic, theme, and mood, i.e., the destruction of all living things (Gen 6:7b) and GOD the Creator's thoughts concerning this plan (Gen 6:7b, c), and, lastly, (c) narrative time, place, and speed of action; the LORD is also the main person of the verbs in the speech (*wayyiqtol* or *qatal*). The disjunctive *waw* (*waw* + non-verb) immediately following the speech marks Gen 6:7 as a unit since it shifts the scene and participants from creation in general (Gen 6:7) to Noah specifically (Gen 6:8).

The next main rhetorical unit is entitled "Initial Divine Comments Concerning Noah" (Gen 6:8). The cohesion of this unit is evidenced by there being analogousness with respect to: (a) participants, namely Noah (Gen 6:8a) and the LORD (Gen 6:8b), (b) topic, theme, mood, and orientation, i.e. the promise of hope provided through the patriarch Noah, and, lastly, (c) narrative time, place, and speed of action (note the absence of any *wayyiqtol* verbs). The *toledoth* formula (Gen 6:9) immediately following Gen 6:8 also delimits this as a distinct unit.

Each of the main rhetorical units of this portion of text are depicted below:

The Corruption of Humanity: Part One—A Prelude to Disaster (Gen 6:5–8)

I. Initial Divine Comments Concerning Humanity (Gen 6:5–6)

II. Divine Speech: "The Great Purge" (Gen 6:7)

III. Initial Divine Comments Concerning Noah (Gen 6:8)

The *toledoth* (Gen 6:9a) constitutes the next main rhetorical unit.[6] While the *toledoth* structurally stands independent from the rest of the text, it

---

5. See Dorsey, *Literary Structure*, 23. Cf. Miller, *Speech*, 400. Though it is unclear who GOD spoke to, it seems best to assume that it was his divine council (angels) since elsewhere the Flood text explicates if GOD is speaking to himself (Gen 8:21; cf. Gen 18:17) or to someone else (Gen 6:13; 7:1; 8:15; 9:1, 8, 12, 17). See Meier, *Speaking*, 9.

6. There is general consensus among scholars of Gen 6:9a being a unit in and of itself. So Dorsey, *Literary Structure*, 51; Longman, *Genesis*, 116; Wenham, *Genesis 1–15*, 157; Waltke and Fredricks, *Genesis*, 121. For more details, see Kempf, "Analysis of Genesis 2:25—3:24," 912–95; Beckerleg, "The 'Image of GOD' in Eden," 28–45. See too McDougall, *Image of God*. Cf. Hamilton who proposes that the unit should be Gen 6:5–10. Hamilton, *Genesis 1–17*, 272. Another scholar proposes the unit should be Gen 6:9–10. See Mathews, *Genesis 1:1—11:26*, 349.

The Corruption of Humanity 87

connects thematically to what follows (Gen 6:9—9:29) because the *toledoth* concerns itself with the life, lineage, and person of Noah (cf. Gen 10:1). Even so, as a boundary marker it stands alone as an independent unit.

The Corruption of Humanity: Part Two—
Hope and Covenant (Gen 6:9-22)

    I.   Toledoth Formula (Gen 6:9a)

After the "*Toledoth* Formula" (Gen 6:9a), the next main rhetorical subunit is entitled "Narratival and Divine Comments Concerning Noah" (Gen 6:9b–10).[7] This section is identified as a unit by virtue of its referential, situational, and structural (relational) coherence, signified by there being correspondence of: (a) participants, that is, Noah (Gen 6:9, 10) and his three sons (Gen 6:10), (b) topic, theme, orientation, and mood, i.e. the moral integrity and uprightness of Noah, which includes his right standing with GOD (Gen 6:9) and some of his life context (Gen 6:9–10), and (c) narrative time, place, and speed of action or pacing (see below for details). Noah is the subject of each verb: the *qaṭal* (Qal) verb "to be" (היה), see Gen 6:9b, the *wayyiqṭol* (Hithpael) verb "to walk" (הלך), see Gen 6:9, and the *wayyiqṭol* (Hiphil) verb "to father" (יול).

    Each of the rhetorical units of this portion of text are depicted below:

The Corruption of Humanity: Part Two—
Hope and Covenant (Gen 6:9-22)

    II.   Additional Narratival Comments Concerning Noah (Gen 6:9b–10)
        1.   description of Noah's character, conduct, and spirituality (Gen 6:9b–c)
            i.   Noah was just—blameless among his contemporaries (Gen 6:9b)

---

7. There is partial consensus concerning the boundaries of this unit. See McKeown, *Genesis*, 52; Mathews, *Genesis 1:1—11:26*, 349. Cf. Sailhamer, *Pentateuch*, 124. Some scholars claim Gen 6:9b–12 could be construed as a single unit introducing the audience to the text's characters (with further subunits therein). See Waltke and Fredricks, *Genesis*, 121. Extending the unit, however, i.e., Gen 6:9b–21, is problematic. Contra Wenham, *Genesis 1–15*, 157.

      ii. Noah walked with G<small>OD</small> (Gen 6:9c)

  2. description of Noah's progeny (Gen 6:10)

      i. Noah fathered three sons (Gen 6:10a)

      ii. The three sons' names were Shem, Ham, and Japheth (Gen 6:10b)

The text turns from Noah and his sons to those who fall outside of his immediate family. This main section is entitled "Narratival and Divine Comments Concerning Humanity" (Gen 6:11–12).[8] It may be differentiated from the units that come before it as evidenced by: (a) the dramatic change in topic, theme, orientation, and mood, i.e. the *in toto*, negative portrayal of the earth and its corruption (Gen 6:11–12) as compared to the altogether positive portrayal of Noah (Gen 6:9–10), (b) the shift in narrative time and place which occurs (cf. Gen 6:11–12 with Gen 6:13), and (c) the shift in participants from Noah and his sons (Gen 6:9–10) to the earth itself (Gen 6:11–12) and G<small>OD</small> (Gen 6:11–12). Accompanying this, the subject of the verbs change from Noah (Gen 6:9–10) to the earth and its inhabitants (Gen 6:11–12) and G<small>OD</small> (Gen 6:12). The end of this unit is also delimited by the divine speech immediately following it (Gen 6:13).

    Each of the rhetorical units of this portion of text are depicted below:

The Corruption of Humanity: Part Two—Hope and Covenant (Gen 6:9–22)

  III. Narratival and Divine Comments Concerning Humanity (Gen 6:11–12)

    1. humanity's depravity—mediated via the narrator (Gen 6:11)

        i. the earth was ruined in the sight of G<small>OD</small> (Gen 6:11a)

        ii. the earth was filled with lawlessness (Gen 6:11b)

    2. humanity's depravity—G<small>OD</small>'s direct adjudications (Gen 6:12)

        i. G<small>OD</small> looked on the earth (Gen 6:12a)

        ii. it was sorely ruined! (Gen 6:12b)

---

8. For details about these verses being a unit, see Mathews, *Genesis 1:1—11:26*, 349; Waltke and Fredricks, *Genesis*, 121; Hamilton, *Genesis 1–17*, 278. It is unnecessary to include Gen 6:11–13. Contra McKeown, *Genesis*, 53.

The Corruption of Humanity

    iii. every creature had ruined its way upon the earth (Gen 6:12c)

The next main rhetorical subunit is entitled "Divine Speech: Make Ready!" (Gen 6:13–21).[9] It hangs together as a divine speech. Its internal coherence is demonstrated through the introductory formula "then GOD said to Noah."[10] Note too the refrain (Gen 6:22; cf. Gen 7:1–4 and Gen 7:5).[11] The first portion of this unit is entitled "Part A–Problem 'Violence'" (Gen 6:13). It makes clear via direct discourse the overarching plans of GOD concerning the earth and its various forms of life. This unit has coherence as evidenced by there being sameness of: (a) topic, theme, orientation, and mood, namely the destruction of all life on earth (Gen 6:13), (b) narratival time and place (cf. Gen 6:13 with Gen 6:14–16), and (c) participants (Gen 6:13).

Each of the rhetorical units of this portion of text and each of the rhetorical units of the following sections will be demonstrated in the graphic portrayal at the end of this main unit.

Following Gen 6:13 is another section entitled "Part B–Solution 'The Ark'" (Gen 6:14–16). The change of topic and theme from destruction (Gen 6:13) to deliverance (Gen 6:14–16) as well as the shift of Noah becoming one of the primary participants (alongside GOD) rather than an addressee (cf. Gen 6:13 with Gen 6:14–16), show the cohesive nature of this section and how it ought to be differentiated from the section(s) surrounding it (cf. Gen 6:14–16 with Gen 6:17).[12]

The referential, situational, and structural (relational) coherence of the next section, entitled "Divine Speech: 'Make Ready!' Part C–Problem 'The Flood'" (Gen 6:17), is evident through correspondence of topic and theme, namely death and destruction by means of the Flood (Gen 6:17) compared to the salvific nature of the ark (Gen 6:14–16). Noah also 'exits the stage.'

The internal coherence of the two primary subsections which comprise the next main unit, entitled "Divine Speech: 'Make Ready!' Part

---

9. There is a general consensus among scholars concerning the boundaries of this unit, albeit many include the refrain (Gen 6:22) as part of the same unit. See Mathews, *Genesis 1:1—11:26*, 349; Sailhamer, *Genesis*, 116; Waltke and Fredricks, *Genesis*, 122; Hamilton, *Genesis 1–17*, 278; McKeown, *Genesis*, 55; Wenham, *Genesis 1–15*, 157.

10. See Dorsey, *Literary Structure*, 23. Cf. Meier, *Speaking*, 59; Miller, *Speech*, 400.

11. See Mathews, *Genesis 1—11:26*, 361; Sailhamer, *Pentateuch*, 124.

12. See Mathews, *Genesis 1—11:26*, 365.

D–Solution 'Covenant/The Ark'" (Gen 6:18–21), is evidenced through uniformity of topic and theme (deliverance, salvation, and redemption as opposed to annihilation, destruction, and doom). There is also the same narratival time (note the *waw*'s) and place. Noah is reintroduced to the scene as are some new participants, including Noah's wife, his sons, and his son's wives—alongside the animal kinds. Hamilton notes the "resumptive pronoun establishes Noah as the person of supreme significance in this paragraph."[13] The second half of this primary subsection is entitled "Plans for Preservation: Part Two" (Gen 6:21). It focuses on food-stuff for the ark's occupants (correspondence of topic).

Each of the rhetorical units of this portion of text are depicted below:

The Corruption of Humanity: Part Two—
Hope and Covenant (Gen 6:9–22)

IV. Divine Speech: "Make Ready!" (Gen 6:13–21)

Part A: problem 'violence' (Gen 6:13)

1. introduction: "God said to Noah" (Gen 6:13a)
2. destruction and devastation (Gen 6:13b–d)
   i. declaration: now is the end (Gen 6:13b)
   ii. declaration: the earth is filled with violence (Gen 6:13c)
   iii. declaration: God will ruin every creature (Gen 6:13d)

Part B: Solution 'The Ark' (Gen 6:14–16)

1. general imperative: fabricate an ark (Gen 6:14a)
2. more specific directives (Gen 6:14b–16d)
   i. build the ark with compartments (Gen 6:14b)
   ii. caulk the ark with pitch (Gen 6:14c)
   iii. build the ark to specific dimensions (Gen 6:15)
      a. initiatory statement (Gen 6:15a)
      b. specificities about the ark's dimensions (Gen 6:15b–d)
   iv. ensure the ark has a vaulted roof (Gen 6:16a)
   v. finish the ark to a cubit from above (Gen 6:16b)

---

13. See Hamilton, *Genesis 1–17*, 283–84.

The Corruption of Humanity

      vi. set a door in the side of the ark (Gen 6:16c)

      vii. construct the ark with three decks (Gen 6:16d)

Part C: problem 'The Flood' (Gen 6:17)

    1. the mechanism of destruction: the Flood (Gen 6:17a–b)

      i. declaration: the Flood will come upon the earth (Gen 6:17a)

      ii. declaration: the Flood will ruin every creature (Gen 6:17b)

    2. re-statement of the extent of the destruction (Gen 6:17c)

Part D: solution 'Covenant/Ark' (Gen 6:18–21)

    1. plans for preservation: part one (Gen 6:18–20)

      i. GOD's covenant with Noah (Gen 6:18a)

      ii. confirmation: Noah will enter the ark (Gen 6:18b)

      iii. confirmation: Noah's family will enter the ark (Gen 6:18c)

      iv. confirmation: chosen animals will enter the ark (Gen 6:19–20)

        a. directives to bring two of every creature (Gen 6:19a)

        b. reiteration of function: 'to keep them alive' (Gen 6:19b)

        c. clarification of gender: 'male and female' (Gen 6:19c)

        d. 'from the birds according to their kinds' (Gen 6:19d)

        e. 'from the beasts according to their kinds' (Gen 6:19e)

        f. 'from creeping things according to kind' (Gen 6:19f)

        g. summative statement (Gen 6:20)

    2. plans for preservation: part two (Gen 6:21)

      i. general imperative for Noah to take food (Gen 6:21a)

      ii. general imperative for Noah to gather it to him (Gen 6:21b)

      iii. final clarifying comment (Gen 6:21c)

The next main rhetorical unit is entitled "Final Narratival Comments Concerning Noah" (Gen 6:22). Since the divine speech which follows this unit (Gen 7:1–4) ends with a similar refrain (Gen 7:5), a pattern is established for helping to delimit the boundaries of this unit (Gen 6:13–21, 22).[14] Lastly, the activities of Noah are recorded via the narrator (Gen 6:22).

Each of the rhetorical units of this portion of text are depicted below:

The Corruption of Humanity: Part Two—
Hope and Covenant (Gen 6:9–22)

    V.   Final Narratival Comments Concerning Noah (Gen 6:22)

It is necessary to argue how Gen 6:9–22 constitutes a rhetorical unit to be differentiated from the rest of the narrative that follows (Gen 7:1–24). The referential, situational, and structural (relational) coherence of these verses is demonstrated, first of all, by means of time. In Gen 6:9–22 the destruction of all life is spoken of in future terms (Gen 6:13, 17. Cf. Gen 6:7). This stands in contrast to the details provided in Gen 7:1–24 pertaining to chronology and the destruction of all life due to the actual presence of the Flood (see Gen 7:4, 6, 7, 10, 11, 12, 13, 17–24). Second, there is a shift in place. In Gen 6:9–22, Noah and company remain outside the ark. In Gen 7:1–24, the people and animals enter the ark (Gen 7:1–3, 5, 7–9, 13–16, 18, 23).

STEP TWO: DETERMINING THE RHETORICAL SITUATION

The second step of rhetorical criticism involves determining the rhetorical situation. As noted in the methodology section, this study proposes to use the category of rhetorical situation in a different way from the majority of rhetorical-critical studies; the inability to determine the situation of the world "behind the text" of the book of Genesis and the Noachian deluge narrative, specifically, requires the interpreter to develop the rhetorical situation from criteria internal to the text. While scholars have recognized this approach is unsatisfactory for placing the text in a specific historical situation, a synchronic, entextualized understanding of rhetorical situation can successfully locate the passage in the situation its words describe and reveal the concerns the rhetor intends to address. This makes it possible to consider how the text's rhetorical strategy would

---

14. See Mathews, *Genesis 1—11:26*, 360–61. Cf. Wenham, *Genesis 1–15*, 153.

The Corruption of Humanity

affect the situation the text describes.[15] An entextualized rhetorical situation offers a way forward through the inevitable frustration of trying to lock the text into a specific historical context, thus permitting the text's persuasive power to have influence beyond the time and place of its original situation. Step four, determining rhetorical effectiveness, also considers how the text may rhetorically relate to (exilic) Israel.[16]

By necessity, the entextualized rhetorical situation will mature, evolve, and develop as the plot unfolds from scene to scene. This is true even if one primary exigence gives clues to other exigences and forms the backdrop to the Genesis Flood narrative, in general. Scripture makes clear the primary exigence of the Flood involves "violence" (חמס), i.e. uncurbed and unmitigated sin and lawlessness (Gen 6:5, 11 and 13. Cf. Gen 8:21–22; 9:1–7). Without help, humanity will implode. Yet, this exigence is not at the forefront of each specific rhetorical unit.

Two secondary exigences also exist. The first is between GOD and the Flood. GOD must act in such a way as to exercise sovereign control over the Flood to ensure he does not destroy that which he has purposed to save.[17] The second exigence is between Noah and GOD. GOD elected Noah to enter into a covenant relationship with himself (Gen 6:18) thus obligating him to "keep self-imposed commitments either on condition of the favored recipients continued faithfulness or as repayment."[18]

Waltke and Fredricks delineate this aspect of the exigence (GOD and Noah) as follows:

> Can GOD count on Noah? To be sure, GOD authors the covenant, but it cannot be effected without Noah's fidelity (see 7:1). If Noah does not build the ark and enter it, not only Noah and all life will perish, but so will GOD's purpose to rule the earth through Adam and his promise to crush the Serpent through the woman's seed. The future of salvation history rides on Noah's faithfulness.[19]

The next component of the exigence (Noah and GOD) is delineated as follows:

---

15. See Barker, *From the Depths*, 68.
16. See McKeown, *Genesis*, 10. Cf. Collins, *Reading Genesis Well*, 125.
17. See Waltke and Fredricks, *Genesis*, 122.
18. Waltke and Fredricks, *Genesis*, 123. See also Kutsch, *TDOT* 1:259.
19. Waltke and Fredricks, *Genesis*, 123.

On the other hand, can Noah count on GOD? GOD calls upon Noah to trust him to keep his threat to wipe out the earth and his promise to preserve him, his family, and the life of all that breathes. If the LORD does not send the threatened Flood, Noah will have wasted years of his life, and of his three sons building the ark, and 'Noah's folly' will become the laughingstock of history. And if GOD does not keep his promise to preserve Noah and his family through the Flood, their faithful service is in vain. The plot develops as the divine and human covenant partners commit themselves to one another.[20]

GOD seeing the ruination of the earth expresses estimation, i.e. GOD "appraised" the earth—and found it wanting (Gen 6:5–6).[21] GOD speaks first to himself (Gen 6:7; cf. Gen 6:3) then to Noah on four occasions: (1) the devastation of the Flood and the imperative to build an ark (Gen 6:13–21), (2) the command to Noah to enter the ark (Gen 7:1–4), (3) the command for Noah to leave the ark (Gen 8:15–17), and (4) the blessings on Noah and his family (Gen 9:1–7), which includes a reiteration of the Noahic covenant (Gen 9:8–11) and its sign (Gen 9:12–17).[22]

It is the Flood itself and these two characters (Noah and GOD) which drive the plot and the two secondary rhetorical exigences of Gen 6:5–22.[23] Interestingly, the narrator feels no need to comment on what Noah might be thinking or feeling concerning what lay before him. Unlike, for instance, Abraham (see Gen 18:16–33), Noah seemingly had no scruples concerning what was to occur. He obeys without question or protest—down to the last cubit (see Gen 6:22).[24]

To summarize, the clues derived from Gen 6:5–8 and 9–22 suggests that aside from the overarching primary tension between humanity's "violence" (חמס) and GOD's merciful, gracious, and benevolent character, there exists at least two secondary exigences. The first secondary exigence is between GOD and the Flood (judgment and salvation). The text presupposes the utter annihilation of all life forms on the earth (judgment). This is demonstrated through the universalistic rhetoric often employed in the text (see step three below). At the same time, the text makes clear

---

20. Waltke and Fredricks, *Genesis*, 123.
21. Knafl, *Forming God*, 239–40. Cf. Speiser, *Genesis*, 51.
22. Knafl, *Forming God*, 240.
23. See Humphreys, *Character of God*, 66–67.
24. See Humphreys, *Character of God*, 66–67. Cf. Greenberger, "Noah," 27–28. See also Dershowitz, "Man of the Land," 364–65; Keiter, "Noah and the Dove," 264.

The Corruption of Humanity

GOD intends to redeem and deliver Noah, certain members of his family, and select beasts from the animal kingdom (salvation). GOD must demonstrate complete control over the Deluge so as to ensure: (a) he destroys all those whom he wishes to annihilate, and (b) he saves all those aboard the ark. The second tension is between Noah and GOD. Much like the first exigence, both judgment and salvation hang in the balance. Noah and GOD must each employ covenant fidelity in order to preserve and redeem all life on earth.

With respect to audience, the second main component of a rhetorical situation, GOD's commands for Noah to build the ark (Gen 6:14) and victual it (Gen 6:22) serves to remind the Israelite community the important role of faithful obedience to GOD (cf. Gen 6:8–9). The third and final component of Bitzer's formulations are constraints. Constraints can include such things as "the degree of interest in the topic that the speaker and audience possess, the capacity for modification of the situation, the risk incurred in responding, the obligation and expectation of a response, the familiarity with a topic, and the immediacy of the situation."[25]

The reader is faced with the issue of divine authority. The question posed is this, "Who will chart the course for your life: you or GOD?"[26] Within Gen 6:5–7, it is evident humanity's appetite for destruction knows no limits. Apart from GOD the Creator's goodness and merciful intervention, humanity would cease to exist. The text suggests the reader to carefully consider how one might live their life in such a way as to not grieve GOD (Gen 6:6). This necessarily involves GOD's regard for faithfulness and the significance of disobedience (cf. Gen 6:8, 18, 22).

STEP THREE: DETERMINING THE RHETORICAL STRATEGY

The third step of this study is to determine and assess the rhetorical strategies which govern the rhetorical units. This step includes commenting on the persuasive nature of the text. The analysis will begin with a fresh

---

25. Barker, *From the Depths of Despair*, 41. See too Bitzer, "Functional Communication," 31–33.

26. McDougall, *Models for Disciple-Making*, A-1:1. See too Neufeld, *Teaching Stones*.

English translation alongside a select commentary of certain grammatical and syntactical features (including text criticism issues).[27]

The arrangement of the analysis is ordered according to the main subunits delineated above in step one, beginning with The Corruption of Humanity: Part One—A Prelude to Disaster (Gen 6:5–8). These main units are (I) "Initial Divine Comments Concerning Humanity" (Gen 6:5–6), (II) "Divine Speech 'The Great Purge'" (Gen 6:7), and (III) "Initial Divine Comments Concerning Noah" (Gen 6:8). With respect to The Corruption of Humanity: Part Two—Hope and Covenant (Gen 6:9–22), the main units are: (I) "*Toledoth* Formula" (Gen 6:9a), (II), "Additional Narrative Comments Concerning Noah" (Gen 6:9b–10), (III) "Narratival and Divine Comments Concerning Humanity" (Gen 6:11–12), (IV) "Divine Speech 'Make Ready!'" (Gen 6:13–21), and, lastly, (V) "Final Narratival Comments Concerning Noah" (Gen 6:22).

The Corruption of Humanity: Part One—A Prelude to Disaster (Gen 6:5–8)

I. *Initial Divine Comments Concerning Humanity (Gen 6:5–6)*

ᵃוירא יהוה ᵇכי רבה רעת ᶜהאדם ᵈבארץ ᵉוכל יצר מחשבת לבו רק רע כל היום

ᶠוינחם יהוה ᵍכי עשה את האדם ʰבארץ ⁱויתעצב אל ʲלבו

> Now the LORD saw the great wickedness of humanity on the earth—every inclination of the thoughts of their minds was only evil continually.
> Then the LORD was remorseful he had made human beings on the earth.
> The LORD was grieved within his innermost being.

---

a. Introductory *waw*. Chisholm, *Exegesis*, 120.

b. Perceptual conjunction. *GBHS* §4.3.4.j. Alongside this, one notes: "Clauses which depend on a transitive verb, especially on what are called *verba cordis*, i.e., verbs denoting any mental act, such as *to see, to hear, to know, to perceive, to believe, to remember, to forget, to say, to think*... as a rule" are usually introduced by this conjunction. GKC §157b. Italics original.

27. See Collins, *Reading Genesis Well*, 29; Shaw, *Speeches of Micah*, 23; Bovard, "Rhetorical Questions," 20; Stewart, "Ethos of the Cosmos," 100; Okoye, *Genesis 1–11*, 18–19.

c. This is a generic (*nomina getilicia*) article. Joüon §137c, *BHRG* §24.4.4.4, Williams, *Hebrew Syntax*, §92. See too Gen 6:6.

d. Spatial preposition. *GBHS* §4.1.5.a.

e. Epexegetical (specification) *waw*. *GBHS* §3.5.4.b. See also *BHRG* §40.23.4.2.6.

f. Sequential *waw*. See *GBHS* §3.5.1.a, Chisholm, *Exegesis*, 120.

g. Evidential conjunction. *GBHS* §4.3.4.b.

h. Spatial preposition. *GBHS* §4.1.5.a or *beth comitantiae*, i.e. a *beth* of accompaniment. See Williams, *Hebrew Syntax*, §248. Cf. Fretheim, *Creation Untamed*, 5, 37, 42.

i. Specification *waw*. *GBHS* §3.5.4.b. See also *BHRG* §40.23.4.2.6.

j. Specification or locative preposition. Williams, *Hebrew Syntax*, §306/308.

Extended Analysis

The text makes explicit the severity of sin by adding "great" (רבה) to Yahweh's assessment of the depraved situation—the same word also used to describe the subterranean waters cast upon the earth as GOD brought his divine judgment upon human sin in the Flood (see Gen 7:11).[28]

Hamilton detects a subtle nuance in the wording of Gen 6:5; "inclination" (יצר) is a nominal form of the same word used in Gen 2:7, 19 to describe humanity's formation from the soil; there "GOD was the potter, fashioning man [sic]. Now man himself [sic] has become the potter, fashioning his [sic] thoughts. What GOD forms is beautiful; what man [sic] forms is repulsive."[29] GOD is no stoic when it comes to bearing witness of evil. As Goldingay asserts: "While Genesis may presuppose that Yahweh has the capacity to be all knowing and may presuppose that he has used that capacity and has foreseen how humanity's action in the world would turn out, the point it makes is that nevertheless Yahweh responds to these events emotionally and conatively within time in the flow of events."[30] The LORD pays careful, heartfelt attention to his creation. He is not so far removed nor calloused so as to be indifferent.

---

28. See *DCH* 7:395–401; Hill, *NIDOTTE* 3:1034–35.

29. Hamilton, *Genesis 1–17*, 273. See too Kidner, *Genesis*, 85. Cf. *DCH* 4:270–71; *HALOT* 1:249; Hartley, *NIDOTTE* 2:506–7; Otzen, *TDOT* 6:264–65.

30. Goldingay, Genesis, 126. Cf. Brueggemann, *Genesis*, 78–79; Mann, *Book of the Torah*, 32.

II. Divine Speech "The Great Purge" (Gen 6:7)

ויאמר יהוה[a]

אמחה את [b]האדם אשר בראתי [c]מעל פני האדמה

[d]מאדם [e]עד בהמה עד רמש [f]ועד עוף השמים [g]כי נחמתי [h]כי עשיתם

> So the LORD said:
> "I will remove humanity, whom I have created, from the face of the ground: human beings, beasts, moving things, up to and including even the birds of the sky—for I am remorseful that I have made them."

---

a. Consequential *waw*. *GBHS* §3.5.1.b, Chisholm, *Exegesis*, 120.

b. The article is generic (*nomina getilicia*). Joüon §137c; *BHRG* §24.4.4.4; Williams, *Hebrew Syntax*, §92.

c. The compound is comprised of a partitive preposition (*GBHS* §4.1.13.f) with a preposition which is spatial/locative in a vertical relationship. *GBHS* §4.1.16.a.1.

d. Inclusive preposition. Williams, *Hebrew Syntax*, §327 (see also §313).

e. The preposition is inclusive. One also notes, "When repeated or used with מִן §327 it can give a range ('from . . . to')." Williams, *Hebrew Syntax*, §313. This stresses the extent of the judgment in creation (see the NET Bible).

f. Accompaniment *waw*. Williams, *Hebrew Syntax*, §436.

g. Evidential conjunction. *GBHS* §4.3.4.a.

h. Perceptual conjunction. *GBHS* §4.3.4.j.

Extended Analysis

The devastating consequences of sin are evident in this passage. It is not only humanity who suffers but all living creatures. This includes (see Gen 6:7) "beasts" (בהמה),[31] "moving things" (רמש),[32] and "birds" (עוֹף).[33]

---

31. Though this term refers mostly to domestic quadruped animals, the nuance here is of all the different varieties of land creatures. *DCH* 2:98–100; *HALOT* 1:111–12; Kiuchi, *NIDOTTE* 1:612–13.

32. Though this term includes insects, it primarily identifies small creeping rodents and reptiles, i.e., creatures that move on the ground. *DCH* 7:500–501; *HALOT* 2:1246; Hill, *NIDOTTE* 3:1127.

33. One notes that though is a generic term for all creatures that fly, thus including

Though Genesis recognizes only humanity as bearing the *Imago Dei*, this verse does not denote a three-fold division of life or a "hierarchy" in the animal order.[34] This is universalistic rhetoric to describe the sum totality of creation.[35] Mathews claims the "omission of 'fish' . . . is due transparently to their innate properties to survive the imminent waters."[36]

One notes the wordplay in Gen 6:7 (cf. Gen 2:7; 3:19) between God's decision to remove "humanity" (האדם) from the "ground" (האדמה).[37] But the LORD does not stand aloof of creation. God was "remorseful" (נחם) he made them (Gen 6:7).[38] The text explicates: (1) the import of sin and how it impugns the mind of God, and (2) the severity of God's judgment. "God not only erases sins, but he erases sinners—he judges them by drowning them."[39]

III. Initial Divine Comments Concerning Noah (Gen 6:8)

ונח מצא חן בעיני יהוה[a]

But Noah found favour in the eyes of the LORD.

---

a. Contrastive (disjunctive) *waw*. Chisholm, *Exegesis*, 126. One scholar states: "GKC 142b takes the word order with the subject first to indicate that the clause provides background information and that the verb should be rendered in the pluperfect. But it is simpler to take the word order as indicating that the clause offers a contrast with what precedes it (DG 142c)." Goldingay, *Genesis*, 112. I agree with this assessment. For more details on so-called "denial of expectation" contrasts, see *BHRG* §40.23.4.2.2.

---

various flying insects (such as bees and such), the nuance here seems to refer, generally, to birds. *DCH* 6:312-13; *HALOT* 1:800; Kiuchi, *NIDOTTE* 3:354; Stiglmair, *TDOT* 10:564-68.

34. Contra Mathews, *Genesis 1:1—11:26*, 345.

35. Hamilton, *Genesis 1-17*, 276.

36. Mathews, *Genesis 1:1—11:26*, 345.

37. For more information on this rhetorical device, see Watson, *Classical Hebrew Poetry*, 237-50.

38. Goldingay notes: "The Vg *paenituit* issues in the English translation 'repented,' which now gives a misleading impression, whereas like the Hebrew verbs, the Latin verb means 'be sorry, regret.'" Goldingay, *Genesis*, 112.

39. Hamilton, *Genesis 1-17*, 275.

Extended Analysis

This verse provides a climactic finish to a dramatic situation. Yahweh's awareness of sin does not just lead to judgment (Gen 6:5–7) but also to salvation (Gen 6:8). Gen 6:8 is the first of many evidences providing the foundation for my assertion GOD ultimately desires life—not death—for all of his creation.[40] As one scholar notes, "When we think about it, perhaps the most surprising element of this story is that he refrains from completely destroying us. Verse 8 is the turning point of the story when it informs the reader of GOD's token of grace in the light of human sin and his declared intention to judge that sin by the flood."[41] The text also communicates the importance of uprightness. It is no accident that GOD chose Noah from among his generations.[42] Through showing grace to Noah GOD demonstrates his purpose to promote and sustain all life.

The Corruption of Humanity: Part Two— Hope and Covenant (Gen 6:9–22)

I. *Toledoth Formula (Gen 6:9a)*

אלה תולדת נח[a]

This is the *toledoth* of Noah.

---

a. For details on the demonstrative, see *IBHS* §17. For more grammatical information, see DG §49.a.

Extended Analysis

The narrator "slows the action to a standstill" within the *toledoth* of Noah (Gen 6:9—9:29), devoting a considerable amount of space and comment to a short span of time, namely the six-hundredth year of Noah's life (see

---

40. See Gilbert, *God Never Meant for Us to Die*, xvii.
41. Longman, *Genesis*, 116.
42. Concerning whether or not GOD showed favour to Noah because of his righteousness, see below.

Gen 6:6 and 11).[43] This is in contrast to the millennia between Adam and Noah delineated in the *toledoth* of Adam immediately preceding the Flood (Gen 5:1—6:8), a narrative time frame of roughly 1600 years or so; it also stands in contrast to the 400 year time period existing between Noah and Abraham in the *toledoth* of Shem, Ham, and Japheth (Gen 10:1—11:9) and the *toledoth* of Shem, in particular (Gen 11:10—11:26), which immediately follow the Noachian deluge narrative.[44]

It, perhaps, cannot be overstated that ancient, biblical genealogies "do not intend to be exhaustive, so we cannot just 'do the math' to get back from Abram to Noah to Adam."[45] Even so, there is good reason to believe the genealogies in Gen 5 and 11 are closed and the above chronology is relatively accurate.[46] Irrespective, the function of this literary device (pacing) is to enable the recipient(s) of the text's message to appreciate the gravity of the narrative and to absorb its significance. Pace communicates emphasis.[47] More text per unit time shows "the importance of the material that the genealogical list is connecting together."[48]

While the *toledoth* of Adam (Gen 5:1—6:8) focuses the narrative of the book of Genesis from creation generally (see Gen 2:4—4:26) to humanity specifically, the *toledoth* of Noah (Gen 6:9—9:29) is even more narrowed—a single individual and his most immediate kin.[49] The reason for this focusing seems to be that Noah and his sons (Shem, Ham, and Japheth) represent "all of living humanity in their families" within the post-Deluge world.[50] Functionally, linear genealogies (those focusing on one offspring per generation, as opposed to segmented genealogies) not

43. Waltke and Fredricks, *Genesis*, 121.

44. These calculations have mostly been derived from Seely, "Noah," 292–93.

45. Longman and Walton, *Lost World of the Flood*, 108.

46. For information about linear vs. segmented genealogies (and genealogies in general), see Thomas, *Generations*, 87–89; Wright, "Genealogies," 345–50; Hill, "Genealogy," 242–46; Walton, "Genealogies," 309–16; Hess, "Genealogies," 58–72. Concerning this passage specifically, see Collins, *Reading Genesis Well*, 181; Levin, "Understanding Biblical Genealogies," 11–46; Sexton, "Evangelicalism's Search for Chronological Gaps," 5–25; Steinmann, "A Reply to Jeremy Sexton Regarding the Genealogies in Genesis," 27–37; Sexton, "Search for Chronological Gaps: A Rejoinder," 39–45; Steinmann, *Genesis*, 20–22.

47. See Gravett et al., eds., *Hebrew Bible*, 70. For more details, see Genette, *Narrative Discourse*, 87–96; Genette, *Narrative Discourse Revisited*, 33–37.

48. Thomas, *Generations*, 88. Cf. Alexander, *Paradise*, 26–27.

49. See Thomas, *Generations*, 127; Mathews, *Genesis 1—11:26*, 44–45.

50. Thomas, *Generations*, 43–44.

only move the attention to the following material but also highlight and draw attention to key figures and persons in the narrative.⁵¹ Here, Noah is the key person (Gen 6:9).

II. *Additional Narratival Comments Concerning Noah (Gen 6:9b–10)*

נח איש צדיק ᵃתמים היה בדרתיו ᵇאת האלהים התהלך נח

ᶜויולד נח שלשה בנים את שם את חם ואת יפת

Noah was a just man, blameless among his contemporaries.
Noah walked with God.
Also, Noah fathered three sons, Shem, Ham, and Japheth.

---

a. Note: certain versions, such as the SamPent and some manuscripts of LXX, tend to reject the asyndetic apposition of two predicative adjectives. See Tal, *BHQ*, 94.

b. This is an instance of a *"fronted* constituent," which is used to "indicate the topic or focus of the sentence that follows." *BHRG* §34.5.1. Details concerning word order are below.

c. Adjunctive *waw*. Williams, *Hebrew Syntax*, §319. See also *BHRG* §40.23.4.2.1#a.

Extended Analysis

Noah was "just" (צדיק).⁵² The text also states he was "blameless" (תמים)⁵³ with respect to his contiguous contemporaries (בדרתיו).⁵⁴ Noah's conduct and behavior were the inverse of the "ever-growing 'avalanche of sin'" plaguing the world.⁵⁵ Given the Bible's penchant for conciseness, the few details provided require one to get "maximum mileage" out of their inclusion.⁵⁶ One function seems to be to create empathy for Noah, i.e.

---

51. Thomas, *Generations*, 88–89. See too Long, *King Saul*, 23–25.

52. *DCH* 7:75; *HALOT* 2:1003; Reimer, *NIDOTTE* 3:748; Koch, *TLOT* 2:1046–62.

53. Alternate renderings include "wholesome," "sound," and "candid." Hamilton, *Genesis 1–17*, 277. Another scholar describes the nuance here as the "serenity of the unclouded relationship between God and the righteous." Olivier, *NIDOTTE* 4:307. Cf. *DCH* 8:643–44; *HALOT* 2:1745.

54. Mathews, *Genesis 1—11:26*, 358; BDB, 190.

55. Clines, *Theme of the Pentateuch*, 70. Cf. Schreiner, *The King in His Beauty*, 12.

56. Ryken, *Words of Delight*, 42. See also Alter, *Narrative*, 126.

we should take Noah's side in the narrative. He is an exemplar (cf. Ezek 14:14, 20).[57] He did not behave as the wicked.[58]

It is written Noah walked (Hitphael) with GOD (Gen 6:9), something only Enoch is said to have done (see Gen 5:22, 24).[59] The appearance of "GOD" at the head of the sentence, an inverted construction more usual in poetry and other figurative usages (cf. Gen 5:22, 24), seems to emphasize "Noah's dependence on the LORD."[60] These comments highlight the "consistent intimacy of Noah's relationship with GOD and exemplifies the Old Testament ideal of piety. Noah is a character to be admired and emulated, especially in light of the extreme wickedness of his generation, with which he is contrasted."[61] These epithets "surely make it likely that the final editor of the flood story saw Noah as good."[62]

With respect to whether or not GOD showed favour to Noah because of his righteousness, it warrants mentioning:

> Noah's survival and role was not earned by his righteousness but was a manifestation of GOD's grace . . . when we hear that Noah was righteous, blameless, and that he walked faithfully, we are to understand that he was a repentant sinner who sought to be holy . . . GOD graciously restored his relationship with him. He then lived in obedience to his GOD.[63]

---

57. Block, *Ezekiel*, 446–47. Cf. Davidson "Noah," 135–37; Kaminski, *Was Noah Good?*, 1–3.

58. Mathews, *Genesis 1—11:26*, 358.

59. One scholar notes, "Later patriarchs 'walked before' GOD (17:1; 24:40; 48:15) and the LORD GOD walked in the garden of Eden (3:8). The priests were expected to walk with GOD (Mal 2:6) and Micah 6:8 describes this as GOD's basic requirements for all persons, though here the verb . . . is used in the qal, not the hithpael. Clearly, then, the phrase suggests a special intimacy with GOD and a life of piety." Wenham, *Genesis 1–15*, 127. See too Goldingay, *Genesis*, 110; Kidner, *Genesis*, 87. Cf. the NET Bible notes. For details on the grammatical form, see *IBHS* 26.1.2. There is, perhaps, "something of the new creation theme being hinted at in this wording." I am indebted to Josh Chalmers for this insight via private communiqué.

60. See Mathews, *Genesis 1—11:26*, 358. Cf. Sasson, "Word-Play," 165–66. See also *BHRG* §34.5.1.

61. Arnold, *Genesis*, 98.

62. Wenham, Review of *Was Noah Good?*, 173.

63. Longman, *Genesis*, 116–17. For more information on this point, namely Noah's righteousness in relation to divine favor, see Wenham, *Genesis 1–15*, 176, Harland, *Value of Human Life*, 52–53, Hamilton, *Genesis 1–17*, 286–87, Clark, "Righteousness of Noah," 262–80, Waltke and Fredricks, *Genesis*, 137, Sailhamer, *Genesis*, 118, McKeown, *Genesis*, 56; Kaminski, *Was Noah Good?*, 194–98; Keiser, "Nuancing Kaminski's *Was Noah Good?*," 195–204.

Nothing is explicitly noted about the spiritual condition or conduct of Noah's wife, his three sons (Shem, Ham, and Japheth) or his son's wives. Walton asserts they probably "enjoy GOD's protection as a corporate group either because Noah's righteousness has been duplicated and imitated by the members of his family, or because the reward of his righteousness includes the deliverance of his loved ones (cf. Lot in Gen. 18–19; Rahab in Josh. 2:12–13)."[64] Walton further states family was considered "an extension of the individual" and that it "hardly constitutes deliverance for Noah alone to be saved if he has no means of propagating the race."[65]

The *toledoth* structure in Genesis provide sufficient rationale why the text names Shem, Ham, and Japheth at this particular time. Since the *toledoth* of Noah (Gen 6:9a) is immediately followed by the *toledoth* of his three sons (Gen 10:1) including such information now (Gen 6:9a) makes sense logically and literarily. While it remains true throughout the rest of the Flood story that Shem, Ham, and Japheth are majorly noted as Noah's sons, with no further attention being given to their specific names (see Gen 6:18 alongside 7:1, 7, 8:16, 18, 9:8), it is reasonable to maintain the text draws attention to their names here because they would become important characters later on (see Gen 9:18–27). Narratively, these three figures would need a certain amount of introduction prior to that time. Their inclusion also helps to retain the literary structure of the text. This does not, however, explain the repetition of the three names in the same order again at Gen 7:13 (cf. Gen 10:1–31). Further analysis will be offered in the next chapter.

Much discussion surrounds the chronology, birth order, and specific positioning of the names in the text.[66] Clearly, Shem is the oldest: thus, he is first.[67] The ordering of the three sons also seems to be euphonic. That is, "Shem, Ham, and Japheth" sounds pleasant to Hebrew ears who tend to put shorter words first.[68] Though the "disqualified son" always takes the second place (Gen 6:10, 7:13, 9:18, 10:1; 1 Chr 1:4) its significance is uncertain.[69]

---

64. Walton, *Genesis*, 311.
65. Walton, *Genesis*, 311. Cf. Steinberg, "Genesis," 279–300.
66. See Ron, "Jubilees," 103–4; Mathews, *Genesis 1—11:26*, 461.
67. Sarna, *Genesis*, 78. Cf. Ron, "Jubilees," 103–4; Wilson, *Genealogy*, 160.
68. So Wenham, *Genesis 1–15*, 201. Cf. Waltke and Fredricks, *Genesis*, 31–32.
69. Mathews, *Genesis 1—11:26*, 461. Cf. Kaminsky, *Yet I Loved Jacob*, 29.

It seems that no noteworthy comments can be made about the meaning of the name Ham (hot?) while the import of Japheth (to enlarge) seems to be clear (see Gen 9:27).[70] Shem's name may, perhaps, mean "renown."[71] Aside from the blessing Noah bestows upon him later (Gen 9:26), the few remarks concerning his lineage (Gen 10:21–31), and the fact he will later become the esteemed father of the Hebrews, no other noteworthy comments can be made.[72]

III. *Narratival and Divine Comments Concerning Humanity (Gen 6:11–12)*

^aותשחת הארץ ^bלפני האלהים ^cותמלא הארץ חמס ^dוירא אלהים את הארץ

^eוהנה נשחתה ^fכי השחית כל בשר את דרכו על הארץ

Now the earth was ruined in the sight of GOD:
    the earth was filled with bloodlust.
And GOD saw the earth—it was ruined!
    For every creature had ruined its way upon the earth!

---

a. Introductory *waw*. Chisholm, *Exegesis*, 120.

b. The compound preposition is perceptual (evaluative discernment). Williams, *Hebrew Syntax*, §372; *GBHS* §4.1.11.c. See also Knafl, *Forming God*, 239–40; Speiser, *Genesis*, 51.

c. Epexegetical (specification) *waw*. *GBHS* §3.5.4.b. See also *BHRG* §40.23.4.2.6.

d. Specifying (focusing) *waw*. Chisholm, *Exegesis*, 122. Cf. *GBHS* §3.5.1.c (epexegetical *waw*).

e. Dramatic (deictic) *waw*. Chisholm, *Exegesis*, 126. Concerning הנה, though some scholars tend to classify this term as an interjection, see *DCH* 2:572–53, or an adverb, see Joüon §105.d, who labels it as a "presentative adverb," it "does not really fit in either of these classes. As opposed to interjections and most ordinary adverbs, it can take a pronominal suffix and, as opposed to ordinary adverbs, it may have scope over a clause or multiple clauses. In fact, it always precedes the clause upon which it has a bearing. Semantically it also differs from the class modal adverbs . . . it does involve the speaker in the content of the clause, but it does not necessarily refer to his or her opinion on the degree of probability of

---

70. See Aaron, "Ham," 732–33, Meiring, "Shem, Ham, Japheth," 223–40. Cf. Horowitz, "Genesis x," 35–43; Lund, *NIDOTTE* 4:693–94, 743–44.

71. See Ross, *NIDOTTE* 4:147–48; Lund, *NIDOTTE* 4:1216–17.

72. Ron, "Jubilees," 103–4; Mathews, *Genesis 1—11:26*, 460–61.

the events or state of affairs." *BHRG* §40.22.1. Although the precise import of the term is often disputed, given the context of Gen 6:12, the function here seems to be to introduce the object of perception in such a manner so as to "color" it with "emotionality." *GBHS* §4.5.2.b. See also category one, "excited perception," within McCarthy, "The Uses of *wᵉhinnēh* in Biblical Hebrew," 332–33. Cf. *IBHS* §40.2; Lamdbin, *Biblical Hebrew*, §135.

f. Causal conjunction. *GBHS* §4.3.4.a. Cf. Lambdin, *Biblical Hebrew*, §135.

Extended Analysis

Within this pericope, the three-fold repetition of "ruined" (שחת) underscores the severity of the situation.[73] As Thomas Schreiner opines: "the account . . . underscores the depth and horror of human sin. Human beings are not stained with a light imperfection . . . the evil that besets the human race is at the core of humanity and is not easily erased. The story . . . reveals that human beings, left to themselves, turn toward violence and evil."[74] The text communicates a state of total depravity.[75] The repetition of "the earth" (הארץ) three times also indicates "the fortunes of humanity and the earth are intertwined."[76] James Chukwuma Okoye states: "GOD responds measure for measure: they [humanity] *hishḥītu* (ruin, pervert, corrupt) the earth; behold me *mashḥitam* (ruining, corrupting) them along with the earth."[77] There is a "stark quality" to GOD's decision to ruin his creation that allows for no middle ground.[78] The usage of "all life" (כל בשר) marks another instance of universalistic rhetoric.

The shift from the narrator's perspective (Gen 6:11) to GOD's direct adjudications (Gen 6:12) serves a specific function—to slow the movement and focus one's attention on the dramatic scene unfolding, namely the "end of all flesh."[79] The use of הנה underscores the significance of said pronouncements and draws attention; it emphasizes the depraved state of

---

73. "Ruin" conveys the sense of both "destroy" and "spoilt." Wenham, *Genesis 1–15*, 170. See too *DCH* 8:327; *HALOT* 2:1469–72; Van Dam, *NIDOTTE* 4:92–93; Vetter, *TLOT* 3:1317–19.

74. Schreiner, *The King in His Beauty*, 12.

75. Humphreys, *Character of God*, 65.

76. Mathews, *Genesis 1—11:26*, 359.

77. Okoye, *Genesis 1–11*, 103.

78. Humphreys, *Character of God*, 65.

79. Ryken, *Words of Delight*, 43. See also Waltke and Fredricks, *Genesis*, 121.

affairs.⁸⁰ Pointedly, "this kind of malaise is a chronic condition, not just a spasmodic lapse."⁸¹

Interestingly, "all life" (כל בשר) is used consistently of both humans and animals within the Noachian deluge narrative (Gen 6:17, 19; 7:15–16, 21; 8:17; 9:11, 15–17). This suggests all living creatures—humans and animals alike—are guilty of moral failure.⁸² The specifics of their failure is that each creature had "ruined their own way" a concept referring not just to one's experience, behavior, or "way of life" (Ps 1:1; 1:6; 146:9; Prov 4:19; 14:2; 15:9; 16:25; Isa 30:21; Jer 12:1) but also (usually) the essence of one's moral character (see Job 31:7; Mal 2:8).⁸³ Fundamental to this meaning is its "covenant overtone. One's path in life ... finds its source and orientation in reference to one's relationship with Yahweh, the GOD of the covenant" (see Ps 32:8; 143:8; Isa 48:17; Jer 42:3).⁸⁴ All life is in pilgrimage to either life or death. The difference of outcome lies strictly in how one chooses to align oneself with the authority of the Creator.

IV. *Divine Speech "Make Ready!" Part A—Problem 'lawlessness' (Gen 6:13)*

ᵃויאמר אלהים לנח

קץ כל בשר בא ᵇלפני ᶜכי מלאה הארץ חמס ᵈמפניהם

ᵉוהנני משחיתם ᶠאת הארץ

Then GOD said to Noah:
"The end of all life has come before me for the earth is filled with bloodlust
through them.
So now I will surely ruin them with the earth!

---

80. The function here is to put the addressee in the perspective of the observing character. GOD is not surprised by what he sees; it is a confirmation of that which was expected. See *BHRG* §40.22.4.1.2.b.

81. Hamilton, *Genesis 1–17*, 273.

82. See Hamilton, *Genesis 1–17*, 279. Cf. Habel and Trudinger, eds., *Ecological Reading*, 86.

83. See *DCH* 2:465; Merrill, *NIDOTTE* 1:989–93.

84. Merrill, *NIDOTTE* 1:989–93. Cf. McComiskey, *Covenants of Promise*, 153.

a. Sequential *waw*. See *GBHS* §3.5.1.a; Chisholm, *Exegesis*, 120.

b. Note: the LXX renders this as καιρός παντός ανθρώπου ἥκει εναντίον μου, i.e. "The time of all humankind has come before me" (NETS). The LES renders it: "The time of all humanity has come before me." This indicates that the "opportune" or "critical" moment" (καιρός) for judgment and destruction had come. See Wevers, *Greek Text of Genesis*, 82–83; Goldingay, *Genesis*, 132.

c. Evidential conjunction. *GBHS* §4.3.4.b.

d. The preposition may be either causal or source. Williams, *Hebrew Syntax*, §319, 322; *GBHS* §4.1.13.a, d. Thus, the translation may be rendered as "by," "through," or "because of them."

e. Consequential *waw*. *GBHS* §3.5.1.b. With respect to הנה, though the function is often to point an addressee to something in the speech situation that is newsworthy, thus emphasizing the immediacy of the events that are pointed out (see *BHRG* §40.22.4.1.1), the context of Gen 6:13 seems to indicate the function is also, perhaps, simply to indicate time. See category six, "time," within McCarthy, "The Uses of *wᵉhinnēh*," 337–39. Cf. Lambdin, *Biblical Hebrew*, §135.2.

f. Note: most versions understand this term to be a preposition (not an accusative particle). Tal, *BHQ*, 94; Hamilton *Genesis 1–17*, 279; Wenham, *Genesis 1–15*, 152. Coordinate or accompaniment preposition. Williams, *Hebrew Syntax*, §343; *GBHS* §4.1.4.a; *IBHS* §11.2.4.a.

Extended Analysis

There is a high concentration of speeches in Noah's Flood (Gen 6:13–21; 7:1–4; 8:15–17, 21–22; 9:1–7, 8–11, 12–16, 17; cf. 6:7). Interestingly, it is always GOD who speaks (cf. Gen 9:25–27). Concerning this, one scholar states:

> Divine monologues lead us directly into Yahweh's mind... This indeed is the value conventionally ascribed to the monologue: it imprints on a speech the mark of *utmost sincerity* and of *absolute truthfulness*... Moreover, what the speaker says will always express faithfully what he thinks, since he is supposed to 'think' the very words of the text.[85]

85. Lapointe, "Monologue," 179–80. All emphases original. Notably, within the book of Genesis, evil is "predominantly used in human speech to represent a perspective, point-of-view, attitude, or psychological state of the speaker towards a given person, situation, or state of affairs. These speech acts entail a degree of subjectivity or individual judgment of their circumstances. However, when the lexeme ... (evil) is used in speech by YHWH Elohim it is directive, declarative, or commissive. This may point to an implicit indication in Genesis that YHWH Elohim is the [only] one who rightly knows what is good and what is evil, acting in regard to situations and people based upon his divine knowledge." Faro, *Evil in Genesis*, 45–46. Cf. Hamilton, *Genesis 1–17*, 280.

GOD's initial announcement to Noah of the carnage to come employs several of the same key terms which were already noted above, including "ruin" (שחת) a double usage of "the earth" (הארץ) and "all life" (כל בשר). Importantly, Gen 6:13 marks the second time (cf. Gen 6:11) the pre-Deluge era is characterized by "violence" (חמס).[86]

The rendering of Gen 6:13b could be construed as either a perfect form or a participle, i.e. "the end of all flesh is coming [or, "has come"] before me."[87] This raises the question whether this is "a past fact, or a scene that passes in front of GOD."[88] It is also possible "end" (קץ) may be a metonymy for what prompted it, namely "violence" (חמס).[89] In any case, when Gen 6:11–13 is coupled with Gen 6:5–7, it becomes evident the Flood is being portrayed here as a "great act of destruction" and a "universal act of judgment."[90]

The use of repetition by GOD in the first announcement "the end of all life has come before me ... I will surely ruin them from the earth!" (Gen 6:13) slows down the literary movement and draws attention to the severity of the indictment.[91] Notably, הנה is used here to garner attention, convey emphasis, and focus the addressee. The text communicates GOD's awareness of the earth and how he has carefully weighed his decision to ruin it by means of the Flood. As Goldingay poignantly puts it: "he is about to act, and you had better believe it."[92]

---

86. While the consistent translation throughout this book as "violence" does not always "do justice to the contexts in which the word is used," I deem it to be sufficient enough for my purposes. Cf. Swart, "In Search of Meaning," 165.

87. Goldingay states: "Three times (cf 6:17; 7:4) Yahweh uses a participle as we do in English if we say 'I'm coming,' when we have not yet begun to move (JM 121e; IBHS 37.6f; GKC 116p)." Goldingay, *Genesis*, 132.

88. Hamilton *Genesis 1–17*, 279. Hence, "I have decided" Speiser, *Genesis*, 47. And, "it has entered into my purpose." Skinner, *Genesis*, 160. For more details, see Wenham, *Genesis 1–15*, 152; Shaviv, "Flood," 534–35.

89. Sarna, *Genesis*, 51.

90. Wenham, "Genesis, Book of," 249. Cf. Mathews, "Genesis," 140–56.

91. Ryken, *Words of Delight*, 43.

92. Goldingay, *Genesis*, 132.

IV. *Divine Speech 'Make Ready!" Part B—Solution 'the ark'* (Gen 6:14–16)

עשה לך תבת עצי ᵃגפר ᵇקנים ᶜתעשה את התבה ᵈוכפרת אתה מבית ᵉומחוץ בכפר

ᶠוזה אשר תעשה אתה

שלש מאות אמה ארך התבה חמשים אמה רחבה ושלשים אמה קומתה ᵍצהר תעשה לתבה

ʰואל אמה תכלנה מלמעלה

ⁱופתח התבה בצדה תשים תחתים שנים ושלשים תעשה

Make for yourself an ark of gopher wood. Use reeds in its construction.
Then caulk it inside and out with pitch. This is how you are to make it:
The ark is to be three hundred cubits in length, fifty cubits in breadth,
    and thirty cubits in height. Make a vaulted roof for the ark.
Then to a cubit finish it from above.
Then set the door of the ark in her side
    —make it lower, second, and third.ʲ

---

a. Note: the versions construe this term either as an adjective (describing the way that the wood was to be shaped/treated) or the material from which the ark itself was actually constructed. "It is therefore a case of establishing the meaning of an unknown word, rather than of textual divergence." Tal, *BHQ*, 94. See the extended analysis for more details.

b. Further discussion of this term and its translation is offered in the extended analysis below.

c. "Verbs which express making, preparing, forming into anything, along with the object proper, take a second accusative of the product." GKC §371.ii. Italics removed.

d. Sequential *waw*. *GBHS* §3.5.1.a; Chisholm, *Exegesis*, 120. The Qal verb is a "denominative from *kōper*; thus the expression smear ... with pitch (*kāpartā ... bakkōper*) is analogous to the expression "season with salt" (*bammerlaḥ timlāḥ*, Lev. 2:13)." Hamilton, *Genesis 1–17*, 281. The idea is that Noah is to cover the ark with pitch (that is, caulking).

e. Accompaniment *waw*. Williams, *Hebrew Syntax*, §436.

f. Explicative *waw*. *BHRG* §40.23.4.2.10; Williams, *Hebrew Syntax*, §434. Not translated.

g. Note: the versions have difficulty translating the *hapax legomenon*. The LXX took this term as a verb denoting the way in which the ark is to be finished while the Syriac understood it to mean the base of the ark. All the other versions translate this term as "light" or "window" (cf. Gen 8:6), apparently from an etymological basis of צהרים "noon." See Tal, *BHQ*, 94.

h. Explicative *waw*. BHRG §40.23.4.2.10; Williams, *Hebrew Syntax*, §434. Spatially terminative participle. *GBHS* §4.1.2.a; Williams, *Hebrew Syntax*, §298.

i. Sequential *waw*. See *GBHS* §3.5.1.a; Chisholm, *Exegesis*, 120.

j. The meaning here is of the three decks of the ark. See Wenham, *Genesis 1–15*, 174.

Extended Analysis

The first series of instructions (Gen 6:14–16) concern the construction of Noah's ark, a topic which has caught the imagination of countless people throughout time.[93] The term originally seemed to refer to a "chest or box-like vessel."[94] A transliteration of the Hebrew term גפר yields *"gopher"* hence the rendering of "gopher wood" in many EVV (KJV, NKJV NAB, NASB, ESV, BBE, CSB, RSV). The exact nature of the wood is uncertain.[95] Some English translations render it as "pine" (see HCSB) or "cypress" (so NEB, NIV 1984, 2011, NRSV, NET). Others opt for "teak wood" (*Message*) or "resinous wood" (NLT).[96]

It has traditionally been understood Noah was to make "rooms," or "compartments" for the ark.[97] More recent linguistic evidence, however, strongly suggests Noah was to use "reeds" (קנים) in the ark's construction (so NJB, NEB, and REB). These were "fastened to the wooden beams of the ark rather than being used for matting or caulking (the latter role

---

93. McKeown, *Genesis*, 55; Patai, *Children of Noah*, 9; Teeple, *Noah's Ark*, 1, 78–122. For details concerning the so-called quest to find Noah's Ark, see Longman and Walton, *Lost World of the Flood*, 165–66; Bailey, *Noah*, 53–115, 203–6. Cf. Ross, *Navigating Genesis*, 179–80; Morris, *Noah's Ark*.

94. *DCH* 8:484; *HALOT* 2:1677–78; Hague, *NIDOTTE* 4:269–72; Sarna, *Understanding Genesis*, 49; Sarna, *Genesis*, 52; Kikawada, *ABD* 4:1129–30; BDB, 1061.

95. *DCH* 2:372; *HALOT* 1:200; Walker, *NIDOTTE* 3:475; Patai, *Children of Noah*, 6.

96. A fairly good overview of the different options are offered in Sarfati, *Genesis Account*, 496–97.

97. Sarna notes: "since the singular *ken* means 'a nest,' the plural is used here in the sense of 'cubicles' for the animals." Sarna, *Genesis*, 52. Cf. NLT "decks and stalls" among other EVV.

being played by the pitch)."⁹⁸ Noah "caulks" (כפר) the ark with "asphalt," i.e., "bitumen," or "pitch" (כפר).⁹⁹ This word is a *hapax legomenon* that has a remarkable parallel with an Akkadian term for "bitumen" or "pitch" (*kupru*) that (similarly) only occurs in connection with "the flood hero's boat in both Atrahasis 3.2.51 and Gilgamesh 11.44, [65], 66."¹⁰⁰

The ark was to be three hundred cubits in length, fifty cubits in breadth, and thirty cubits in height. This is roughly 134 meters (440 feet) long, 22 meters (73 feet) broad, and 13 meters (44 feet) high given the 18" (45.7 cm) cubit, i.e. the standard construction formula found in Exod 25:10, 17, 23.¹⁰¹ The displacement of the vessel is about 43, 000 tons.¹⁰² Noah was to make a "vaulted roof" (תעשה).¹⁰³ He was also supposed to finish the ark from above "to a cubit" (Gen 6:16). Concerning this, James Franklin Armstrong states:

> If . . . a gable-type roof be postulated, the 'one cubit upward' can refer to the elevation of the crease of the roof above the level of the tops of the walls. In modern architectural terms, the 'one cubit' would be the height of the kingposts between which the ridgepiece is laid. It is not necessary to assume that when the ancients did construct gable-type roofs they used exactly the same components as are employed in the present day. All that is required is that such roofs were elevated along the center-line, gradually sloping down to meet the tops of the walls. According to the argument that has been presented, the roof of Noah's ark was conceived as having a four per-cent pitch (1 cubit

---

98. Day, *From Creation to Babel*, 122. For more details, see McCann, "Woven of Reeds," 113–40; Longman and Walton, *Lost World of the Flood*, 77–78; Wenham, *Genesis 1–15*, 173. Cf. *DCH* 7:263.

99. *DCH* 4:455; *HALOT* 1:495; Carpenter, *NIDOTTE* 2:711.

100. Day, *From Creation to Babel*, 118. See too Wenham, *Genesis 1–15*, 173; Cohen, *Hapax*, 33–34.

101. See Wenham, *Genesis 1–15*, 173. Some scholars reckon that the ark should be measured by the large (medium) cubit, 17.52" (44.5 cm). See Fuller, *NIDOTTE* 1:423; *DCH* 1:310–11. Cf. Mathews, *Genesis 1—11:26*, 364.

102. See Hamilton, *Genesis 1–17*, 282.

103. This unique word has been variously rendered as "light" (ASV), "window" (AV), "course of windows" (Knox), "opening" (NAB, NJPS), and "casement." Driver, *Genesis*, 8. Given the ark was intended to withstand a torrential downpour, not to mention the common word for roof, גג, refers to a flat surface, it is possible this refers to a pitched roof, which is much more appropriate for a sea-worthy vessel. That the boat of Utnapishtim has also been conceived as having a vaulted construction lends further credence to this rendering. See *DCH* 7:90; Carpenter and Grisanti, *NIDOTTE* 1:815–16; Hamilton, *Genesis 1–17*, 282–83; "Armstrong, "Short Notes," 328–33.

elevation—25 cubits from wall to ridge), quite adequate to permit the water of the rains to flow off.[104]

That "no rudder or sail is mentioned" makes evident Noah's ark "was not designed to be navigated. Consequently, the fate of the company aboard was left in the hands of GOD."[105] The text communicates the sovereignty of GOD and the need to trust GOD with one's very life.

Many scholars have noted the ark is described as being in the shape of something often considered to be a seaworthy vessel.[106] To say it differently, the relations between the height, length, and width of the ark are usually understood to pertain to something reckoned to be "shipshape" for sea-faring, i.e. "a type of vessel characterized by a comparatively narrow beam combined with considerable length of hull and shallowness of draught."[107] This would make the ark extremely capable of withstanding inclement weather with respect to pitch, yaw, and roll (list and heel).[108] Hamilton, for instance, asserts: "the size of Noah's ark possibly suggests that it was large enough and strong enough to weather the Flood, and that it contained enough space (an approximate total deck area of 95,700 sq. ft.) to accommodate all the animals."[109] Great effort has also been expended by certain members of the academic community to bolster the assertion the biblical ark was an effective nautical vessel able to accommodate each of the biblical kinds of animals.[110] In this sense, the text conveys GOD's knowledge, understanding, and wisdom.[111]

The Deluge vessel constructed by Utnapishtim in the Gilgamesh Epic was unsuitable for sea travel by virtue of it being quadrangular, one hundred twenty cubits by one hundred twenty cubits by one hundred

---

104. Armstrong, "Short Notes," 333. See too Goldingay, *Genesis*, 132. Cf. Hamilton, *Genesis 1–17*, 283; Wenham, *Genesis 1–15*, 173–74; Sarna, *Genesis*, 52, 356.

105. Walton, *Genesis*, 312.

106. See Hamilton, *Genesis 1–17*, 282; Waltke and Fredricks, *Genesis*, 135; Mathews, *Genesis 1—11:26*, 363. Cf. Cohn, *Noah's Flood*, 38–133; Wenham, *Genesis 1–15*, 173.

107. Patai, *Children of Noah*, 4. See also Longman and Walton, *Lost World of the Flood*, 77.

108. See Ramm, *Christian View of Science and Scripture*, 157; Filby, *Flood Reconsidered*, 93.

109. Hamilton, *Genesis 1–17*, 282. Cf. Griffin, *Creation and the Flood*, 147–48.

110. See, for instance, Welch, ed., *Noah's Ark*; Lovett, *Noah's Ark*; Griffith and Miller, *Johannes Buteo*; Woodmorappe, *Noah's Ark*; Ross, *Navigating Genesis*, 173–82.

111. Cf. Longman and Walton, *Lost World of the Flood*, 39.

twenty cubits, i.e. a perfect cube or ziggurat-shape (dimensions that recapitulate sacred space).[112] Given the unique terminology shared by the Bible and the ANE Flood texts, it is thought-provoking to consider "there is no evidence to suggest that the ark in Genesis recapitulates sacred space. The rectangular dimensions suggest instead that it recapitulates the standard shape of boats."[113]

Even so, the dimensions of the ark describe "a boat like no other boat ever built in antiquity."[114] That is to say, "no seagoing ships even approaching such large dimensions were built by either the Greeks or the Romans even at the most advanced stage of their technical development of shipbuilding, when magnificent triremes were being constructed in Attic shipyards."[115] Given the ark was designed to withstand colossal storms, it is peculiar how Noah's incredible contribution to nautical engineering "vanished without a trace, and the seafarers returned to their hollow logs and reed rafts. Like a passing mirage, the ark was here one day and gone the next, leaving not a ripple in the long saga of shipbuilding."[116] As Walton notes:

> Prior to the invention of sea-worthy vessels which could carry sailors and cargo through the heavy seas of the Mediterranean, most boats were made of skin or reeds and were designed to sail through marshes or along the river bank. They were used for fishing or hunting and would not have been more than 10 feet in length. True sailing ships, with a length of 170 feet, are first depicted in Old Kingdom Egyptian art (ca. 2500 BC) and are described in Ugaritic (1600–1200 BC) and Phoenician (1000–500 BC) texts. Even this late they generally navigated within sight of land, with trips to Crete and Cyprus as well as the ports along the coasts of Egypt, the Persian Gulf, and Asia Minor.[117]

This aspect of the Brobdingnag structure seems to defy naturalistic explanation since ship building was a long, expensive process often acquired

---

112. Crawford, "Noah's Architecture," 1–22; Wenham, *Genesis 1–15*, 173; Walton *Genesis*, 312; Mathews, *Genesis 1—11:26*, 363; Longman and Walton, *Lost World of The Flood*, 77; Blenkinsopp, *Creation*, 138; Holloway "What Ship Goes There," 328–55; Bailey, "Noah's Ark," 1131; Baily, *Noah*, 19; Hendel, "Ark," 128–29.

113. Longman and Walton, *Lost World of the Flood*, 77.

114. See Longman, *Genesis*, 117. See also, Stein, ed., *The Sea*, 5–52.

115. Patai, *Children of Noah*, 5. See also Casson, *Ships and Seafaring*, 60–77.

116. Moore, "Impossible Voyage," 3. Cf. Burlet, "Cosmos to Chaos," 121.

117. Walton et al., eds., *IVP Background*, 36–37. See also Patai, *Children of Noah*, 5.

through millennia of apprentice and multiple life and death experiences.[118] It also provides rationale for why many people stand against a conventional, straight-forward understanding of the ark's dimensions.[119]

But if the numbers themselves are not to be understood as having their historically referential sense, that is, if Noah's ark was not actually the size the text seems to indicate, what does the math mean? Where did the dimensions come from? What do they signify or represent? What function do they serve? By what criteria are readers to adjudicate these matters?

One intriguing idea for reducing the size centers on changing the unit of measurement from a "cubit" (אמה), the distance from the elbow to the fingertips, to a "hand span" (זרת), the distance between the tips of one's thumb and their little finger when the fingers are spread apart.

Robert M. Best begins his analysis by noting how numerous cargo ships have an inside clearance of about 6 feet (tall enough for the vast majority of standing animals and many adult workers), a number less than half of what the dimensions of the ark are recorded as being.[120] Best opines:

> If the meaning of cubit changed or was mistranslated or if cubits was an editorial gloss, the size of Noah's barge could have been much smaller . . . [t]he source text used by an editor of Genesis 6:15 may have omitted the unit of measurement, just as we omit inches in the expression 'two by four.' A story teller or editor may have added cubits to the story. Alternatively, an archaic sign or pictograph for hand spans may have been used that was unfamiliar to an ancient translator who assumed it meant cubits. A barge measuring 300 hand spans in length would be about 200 feet (61 m) long.[121]

While it is true Best's calculations would produce a boat much more in alignment with our knowledge of wooden boat making and early engineering the lack of textual evidence among the ancient versions render speculation on this matter fruitless. The idea should be abandoned.

Another proposal to account for the dimensions of the ark is to conjecture the scribe(s) employed a "fanciful exaggeration" in their accounting.[122] Raphael Patai asserts such extensive hyperbole would have

---

118. See Casson, *Ships and Seafaring*, 17; Rawson and Tupper, *Ship Theory*, 2, Unger, *Medieval Technology*, 50–61. Cf. Moore, "Impossible Voyage," 1–43.

119. Sarna, *Understanding Genesis*, 38. Cf. Welch ed., *Noah's Ark*, 15.

120. See Best, *Noah's Ark*, 81.

121. Best, *Noah's Ark*, 81. Italics original.

122. Patai, *Children of Noah*, 5.

"appeared necessary when telling about a ship that played a crucial role in the ancient mythical history of the world."[123] This is especially so, Patai maintains, when one considers the ark was designed to hold at least two members of every kind of animal.[124]

Patai also claims a number of scribes would have observed various ships at port, the largest of which, in Talmudic times, were described as "having had a capacity of 10, 000 talents or amphorae, which is equal in burden to about 250 tons."[125] Given these things, Patai states:

> It would therefore appear as probable that the author of the passage about the ark of Noah, after observing the proportions of the ships available to his inspection, solved rather simply the difficulty of having to describe a vessel that could carry a great magnitude of animals: he multiplied the measurements of the ships he saw by a round number, such as seven, or ten; then, ignoring the units under ten, he arrived at the arbitrary sizes of 300, 50, and 30 cubits for the length, breadth, and height of Noah's ark. From the fact that the ratio of beam to length is one to six we can infer that the basis of the calculation was the dimensions of a slender galley propelled by oars, rather than the average measurements of tubby merchantmen such as the grain ships that ran from Alexandria to Rome during the period when Rome held Egypt in her grip.[126]

By way of critique, Patai's time periods cannot be reconciled with the evidence of the text since the Pentateuch shows numerous signs the implied readers experienced the apostasy of Israel, the devastation of Jerusalem, and the deportation to Babylon which began with Judah in 587 BC.

Patai's argument is also unconvincing in that it fails to argue why any scribe would have chosen to make their calculations from a vessel (the slender galley) so dissimilar from the type of craft they were actually attempting to comment on (the ark) when they had available to them something much more in keeping with its cargo-preserving function (the grain ship). The problem becomes even more acute when one considers the "blueprints" of the ark intimate it was not designed to be navigated (hence the absence of any rudder/sail system) or even physically maneuvered by personnel; "the fate of the company aboard was [entirely] left in

---

123. Patai, *Children of Noah*, 5.
124. Patai, *Children of Noah*, 5.
125. Patai, *Children of Noah*, 5 (see also 39–46).
126. Patai, *Children of Noah*, 5.

the hands of God."¹²⁷ Alongside this, Patai fails to determine how a scribe would have chosen between the two round numbers he offers, seven and ten, or why a scribe would have selected those figures, in particular, from among any other number, such as three, five, twelve, or forty (why not!) which are also known to contain symbolic meanings.¹²⁸ In sum, Patai's work is founded on a construct that does not account for the literary features of the text or make much logical sense.

With respect to hyperbole, it is understood the vessel constructed by Utnapishtim was completely unsuitable for sea travel. This is by virtue of it being a quadrangular (120 cubits by 120 cubits by 120 cubits), i.e. a perfect cube or ziggurat-shape–dimensions recapitulating sacred space (possibly the seven-stepped ziggurat shrine in Babylon); the base itself measured one *ikū* (equivalent to about 3, 600 square meters) and the vessel was divided into nine parts.¹²⁹ Lloyd R. Bailey communicates these dimensions reflect a preoccupation with the "idealized number" given the Mesopotamian penchant for the sexagesimal system and the fact the ship's length, width, and height are all multiples of sixty.¹³⁰ While the vessel was said to be covered with pitch and equipped with punting poles there is no true concern for "realism and verisimilitude" in the descriptions of the ship.¹³¹ It is fitting to remember the Gilgamesh scribe was "a poet not a carpenter."¹³² In brief, the numbers are rhetorical edifices (not construction-type blueprints) erected to convey the import of the craft itself.¹³³

When Enlil urged Atrahasis to tear down his house of reeds and to build a boat covered with a roof and slimed with pitch, the physical impossibility of building a coracle the size the text requires (the floor area of the boat equaled 3, 600 square meters, the diameter nearly 70 meters,

---

127. Walton, *Genesis*, 312.

128. See Ryken et al., eds., *DBI*, 599.

129. As noted above, see Crawford, "Noah's Architecture," 1–22; Wenham, *Genesis 1–15*, 173; Walton, *Genesis*, 312; Mathews, *Genesis 1—11:26*, 363; Longman and Walton, *Lost World of The Flood*, 77; Blenkinsopp, *Creation*, 138; Holloway, "What Ship Goes There," 328–55; Bailey, "Noah's Ark," 1131; Baily, *Noah*, 19; Hendel, "Ark," 128–29.

130. Bailey, *Noah*, 19.

131. Blenkinsopp, *Creation*, 138.

132. Best, *Noah's Ark*, 82.

133. Blenkinsopp, *Creation*, 138.

and the walls roughly 6 meters high) is seemingly irrelevant.[134] As Irving Finkel assesses:

> This is a GOD speaking ... who is not concerned with the theoretical nature of circles but with reinforcing the image of a round boat; unlike any other boat, it has neither prow nor stern but is the same width—or as we would say, diameter—in all directions. Enki's instructions to build a coracle were very specific ... and his servant Atra-hasīs had to be clear on this.[135]

Some evangelicals argue the ark's dimensions are, also, perhaps "hyperbolic numbers ... purposefully exaggerated for rhetorical effect to make a (theological) point."[136] More specifically, Longman and Walton state:

> In light of the recognition of academic arithmetic in the ancient world and the practice noted in iconography to supersize that which is important, we suggest that in the dimensions ... more than hyperbole is going on. That is, we are not suggesting that the boat was actually only half the stated size and they doubled it to aggrandize the size of the vessel. The dimensions are not relative to the actual size. Alternatively, the dimensions can be viewed as devised with a rhetorical effect in mind. Neither jibes by skeptics about the impossibility of the vessels nor the apologetic defenses of practicality and realism are to the point. Both groups are reading the text through their modern filters and thereby expect to conform how such information would be conveyed in our current-day cultural river.[137]

Though the biblical ark may appear to be monstrous in size, its scope is nothing compared to the Armenian account of Eusebius' *Chronicles*, where the length of the vessel is given as fifteen furlongs (nearly two miles!) or Berosus's claim it was five stadia long and two stadia broad. To be clear, this is about 914 m (3000 feet) long and 366 m (1200 feet) broad.[138]

---

134. Finkel, *The Ark Before Noah*, 126, 161.

135. Finkel, *The Ark Before Noah*, 126.

136. Longman and Walton, *Lost World of the Flood*, 38.

137. Longman and Walton, *Lost World of the Flood*, 76. See too Griffin, *Creation and the Flood*, 167–72. Cf. Stallings, *Genesis Cataclysm*, 3–11. Interestingly, Finkel disregards the possibility that the cuneiform tablet he discovered uses hyperbole. See Sigler, "Genesis Flood & Hyperbole: Part Two." No pages. Online.

138. Patai, *Children of Noah*, 5. For more details, see Day, *From Creation to Babel*, 61–76.

The Corruption of Humanity

In sum, as a salvific vehicle *par excellence* the Ark's presence within the Noachian deluge narrative conveys the grandeur, majesty, wisdom, and sovereignty of GOD. It also shows GOD's compassion, care, and sensitivity for all life. The massive size of this "handmade wooden craft staggers the imagination, and its seaworthy proportions incite admiration."[139]

IV. Divine Speech "Make Ready!" Part C—Problem 'the flood' (Gen 6:17)

ואני [b]הנני מביא את המבול מים על הארץ [c]לשחת כל בשר אשר בו רוח חיים [d]מתחת [e]השמים[a]

כל אשר בארץ יגוע

> But I am surely bringing the Flood as water upon the earth, soon, in order to ruin every creature that has the breath of life in it under the sky.
> Everything that is on the earth shall perish.

---

a. Dramatic (disjunctive) *waw*. Chisholm, *Exegesis*, 126–27. The separate pronoun serves to give "strong emphasis." See GKC §135.d.

b. The function here is to introduce a fact upon which the following statement is based. Lambdin, *Biblical Hebrew*, 168–70. Cf. *IBHS* §16.3.6.b. See also category three, "occasion," in McCarthy, "The Uses of *wᵉhinnēh*," 334–36. Cf. Muraoka, *Emphatic Words*, 140.

c. Note: for text-critical details on the *piel*, see Tal, *BHQ*, 95.

d. The compound is locative carrying the force of only one of the particles (vertical relationship). See *GBHS* §4.1.18.a and §4.1.13.i alongside Williams, *Hebrew Syntax*, §349.

e. The syntax of the total construction of the sentence here conveys an imminent future nuance, see GKC §116p and §131kN; Joüon §119n; Lambdin, *Biblical Hebrew*, 168–70.

Extended Analysis

While the first series of instructions pertain to the construction of Noah's ark (Gen 6:14–16), this verse marks a shift in the speech to the destruction of all life (Gen 6:17). It is also the second occurrence of הנה within the same speech (Gen 6:13–21). A contrast exists "between what GOD is

---

139. Waltke and Fredricks, *Genesis*, 135. Cf. Griffin, *Creation and Flood*, 146.

doing and what Noah must do, vv 14–16, 21)."[140] As one scholar notes, "the sense is, 'When you, Noah, have built the ark, I, GOD, will act.'"[141] The text conveys GOD's sovereignty over all of his creation—both to give life (salvation) and to take it away (judgment).[142]

This is the first time the technical term for "Flood" (מבול) is used.[143] To be clear, Gerhard von Rad asserts that "the Hebrew *mabbuwl* is not actually a regular word for flood. In fact, it does not refer to any sort of normal flood understanding at all, but rather 'it is a technical term for a part of the [phenomenological] world structure, namely the heavenly ocean,' which carries with it' the same realistic and cosmological ideas as in Gen., ch. 2.'"[144]

The context of the passage makes clear the Flood is no mere force of nature but a "cosmic water-weapon wielded by deity."[145] The withholding of the word until now could be part of the literary art of tension-building.[146] Given the text has yet to reveal GOD's intentions to save anyone other than Noah (see Gen 6:14; cf. Gen 6:8) the mood is pensive and grim.

The language used for the devastation is brutal. "The Flood" (מבול) will come upon the "land" (ארץ) "ruining" (שחת) "all life" (כל בשר).[147] Everything will perish (Gen 6:17).[148] Wenham states: "'beneath the heaven' may be a poetic alternative to 'upon the earth'" and, as such, a possible contrast to "'beneath the waters' ... thereby excluding fishes [sic] and

---

140. Wenham, *Genesis 1–15*, 152.

141. Sarna, *Genesis*, 52.

142. Wenham, *Genesis 1–15*, 174.

143. For lexical details, see *DCH* 5:124–25; *HALOT* 1:541; Grisanti, *NIDOTTE* 2:835–37; Sarna, *Genesis*, 53.

144. Stallings, *Genesis Cataclysm*, 26 quoting von Rad, *Genesis*, 128. Stallings maintains, "this notion is further confirmation of the global Flood image that is inherently built into the biblical text." Stallings, *Genesis Cataclysm*, 26. Italics original. See too Chaffey and Lisle, *Old Earth Creationism on Trial*, 89. Cf. Goldingay, *Genesis*, 143.

145. Walton, *Genesis 1–15*, 313.

146. Mathews, *Genesis 1—11:26*, 355.

147. The NET Bible notes: "the Hebrew construction here is different from the previous two; here it is רוּחַ חַיִּים ... rather than נֶפֶשׁ חַיָּה ... or נִשְׁמַת חַיִּים ... [i]t refers to everything that breathes." Cf. Mathews, *Genesis 1—11:26*, 366.

148. Perish is essentially equivalent "to the common word 'die' (*mût*, Num 20:29), but it often is associated with the departure of a person's vital 'breath' (e.g., Gen 25:8, 17; 35:39), hence translated at times 'expire.'" Mathews, *Genesis 1—11:26*, 366. See *DCH* 2:335; *HALOT* 1:184; Merrill, *NIDOTTE* 1:835; Ringgren, *TDOT* 2:438–39.

other water creatures from destruction."[149] It is also possible the text utilizes *merismus*; that is, "under heaven" and "on earth" is universalistic language signifying all creatures everywhere.[150]

IV. *Divine Speech "Make Ready!" Part D—Solution 'covenant' (Gen 6:18–21)*

[a]והקמתי את בריתי [b]אתך [c]ובאת אל התבה אתה [d]ובניך ואשתך ונשי בניך אתך

[e]ומכל החי מכל בשר שנים מכל תביא אל התבה להחית אתך זכר [f]ונקבה יהיו

מהעוף למינהו [g]ומן הבהמה למינה מכל רמש האדמה למינהו

שנים מכל יבאו אליך להחיות

[h]ואתה קח לך מכל מאכל אשר יאכל [i]ואספת אליך [j]והיה לך [k]ולהם לאכלה

But I will set up my covenant with you.
    Thus you shall come into the ark—you, and your sons, and your wife, and the wives of your sons with you.
    Also, from all living things, from every creature, bring two from every [kind] into the ark in order to keep (them) alive with you—male and female they shall be: from the birds according to their kinds, and from beasts according to their kinds, from every creeping thing of the ground, according to their kinds.
    Two from every [kind] shall come to you in order to keep [them] alive.
    Alongside this, you must take for yourself from every [kind] of food which is edible and gather it to you. Thus it shall be for you and for them for food."

---

a. Climactic *waw*. Chisholm, *Exegesis*, 132. For more details see the NET Bible and GKC §72w.

b. The preposition could have the nuance of advantage. See Williams, *Hebrew Syntax*, §341.

c. Consequential *waw*. GBHS §3.5.1.b.

---

149. Wenham, *Genesis 1–15*, 174. See too Okoye, *Genesis 1–11*, 103.

150. For more information on *merismus*, see Watson, *Classical Hebrew Poetry*, 31.

d. This *waw* (and the two that follow) signify accompaniment. Williams, *Hebrew Syntax*, §436.

e. Synchronic *waw* (displaying simultaneous action). Chisholm, *Exegesis*, 126; GBHS §3.5.4.b. Separative preposition. GBHS §4.1.13.f; Williams, *Hebrew Syntax*, §315.

f. This coordinative *waw* joins opposites. Williams, *Hebrew Syntax*, §430a and §431.

g. Coordinative *waw*. Williams, *Hebrew Syntax*, §430a.

h. Synchronic *waw* (displaying simultaneous action). Chisholm, *Exegesis*, 126; GBHS §3.5.4.b. The adverb (in compound form with the *waw*) indicates a "logical . . . shift in the argument or flow of the discourse without a break in the theme." GBHS §4.2.14.b.

i. Synchronic *waw* (displaying simultaneous action). Chisholm, *Exegesis*, 126; GBHS §3.5.4.b.

j. Consequential *waw*. GBHS §3.5.1.b.

k. Accompaniment *waw*. Williams, *Hebrew Syntax*, §436. The preposition shows possession. GBHS §4.1.10.f; IBHS §9.7a–c; Joüon §130.

Extended Analysis

The phrase "you, your sons, your wife, and your sons' wives" (Gen 6:18) seem to illustrate the "basic unit of biblical society consisted of a man, his wife, his married sons and daughters-in-law and their children, rather than the modern nuclear family."[151] Chronologically, the fact the wives of Noah's sons are mentioned (Gen 6:18) seems to imply they are already married when GOD gave Noah the command to build the ark; this means Noah had roughly seventy years to finish the task of completing the ark.[152] While no emotional response is provided in the text, GOD's words would likely give "the fearful band" the "security" it needs "for the disaster unfolding before them."[153] Comments concerning the enumeration of the ark's human inhabitants will be made in those sections repeating the order (Gen 7:7, 13; 8:16, 18). Comments about the Noahic covenant,

---

151. Wenham, *Genesis 1–15*, 175.

152. This calculation assumes Noah was five hundred years old when Japheth was born (Gen 5:32) and that Noah was six hundred years old when the Flood came (Gen 7:6). Some scholars calculate it as being eighty-one years. See LaHaye and Morris, *Ark on Ararat*, 248. Cf. Wilson, *Genealogy*, 160; Hordes, "Noah," 217.

153. Mathews, *Genesis 1—11:26*, 367.

specifically, will be given in conjunction to the time after the Flood (Gen 8:20—9:17).

As noted above, while the first series of instructions pertain to the construction of Noah's ark (Gen 6:14–16), in the second series of instructions (Gen 6:19–21), Noah must bring the pairs of animals (male and female) into the life-saving vessel (Gen 6:19–20) and victual it (Gen 6:21). This imperative could be an echo of the giving of food for all creatures at creation (Gen 1).[154]

It is, however, unproductive to speculate on why there is no command to bring aboard water.[155]

The list of animals develops from being more general (two of every creature—male and female) to somewhat more specific (birds, beasts, and moving things). There is no hierarchy or particular ranking of life. The text persuasively argues all of the animal kinds are of value and precious to GOD who has chosen to save representatives of every kind of life (cf. Jonah 4:11).

Lastly, it is interesting the Hebrew term for the "ark" (תבה) occurs seven times, in total, within the divine speech (Gen 6:14–2x, Gen 6:15–1x, Gen 6:16–2x, Gen 6:18–1x, Gen 6:19–1x).[156] In this way, the text communicates GOD's mercies in providing refuge and comfort.

V. *Final Narratival Comments Concerning Noah (Gen 6:22)*

[a]ויעש נח [b]ככל אשר צוה אתו אלהים כן עשה

So Noah did according to all that GOD commanded him
  —thus he did.

---

a. Summarizing or concluding *waw*. Chisholm, *Exegesis*, 123.

b. The preposition denotes "agreement between trajector x and landmark y." *BHRG* §39.10.

154. I am indebted to Rick Wadholm Jr. for this insight via private communiqué.

155. McKeown presumes the reason for this is because it is not in short supply, but questions arise concerning contamination and other issues. McKeown, *Genesis*, 55. Cf. Okoye, *Genesis 1–11*, 103.

156. Sarna, *Genesis*, 52.

Extended Analysis

This portion of text concludes with the refrain Noah did according to all GOD commanded (Gen 6:22).[157] This is the first of two refrains which occur in connection with two critical acts: (1) building the ark (Gen 6:22), and (2) entering it (Gen 7:5).[158] Meier Sternberg notes this as a *forecast → enactment* sequence.[159] This rhetorical device functions as an "indirect means of characterizing the giver or the addressee of an order or their relations."[160] The characterization of all parties is positive. The text communicates Noah is worthy of empathy and support.

Summary

There are two main emphases within this pericope: judgment and salvation. The account begins by communicating the need for GOD to do something about the earth's depraved state of affairs. Evil grew to such an extent that sin was pervasive throughout all creation (Gen 6:5–7). Noah, however, found favour in the eyes of the LORD (Gen 6:8). The text notes certain aspects about Noah and affirms his righteousness (Gen 6:9–10). Despite the corruption of the earth and GOD's decision to destroy all things along with the earth itself (Gen 6:9 11–13) GOD spared Noah's life by commanding him to build and victual an ark (Gen 6:14–16). While GOD makes clear all life outside the ark will die (Gen 6:17) the text also notes the covenant made with Noah (Gen 6:18), the salvific nature of the ark (Gen 6:19–21), and Noah's marked obedience to GOD (Gen 6:22).

STEP FOUR: DETERMINING THE RHETORICAL EFFECTIVENESS

The fourth step of the model involves determining the rhetorical effectiveness of the text. Within this stage, the rhetorical critic seeks to answer to what degree the discourse was a "fitting response to the exigency that

---

157. See DG §147.c for more grammatical information about the appositional phrasing.
158. Waltke and Fredricks, *Genesis*, 123.
159. Sternberg, *Poetics*, 388.
160. Sternberg, *Poetics*, 388.

occasioned it."[161] The primary exigence of the entextualized rhetorical situation pertains to humanity's "violence" (חמס). There is also the secondary exigence of potential covenant infidelity on the part of GOD and Noah alongside the exigence of the Flood which must be controlled and stabilized so as to permit life aboard the ark to exist. Concerning the latter, it is not evident at this time that GOD displayed his sovereignty over this situation. With respect to the other exigences, however, while the text does provide some inklings concerning such, we will have to wait for future chapters in order to bring resolution to these problems.

Those persons privy to the Flood account in the exilic/postexilic period would have identified with many of the sentiments found in this pericope (Gen 6:5–8 and 9–22).[162] As James McKeown notes: "They too had suffered, not the destruction of a flood, but the brutality of an expansionist regime."[163] This passage offers the consolation "GOD is not unfeeling or uncaring but actually shares the suffering of his recalcitrant creation."[164] Notably, the Flood itself would prove to be a source of hope for a downcast Israel (see Isa 54:9). As John Oswalt proclaims:

> There is no discontinuity between the GOD of Noah and the GOD of the postexilic era. Just as his compassion prevented him from completely destroying the world then and led him to bind himself from that sort of destruction in the future, so here it is his compassion that leads him to bring an exile to an end and to swear not to pour out his anger on them.[165]

The compassionate GOD of Israel ensures that his promise of peace would endure forever.[166]

CONCLUSION

This chapter analyzed the text of Gen 6:5–8 and 9–22 via the four steps of the rhetorical-critical method delineated in chapter 2. Step one was determining the rhetorical units. This process demonstrated Gen 6:5–8 was constructed of several main rhetorical subsections, namely: (I) "Initial

---

161. Möller, *Prophet in Debate*, 42. See also Ahn, *Persuasive Portrayal*, 31.
162. McKeown, *Genesis*, 52. Cf. Peterson, *Genesis*, 65–67.
163. McKeown, *Genesis*, 52.
164. McKeown, *Genesis*, 52.
165. Oswalt, *Isaiah 40–66*, 422. Cf. Smith, *Isaiah 40–66*, 484–85.
166. See Beyer, *Encountering Isaiah*, 217.

Divine Comments Concerning Humanity" (Gen 6:5–6), (II) "The Great Purge" (Gen 6:7), and (III) "Initial Divine Comments Concerning Noah" (Gen 6:8). It was also demonstrated Gen 6:9–22 was constructed of several main rhetorical subsections: (I) *Toledoth* Formula" (Gen 6:9a), (II) "Additional Narratival Comments Concerning Noah" (Gen 6:9b-10), (III) "Narratival and Divine Comments Concerning Humanity" (Gen 6:11–12), (IV) "Divine Speech: Make Ready!" (Gen 6:13–21), and (IV) "Final Narratival Comments Concerning Noah" (Gen 6:22). Each of these sections are also capable of being subdivided into even smaller rhetorical units.

In step two, determining the rhetorical situation, it was made clear the primary exigence of Noah's Flood pertains to humanity's inability to relate to GOD, one another, and creation in a way that honors, serves, and pleases GOD. A secondary exigence also exists, namely the potential risk of covenant infidelity on the part of GOD and Noah. Lastly, a third (but lesser) exigence pertains to the Flood which must be controlled and stabilized so as to permit all life coming aboard the ark to exist. In step three, determining the rhetorical strategy, it was shown the text employs a variety of literary devices giving it aesthetic appeal and rhetorical effect. The text communicated both GOD's judgment by means of the Flood and GOD's salvation by means of the ark and the covenant with Noah (see below). With respect to step four, determining the rhetorical effectiveness, though the text underscores Noah's fidelity to the covenant initiated by GOD it was indeterminate within the confines of the pericope (Gen 6:9–22) to what degree GOD would remain true to his word and to what degree he would display his sovereignty over the Flood. This step also noted how the Deluge had a comforting effect upon the post-Flood Israelite community.

With respect to universalistic language, the Hebrew term "all" (כל) occurs two times (Gen 6:5) in the first portion of text this chapter surveyed (Gen 6:5–8). Both of these occurrences pertain to negative evaluative judgments of humanity by GOD concerning their wickedness. In the second portion of text this chapter surveyed (Gen 6:9–22), the Hebrew term "all" (כל) occurs nine times in total. Four times (roughly 44 percent of all of the occurrences here) the sense relates judgment (Gen 6:12, 13, 17x2). Everything corrupted their way upon the earth (Gen 6:12). GOD declared the end of all life (Gen 6:13). GOD repeated that he would destroy all life (Gen 6:17x2).

The Hebrew term "all" (כל) also occurs five times (roughly 56 percent) with the sense relating to salvation (Gen 6:19x2, 20, 21, 22). That is, God required two of every kind of animal to be brought into the ark by Noah (Gen 6:19x2, 20). God required all sorts of food be stored in the ark (Gen 6:21). Lastly, Noah obeyed and did according to all God required him (Gen 6:22).

Alongside this, while the text does note the destructive power of the Flood (Gen 6:17) and the reason for its existence (see Gen 6:11–13; cf. Gen 6:5–7), only four verses (roughly 29 percent) within Gen 6:9–22 focus on judgment and the Flood (Gen 6:11, 12, 13, 17; cf. Gen 6:5–7). To compare, a good portion more text, i.e., ten verses (roughly 71 percent), was devoted to either: (a) explicitly salvific aspects, i.e., details concerning either the ark or God's covenant (Gen 6:14–16, 18–21) or (b) positively characterizing Noah within the narrative (Gen 6:9–10, 22; cf. Gen 6:8).

To conclude, this book contends the text of the Noachian deluge narrative categorically underscores all God did to preserve life in spite of the disaster. Despite the picture of devastation that the narrative depicts, the prominent emphasis of the text is on deliverance and redemption i.e., salvation, not judgment. The focus of the Genesis Flood is acutely bent towards God's salvific rather than punitive purposes.

The arc of salvation within the Flood narrative can be broken down into two main ideas. First, God's intention for creation is not thwarted and, secondly, God commits himself to his intentions of creation. His intention for creation can be stated as thus: the establishment of order via covenant showing the sanctity of human life and the upholding of all life.

The text of Gen 6:5–8 alongside Gen 6:9–22 (as a whole) markedly bolsters this assertion as demonstrated through the universalistic language summation and the preceding analysis.

4

It Cometh!
(Genesis 7:1–24)

INTRODUCTION

IN THE PREVIOUS CHAPTER's analysis (Gen 6:5–8 and 9–22), it was made clear GOD was resolute in his endeavor to redeem creation by means of saving Noah, his immediate family, and all forms of animal life via the ark—a colossal nautical vessel of salvation. That the ark was to be the salvific vehicle from the Flood was made clear through divine speech (Gen 6:18–21) and is reaffirmed here (Gen 7:1–3, 7–9, 13–16, and 23). The text's comment "the LORD closed it behind him" (Gen 7:16), namely the door, provides assurance that despite the catastrophe to come, GOD's hand would rest upon all the ark's inhabitants. While Gen 7:17–24 places the most emphasis of the entire Noachian deluge narrative upon the totality of the devastation involved in the Flood, it behooves us to remember all those together with Noah inside the ark were spared via the LORD's great mercy (Gen 7:23). Nothing can thwart GOD's plans to save his creation.

STEP ONE: DETERMINING THE RHETORICAL UNITS

As in the previous chapter, the first step of the rhetorical-critical, rhetoric as persuasion, model this study utilizes is to determine the boundaries of each of the rhetorical units of the text. This is done by looking at various signals demarcating the discourse units (aperture and closing). The

It Cometh!

same vocabulary and schematics for rhetorical units used in the previous chapter are used here.

The first main rhetorical unit is entitled "Divine Speech: 'Enter!'" (Gen 7:1–4).[1] The unit hangs together as a divine speech. Its referential, situational, and structural (relational) coherence is best demonstrated by means of the introductory formula "then the LORD said to Noah" (Gen 7:1) and the refrain that marks the end of the speech (Gen 7:5). Gen 7:1–5 follows a similar pattern and structure as Gen 6:13–22, i.e. a divine speech (Gen 7:1–4, cf. Gen 6:13–21) followed by the text's affirmation of Noah's obedience to GOD (Gen 7:5, cf. Gen 6:22).[2]

The text's coherence is also signified through consistency of: (a) narratival time (cf. Gen 7:1–4 with vv. 6, 10), (b) place (cf. Gen 7:1–5 with vv. 6–9), (c) participants, including GOD (Gen 7:1, 4), Noah (Gen 7:1–2), and the inhabitants of the ark (Gen 7:1–3), (d) speed of action alongside frequent repetition of key words (Gen 7:2–4), and (e) topic, theme, and mood that is, the preservation of life for those aboard the ark and the death of all those outside.[3]

Each of the rhetorical subunits of this portion of text are depicted below:

It Cometh! (Gen 7:1–24)

I. Divine Speech "Enter!" (Gen 7:1–4)
   1. preface (Gen 7:1a)
   2. directives: enter the Ark (Gen 7:1b–3)
      i. directives concerning human beings (Gen 7:1b–c)
         a. divine imperative for Noah to enter the ark (Gen 7:1b)

---

1. A number of scholars place Gen 7:1–4 together with Gen 7:5 as one unit, i.e., Gen 7:1–5. See Waltke and Fredricks, *Genesis*, 138; McKeown, *Genesis*, 56; Sailhamer, *Genesis*, 116; Keiser, *Genesis 1–11*, 129. This scheme does not reckon with the "divine speech + refrain" pattern the text employs. Albeit, this is better than the alternative division many other scholars offer, namely placing Gen 7:1–4 in the same unit as Gen 7:5–10 or extending the unit, i.e., Gen 7:5–16. See Mathews, *Genesis 1—11:26*, 370; Hamilton, *Genesis 1–17*, 288; Wenham, *Genesis 1–15*, 157.

2. Hamilton, *Genesis 1–17*, 288.

3. See Hamilton, *Genesis 1–17*, 288. Cf. Sailhamer, *Pentateuch*, 126.

        b. inclusion of all of Noah's household (Gen 7:1b)

        c. further clarification (Gen 7:1c)

    ii. directives concerning animals (Gen 7:2–3)

        a. specifics that pertain to clean animals (Gen 7:2a)

- groupings (sevens)/gender (male and female)

        b. specifics pertaining to animals that are not clean (Gen 7:2b)

- groupings (pairs)/gender (male and female)

        c. specifics that pertain to birds (Gen 7:3a)

- groupings (sevens)/gender (male and female)

        d. explanatory comment (Gen 7:3b)

  3. comments concerning the Flood (Gen 7:4)

    i. countdown (Gen 7:4a)

    ii. duration (Gen 7:4b)

    iii. consequence (Gen 7:4c)

II. Noah's Obedient Faithfulness (Gen 7:5)

The next main rhetorical subunit is entitled "Initial Recounting of the Entry into the Ark" (Gen 7:6–9).[4] It is identified as a unit by virtue of its referential, situational, and structural (relational) coherence signified by there being sameness of: (a) time (cf. Gen 7:6 with Gen 7:10, 11, 12, 13), (b) place (cf. Gen 7:7–9 with Gen 7:13–16), (c) participants, namely Noah (Gen 7:6, 7, 9), Noah's kin (Gen 7:7), and the animals GOD chose (Gen 7:8–9), and (d) topic, theme, and mood, i.e., salvation from the onslaught of the Flood (Gen 7:6–9).

Each of the rhetorical subunits of this portion of text are depicted below:

---

4. A number of scholars disregard the temporal shift occurring between Gen 7:6–9 and Gen 7:10–12. That is, they keep Gen 7:10 with Gen 7:6–9 as one and the same unit (Gen 7:6–10). See Waltke and Fredricks, *Genesis*, 138; Mathews, *Genesis 1—11:26*, 374; Keiser, *Genesis 1–11*, 129.

It Cometh! (Gen 7:1–24)

III. Initial Recounting of the Entry into the Ark (Gen 7:6–9)

1. temporal clarification (Gen 7:6)
2. human entry into the ark (Gen 7:7)
   i. delineation of persons (Gen 7:7a)
   ii. clarification for entry (Gen 7:7b)
3. animal entry into the ark (Gen 7:8–9)
   i. delineation of animals (Gen 7:8–9b)
      a. clean animals (Gen 7:8)
         - groupings (pairs)/gender (male and female)
      b. animals that are not clean (Gen 7:8)
         - groupings (pairs)/gender (male and female)
      c. birds (Gen 7:8)
         - groupings (pairs)/gender (male and female)
      d. every creature that creeps on the ground (Gen 7:8)
         - groupings (pairs)/gender (male and female)
   ii. clarifying comment (Gen 7:9b)

The next main unit is entitled "Narration of the Flood: Part A 'It Cometh'" (Gen 7:10–12).[5] It is identified as a rhetorical unit by virtue of its referential, situational, and structural (relational) coherence signified by there being correspondence with respect to: time (cf. Gen 7:10–12 with Gen 7:13), (b) place (cf. Gen 7:10–12 with Gen 7:13–16), (c) participants, namely Noah (Gen 7:11 cf. Gen 7:13), the Flood (Gen 7:10), and all its mechanisms (Gen 7:11–12), and (d) sameness of topic, theme, and mood, i.e., the ensuing Flood (Gen 7:10–12). In this way, the destructive capacity of the hydrologic phenomena which surrounds the Flood (Gen 7:10–12) may be compared to the salvific nature of the ark (Gen 7:7–9). This helps to differentiate this section from the preceding unit. Alongside this, Gen 7:6–9 represents "Noah's fulfillment of the divine imperative" (see Gen 7:1) while Gen 7:10 represents the "fulfillment of the divine

---

5. Some scholars choose to include Gen 7:10–12 in Gen 7:11–16 (as a unit together). See Waltke and Fredricks, *Genesis*, 138. This proposal, however, ignores the distinguishing features which mark it as an independent unit.

indicative (a promissory note) of v. 4. Noah does what God says. And God does what God says."⁶

Each of the rhetorical subunits of this portion of text are depicted below:

It Cometh! (Gen 7:1–24)

IV. Narration of the Flood: Partial Recounting of the Entry into the Ark (Gen 7:6–9)

1. initial comment (Gen 7:10)
    i. temporal clarification (Gen 7:10a)
    ii. re-statement about the Flood (Gen 7:10b)
2. second comment (Gen 7:11)
    i. temporal clarification (Gen 7:11a)
    ii. mechanical clarification (Gen 7:11b)
3. final comment (Gen 7:12)
    i. initial statement (Gen 7:12a)
    ii. temporal clarification (Gen 7:12b)

The next main rhetorical unit is entitled "Second Recounting of the Boarding of the Ark" (Gen 7:13–16).⁷ It has cohesion based upon several factors, namely sameness of: (a) time and speed of action (cf. Gen 7:13 with 7:17–20), (b) participants, i.e., Noah (Gen 7:13, 14, 15), his kin (Gen 7:13, 14, 15), and the animals (Gen 7:14, 15), (c) narratival pace and action (cf. Gen 7:13–16 with Gen 7:17–20), (d) place and space—proximity to the ark (cf. Gen 7:13–16 with Gen 7:17–20), and (e) topic and theme, i.e., the ark as a salvific vehicle that provides shelter and protection from the Flood (cf. Gen 7:13–16 with 7:17–22, 24)

Each of the rhetorical subunits of this portion of text are depicted below:

---

6. Hamilton, *Genesis 1–17*, 289.
7. Cf. Waltke and Fredricks, *Genesis*, 138; Keiser, *Genesis 1–11*, 129.

It Cometh! (Gen 7:1–24)

    V. Second Recounting of the Boarding of the Ark (Gen 7:13–16)
        1. human entry into the ark (Gen 7:13)
            i. temporal clarification (Gen 7:13a)
            ii. occupant clarification (Gen 7:13b)
        2. animal entry into the ark (Gen 7:14–16b)
            i. occupant clarification (Gen 7:14–16a)
                a. domestic beast
- groupings (pairs)/gender (male and female)

                b. everything that creeps on the earth
- groupings (pairs)/gender (male and female)

                c. everything that flies//every bird, every wing
- groupings (pairs)/gender (male and female)

            ii. theological clarification (Gen 7:16b)
        3. theological affirmation (Gen 7:16c)

The next main section is entitled "Narration of the Flood: Part B "The Waters Prevail" (Gen 7:17–24).[8] There is a pronounced change of pace in this section as the narrator severely slows the action down—repeating the essence of the Flood's onslaught and destruction three times for emphasis (Gen 7:18, 19, 20). The Flood also acts as a new participant of many of the verbs (Gen 7:17–20, 24). The referential, situational, and structural (relational) coherence of this unit is further demonstrated by sameness of: (a) place (differentiated from the previous section by the 'bird's eye' view of the ark and the Flood), participants, namely the inhabitants of the ark (Gen 7:23), all those creatures and human beings outside of it (Gen 7:21–23), and the Flood itself, a new 'actor' (see Gen 7:17–20, 24), (c) topic, theme, and mood, namely the reversal of creation (the cosmos becoming chaos), and (d) frequent word repetition throughout the unit (Gen 7:18, 19, 20, 24), that is, the waters "prevailed" (גבר).

---

8. There is a broad consensus of scholars regarding this to be a unit. See Waltke and Fredricks, *Genesis*, 139; Mathews, *Genesis 1—11:26*, 379; McKeown, *Genesis*, 58; Hamilton, *Genesis 1–17*, 295; Wenham, *Genesis 1–15*; 182; Keiser, *Genesis 1–11*, 129. Cf. Sailhamer, *Genesis*, 116.

The following schematic highlights the series of events which unfold in this account.

Series One

Initial Summative Announcement	Thus every creature that moved perished:	Gen 7:21a
Clarification and Specifics	the bird, and the cattle, and the beast, all the swarming creatures on the earth, and every human.	Gen 7:21b–d
Concluding Summative Statement	Yes! Even humans to whom GOD gave the breath of life in their nostrils. Everything that was on the dry ground died.	Gen 7:22a–b

Series Two

Initial Summative Announcement	So he wiped away every living thing which was upon the face of the ground—	Gen 7:23a–b
Clarification and Specifics	humans, beasts, moving things, even the birds of the sky,	Gen 7:23c–d
Concluding Summative Statement	they were all wiped away from the earth.	Gen 7:23e

Each of the rhetorical subunits of the above section are depicted below:

It Cometh! (Gen 7:1–24)

    VI. Narration of the Flood: Part B "The Waters Prevail" (Gen 7:17–24)

        1. the ark in relation to the Flood (Gen 7:17–18)

            i. temporal clarification (Gen 7:17a)

            ii. Ark's movement—part one (Gen 7:17b–c)

            iii. Flood devastation (Gen 7:18a–b)

            iv. Ark movement—part two (Gen 7:18c)

2. the prevailing of the Flood (Gen 7:19–20)

   i. water (Gen 7:19a)

   ii. water and the mountains (Gen 7:19b–20)

3. the consequences of the Flood (Gen 7:21–23)

   i. devastation (Gen 7:21–23e)

   ii. deliverance (Gen 7:23f–g)

4. summative comment (Gen 7:24)

   i. summative conclusion (Gen 7:24a)

   ii. temporal clarification (Gen 7:24b)

Gen 7:1–24 constitutes a rhetorical unit which ought to be differentiated from the rest of the narrative (Gen 8:1–22). The referential, situational, and structural (relational) coherence of these verses is demonstrated through recognizing the disjuncture of Gen 8:1. The flow of the account changes with the direction of the water.[9] Joseph Blenkinsopp states: "the pivot of the narrative, the *peripateia*, occurs at this point, with the flood water at its highest point . . . GOD remembered Noah, the water began to recede and the vessel was grounded on Mount Ararat."[10]

STEP TWO: DETERMINING THE RHETORICAL SITUATION

In the analysis of Gen 6:9–22 it was noted there were multiple exigencies. The primary exigence of the Flood account pertains to human "violence" (חמס). This tension, though, is not at the forefront of each of the main sections of the Noachian deluge narrative. For example, in Gen 7:1–24, the secondary tension between GOD and the Flood is at center stage. GOD must exercise complete control over the water so as to: (1) ensure judgment flows effectively from his hand, and (2) ensure the safety and preservation of all those whom he wishes to save on earth.

The tension between judgment and salvation was (mostly) muted in the analysis of Gen 6:9–22 because no rain had yet appeared (see Gen 6:13, 17). The balance between judgment and salvation is noted at four different intervals in Gen 7:1–24. The first instance occurs prior to the

---

9. See Mathews, *Genesis 1—11:26*, 382.
10. Blenkinsopp, *Creation*, 142.

Flood event (Gen 7:1–4). At this time, Yahweh commanded Noah (and company) to enter the ark (Gen 7:1–3). GOD was about to send forty days and forty nights of rain and "blot out every living thing" he had made from upon the face of the ground (Gen 7:4). The hope of salvation, however, is also made clear (Gen 7:5).[11]

The second instance is a restatement. The text reads: "the Flood waters came upon the earth" (Gen 7:6). Those select few individuals and animals appointed for salvation then entered the ark (the mechanism of salvation) as GOD had commanded Noah (Gen 7:7–9). The third occurrence provides more details. The narrator underscores the means of judgment, noting the Flood waters were upon the earth (Gen 7:10), the fountains of the great deep had burst open (Gen 7:11), the windows of heaven were opened (Gen 7:11), and the rain fell upon the earth for forty days and forty nights (Gen 7:12). The text also makes clear Noah and company safely entered the ark—indeed, the LORD himself shut them in (Gen 7:13–16).

The fourth, final occurrence follows a somewhat different pattern. The text explains how the water rose and bore up the ark so it was raised from above the earth (Gen 7:17) and how the ark went on the surface of the water (Gen 7:18). This note signifies the safety of the inhabitants from crashing. Noah and company were "in good hands" despite the absence of rudder or sail.[12]

In contrast to this, three times it is explicitly noted how the waters prevailed (see Gen 7:18–20).

In the end, "Noah was the only remnant, alongside those with him in the ark" (Gen 7:23).

It seems; therefore, it is the "picture of Noah's salvation the author wants his readers to take a long look at."[13] The rest of the text (Gen 7:17–24) continues to place great emphasis on judgment (Gen 7:21–23). The account closes on the sober note: "the waters prevailed upon the earth one hundred and fifty days" (Gen 7:24).

Concerning the secondary exigence between GOD and Noah and the covenant, "the future of salvation history" depends on the survival of Noah and company.[14] The question remains:

---

11. See Harper, "It's All In The Name," 42.
12. Cf. McKeown, *Genesis*, 58–59.
13. See Sailhamer, *Pentateuch*, 124.
14. Waltke and Fredricks, *Genesis*, 123. See also McKeown, *Genesis*, 56.

It Cometh!

Can Noah count on God? God calls upon Noah to trust him to keep his threat to wipe out the earth and his promise to preserve him, his family, and the life of all that breathes. If the Lord does not send the threatened Flood . . . [a]nd if God does not keep his promise to preserve Noah and his family through the Flood, their faithful service is in vain. The plot develops as the . . . covenant partners commit themselves to one another.[15]

In the last chapter's analysis, Noah's complete obedience was underscored (Gen 6:22). A similar pattern emerges at the end of this (second) divine speech as well (Gen 7:5).

Referent	Hebrew
Gen 6:22	ויעש נח ככל אשר צוה אתו אלהים כן עשה
Gen 7:5	ויעש נח ככל אשר צוהו יהוה

As Collins states, "On the literary side, the linguistic peak often has some bearing on the resolution of the central conflict of the narrative."[16] Here, "the reiteration of Noah's obedience (7:5) confirms that he has fulfilled his part of the covenant stipulations and now he can do no more than wait for God to provide the protection that he has promised."[17] The text further underscores Noah's obedience and how everyone entered the ark (Gen 7:7–9, 13–14, 15–16).

Turning from exigence to audience, the virtues of fidelity to God is made explicit for "only Noah was left, together with those that were with him in the ark" (Gen 7:23b). In this way, "the author's point could not be clearer. Obedience to God's will is the way to salvation."[18] Arguably, "Noah's behavior contrasts with that of Adam, who lost the protective environment . . . through disobedience. Noah through obedience receives protection."[19]

---

15. Waltke and Fredricks, *Genesis*, 123.
16. Collins, *Reading Genesis Well*, 166.
17. See McKeown, *Genesis*, 57.
18. Sailhamer, "Genesis," 125.
19. McKeown, *Genesis*, 57.

STEP THREE: DETERMINING THE RHETORICAL STRATEGY

This step involves determining and assessing the rhetorical strategies governing the rhetorical units. As in the preceding chapter, the analysis will begin with a fresh, English translation alongside a commentary of grammatical/syntactical features (including text criticism issues).

The analysis will be divided into the main subunits of step one, namely: (I) "Divine Speech 'Enter!'" (Gen 7:1–4), (II) "Narratival Comments Concerning Noah's Obedience" (Gen 7:5), (III) "Initial Recounting of the Entry into the Ark" (Gen 7:6–9), (IV) "Narration of the Flood: Part A 'It Cometh,'" (Gen 7:10–12), (V) "Second Recounting of the Boarding of the Ark" (Gen 7:13–16), and (VI) "Narration of the Flood: Part B 'The Waters Prevail'" (Gen 7:17–24).

I. *Divine Speech "Enter!" (Gen 7:1–4)*

ᵃויאמר ᵇיהוה לנח

בא ᶜאתה ᵈוכל ביתך אל התבה ᵉכי ᶠאתך ראיתי צדיק ᵍלפני בדור הזה

מכל הבהמה הטהורה תקח לך שבעה ʰאיש שבעה ⁱואשתו

ʲומן הבהמה אשר לא טהרה ᵏהוא ˡשנים איש ᵐואשתו

ⁿגם מעוף השמים שבעה שבעה זכר ונקבה

לחיות זרע על פני כל הארץ

ᵒכי לימים עוד שבעה אנכי ממטיר על הארץ ארבעים יום וארבעים לילה

ᵖומחיתי את כל ᵍהיקום אשר עשיתי מעל פני האדמה

Then the LORD said to Noah:
"Go—you and all your house—into the ark!
For you have I seen as just before me in this generation.
From all the clean beasts, take with you seven pairs
    —a male and his mate.
Also, from the beast which is not clean, (take) a pair
    —a male and his mate.

It Cometh!   139

Even from the birds of the sky (take) a pair—male and female—in order to keep seed alive upon the face of the earth.
For in seven days I will cause it to rain upon the earth forty and forty nights.
Thus I will blot out every living thing that I have made from upon the face of the ground."

---

a. Narratival *waw*. See *GBHS* §3.5.1.c. Cf. Chisholm, *Exegesis*, 120 (introductory *waw*).

b. Note: the SamPent reads "God" while the LXX reads "LORD God." See Wenham, *Genesis 1–15*, 153. Wevers states: "in view of Gen's apparent indifference with respect to the divine name its double name is text critically of little use." Wevers, *Greek Text of Genesis*, 89.

c. The use of the personal pronoun "is not pleonastic or emphatic; it serves merely to represent the referent of the pronoun as the chief actor among other actors." *IBHS* §16.3.2.c.

d. Synchronic *waw*. Chisholm, *Exegesis*, 126.

e. Causal conjunction. *GBHS* §4.3.4.a; Williams, *Hebrew Syntax*, §444.

f. The direct object is placed first for emphasis. See Wenham, *Genesis 1–15*, 153. For more details concerning the use of fronting here (constituent focus) consult *BHRG* §47.2.2.a.

g. The compound preposition is perceptual (evaluative discernment). Williams, *Hebrew Syntax*, §372; *GBHS* §4.1.11.c. Cf. *IBHS* §11.3.1.a (referential).

h. On the distributive use of numbers here, see *IBHS* §7.2.3, 16.6c, 39.3.2a; Joüon §142p. One scholar states "[s]even seven . . . presumably means seven pairs." Bandstra, *Handbook*, 384. Cf. GKC §134.q.

i. This coordinative *waw* joins opposites. Williams, *Hebrew Syntax*, §430a and §431. Note: given these terms usually refer to human beings, "the versions rejected the isolated metaphorical terms in favor of the discriminatory ones." Tal, *BHQ* 95.

j. Synchronic *waw*. Chisholm, *Exegesis*, 126. Partitive preposition. *GBHS* §4.1.13.f.

k. The retrospective pronoun is usually added in negative sentences. GKC §138b.

l. Note: "the versions repeat the number . . . in order to stress the distributive." Tal, *BHQ*, 95.

m. This coordinative *waw* joins opposites. Williams, *Hebrew Syntax*, §430a and §431.

n. Note: the Syriac and LXX discriminate between "clean" and "unclean" birds. Tal, *BHQ*, 95; Wevers, *Notes on the Greek Text of Genesis*, 90.

o. Causal conjunction. *GBHS* §4.3.4.a; Williams, *Hebrew Syntax*, §444.

p. Consequential *waw*. Chisholm, *Exegesis*, 132; *GBHS* §3.5.1.b. See also *IBHS* §37.7.2.a.

q. This is a rare word that occurs only here and two other places (Gen 7:23; Deut 11:6). It indicates "living form," "substance," or "existence." *DCH* 4:273; *HALOT* 1:430; Coppes, *TWOT* 2:793; Brensinger, *NIDOTTE* 2:519.

Extended Analysis:

Divine speeches dominate the beginning of the Flood narrative (Gen 6:13–21 and Gen 7:1–4; cf. Gen 6:7).[20] While the preface of the speech (Gen 7:1a) clarifies the interlocutor and the recipient (cf. Gen 6:13), it differs from it in the way it refers to the Deity.[21]

Referent	Hebrew
Gen 6:13	ויאמר אלהים לנח
Gen 7:1a	ויאמר יהוה לנח

Those who perceive a doublet in the text often appeal to this type of phenomenon in order to support their case, i.e., the scribe of one of the Flood stories (J) uses only the *tetragrammaton* in reference to the Deity (see Gen 7:1) while the scribe of the other Flood story (P) uses only *elohim* to refer to the Deity (see Gen 6:13).[22] ANE literature, however, reveals deities were often referred to by more than one name in accounts having no record of being compiled from "interwoven source documents."[23] Theme (mood) and context seem to drive the usage of divine epithets in the HB/OT rather than divergent sources.[24]

While not identical, the divine speeches make essentially the same point: humanity is so evil God has resolved to destroy the earth.

20. Harper, "It's All In The Name," 42.
21. Hamilton, *Genesis 1–17*, 285.
22. See Hamilton, *Genesis 1–17*, 285.
23. Steinmann, *Genesis*, 12. See too Shaviv, "Flood," 527–31.
24. Hamilton suggests the *tetragrammaton* only occurs where there is "special reason" for it, i.e., when the thematic participant is Yahweh himself. Hamilton, *Genesis 1–17*, 286. Others argue: "the more generic name *Elohim* is often used to emphasize God's general relationship to his creatures" and "God's proper name *Yahweh* highlights his covenant relationship with individuals and groups." Steinmann, *Genesis*, 12. The *tetragrammaton* might occur in Gen 7:1 due to its close proximity and relationship to Gen 6:18–20. Cf. Longacre, "Discourse Structure," 235–62; Wenham, "Pentateuchal Source Criticism," 87. For a different perspective, see Friedman, *Sources Revealed*, 42.

"Paradoxically, nothing is to be lost, representatives of everything are to be saved."[25] In this particular divine speech (Gen 7:1-4), however, in inverse to the preceding divine speech (Gen 6:13-21), "the motivating problems are only implicit and the emphasis is on salvation: the righteousness of Noah, the preservation of seed."[26]

Noah's household is repeatedly defined throughout the Flood as being comprised of himself, his three sons, Shem, Ham, and Japheth, his wife, and his three daughter-in-laws (Gen 6:18, 7:7, 13, 8:16, 18).[27] In the first portion of the second divine speech (Gen 7:1), however, the text is abbreviated to the command for Noah "and all his household" to enter the ark without the explicit delineation of who such members are (cf. Gen 7:13). It seems a principle of solidarity is being employed where the members are subsumed under the patriarchal figure-head.[28] The text seems to insinuate Noah's righteousness is why his immediate household are able to be included (see Gen 7:1; cf. Ezek 14:14, 20).[29] As one scholar puts it: "we are told for the first time explicitly that the salvation of Noah and his family is due to his virtuous character."[30]

In another divine speech (Gen 6:13-21), Noah was instructed to take (only) two of every kind of animal (see Gen 6:19-20). In this speech (Gen 7:1-4), the LORD required seven pairs of each type of "clean" (טהור) animal.[31] Alongside this, Noah must also be sure to include a pair—a male and his mate—of every kind of animal that is not clean to come aboard the ark (Gen 7:2-3).[32] The text notably avoids using the word for "unclean" (טמא).[33]

The reason for this final set of instructions remains uncertain.[34] It is possible "the purpose of the larger number is to provide animals for

---

25. Harper, "It's All In The Name," 42.

26. Harper, "It's All In The Name," 42.

27. Arnold, *Genesis*, 102.

28. See Steinberg, "Genesis," 286-88.

29. See McKeown, *Genesis*, 56.

30. Mathews, *Genesis 1—11:26*, 370. See also Skinner, *Genesis*, 152.

31. For lexical details, see *DCH* 3:343; *HALOT* 1:369-70; Averbeck, *NIDOTTE* 2:338-53, 4:477-86.

32. For details concerning the rendering "a male and his mate" see Joüon §145a. For more grammatical information about the clause itself, see DG §49.b.

33. Notably, humans were commanded not to eat any type of meat before the Flood (cf. Gen 1:29; 9:4).

34. Those scholars who adhere to doublets within the Flood narrative "find further

sacrifice or food without wiping out the species."³⁵ If one reads Gen 6:19–20 as a general statement and the keyword as a "collective for pairs," the contradiction between the texts disappears.³⁶ This communicates God's care for creation since the animals receive the same level of compassion as Noah does. "If nothing else, their inclusion in those who are delivered is partial confirmation of the fact that in the OT 'sinful' is not normally a synonym for 'unclean,' especially in the cultic sections of the OT."³⁷

The function of the seven days is unclear. As such, it goes beyond the text to assume the animals occupied the ark for the duration of the seven days or that seven days were required for all the animals to be accommodated on board.³⁸ Orchestrating ways to wrangle the animals onto the ark are also unnecessary (see Gen 7:15). Notably, the Gilgamesh Epic reckons only seven days to build a craft of a much different scale and a Flood that lasts only seven days.³⁹

Forty is a conventional number for "a long time" (Ex 24:18; Num 13:25; 1 Sam 17:16; 1 Kgs 19:8) and possibly representing the introduction of "a new age" (Gen 25:20; 26:34; cf. Acts 1:3).⁴⁰ Forty is associated with hardship, affliction, punishment, and judgment (Ezek 4:6; cf. Jonah 3:4 and Matt 4:2).⁴¹ Given such, some scholars assert the usage of a "preferred number" indicates that it is not "purely rational" math.⁴² Clearly, the Flood's function was to destroy all life—blotting out every living thing that God made via forty days and forty nights of "rain."⁴³

---

support for their position in the fact that two different numbers of animals are cited here." Hamilton, *Genesis 1–17*, 287.

35. McKeown, *Genesis*, 57. One notes, however, that the animals are boarded according to their kind(s) and not according to species. See Wood and Murray, *Pattern of Life*. Cf. Goldingay, *Genesis*, 132; Collins, *Reading Genesis Well*, 278.

36. See Hamilton, *Genesis 1–17*, 287; Mathews, *Genesis 1—11:26*, 371; Walton, *Genesis*, 315–16; Hartley, *Genesis*, 100–101, 107. Cf. Arnold, *Genesis*, 102–3. Since "seven-seven" is qualified as male and female, only seven pairs match the description and line up with the grammatical use of distributives used here to express pairing. So TNIV, NIV 2011, HCSB, RSV, NRSV, NLT, NCV, ESV, NET, CEB. Contra NIV 1984, KJV, NKJV, NASB.

37. See Hamilton, *Genesis 1–17*, 288.

38. See Mathews, *Genesis 1—11:26*, 374. Cf. Waltke and Fredricks, *Genesis*, 138.

39. See Smith, *Babylon*, 512–16. Cf. Blenkinsopp, *Creation*, 139.

40. Waltke and Fredricks, *Genesis*, 138. See too Sarna, *Genesis*, 54.

41. See Ryken et al., eds., *DBI*, 305; Hodge, *Days of Genesis*, 150–52.

42. See Hill, "Numbers of Genesis," 243. Cf. Waltke and Fredricks, *Genesis*, 138.

43. This word refers to a "regular rainfall. It is not normally a torrential downpour.

II. *Narratival Comments Concerning Noah's Obedience (Gen 7:5)*

ויעשׂ נחa בּככלb אשׁר צוהו יהוה

So Noah did according to all that the LORD commanded him.

---

a. Summarizing or concluding *waw*. Chisholm, *Exegesis*, 123.
b. The preposition denotes "agreement between trajector x and landmark y." *BHRG* §39.10.

Extended Analysis

As in the previous speech, an imperative is given to Noah by GOD (Gen 6:13–21; 7:1–4). The text then records Noah's fulfillment of the divine command (Gen 6:22; 7:5).[44] Given the text offers only one verse concerning the construction and preparation of the ark for entry (Gen 6:22) but devotes a considerable amount more space to reiterate all of the personnel who are to board the ark (Gen 7:1–4), it is reasonable to conclude "the narrator wishes to insist that the latter events were much more important than the actual building of the ark."[45] Hamilton contends:

> Presumably the writer could have supplied myriads of details about Noah's erection of the ark and the assembling of the animals, but he did not. Noah's rather long and complicated exploits are condensed into these words: he did it! Not a note about his expertise in construction and zoology. By condensing Noah's considerable achievements into an unbelievably skeletal statement, the author concentrates on one fact only, Noah's obedience to and successful completion of the divine mandate.[46]

What makes this storm so potent is that it is to last forty days and nights." Hamilton, *Genesis 1–17*, 288. Cf. Goldingay, *Genesis*, 133; Wenham, *Genesis 1–15*, 181. For further lexical information, see *DCH* 5:240–41; Futato, *NIDOTTE* 1:900–902.

44. Hamilton, *Genesis 1–17*, 288.
45. Wenham, *Genesis 1–15*, 178.
46. Hamilton, *Genesis 1–17*, 288.

The refrains are turning points in the "developing story line" indicating "the flood will only take place upon Noah's faithful completion of the assigned tasks."[47]

III. Initial Recounting of the Entry into the Ark (Gen 7:6–9)

ᵃונח בן שש מאות שנה ᵇוהמבול ᶜהיה מים על הארץ

ᵈויבא נח ᵉובניו ואשתו ונשי בניו אתו אל התבה מפני מי המבול

מן הבהמה הטהורה ומן הבהמה אשר איננה טהרה ומן העוף

ᶠוכל אשר רמש על התבה שנים שנים באו אל נח אל האדמה

זכר ᵍונקבה כאשר צוה אלהים את נח

Now Noah was six hundred years old when the waters came upon the earth.
Then Noah, his sons, his wife, and his son's wives with him went into the ark in order to escape the waters of the Flood.ʰ
From the clean beast, from the beast that is not clean, and from the bird, from every creature that moves on the ground, by pairs they went with Noah into the ark—male and female—as God commanded Noah.

---

a. Introductory (disjunctive) *waw*. Chisholm, *Exegesis*, 124. Cf. *GBHS* §3.5.1.c (narratival *waw*). See too\ Joüon §166g. (observation *waw*).

b. See GKC §164a for further information on the temporal nature of this disjunctive clause.

c. The verb carries the nuance "to come." BDB 225. Note: though the disjunctive *zâqēph qāṭôn* here makes the following phrase become appositional to the previous one, the LXX puts the phrase in the genitive, i.e., "flood of waters." See Tal, *BHQ*, 95; Wevers, *Notes on the Greek Text of Genesis*, 92.

d. Sequential *waw*. *GBHS* §3.5.1.a. Cf. Chisholm, *Exegesis*, 124 (consequential *waw*).

e. This *waw* (and the following two) show accompaniment. Williams, *Hebrew Syntax*, §436; *GBHS* §4.3.3.e.

f. Summarizing or concluding *waw*. Chisholm, *Exegesis*, 123

g. This coordinative *waw* joins opposites. Williams, *Hebrew Syntax*, §430a and §431.

47. Mathews, *Genesis 1:1—11:26*, 373.

h. Hebrew reads "from before the face of the waters of the Flood." A precedent for the English translation of "escape" is found in the NIV 1984, NIV 2011, NRSV, NJB, and the GNB. Other EVV render the clause as causal, i.e., "because of the waters" (see AV, NASB, NJPS, NAB).

Extended Analysis

The general statement "Noah did according to all that the LORD had commanded him" (Gen 7:5) is particularized in these verses which detail the occupant's entry into the ark (Gen 7:6–9).[48] It is written Noah was "six hundred years of age" when the Flood came.[49] This is noteworthy since the Flood is the only event in Genesis dated so precisely. While other chronologies in Scripture include regnal years, earthquakes, and such, here it is the age of Noah himself—a prominent patriarchal figure.[50] It is not by chance the rain fell "precisely on the day GOD had forewarned one week earlier (v. 4). Noah's confidence is not misplaced."[51]

The initial recounting of the entry into the ark (Gen 7:7–9) proceeds logically from the divine imperative to enter the ark (Gen 7:1). The text reads as though "they scramble on board just 'before the waters of the flood,'" adding an element of suspense to the narrative.[52] Noting each specific occupant boarding the vessel, i.e., Noah, his sons, his wife, his son's wives, clean animals, animals that are not clean, and every moving thing (Gen 7:7–8), underscores GOD the Creator's desire to save every form of life. The fact the animals were male and female (Gen 7:9) brings fecundity to mind and the hope of offspring (cf. Gen 1:20–22, 24–30 and 7:3).

---

48. Hamilton, *Genesis 1–17*, 288.

49. "Literally, 'in the year of six-hundred, the year': with compound numbers 'year' can be repeated" (cf. GKC 1340). Goldingay, *Genesis*, 133. For more details on the idiom for age with respect to Noah, see *IBHS* §9.5.3.b.

50. Wenham, *Genesis 1–15*, 178–79.

51. Mathews, Genesis 1:1—11:26, 374.

52. Mathews, Genesis 1:1—11:26, 374.

IV. *Narration of the Flood: Part A "It Cometh" (Gen 7:10–12)*

^aויהי לשבעת הימים ^bומי המבול היו על הארץ

בשנת ^cשש מאות^d לחיי נח בחדש השני בשבעה עשר יום שנה ^eלחדש

ביום הזה נבקעו כל מעינת תהום רבה ^fוארבת השמים נפתחו

^gויהי הגשם על הארץ ארבעים יום ^hוארבעים ⁱלילה

Now seven days passed.
Then the Flood waters were upon the earth.
In the six hundredth year of Noah's life, in the second month, on the
    seventeenth day of the month, on that day, all the fountains of the great
    deep burst open and the windows of heaven were opened.
At the same time, the rain was upon the earth
    —forty days and forty nights.

---

a. Introductory *waw*. Chisholm, *Exegesis*, 120. Cf. *GBHS* §3.5.1.c (narratival *waw*).
b. Dramatic *waw*. Chisholm, *Exegesis*, 126.
c. Note: SamPent and LXX "prefer the determined numeral, in line with Lev 25:11" where the MT "also has the determined form." Tal, *BHQ* 95.
d. Such repetition is not unusual in this type of construction. See GKC §134o; Joüon §142o.
e. This preposition and the one following are temporal. Williams, *Hebrew Syntax*, §241.
f. Note: LXX makes the Flood "exactly one year long (cf. 8:14)." Tal, *BHQ* 95, 96.
g. Synchronic *waw*. Chisholm, *Exegesis*, 126.
h. This coordinative *waw* joins opposites. Williams, *Hebrew Syntax*, §430a and §431.
i. On the use of plurals here for singular numbers, see Hamilton, *Genesis 1–17*, 290.

Extended Analysis:

The text twice notes Noah was six hundred years of age when the Flood began (Gen 7:6, 11). Some scholars suggest (60 x 10) "was considered

It Cometh!

to be a perfect number in the sexagesimal system, and was symbolic of Noah's perfection as a person."[53] In a similar manner, one individual states: "it has been suggested that an age of 600 years may be related to the Sumerian *ner* which equals 600 . . . a learned loan word in Babylonian, or to Ziusudra, who according to one tradition ruled 600 *ner* until the flood came . . . but this may be just coincidence."[54]

While this connection may be stimulating to consider, it is difficult to construe any significance beyond the ordinary in terms of why the Flood would have been said to have occurred not just in the six hundredth year of Noah's life but also, specifically, in "the second month, on the seventeenth day of the month, on the same day" (Gen 7:11). As it stands, the precise significance of many of the chronological details of the Flood remain an enigma.[55]

With respect to the specific mechanics concerning the Flood, there are many mysteries. Though it is written "all the springs belonging to the great deep were broken up," no scholarly consensus exists as to what those "springs" are.[56] One scholar suggests "geysers" which spray up from "wells deep underground."[57] The same sort of challenges arise concerning the so-called "great deep."[58] In any case, the "floodgates of the sky" work alongside and with these diverse machinations to provide the engine for the Flood.[59]

Whatever the mechanics involved, the "the cosmic phenomena described . . . represents a reversal of creation, or 'uncreation' as it has been

53. Hill, "Numbers of Genesis," 247.

54. Wenham, *Genesis 1–15*, 179.

55. For more details in this regard, see Davidson and Turner, *Manifold Beauty*, 128–33; Wenham, *Genesis 1–15*, 178–81; Barré, "Flood Chronology," 3–20; Sarna, *Genesis*, 376. Cf. Boyd and Snelling, eds., *Chronology*, 189–298.

56. For more details, see *DCH* 5:397; *HALOT* 1:612; Beyer, *NIDOTTE* 2:1018–19.

57. Miller, *Complete Guide to the Bible*, 14.

58. Though traditionally understood to be derived from Tiamat of the Babylonian Enuma Elish, the term indicates: (i) the primeval ocean which surrounded the earth at the beginning of the creation week (see Gen 1:2), (ii) subterranean waters, i.e., the lower parts of a so-called three storied universe, or (iii) a (poetical) term for the open sea. See *DCH* 8:593–94. For information against the Babylonian connection, see Heidel, *Babylonian Genesis*, 98–101; Tsumura, *Creation and Destruction*, 36–53. For other lexical details, see *DCH* 7:552–53; *HALOT* 2:1690–91; Grisanti, *NIDOTTE* 4:275–77; Hasel, "Fountains of the Great Deep," 67–72; Hasel "Biblical View," 77–95; Wolde, "Creation out of Nothing, 157–76; Collins, *Reading Genesis Well*, 166.

59. See *Journal of the Creation Theology Society* (2022) for more information on these different aspects,

called . . . as the sky dome was created to keep the heavenly waters from falling to earth (1:6–7), here the opened 'windows of the heavens' reverse that created function (7:11). When the 'fountains of the great deep [*tĕhôm*]' burst forth (7:11), the cosmic order that had been fashioned from water chaos returns to watery chaos."[60] The effect of sin is clear—the cosmos is now chaos once again.

V. *Second Recounting of the Boarding of the Ark (Gen 7:13–16)*

בעצם היום הזה[a]

בא נח [b]ושם וחם ויפת בני נח ואשת נח [c]ושלשת נשי בניו אתם אל התבה

המה וכל החיה למינה וכל הבהמה למינה וכל הרמש הרמש על הארץ למינהו

וכל העוף למינהו כל צפור כל כנף

[d]ויבאו אל נח אל התבה שנים שנים מכל הבשר אשר בו רוח חיים

[e]והבאים זכר [f]ונקבה מכל בשר באו כאשר צוה אתו אלהים

[g]ויסגר יהוה בעדו

On that very same day, Noah, Shem, Ham, and Japheth, the sons of Noah, and
  Noah's wife, and the three wives of his sons, with them, entered the ark.
Them and every living animal after its kind—including every kind of domestic
  beast, alongside every moving thing that moves on the earth after its kind,
  and everything that flies after its kind: every bird—every wing.
They came with Noah into the ark,[h]
  pairs of every creature in which there was the breath of life. Those that
  entered, male and female of all life, went in, coming just as God had commanded him.
Then the LORD shut them in.

---

a. On the use of substantives to represent pronominal ideas (here understood to be a metaphor to communicate the idea of "self same/very same"), see GKC §139g; Joüon §147a.

60. Arnold, *Genesis*, 103.

b. This *waw* (and the ones that follow unless indicated otherwise) signify accompaniment. Williams, *Hebrew Syntax*, §436; *GBHS* §4.3.3.e.

c. The construction of the numerals is rare. GKC §97c; Wenham, *Genesis 1–15*, 182.

d. Summarizing or concluding *waw*. Chisholm, *Exegesis*, 123.

e. Summarizing or concluding *waw*. Chisholm, *Exegesis*, 123.

f. This coordinative *waw* joins opposites. Williams, *Hebrew Syntax*, §430a and §431.

g. Sequential *waw*. See *GBHS* §3.5.1.a; Chisholm, *Exegesis*, 120.

h. The preposition either is spatially terminative (see *GBHS* §4.1.2.a; Williams, *Hebrew Syntax*, §298) or shows accompaniment (Williams, *Hebrew Syntax*, §304). The translation can thus be "they came with Noah into the ark" or "they came to Noah inside the ark." Hamilton, *Genesis 1–17*, 291.

Extended Analysis:

This passage differs from the first entry with respect to its tone, detail, and pacing. The narrative is slowed down. This enables one to appreciate the grandeur of the acts of GOD in imparting his salvation.[61] It is interesting how the text makes explicit the fact that the wife of Noah entered the ark (Gen 7:13).[62] Elsewhere, the name Noah is not mentioned. It is either "his wife" (Gen 7:7, 8:18) or "your wife" (Gen 6:18, 8:16). It is thus possible the text is seeking to draw attention to Noah himself or, perhaps, the import of his name "rest."[63] Alongside this, there is no differentiation between clean and so-called unclean animals.[64] In sum, Wenham states:

> The entry into the ark is here described again (cf, vv 7–9), but with extra details giving the whole occasion a 'festive tone' as befits an act which marks one of the turning points in human history. Noah's great act of obedience not merely saved himself

61. Sailhamer, "Genesis," 125. See too Sailhamer, *Pentateuch*, 126.

62. While scholasticism offers over one hundred possible names for Noah's wife, "some rabbinical legends tell us that Noah's wife was called Naamah because her deeds were pleasant. These legends also tell of another Naamah whose name means 'great singer.' The name, a variation of the name Naomi (which means 'sweet' or 'pleasant') is usually given three syllables (Na-ah-mah or Nay-ah-mah)." See Bartoletti, *Naamah and the Ark at Night*, no pages. Cf. Dalton, *Children's Bibles in America*, 203.

63. See Wenham, *Genesis 1–15*, 182; See Bartoletti, *Naamah and the Ark at Night*, no pages.

64. For details as to how this concerns 'J' and 'P' sources, see Blenkinsopp, *Creation*, 139–40.

but made possible the new world order, whose safety would be guaranteed by covenant. These verses thus portray the founders of the new humanity and new animal kingdom processing in a double column into the ark. As each group embarks, its name is called and recorded for posterity.[65]

GOD is keen to offer his aid to all whom he wishes to save—the one door being a token. One scholar goes so far as to call it "[a]n act of paternal love."[66] In the Babylonian account of the great Deluge, the flood hero, Uta-napishti, closed the hatch.[67]

VI. *Narration of the Flood: Part B "The Waters Prevail" (Gen 7:17–24)*

[a]ויהי המבול ארבעים יום על הארץ [b]וירבו המים [c]וישאו את התבה

[d]ותרם מעל הארץ [e]ויגברו המים [f]וירבו מאד על הארץ [g]ותלך התבה על פני המים

[h]והמים גברו מאד [i]מאד על הארץ [j]ויכסו כל ההרים הגבהים אשר תחת כל השמים

חמש עשרה אמה [k]מלמעלה גברו המים [l]ויכסו ההרים [m]ויגוע כל בשר הרמש על הארץ

בעוף [n]ובבהמה ובחיה ובכל השרץ השרץ על הארץ וכל האדם

כל אשר נשמת רוח חיים באפיו מכל אשר בחרבה מתו

[o]וימח את כל היקום אשר על פני האדמה מאדם עד בהמה עד רמש [p]ועד עוף השמים

[q]וימחו מן הארץ

[r]וישאר אך נח [s]ואשר אתו [t]בתבה

[u]ויגברו המים על הארץ חמשים [v]ומאת יום

Now the Flood lasted forty days upon the earth.
The waters increased—they bore up the ark.
Then it (the ark) was raised from

---

65. Wenham, *Genesis 1–15*, 181.
66. Okoye, *Genesis 1–11*, 104.
67. See George, *Gilgamesh*, 91; Sargent, "Wind, Water, and Battle Imagery," 153; Wenham, *Rethinking Genesis*, 50.

> above the earth; the waters prevailed.
>> In fact, they increased greatly upon the earth.
>> Thus the ark went on the face of the water.
> Alongside this, the waters continued to prevail—they were exceedingly great on the earth—so great as to cover all the high mountains that were under all the heavens. Fifteen cubits from above the waters prevailed.
> Then the mountains were covered.
> Thus every creature that moved on the earth perished: the birds, the cattle, the beasts, all the swarming creatures that swarm on the earth, even every human. Yes! Even people to whom GOD gave the breath of life in their nostrils. Everything on the dry ground, died.
> So he wiped away every living thing which was upon the face of the ground–from humans, beasts, moving things, and the birds of the sky.
>> They were wiped away from the earth.
> Thus Noah was the only remnant, alongside those with him in the ark.
> So the waters prevailed over the earth one hundred and fifty days.

---

a. Narratival *waw*. See *GBHS* §3.5.1.c. Cf. Chisholm, *Exegesis*, 120 (introductory *waw*).

b. Sequential *waw*. *GBHS* §3.5.1.a; Chisholm, *Exegesis*, 120.

c. Consequential *waw*. *GBHS* §3.5.1.b.

d. Sequential *waw*. See *GBHS* §3.5.1.a; Chisholm, *Exegesis*, 120.

e. Sequential *waw*. See *GBHS* §3.5.1.a; Chisholm, *Exegesis*, 120.

f. Explicative *waw*. Williams *Hebrew Syntax*, §434.

g. Consequential *waw*. *GBHS* §3.5.1.b.

h. Synchronic *waw*. Chisholm, *Exegesis*, 126.

i. The intensification of attributes by means of repetition is for rhetorical emphasis. GKC §133k.

j. This *waw* is considered "complex" with respect to aspect. See *IBHS* §33.3.1.a.

k. "The local extent of a verbal action can ... stand as an accusative of place" (so *IBHS* §10.2.2.b), an accusative of extent (so GKC §118h; Wenham, *Genesis 1–15*, 153), or, alternatively, one may view this clause as "an accusative of measure." Joüon §126j.

l. Sequential *waw*. *GBHS* §3.5.1.a. Cf. Chisholm, *Exegesis*, 124 (consequential waw).

m. Consequential *waw*. *GBHS* §3.5.1.b.

n. This waw and the ones which follow (unless indicated otherwise) are coordinative *waws*. Williams, *Hebrew Syntax*, §430a.

o. Sequential *waw*. *GBHS* §3.5.1.a. Cf. Chisholm, *Exegesis*, 124 (consequential *waw*).

p. Coordinative *waw*. Williams, *Hebrew Syntax*, §430a.

q. Summarizing *waw*. Chisholm, *Exegesis*, 123.

r. Concluding *waw*. Chisholm, *Exegesis*, 123.

s. Coordinative *waw*. Williams, *Hebrew Syntax*, §430a.

t. Note: 4Q370 (column I, line 6) adds "'the mighty ones' to the list of those who perished" providing "a separate clause for 'the mighty ones,' emphasizing their death . . . (and the giants did not escape.)" Lyon, *Qumran Interpretation*, 117–18, 144. Cf. 1 En 89:5–6; Sir 16:7; Wis 14:6–7; 3 Macc 2:4. For more details concerning this, including other mythological, i.e., fantastic, creatures on Noah's ark, please see Shemesh, "Religious Literature," 235–55.

u. Summarizing or concluding *waw*. Chisholm, *Exegesis*, 123.

v. Coordinative *waw*. Williams, *Hebrew Syntax*, §430a.

Extended Analysis

This marks the climax (or peak) of the narrative.[68] It is the "zone of maximum linguistic turbulences—that is, there are [significant] textual devices that draw attention to the event."[69] It is written (Gen 7:17–24) the Flood came upon the earth and the water increased (Gen 7:17) and (four times!) "the water prevailed" (Gen 7:18, 19, 20, 24). The term "prevail" is being used here in the military sense ('triumphed').[70] Another scholar states: "Gen portrays the waters . . . battling against life . . . on earth and emerging victorious."[71]

As Keiser states, these sections "provide descriptions of the flood using recapitulation, that is, each section picking up the narrative at a point in time in the midst of the prior section, but carrying the narrative further forward."[72] The text communicates sin's import and GOD's judgment. When GOD created the world, he separated the waters above from

---

68. Mathews, *Genesis 1—11:26*, 354; Wenham, *Genesis 1–15*, 183; Licht, *Storytelling in the Bible*, 113–14.

69. Collins, *Reading Genesis Well*, 163.

70. See Wenham, *Genesis 1–15*, 150, 82–83; Waltke and Fredricks, *Genesis*, 140; Sargent, "Wind, Water, and Battle Imagery," 81.

71. Wevers, *Genesis*, 97.

72. Keiser, *Genesis 1–11*, 129.

the waters below (see Gen 1:6–7). "Now, in an act of uncreation, he reverses the process and returns all to *tohu wa-bohu* (watery wilderness!)."[73]

The "drenching" or "covering" of the mountains could also represent a type of spiritual conquest over the powers that presumably lived there since the Sumerians considered their temples (ziggurats) to be "mountains," É. kur, or a "house of the mountain/mountain house."[74]

That the water prevailed an additional fifteen cubits, that is, approximately seven meters or just over twenty two feet (half the height of the ark) upward indicates the ark would have been safe from scraping bottom while floating above the waters.[75] This communicates not only the sovereignty and wisdom of GOD but also his compassion for the life aboard the ark.

Strikingly, "the sequence of annihilation, 'birds, domestic animals, wild animals, all swarming creatures that swarm on the earth, and all human beings' (7:21), follows closely that of creation itself in Gen 1:1—2:3."[76] The Creator who first gave the breath of life (Gen 2:7) now removes it (Gen 7:22).[77] In the words of one scholar, "the narrator's camera lingers longest over the destruction of life by the flood."[78] Another individual puts it: "we see water everywhere, as though the world had reverted to its primeval state at the dawn of Creation, when the waters of the deep submerged everything. Nothing remained of the teeming life that had burst forth upon the earth."[79] The text makes clear everything died.[80] Mathews notes: "'Perished' and 'wiped out' (vv. 21, 23) occur earlier in the flood narrative (e.g., 6:7, 17) but 'died' is new to the story and only occurs here (cf. 9:29)."[81] Wenham points out: "Elsewhere in Genesis 'expire and die'

---

73. Okoye, *Genesis 1–11*, 104. Cf. Hamilton, *Genesis 1–17*, 275; Turner, *Plot*, 38.

74. See Hill, "Noachian Flood," 173; Roaf, "Palaces and Temples," 425. Cf. Stallings, *Genesis Cataclysm*, 24–25.

75. Wenham, *Genesis 1–15*, 183. See too Ramm, *Christian View of Science and Scripture*, 164.

76. Arnold, *Genesis*, 103. See also Sailhamer, "Genesis," 125.

77. Wenham, *Genesis 1–15*, 183.

78. Wenham, *Genesis 1–15*, 183.

79. Cassuto, *Genesis*, 2:97.

80. The NET Bible states: "The MT reads נִשְׁמַת רוּחַ חַיִּים (nishmat ruakh khayyim, "breath of the breath/spirit of life"), but the LXX and Vulgate imply only נִשְׁמַת חַיִּים (nishmat khayyim). Either the LXX translator omitted translation of both words because of their similarity in meaning, or the omission in LXX shows that the inclusion of רוּחַ in the MT is the addition of an explanatory gloss."

81. Mathews, *Genesis 1—11:26*, 381.

are used in quick succession . . . Here the members of this standard word pair are spaced out . . . Such slowing of pace regularly marks the climax of a narrative."[82] The text communicates the sober reality: "the soul that sins shall die" (Ezek 18:20) and "the wages of sin is death" (Rom 6:23). The text also stirs a sense of deep reverence for GOD who is both merciful and mighty.

In the midst of so much judgment "GOD is committed to salvage operations. Noah and his family are saved; the world and human civilization are salvaged. Salvaging involves retrieving that which is valuable from the wreckage. This concept is at the heart of Israel's remnant theology."[83] Given such, "the contrast between those wiped out *mḥh* and Noah *nḥ* is deliberately highlighted by using the similar verb with the proper name."[84]

According to the lunar calendar, the 150 days here would cover at least the first five months from the coming of the Flood (Gen 7:11) to the grounding of the Ark upon the mountains of Ararat (Gen 8:3–4).[85] "Evidently the first forty days of heavy rain (7:12) were followed by 110 days of the waters' triumph. 8:4 makes plain that at least toward the end of the five months, the waters had begun to fall."[86] Hamilton argues: "Flood begins (1st of 40 days) on Noah's 600th year, 2nd month, 17th day (7:11). Ark rests on mountain on Noah's 600th year, 7th month, 17th day (8:4), i.e. 150 days later, possibly to be understood as 5 months of 30 days each."[87] Aspects of chronology will be returned to in the next section (Gen 8:1–22).

Summary

Two main emphases exist in this pericope (Gen 7:1–24): judgment and salvation. The text communicates the nocuous effects of disobedience to GOD. The cosmos became chaos on account of sin (Gen 7:4, 10–12, 17–24). At the same time, GOD himself closed the door of the ark. A great token of his mercy, love, and ultimate salvation (Gen 7:16). As far-reaching

---

82. Wenham, *Genesis 1–15*, 183.
83. Walton, Genesis, 337–38. Cf. Hasel, "Semantic Values," 152–69.
84. Wenham, *Genesis 1–15*, 183.
85. Mathews, *Genesis 1:1—11:26*, 382; Wenham, *Genesis 1–15*, 183.
86. Wenham, *Genesis 1–15*, 183.
87. Hamilton, *Genesis 1–17*, 298. For further information on this matter, see Steinmann, *Genesis*; 99; Boyd and Snelling, eds., *Chronology*, 231–756; Sarna, *Genesis*, 376.

and all-encompassing as the Flood water's triumphs are (Gen 7:4, 10–12, 17–24) God's efforts to save his created ones (both human and animals) are equal and then some. This is evidenced by Yahweh's compassion for all the inhabitants who boarded the ark (Gen 7:1–4, 6–9, 13–16, 23). The text's emphasis on Noah's virtue (Gen 7:1), his faithfulness to God (Gen 7:5), and his salvation from the onslaught of the Flood (see Gen 7:23, cf. Gen 7:4), make clear God's power and purpose to save. The earth will teem with life once again because of God's mercy and love.

STEP FOUR: DETERMINING THE RHETORICAL EFFECTIVENESS

This chapter outlined the rhetorical units comprising the text of Gen 7:1–24 (step one) and made clear the entextualized rhetorical situation, showcasing its exigences (step two). This chapter also commented on the various strategies that the text employed for aesthetic (literary) and rhetorical effect (step three). Step four determines the rhetorical effectiveness of the text.

With respect to exigence, the power of the Flood seems almost completely unstoppable, insurmountable, and uncontrollable.[88] Concerning the exigence of covenant fidelity, however, Noah was fully obedient to God (Gen 7:6). Also, since the LORD himself safely shut the occupants of the ark inside (Gen 7:16), it is clear that each party sought to fulfill the stipulations necessary to keep the covenant. In this way, one may consider that portion as being resolved.

Another resolved exigence involves the sheer preponderance of sin. With only Noah and company remaining, there are few people left to carry out "violence" (חמס). Yet, less cataclysmic ways to curb humanity's sinful proclivities must still be found (cf. Gen 8:20–22 and 9:1–17).

Concerning the exilic and post exilic context of the Israelites, McKeown states:

> The account of Noah and his ark is often romanticized as a children's story with the emphasis on the animals that are rescued. However, it is also a horror story in which human beings—men women, and children—and . . . animals are swept away by the merciless floodwaters. To ancient readers who had suffered

---

88. For further details to this end, see Sargent, "Wind, Water, and Battle Imagery" 80–81.

calamities such as the exile, it is this horror dimension that would have been analogous to their situation.[89]

As noted, out of the entirety of the Noachian deluge narrative, Gen 7:17–24 offers the clearest depiction of the severity of the Flood. "Outside the ark, nothing survives."[90] The cataclysmic nature of the Flood is all-encompassing and terrifying. As McKeown contends:

> While the fate of those outside the ark is inevitable and terrible, the fate of those inside is not enviable. Since the ark has no rudder, they have no control over their destination and all they can do is wait and hope. Exiled Israelites probably saw themselves in a similar situation to those in the ark. Both shared that most debilitating sense of uncertainty combined with an inability to control their own destiny.[91]

One remembers, though, the LORD closed the door of the ark behind them (see Gen 7:16). In light of this, it may safely be said that no matter where GOD's people are and however great a storm they might face, GOD's mercies and grace shall always be present with them (Gen 7:23).

CONCLUSION

This chapter analyzed the text of Gen 7:1–24 by means of the rhetorical-critical, rhetoric as persuasion, method outlined in chapter 2 of this study. Step one involved determining the rhetorical units. It was demonstrated the text was constructed of several main rhetorical subsections, namely (I) "Divine Speech: 'Enter!'" (Gen 7:1–4), (II) "Noah's Obedient Faithfulness" (Gen 7:5), (III) "Initial Recounting of the Entry into the Ark" (Gen 7:6–9), (IV) "Narration of the Flood: Patrial recounting of the Entry into the Ark" (Gen 7:10–12), (V) "Second Recounting of the Boarding of the Ark" (Gen 7:13–16), and (VI) "Narration of the Flood: Part B 'The Waters Prevail'" (Gen 7:17–24). The analysis also determined each of these main subsections consist of a various number of other subunits (which need not detain us).

In step two, determining the rhetorical situation, it was again asserted that though the primary exigence of the rhetorical situation pertains

---

89. McKeown, *Genesis*, 58. For exhaustive details, see Dalton, *Children's Bibles in America*.

90. McKeown, *Genesis*, 58.

91. McKeown, *Genesis*, 58–59.

to humanity's "violence" (חמס) this aspect of the rhetorical situation is not necessarily resolved since only a portion of the problem is addressed. It remains indeterminate how God will seek to prevent the situation from compounding once humanity begins to multiply again on the earth. With respect to the potential risk of covenant infidelity on the part of God and Noah, this secondary exigence was effectively resolved. The other secondary exigence concerning the Flood and salvation was not resolved.

Concerning step three, determining the rhetorical strategy, a number of literary devices were noted which had both aesthetic appeal and rhetorical efficacy. It was specifically noted how the text communicated both God's judgment and his salvation. Concerning step four, determining the rhetorical effectiveness, though a number of exigencies were resolved, further analysis concerning the triumph of the Flood is needed. This section also noted the marked effect this pericope and the Flood would have upon an exilic/post-exilic Israel community.

With respect to universalistic language, the Hebrew term "all" (כל) occurs twenty-three times within the portion of text this chapter analyzed (Gen 7:1–24). Ten times (roughly 43 percent of all of the occurrences here) the sense relates judgment (Gen 7:4, 11, 19x2, 21x3, 22x2, 23). God declares he is going to wipe out every living creature he made (Gen 7:4), all of the fountains of the great deep opened up (Gen 7:11), all the high mountains under the whole heaven were covered (Gen 7:19x2), every living thing that moved on the earth died (Gen 7:21), all the creatures that swarmed over the earth were wiped out (Gen 7:21), every human being who was not inside the ark died (Gen 7:21), everything that was on dry ground died (Gen 7:22x2), and God blotted out every living thing on the earth (Gen 7:23).

The Hebrew term "all" (כל) also occurs thirteen times (roughly 57 percent) with the sense relating to salvation (Gen 7:1, 2, 3, 5, 8, 14x6, 15, 16). Before the Flood, Noah and his whole family entered the ark (Gen 7:1) alongside every kind of clean animal (Gen 7:2). This was done so as to keep life from dying out throughout all the earth (see Gen 7:3). The text also makes clear Noah did according to all God commanded him (Gen 7:5). During the onset of the Flood, it is written every moving thing entered the ark (Gen 7:8) alongside every kind of wild animal (Gen 7:14), all livestock (Gen 7:14), everything that moves along the ground (Gen 7:14), and every bird according to its kind (Gen 7:14). All flying things (Gen 7:14), i.e., everything with wings entered the ark (Gen 7:14). Pairs of all creatures came into the ark (Gen 7:15). Males and females of every kind of animal came (Gen 7:16).

While many verses, i.e., fourteen (roughly 58 percent), of Gen 7:1–24 underscore the catastrophic nature of the Flood (Gen 7:4, 6, 7, 10, 11, 12, 17–24), a good portion of the narrative (ten verses, i.e., roughly 42 percent) also recounts the parade of people and animals entering the ark (Gen 7:1–3, 7–9, 13–16). The narrator's comment that "the LORD closed it behind him" (Gen 7:16), namely the door, provides assurance that, despite the dangers of the Flood, GOD spared Noah and all life aboard the ark—the cradle of life (Gen 7:23).

To conclude, this book contends the text of the Noachian deluge narrative categorically underscores all GOD did to preserve life in spite of the disaster. Despite the picture of devastation that the narrative depicts, the prominent emphasis of the text is on deliverance and redemption i.e., salvation, not judgment. The focus of the Genesis Flood is acutely bent towards GOD's salvific rather than punitive purposes.

The arc of salvation within the Flood narrative can be broken down into two main ideas. First, GOD's intention for creation is not thwarted and, secondly, GOD commits himself to his intentions of creation. His intention for creation can be stated as thus: the establishment of order via covenant showing the sanctity of human life and the upholding of all life.

While Gen 7:1–24 may not be thought of as directly bolstering this assertion, considering that this is the trough of the entire Flood account (see Gen 7:17–24), the statistics relating to universalistic language and its relation to salvation remain quite strong. In addition, when these statistics are coupled with the rest of the narrative, as a whole, the case becomes much stronger.

5

After the Rain
The Flood Subsides (Gen 8:1–22)

INTRODUCTION

THE FIRST CHAPTER OF textual analysis in this book studied Gen 6:5–8 and 9–22 of the Noahic Flood. It was there determined that despite the prevalence of human sin and the dynamic way GOD chose to deal with it (see Gen 6:13, 17) nothing could thwart Yahweh's plan to restore order via covenant (Gen 6:18). GOD's purpose was salvation. GOD commanded Noah to build an ark so as to save all life on earth (Gen 6:14–16, 18–21). Noah obeyed all GOD's instructions (Gen 6:22).

In the previous chapter, while the text placed a high degree of emphasis on the universal scope and devastative impact of the waters of the Flood, the most, in fact, of the entire Deluge account (see Gen 7:17–24), Noah and all those with him in the ark were spared because of GOD's great mercy and love (Gen 7:23; cf. Gen 7:16). Still, however, the water prevailed (Gen 7:24).

Gen 8:1–22 thus functions as the pivot point of the narrative structure of the Noachian deluge with Gen 8:1 being the key turnaround of the entire construct. The chaos of the cosmos will be returned to order as the waters decrease and the ark comes to rest (Gen 8:1–4). The text communicates that despite the devastation GOD upended on the earth, death and despair do not have the last word. GOD promises to never again curse the ground on account of humanity and to never again destroy every living being as he had just done (Gen 8:21–22). It is a new beginning.

This chapter will proceed in the same manner as the previous two analyses. The first step is to determine the rhetorical units of Gen 8:1–22. In addition, as in the previous chapters, each of the main rhetorical units of this specific pericope will be broken down into smaller subunits following the same procedure(s) and using the same terms used prior. The rest of the chapter will unfold according to the remaining steps of the rhetorical-critical method outlined in chapter 2.

STEP ONE: DETERMINING THE RHETORICAL UNITS

The first main subunit is entitled "The Waters Abate" (Gen 8:1–5).[1] It has referential, situational, and structural (relational) coherence signified by there being basic sameness of: (a) place (note how all of the events take place on board the ark), (b) participants, i.e., GOD (Gen 8:1), Noah (Gen 8:1), and all the other animals and human beings on board the ark with Noah (Gen 8:1), and (c) topic, theme, and mood, namely the reversal of the Flood waters upon the earth and the beginning of a new creation (Gen 8:1–5; cf. Gen 7:17–24). In addition, while numerous chronological details are contained in this pericope (Gen 8:3, 4, 5) they each cover a single incident—namely the summative reversal of the Flood. There are four temporal markers: (1) the waters decreasing and the initial time period of 150 days (Gen 8:3), (2) the ark resting on the mountains of Ararat on the seventh month on the seventeenth day due to the waters decreasing (Gen 8:4), (3) the waters decreasing steadily until the tenth month (Gen 8:5a), and finally, (4) the tops of the mountains becoming visible on the first day of the tenth month (Gen 8:5b). Alongside this, in Gen 8:1–5 it is either GOD or the waters dominating the subject of the verbs (cf. Gen 8:4 where the ark comes to rest). This contrasts with Gen 8:6–14 where the primary participants are Noah, the raven, and the dove. Lastly, Gen 8:6 begins with the *wayyiqtol* verb ויהי "Now it was . . ." (cf. EVV), indicating a new scene has begun.

1. See Van Pelt, ed., *Basics of Hebrew Discourse*, 70. The demarcation of Gen 8:1–5 being a unit is generally uncontested by scholars. See Hamilton, *Genesis 1–17*, 299; Wenham, *Genesis 1–15*, 183. Albeit, a number of scholars choose to subdivide Gen 8:1a as being its own scene. Cf. Mathews, *Genesis 1—11:26*, 384; Waltke and Fredricks, *Genesis*, 140–41. Outliers include Sailhamer, *Pentateuch*, 126–27. From both a literary and grammatical point of view, however, GOD "remembering" Noah requires certain actions on Yahweh's part. As such, Gen 8:1 (and what follows) must go hand in glove. The decision of some scholars to extend the unit (Gen 8:1–14), is indefensible. Cf. McKeown, *Genesis*, 59; Kidner, *Genesis*, 92.

After the Rain 161

This section (Gen 8:1–5) may be differentiated from Gen 7:17–24 because of the change in topic, theme, and mood. While the previous unit notes how Noah and company were safe on the ark (Gen 7:23) the overall emphasis is on the cataclysmic nature of the Flood (Gen 7:17–24). The somber note on which the previous pericope ended, namely "the waters prevailed upon the earth one hundred and fifty days" (Gen 7:24), stands in stark contrast to the unbridled hope and optimism which now resonates within the text: "GOD remembered Noah . . ." (Gen 8:1).

Each of the rhetorical subunits of the above portion of text are depicted below:

After The Rain: The Flood Subsides (Gen 8:1–22)

I. The Waters Abate (Gen 8:1–5)
   1. GOD remembers (Gen 8:1)
      i. GOD remembers Noah (Gen 8:1a)
      ii. GOD remembers the animals (Gen 8:1b)
   2. GOD acts (Gen 8:1–3)
      i. GOD causes the wind to blow (Gen 8:1c)
      ii. GOD calms the waters (Gen 8:1d)
      iii. GOD closes the fountains of the great deep (Gen 8:2a)
      iv. GOD closes the floodgates of the sky (Gen 8:2b)
      v. GOD restrains the rain from the sky (Gen 8:2c)
   3. The waters recede (Gen 8:3)
   4. The Ark comes to rest (Gen 8:4)
      i. calendar (Gen 8:4–5a)
      ii. mountains become visible (Gen 8:5)

The next main subunit is entitled "After the Rain" (Gen 8:6–14).[2] While the events which transpired in Gen 8:1–5 all took place on board the ark,

---

2. The demarcation of these verses being a unit is generally uncontested. See Mathews, *Genesis 1—11:26*, 386; Hamilton, *Genesis 1–17*, 302; Wenham, *Genesis 1–15*, 185; Waltke and Fredricks, *Genesis*, 141. Cf. Sailhamer, *Pentateuch*, 126–27; Sailhamer, *Genesis*, 116.

the literary viewpoint was at a distance. That is, the ark was still adrift (cf. Gen 8:4). In Gen 8:6–14, the viewpoint is aboard the ark (up close) as it remains stationary on top of the mountains of Ararat. The coherence of this unit is made clear through analogousness of: (a) place, (b) participants, i.e., Noah (Gen 8:6–13), the raven (Gen 8:7), and the dove (Gen 8:9–12), and (c) topic, theme, and mood. Concerning chronology, while the details recorded in this pericope do take place over an extended period of time (see Gen 8:6, 8, 10, 12, 13, 14) the unit itself still covers a single incident—the ground becoming dry after the Flood. Lastly, Gen 8:15 marks a divine speech, demarcating a new unit.

Each of the rhetorical subunits of the above section are depicted below:

After The Rain: The Flood Subsides (Gen 8:1–22)

    II. After the Rain (Gen 8:6–14)

        1. Noah, the window, and the raven (Gen 8:6–7)

            i. chronological marker (Gen 8:6a)

            ii. Noah and the window (Gen 8:b)

            iii. Noah and the raven (Gen 8:7)

        2. Noah and the dove (Gen 8:8–12)

            i. initial sending of the dove (Gen 8:8–9)

                a. initial sending of the dove to inspect the floodwaters (Gen 8:8)

                b. initial return of the dove (Gen 8:9a)

                c. narratival comments with respect to the water (Gen 8:9b)

                d. Noah taking the dove (Gen 8:9c)

            ii. second sending of the dove (Gen 8:10–11)

                a. calendar (Gen 8:10a)

                b. second sending of the dove (Gen 8:10b)

                c. second return of the dove (Gen 8:11a)

                d. Noah's knowledge about the flood (Gen 8:11b)

After the Rain

      iii. third sending of the dove (Gen 8:12)

          a. calendar (Gen 8:12a)

          b. no return (Gen 8:12b)

The next main subunit is entitled "Disembarking the Ark" (Gen 8:15–19).[3] It contains a divine speech (Gen 8:16–17). The cohesion of this subunit is evidenced by the introductory formula and the refrain (Gen 8:18–20; cf. Gen 6:13–21 and 22; 7:1–4 and 5).[4]

Each of the rhetorical subunits of the above section are depicted below:

After The Rain: The Flood Subsides (Gen 8:1–22)

    III. Disembarking the Ark (Gen 8:15–19)

        1. preface (Gen 8:15)

        2. divine directive to leave the ark (Gen 8:16–17)

            i. directives concerning human beings (Gen 8:16)

            ii. directives concerning animals (Gen 8:17)

        3. fulfillment of the disembarking (Gen 8:18–19)

The next main subunit is entitled "Noah's Sacrifice and God's Promise" (Gen 8:20–22).[5] Like Gen 8:15–19, it contains a divine speech (Gen 8:21–22). The cohesion of this subunit is thus demonstrated by the introductory formula (see Gen 8:21).[6] One also notes that immediately following this speech there is another divine speech (Gen 9:1–7). The

---

    3. Gen 8:15–19 as a unit is generally uncontested. See Mathews, *Genesis 1—11:26*, 390; Sailhamer, *Genesis*, 116; Kidner, *Genesis*, 92; Wenham, *Genesis 1–15*, 185; Waltke and Fredricks, *Genesis*, 141; Hamilton, *Genesis 1–17*, 307. Problems relating to extending the unit (Gen 8:15–22) will be addressed below. Cf. McKeown, *Genesis*, 60.

    4. See Dorsey, *Literary Structure*, 23. Cf. Meier, *Speaking*, 9; Miller, *Speech*, 400.

    5. Some scholars do not divide the third (Gen 8:15–19) and fourth main subunit (Gen 8:20–22), keeping both sets under one title, "Noah Leaves the Ark." See Hamilton, *Genesis 1–17*, 306. This division, however, does not account for the differences in time, place, and participants of the units. Cf. Mathews, *Genesis 1—11:26*, 390; Waltke and Fredricks, *Genesis*, 142. The end of this section discusses scholars who combine 8:20–22 with 9:1–17 (Gen 8:20—9:17). These include Wenham, *Genesis 1–15*, 188; Sailhamer, *Pentateuch*, 128; Sailhamer, *Genesis*, 116.

    6. See Dorsey, *Literary Structure*, 21. Cf. Meier, *Speaking*, 9; Miller, *Speech*, 400.

cohesion of this unit is also signified by there being agreement of: (a) place, that is, the participants are all outside of the ark as compared to inside, (b) participants, i.e., Noah (Gen 8:20) and GOD (Gen 8:21–22), (c) narratival speed of action (one notes the rhetorical unit spans a single incident, namely Noah's sacrifice to GOD), and (d) the promise of sustained salvation (similar mood/topic/theme). There is also a logical order to the events which transpire in this unit (Gen 8:20–22). That is to say, Noah offers a sacrifice to the LORD upon the altar (Gen 8:20) and GOD responds (Gen 8:21–22).

Each of the rhetorical subunits of the above section are depicted below:

After The Rain: The Flood Subsides (Gen 8:1–22)

  IV. Noah's Sacrifice and GOD's Promise (Gen 8:20–22)

   1. Noah's sacrifice to Yahweh (Gen 8:20)
   2. divine speech (Gen 8:21–22)
      i. 'never again' promises (Gen 8:21)
         a. curse the ground
         b. destroy every living thing
      ii. 'forevermore' promises (Gen 8:22)

As noted above, Gen 8:1–22 is, itself, a rhetorical unit. The cohesion of these verses is demonstrated through recognizing that each of the events which transpired in the pericope temporally occurred after GOD had remembered Noah (Gen 8:1) and after the reversal of the Flood (Gen 8:2–5). There is also a clear difference in topic, theme, and mood when one compares the prevailing of the Flood in Gen 7:17–24 with the hope and promise of Gen 8:1–22. Lastly, as noted above, Gen 9:1 begins with a divine speech, thereby marking a new unit.

STEP TWO: DETERMINING THE RHETORICAL SITUATION

This set of verses (Gen 8:1–22) brings closure to many of the secondary exigencies which comprise the entextualized rhetorical situation of the

Flood account. With respect to Noah, the covenant, and Yahweh, it is clear Noah is the same righteous, faithful, and obedient individual he was at the beginning of the account (see Gen 6:9, 22; 7:5, 7, 13, 15, 23; 8:6–13, 18, 20).[7] Noah obeyed at the first command of God to leave the ark (Gen 8:18, 19). It is reasonable to conclude Noah knew he was not supposed to live in the ark indefinitely. The ark was intended to be a temporary shelter, not a permanent home. Noah's initiative with the raven and the dove should also be thought of as further depictions of Noah's virtuous character as one who sought to obey God in all things. To put the matter differently, as a narrative, despite an acute knowledge of the ground being dry (Gen 8:13, 14), Noah's decision to not leave the ark seems to indicate that he deemed it necessary to hear from God before leaving. Since it was at God's command Noah both built and entered the ark why should he not wait for God's command prior to leaving it?

The narrator's comment how the LORD looked on Noah's sacrifice and received it, i.e., Yahweh "smelled the soothing aroma" (Gen 8:21), also speaks to Noah's good and godly character since God does not receive every offering in this way (cf. Gen 4:1–7).[8] In short, Noah fulfilled his covenant obligations. There is nothing more that Noah can do to either: (a) break the covenant God made with him, or (b) add to it. This portion of the exigence is resolved in full.

Concerning the other covenant partner, the text makes clear God was the one who remembered Noah and company (Gen 8:1). To this end, Mathews states:

> The expression 'remembered' (zākar) does not mean 'calling to mind' here; it is covenant language, designating covenant fidelity (e.g., The Fourth Commandment, Exod 20:8; cf. Luke 1:72). God is acting in according with his earlier promise to Noah (6:18). We find the same expression in the Noachic covenant, where the LORD commits to carrying out his promises (8:21) and establishes the covenant sign of the rainbow (9:14–15) . . . People of the covenant, whether yesterday or today, are expected to exercise covenant allegiance by 'remembering' the LORD (e.g., Deut 8:18; Ps 103:18). Israel's GOD had remembered Noah, and by this Israel too was incited to remember the LORD of Sinai.[9]

---

7. See Okoye, *Genesis 1–11*, 104–5.

8. See Waltke, "Cain and His Offering," 363–72. Cf. Youngblood ed., *Genesis Debate*, 130–47.

9. Mathews, *Genesis 1—11:26*, 382–83. See too Collins, *Reading Genesis*, 87.

Since the analysis of Gen 9:1–17 will provide additional details concerning the full resolution of this exigence, it will be left until that time to provide more details on this particular point.

To conclude, the Deluge is now finally over. The text affirms this four different times: (1) God caused a wind to pass over the earth—causing the waters to subside (Gen 8:1), (2) the waters steadily decreased (Gen 8:1, 3, 5), and (3) the fountains of the deep, the floodgates of the sky, and the rain from the heavens, i.e., all of the mechanisms which produced the Flood, stopped completely (Gen 8:2). While the text does not state God caused the fountains of the deep and the floodgates of the sky to actually close, it is written elsewhere in the Flood narrative that God would "bring the flood of water upon the earth to destroy all flesh in which is the breath of life" (Gen 6:17, see also Gen 6:13). It seems evident the sovereignty of God had to be involved in these matters. This point is also supported by the miraculous timing of the Flood. That is, it was on the very same day Noah and company entered the ark that "the water of the Flood came upon the earth" (Gen 7:10) and "all the fountains of the great deep burst open and the floodgates of the sky were opened" (Gen 7:11). Lastly, (4), the text records via divine speech how God will never again destroy every living thing by means of a Flood (Gen 8:21–22). God could not make this promise unless he himself was in complete control of the Flood (see Ps 29:10; cf. Isa 40:22).

In sum, God was exercising his sovereign care over all aspects of the Deluge so as to: (1) ensure that the Flood would destroy all those whom God wished to "wipe away" (Gen 6:7, 13, 17; 7:4, 17–24), and (2) ensure the ark had fulfilled its salvific purpose (Gen 6:14, 18–21; 7:1–5, 7–9, 13–16, 23; 8:1, 16–19). Now that the annihilation of the world was complete—the cosmos becoming chaos—and the Deluge and the ark had both fulfilled their purposes, God states, unequivocally, that he would never again destroy every living thing as he had just done with the catastrophe of the Flood (Gen 8:21). The exigence concerning God and the Flood is resolved.

Turning to the second key component of the rhetorical situation, namely audience, it is once again made clear how Noah does not fit the traditional scheme of "indictment and sentence."[10] In the words of Brueggemann:

---

10. Brueggemann, *Genesis*, 79.

After the Rain 167

> Noah is righteous and blameless. He walks with GOD (vv. 6:9; 7:1; cf. 5:2). In this dismal story of pain, there is one who embodies a new possibility ... [t]he narrator wants the listening community to turn to Noah, to consider that in this troubled exchanged between creator and creation there is the prospect of fresh alternative. Something new is at work in creation. Noah is the new being ... He is the fully responsive man who accepts creatureliness and lets GOD be GOD.[11]

The implications of this for determining the constraints of the rhetorical situation are far-reaching. If GOD's mercies are so all-encompassing that even the Flood is not truly an end, but actually a new beginning, and if the same grace GOD extended to Noah is being offered to all creation (Gen 8:21–22), then every day is a new opportunity for Yahweh's glory to abound.[12]

STEP THREE: DETERMINING THE RHETORICAL STRATEGY

This step centers on assessing the rhetorical strategies the text employs to make its persuasive appeal. As in the previous two chapters of this study, the analysis will begin with a fresh, English translation along with a commentary of certain grammatical/syntactical features (including text criticism issues). The analysis is divided according to the main subunits: (I) "The Flood Waters Abate" (Gen 8:1–5), (II) "After the Rain" (Gen 8:6–14), (III) "Disembarking the Ark (Gen 8:15–19), and (IV) "Noah's Worship and GOD's Promise" (Gen 8:20–22).

After The Rain: The Flood Subsides (Gen 8:1–22)

I. *The Flood Waters Abate (Gen 8:1–5)*

ויזכר אלהים את נח [a] ואת כל החיה ואת כל הבהמה אשר אתו בתבה [b]

---

11. Brueggemann, *Genesis*, 79. Notably, however, Paul does not use Noah as a type of "Adam" (1 Cor 15:20–27, 44–49; Rom 5:12–21). For more details, see Carson, "Adam in the Epistles of Paul," 28–43.

12. See Hodge, *Days of Genesis*, 139.

ᶜויעבר אלהים רוח על הארץ ᵈוישכו המים ᵉויסכרו מעינת תהום ᶠוארבת השמים

ᵍויכלא הגשם מן השמים ʰוישבו המים מעל הארץ ⁱהלוך ושוב

ʲויחסרו המים מקצה חמשים ומאת יום

ᵏותנח התבה בחדש השביעי בשבעה עשר יום לחדש על ᵐהרי אררט

ᵐוהמים היו הלוך

ⁿוחסור עד החדש העשירי בעשירי ᵒבאחד לחדש נראו ראשי ההרים

Nowᵖ GOD remembered Noah, along with all the wild animals, and all the other animals with him in the ark.

Thus GOD caused a wind to blow on the earth. As a result, the waters calmed. (The springs of the deepᑫ had been closed, along with the windows of heaven. Thus the rain from the sky was restrained).ʳ

So the waters kept receding steadily from upon the earth.

The waters had gone down at the end of 150 days.

Then the ark rested in the seventh month, on the seventeenth day of the month, among the mountains of Ararat.ˢ

But the waters continued to exist—they diminished until the tenth month; in the tenth month, on the first day of the month, the tops of the mountains were able to be seen.

---

a. Narratival *waw*. *GBHS* §3.5.1.c. Cf. Chisholm, *Exegesis*, 120 (introductory *waw*).

b. This *waw* and the one that follows it are both accompaniment *waw*s. Williams, *Hebrew Syntax*, §436.

c. Consequential *waw*. *GBHS* §3.5.1.b. See *IBHS* §27.2.b for more details on the Hiphil here.

d. Consequential *waw*. *GBHS* §3.5.1.b; Chisholm, *Exegesis*, 120.

e. Supplemental or parenthetical *waw*. Chisholm, *Exegesis*, 122.

f. Accompaniment *waw*. Williams, *Hebrew Syntax*, §436.

g. Consequential *waw*. *GBHS* §3.5.1.b; Chisholm, *Exegesis*, 120.

h. Resumptive *waw*. Chisholm, *Exegesis*, 121.

i. The intensifying infinitive comes along the main verb of motion in order to signify repetition or continuance. See GKC §113u; Joüon §123s; *IBHS* §35.3.2.c

j. Consequential *waw*. *GBHS* §3.5.1.b. Note: the MT is more likely than the Sam-Pent due to the preference of the latter for uniform spelling despite the fact that its rendering is actually more usual in temporal phrases than the MT. See Wenham, *Genesis 1–15*, 153; Tal, *BHQ*, 98.

k. Sequential *waw*. Chisholm, *Exegesis*, 120; *GBHS* §4.1.13.a.

l. It is possible the plural is being used here to denote an indefinite singular, i.e., "one of the mountains." See GKC §124o. It could also have the sense of "mountain range." So Speiser, *Genesis*, 53.

m. Coordinative/conjunctive waw. Williams, *Hebrew Syntax*, §430a

n. Explicative *waw*. Williams, *Hebrew Syntax*, §434.

o. For the day of the month with a cardinal, see GKC §129f, 134p; Wenham, *Genesis 1–15*, 153.

p. Though many EVV offer a disjunctive conjunction here, i.e., "but" (see, for example, NET, NIV 1984, NIV 2011, ESV, NASB, NLT, RSV, and NRSV), this is not a *waw* + non-verb form. Though the rhetorical nuance of the Flood account, as a whole, forbids rendering the *waw* as the simple conjunction "and" (contra the KJV and BBE), one should also not leave the *waw* untranslated altogether (contra the CEB and HCSB) since it is foundational for determining the flow of the units. Lastly, though the NKJV offers the rendering "then," the *waw* is not merely sequential but either a narrative *waw* or an introductory *waw* (see above).

q. See the NIV 1984/NIV 2011 for a precedent of this rendering. Cf. NET, NASB, ESV, BBE, KJV, NKJV, and NRSV "fountains of the deep." The NLT rendering "underground waters" and *The Message*, "underground springs," fail to clarify the nuances associated with "the deep."

r. A "pluperfect" rendering helps to communicate the idea the sources of water would have stopped before the waters began to recede. Cf. the NIV 1984/NIV 2011 "had gone down," and the NRSV/REB "had abated." See *IBHS* §33.2.3.a; GKC §111q; Joüon §118 d; Collins, "*Wayyiqtol* as 'Pluperfect,'" 117–40; Wenham, "Pentateuchal Source Criticism," 89–92; Mathews, *Genesis 1–11:26*, 385.

s. While the ark may have come to rest on a particular mountain within the chain itself (see the details below for specifics concerning Ararat), to say the ark came to rest "on" a mountain chain is absurd (cf. EVV). The preposition, though, indicates a spatial relationship wherein *x* is "above," "over," or "upon" *y* (*BHRG* §39.20.i.a; *GBHS* §4.1.16.a.i.). Walton, however, suggests "it may be preferable ... to translate that the ark came to rest *against* the mountains." Walton, *Genesis*, 328. Emphasis original.

Extended Analysis

At long last, the redemption that was only hinted at in the previous units of text (Gen 6:14–21; 7:1–4, 7–9, 13–16, 23) is made manifest within the first verse of this unit (Gen 8:1). The text communicates GOD's faithfulness. Interestingly, the text makes no mention of either Noah's righteousness (cf. Gen 6:9, 7:1) or his obedience to GOD (cf. Gen 6:22, 7:5) in connection to GOD's remembrance of him (Gen 8:1). The covenant (which will be the source of much of the discussion of Gen 9:9–17) is also not mentioned (cf. Gen 6:18). Hamilton states: "By trimming the description of the divine remembrance as much as possible, the point is made that when all appears helpless GOD intervenes to prevent tragedy."[13] The text communicates the richness of GOD's mercy and love which extends even to the animal kingdom (Gen 8:1; cf. Jonah 4:11).[14]

With respect to GOD "remembering" (זכר) this is "not the retention or recollection of a mental image, but a focusing upon the object of memory that results in action."[15] To state again, GOD remembering Noah "is not only evidence of his compassion, but it also translates into action."[16] As another scholar puts it: "When GOD remembers, he acts, sets things in motion."[17] Truly, "it is only the remembering of GOD that gives hope and makes new life possible."[18]

In this instance (Gen 8:1), GOD remembering the ark's inhabitants directly relates to "causing a wind to blow over the earth."[19] This comment is similar to the beginning of creation: "blowing wind, retreating waters, and the emergence of drying land dominate the telling of the deluge's reversal. The language echoes the description of Genesis 1, showing that GOD has set about making a new creation."[20] The "wind" (רוח) "heralds the reimposition of order."[21] The text communicates the sovereignty of GOD over wind, water, and all of the forces of creation/nature.

---

13. Hamilton, *Genesis 1–17*, 299.
14. See Okoye, *Genesis 1–11*, 104; Linzey and Cohn-Sherbok, *After Noah*.
15. Sarna, *Genesis*, 56.
16. Wevers, *Genesis*, 101. See too Childs, *Memory*, 34.
17. Okoye, *Genesis 1–11*, 104.
18. Waltke and Fredricks, *Genesis*, 141. See also Blenkinsopp, *Creation*, 142.
19. Though some EVV render this as a "divine wind," cf. the NEB and the AB which render this clause as "a mighty wind that swept over the surface of the waters" and "an awesome wind sweeping over the water" respectively, the text suggests otherwise. See Bediako, "Spirit/Wind," 78–84. In addition, though many EVV choose to render the latter half of this phrase as "pass over" (see NASB, ESV, NLT, and HCSB) rather than "blow over," there is no tangible difference between the two. For details, see Sargent, "Wind, Water, and Battle Imagery," 3
20. Mathews, *Genesis 1—11:26*, 383. Cf. Sailhamer, "Genesis," 113.
21. Sarna, *Genesis*, 56.

The Flood is over. The waters are now "humbled" before Yahweh.[22] Mathews states the deep is now "no longer 'great.'"[23] The Flood is not a "freak of nature. Both its commencement and completion are divinely ordained and divinely controlled."[24] The text communicates how everything issues from "GOD's sovereign will" and how all of creation are under his "undisputed control" and sovereignty.[25]

With respect to comparative analysis, within the Sumerian Flood account, Ziusudra prostrates himself before Utu, the sun-GOD, after he leaves his ship for "it is the sun that has just come out and illuminated the earth and the sky."[26] Hamilton goes so far as to state that since the sun plays no role in the drying up of the Flood waters this could indicate a "deliberate dissociation in biblical thought between the Flood's end and a sun deity."[27]

While the chronology of the Flood is an enigma, calendar plays a large role in Gen 8:3–5. Many specific dates and times are noted in a few short verses.[28] The process culminates with the ark coming to rest in the seventh month, on the seventeenth day of the month (Gen 8:4).[29] It is possible a wordplay exists here as well. "The verb *came to rest*, Heb. *Tānaḥ*, is that from which the name Noah (Heb. *Nōaḥ*) is derived. Thus, one might say that the ark 'noah-ed' on one of the mountains of Ararat."[30] Another scholar states there is "clearly a paronomastic allusion to Noah's name" here.[31] The text communicates the wisdom and sovereignty of GOD.

---

22. Sargent, "Wind, Water, and Battle Imagery," ii.

23. Mathews, *Genesis 1—11:26*, 385.

24. Hamilton, *Genesis 1-17*, 300.

25. Sarna, *Genesis*, 56.

26. Hamilton, *Genesis 1-17*, 300. See also *ANET*, 44.

27. Hamilton, *Genesis 1-17*, 300.

28. "To make sense of the last part of the verse, one must attribute to the verb inceptive force ... that is, it describes the beginning of a process not the conclusion of that process." Hamilton, *Genesis 1-17*, 300. This means the period of "abatement could have begun already within the 150-day period." Mathews, *Genesis 1—11:26*, 385.

29. This refers to the mountainous region Urartu located north of Mesopotamia (modern day eastern Turkey). Yamauchi, *Foes from the Northern Frontier*, 29-32; Wenham, *Genesis 1-15*, 184-85; Hamilton, *Genesis 1-17*, 301. This is in contrast to *Jubilees* (5:28, 7:1) and 1QapGen which identify Mount Lubar as the landing point. See Mathews, *Genesis 1—11:26*, 386; Lyon, *Qumran Interpretation*, 59-64.

30. Hamilton, *Genesis 1-17*, 301. All emphases original.

31. Wenham, *Genesis 1-15*, 184.

The waters diminished until the tenth month; on the first day of the month, seventy three days later, the tops of the mountains were seen (Gen 8:5).[32] The temporal conundrums the interpreter faces are numerous.[33] Even so, the text communicates GOD's power over all aspects of creation as well as his sustaining hand of grace and faithful provision to all life on earth.

II. *After the Rain (Gen 8:6–14)*

^aויהי מקץ ארבעים יום ^bויפתח נח את חלון התבה אשר עשה

וישלח את הערב ויצא יצוא ^cושוב עד יבשת ^dהמים מעל ^eהארץ

וישלח את היונה מאתו לראות הקלו המים מעל פני האדמה

^fולא מצאה היונה מנוח לכף ^gרגלה

^hותשב אליו אל התבה כי מים על פני כל הארץ

ⁱוישלח ידו ^jויחל עוד שבעת ימים אחרים ויקחה ויבא אתה אליו אל התבה

ותבא אליו היונה לעת ויסף שלח את היונה מן התבה ^kערב

^lוהנה עלה זית טרף בפיה וידע נח כי קלו המים מעל הארץ

וייחל עוד שבעת ימים אחרים וישלח את היונה

^mולא יספה שוב אליו עוד

ⁿויהי באחת ^oושש מאות שנה בראשון באחד לחדש חרבו המים מעל הארץ

---

32. Sarna, *Genesis*, 57. For further information on this point, see Domeris, *NIDOTTE*: 2:675; Harris, *TWOT* 1:449; Wenham, Genesis, 325–30; Martin, *Solving the Riddle*, 19–21. Walton suggests the Flood "covered all the elevated places . . . within eyesight of the . . . ark." Walton, *Genesis*, 328. See too Sailhamer, *Genesis Unbound*, 53–72.

33. Hamilton states: "I see no credible way of harmonizing the information of v. 5 with v. 4. V. 4 clearly states that the ark rested on one of the mountains of Ararat in the 17th day of the 7th month. Yet v. 5 states that no mountaintop was spotted until the first day of the 10th month.'" Hamilton, *Genesis 1–17*, 301.

After the Rain

^pויסר נח את מכסה התבה

^qוירא ^rוהנה חרבו פני האדמה

^sובחדש השני בשבעה ^tועשרים יום לחדש יבשה הארץ

Now it was the end of forty days.
Noah opened the window in the ark he had made.
> He sent forth the raven and it keptflying back and forth repeatedly^u
> until the water dried up from on the earth.
> Then he sent forth a dove from himself, in order to see whether they—the waters—had subsided from upon the surface of the ground. But the dove could find no place to set her foot. So she returned to him to the ark, for water was on the surface of the entire earth. So he put forth his hand and he took her and he brought her to himself to the ark.

Then he waited until seven more days and sent the dove again out of the ark.
Then the dove came to him by evening time, now with a freshly plucked
> olive leaf in her beak!

Then Noah knew that the waters had subsided from upon the earth.
Then he waited until seven more days (passed) and he sent forth the dove.
But she did not return to him again.^v
Now it was in the six hundred and first year [of Noah's life], in the first month,
> on the first [day] of the month, the waters were dried from on the earth.

Then Noah removed the covering of the ark.
And he saw that the face of the ground was dried up!
In the second month, on the twenty seventh day of the month, the earth was dry.

---

a. Narratival *waw*. See *GBHS* §3.5.1.c. Cf. Chisholm, *Exegesis*, 120 (introductory *waw*).

b. Sequential *waw*. *GBHS* §3.5.1.a. Unless indicated otherwise, all *waw*s here are sequential.

c. Instances where a second infinitive absolute is coordinated with the first express "either an accompanying or antithetical action or the aim to which the principal action is directed." GKC §113s. In this particular case, it expresses the "simultaneity or quasi-simultaneity of a second action . . . 'and he went out just to come back again (soon).'" Joüon §123m.

d. "Where a verb has two infinitive forms . . . one was used as *nomen regens* in preference to the other. Thus in Gn 8.7 עַד־יְבֹ֥שֶׁת הַמָּ֖יִם† there probably is a genitive." Joüon §124h.

e. Note: the LXX inserts "to see if the water had dried" assimilating Gen 8:7 to Gen 8:8. See Wenham *Genesis 1–15*, 154; Sarna, *Genesis*, 57.

f. Contrastive (or, perhaps, dramatic) *waw*. Chisholm, *Exegesis*, 126.

g. For details on the word order that is used in this verbal clause, see Joüon §1550 and 153.

h. Though the *waw* is sequential (*GBHS* §3.5.1.a) the nuance is consequential (*GBHS* §3.5.1.b). For further information on the *telic* sense of the verb here, see *IBHS* §33.3.1.b.

i. Though the *waw* is sequential (*GBHS* §3.5.1.a) the nuance is consequential (*GBHS* §3.5.1.b).

j. Sequential waw. GBHS §3.5.1.a. Unless indicated otherwise, all *waw*s here are sequential.

k. For details on this being "motion in time and not point in time, i.e., 'by' and not 'at,'" see Hamilton, *Genesis 1–17*, 302. Cf. Meek, "Old Testament," 236–38.

l. The construct here is "for dramatic effect to invite the audience to step into the story and see what a bystander or one of the characters saw." Chisholm, *Exegesis*, 126. Cf. *GBHS* §4.5.2.c.4. (temporal). See also Lambdin, *Biblical Hebrew*, 168–70.

m. Contrastive (or, perhaps, dramatic) *waw*. Chisholm, *Exegesis*, 126.

n. Narratival *waw*. See *GBHS* §3.5.1.c. Cf. Chisholm, *Exegesis*, 120 (introductory *waw*).

o. Coordinative waw. Williams, *Hebrew Syntax*, §430a.

p. Sequential *waw*. GBHS §3.5.1.a. For information on the verbal form here, see GKC §72t, aa.

q. Sequential *waw*. GBHS §3.5.1.a.

r. The construction here assumes there is no anticipation of the ensuing event, i.e., it is a surprise. See Joüon §177i; Wenham, *Genesis 1–15*, 154.

s. Concluding *waw*. Chisholm, *Exegesis*, 127. Temporal preposition. *GBHS* §4.1.5.b.

t. Coordinative *waw*. Williams, *Hebrew Syntax*, §430a.

u. Goldingay notes that "the idiomatic expression begins with a finite verb followed by its infinitive absolute, "it went out in going out,' i.e., 'it went out repeatedly,' then adds a second infinite absolute from a different root so that in effect there is an ellipses of the related second finite verb. See *IBHS* §135.3c; JM 123m; GKC 111s; DG 101c." Goldingay, *Genesis*, 135. See too *IBHS* §35.3.2.c for a defense of this translation. Cf. NIV 1984, NIV 2011, NET, NKJV.

v. See BDB 414 for a defense of this reading. It is possible there is a pleonasm in Hebrew. For further information on the LXX rendering, see Lee, *Greek*, 214.

Extended Analysis

Noah waits for forty days to open the hatch of the ark (Gen 8:6). Noah first sends "the raven" (ערב).[34] Next, Noah sends a "dove" (יונה).[35] The two birds were sent out in order to discern the suitability of the earth for habitation (Gen 8:7–8). The use of birds for reconnaissance is well founded.[36] The order of raven to dove also makes logical sense: "the raven is a carrion eater and did not return because it found food on the mountain peaks. The dove is a valley bird . . . it was released in order to determine whether the lower-lying areas were habitable."[37]

From an ANE perspective, "Heidel compared the Babylonian version unfavorably with the account in Genesis supposing that 'by releasing the raven first, Noah . . . displayed greater wisdom than Utnapišti, who . . . sent the raven out last'. This statement, based as it was on a theory of bird behavior extrapolated from the biblical account and thence unaltered to the cuneiform tradition, is methodologically suspect. The Babylonian order of birds may have had a different rationale from that which informed the Hebrew story."[38]

Yitzchak Etshalom states:

> The three 'missions' of the dove seem to be unusual—after all, if the land was already visible well before Noah sent out the dove the first time, why did it not find any rest? And why did it return after its second voyage—but with an olive branch . . . And if it was able to gain access to such trees, why did it come back at all—after all, when it was sent the third time and evidently found the water yet lower, it didn't return.[39]

---

34. See Goldingay, *Genesis*, 134; GKC §126r; *HALOT* 1:879; Kiuchi, *NIDOTTE* 3:524.

35. See *HALOT* 1:402; Kiuchi, *NIDOTTE* 2:425–26.

36. Wachsmann, *Seagoing Ships and Seamanship*, 300, 371. See too Marcus, "Mission of the Raven," 71–80; Heras, "'The Crow' of Noe," 131–39.

37. Hamilton, *Genesis 1–17*, 304–5. See too Keiter, "Dove," 262. Oddly, one scholar states: "the two birds are really one bird, but in two different versions of the story. The dove is the one bird sent out in the Yahwist's flood story, while the raven is the one bird sent out in the Priestly account of the flood." Moberly, "Raven," 348. See too Noort, "Flood," 9.

38. Smith, *Babylon*, 516–17. Cf. Waltke and Fredricks, *Genesis*, 141; Wenham, *Genesis 1–15*, 186; Jacobus, "Birds," 85–112.

39. Etshalom, *Between the Lines*, 2.

Arnold opines "the three trips of the dove illustrate the degrees of readiness of earth."[40] Clues to the process involved may be derived from what immediately follows. After the episode of the birds, there is a dual reporting of the situation. One is from the perspective of Noah. The other comes from the narrator. Each of these reports involve calendar and a statement concerning the condition of the earth with respect to water. Concerning the first report:

> It is vital to view the narrative from a 'real-world' perspective, remembering that the characters only know what they know and that the various questions posed, observations made and tests passed (or not) may be designed to further the actor's grasp of the situation. We find ourselves at the disadvantage of having read the story so many times that, in this instance (for example) we already know that the earth is completely dry (well, at least by the end of the narrative). We have to sensitize ourselves to the reality that Noah doesn't know that—to anticipate the questions in his mind and view his actions in that light—as intelligent and thoughtful attempts to give him the information necessary to move forward.[41]

In this way, the text is persuasive in fostering additional support and empathy for Noah.

The second report merely states: "in the second month, on the twenty seventh day of the month, the earth was dried up" (Gen 8:14). If one compares the calendar of these dates with those of the beginning of the narrative an interesting point emerges.[42]

- Flood begins (Gen 7:11): 17th day/2nd month/600th year of Noah
- Flood has gone (Gen 8:14): 27th day/2nd month/601st year of Noah

In brief, Noah's Flood lasted "twelve months and eleven days, the exact period required to equate the year of twelve lunar months, 354 days, with the solar year of 365 days."[43]

---

40. Arnold, *Genesis*, 105.

41. Etshalom, *Between the Lines*, 4.

42. The following schematic (with slight modifications) comes from Hamilton, *Genesis 1–17*, 305.

43. De Vaux, *Ancient Israel*, 1:188–89. See also Larsson, "Noah-Flood Complex," 75–77. For more details, see Cooper and Goldstein, "Calendars," 1–20.

From the narrator's perspective, "one gets a strong impression that Noah does not wish to leave the ark precipitately."[44] This bespeaks the virtuous character of Noah who waits for a divine signal to leave that which he has been commanded to enter. This sequence "'subtly lets us witness the waiting and hoping of those enclosed in the ark'. Noah's resourcefulness comes to light, and above all, in 13, 14, his self-discipline as he patiently awaits God's time and word."[45] The text communicates support and empathy for Noah.

The olive leaf was "fresh" (טרף זית).[46] This confirms the "earth was again yielding its herbage (as 1:11–12, 30)."[47] Sarna states, "The rare noun *taraf* connotes that it was freshly removed from the tree and was not flotsam, a sure sign that plant life had begun to renew itself."[48] Another scholar maintain the olive leaf "represents a new beginning, the world coming to life once again."[49] The depiction of an olive leaf may also prompt one to "reflect on" possible relationships with the menorah, which is fueled by olive oil alongside, perhaps, certain other cultic matters, such as the perfumed anointing oil.[50] To this end, one scholar asserts: "The olive tree, one of the earliest to be cultivated in the near East, is an evergreen. It is extraordinarily sturdy and may thrive for up to a thousand years. Thus it became symbolic of God's blessings of regeneration, abundance, and strength, which is most likely the function it serves here."[51] The text communicates God's desire for beauty and fertility.[52]

Although some seek to connect the "covering" (מכסה) of the ark (cf. Gen 6:16) and the "cover" (מבסה) for the tent of meeting (e.g., Exod 26:14; 35:11; 36:19; Num 3:25), it seems there are corresponding physical components involved in both structures, such as a "tarpaulin of skins" of sorts; thus, this particular aspect of the ark seems to have no cultic bearing or significance.[53]

---

44. Hamilton, *Genesis 1–17*, 302.

45. Kidner, *Genesis*, 92.

46. See Gevaryahu, "Dove," 172–75. For more lexical information, see *DCH* 3:376; *HALOT* 1:380.

47. Mathews, *Genesis 1:1—11:26*, 388.

48. Sarna, *Genesis*, 58.

49. Gevaryahu, "Dove," 173.

50. Mathews, *Genesis 1:1—11:26*, 388. See too Wenham, *Genesis 1–15*, 187.

51. Sarna, *Genesis*, 58.

52. See Wenham, *Genesis 1–15*, 187.

53. *DCH* 4:271; *HALOT* 1:581; Pan, *NIDOTTE* 2:677. For more details, see Kidner,

III. *Disembarking the Ark (Gen 8:15–19)*

וידבר אלהים אל נח לאמר^a

צא מן התבה אתה ^bואשתך ובניך ונשי בניך אתך

^cכל החיה אשר אתך מכל בשר

בעוף^d ובבהמה ובכל הרמש הרמש על הארץ ^eהיצא אתך

^fושרצו בארץ ^gופרו ורבו על הארץ ^hויצא נח

ⁱובניו ואשתו ונשי בניו אתו ^jכל החיה כל הרמש וכל העוף

כל רומש על הארץ למשפחתיהם יצאו מן התבה

Then GOD spoke to Noah:
"Exit the ark, you and your wife and your sons and your son's wives with you!
>From every living creature living creature with you, from all animals—of birds, of domesticated beasts, and of every moving thing that moves on the earth—bring (them) out with you!^j Thus they shall abound on the earth!^k They shall be fruitful! They shall multiply on the earth!"
So Noah went out, and his sons, and his wife, and the wives of his sons with him. Every living creature, every moving thing, and every bird. Everything that moves on the earth, according to their families, went out of the ark.

---

a. Sequential *waw*. GBHS §3.5.1.a.
b. This *waw* and the two that follow it are coordinative. Williams, *Hebrew Syntax*, §430a.
c. Note: various versions add "and" here (Cf. Gen 8:17). See Wenham, *Genesis 1–15*, 154.
d. This *waw* and the one that follows it are both coordinative. Williams, *Hebrew Syntax*, §430a.
e. For more details on the form of this verb (including the *ketiv qere* variant) see GKC §69v, 70b; Hamilton, *Genesis 1–17*, 306–7.

Genesis, 92; Mathews, *Genesis 1:1—11:26*, 388; Wenham, *Genesis 1–15*, 187. Cf. Powell and Powell, "Noah's Ark," 1–27.

f. Consequential *waw*. Chisholm, *Exegesis*, 132, *GBHS* §3.5.1.b. The verbal form here also (possibly) carries an imperatival nuance. See Driver, *Tenses in Hebrew*, 124–25.

g. This *waw* and the one that follows it are both coordinative. Williams, *Hebrew Syntax*, §430a.

h. Though the *waw* is sequential (*GBHS* §3.5.1.a) because the action comes after an imperative, the nuance is consequential. Chisholm, *Exegesis*, 132, *GBHS* §3.5.1.b. For details on the use of a singular verb with a plural subject, see GKC §146f; Wenham, *Genesis 1–15*, 154.

i. This *waw* and the three that follow it are each coordinative. Williams, *Hebrew Syntax*, §430a.

j. Note: though the LXX suggests "and all domesticated animals" the "MT may be preferable. Had Noah let out all the domesticated animals and birds, he would have had none to sacrifice. Cf. v 17 where he is instructed to release some of the birds and domesticated animals." Wenham, *Genesis 1–15*, 154. For more grammatical information about the Hebrew underlying this verse, see Goldingay, *Genesis*, 135.

k. It is difficult to communicate the sense of the Hebrew (cf. Gen 1:21). English variants include "spread over the earth" (HCSB), "increase" (NET), "multiply" (NIV 1984, 2011), "breed abundantly" (NASB, KJV, RSV), and "swarm" (ESV). See NRSV/NKJV for a precedent in English of "abound."

Extended Analysis

As noted above, Noah seems extremely reticent to disembark despite his acute knowledge the earth is no longer water inundated. "Why not just leave the ark? Evidently, when Noah's future is at stake, he subordinates his own experiments, however noble and adroit, to a message from GOD."[54] It is interesting this is the only time Noah heard the voice of GOD from inside the ark. As has been the case in the other divine speeches (Gen 6:13–21 and Gen 7:1–4), however, GOD speaks directly to (and only to) Noah (Gen 8:15–17; cf. Gen 9:1–7, 8–11). It is thus assumed Noah relays the information to all parties involved in an expedient and reliable manner.[55]

Once Noah hears from GOD, Noah responds promptly obeys, leaving the ark *en masse* (Gen 8:18–19. Cf. Gen 6:22; 7:5). John Calvin states: "How great must have been the fortitude of the man, who, after the incredible weariness of a whole year, when the deluge has ceased, and new life has shone forth, does not yet move a foot out of his sepulcher, without

54. Hamilton, *Genesis 1–17*, 307.
55. Hamilton, *Genesis 1–17*, 307.

the command of God."⁵⁶ The text communicates the need for faithful obedience and garners empathy for Noah.⁵⁷

Noah's departure from the ark is noted through a four-fold repetition of the verb יצא: (1) Qal imperative (Gen 8:16), (2) Hiphil imperative (Gen 8:17), (3) Qal *yiqtol* with *waw* (Gen 8:18), and Qal *qatal* (Gen 8:19). Hamilton argues that by highlighting this verb, the text "emphasises the departure from the ark. Noah and his companions are not consigned to an ark existence. The ark is . . . only a shelter, not a domicile."⁵⁸ The significance of the imperative to leave the ark and the recitation of the act itself by the narrator highlights the redemptive nature of God to begin life anew. Longman proclaims:

> The flood was an act of un-creation in which God reverted the earth to its pre-creation state of *tohu wabohu* ('formless and empty,' 1:2). Not surprisingly then, we begin to encounter language that echoes language of the first creation. We move now from un-creation to re-creation.⁵⁹

The text communicates God's desire to redeem and restore all life and his plan for salvation.

IV. *Noah's Sacrifice and God's Promise (Gen 8:20–22)*

ᵃויבן נח מזבח ליהוה

ᵇויקח מכל הבהמה הטהורה ᶜומכל העוף הטהר ᵈויעל עלת במזבח

ᵉוירח יהוה את ריח הניחח

ᶠויאמר יהוה אל לבו

ᵍלא אסף לקלל עוד את ʰהאדמה ⁱבעבור האדם כי יצר לב האדם רע מנעריו

ʲולא אסף עוד להכות את כל חי כאשר עשיתי

---

56. Calvin, *Genesis*, 280. Cf. Waltke and Fredricks, *Genesis*, 142.

57. See Mathews, *Genesis 1—11:26*, 391.

58. Hamilton, *Genesis 1–17*, 307. Cf. Hodge, *Days of Genesis*, 146–50.

59. Longman, *Genesis*, 119–20. See also Sailhamer, "Genesis," 129; Sarna, *Genesis*, 59.

After the Rain

עד כל ימי הארץ

זרעˡוקציר וקר וחם וקיץ וחרף ויום ולילה לא ישבתוᵏ

Then Noah built an altar to the LORD and he took of every clean animal and of every clean bird and he offered burnt offerings on the altar.
Then the LORD smelled the pleasing odor and the LORD said to himself:ᵐ
> "I will never again curse the ground anymore, due to humanity.
> Though the inclination of humanity's minds are evil from youth.
> Nor will I again anymore destroy all life as I have just done.
>> Yet all the days of the earth:ⁿ
>>> Seedtime and Harvest
>>> Cold and Heat
>>> Summer and Winter
>>> Day and Night
>> Shall not cease."

---

a. Sequential *waw*. *GBHS* §3.5.1.a.

b. Sequential *waw*. *GBHS* §3.5.1.a.

c. Coordinative *waw*. Williams, *Hebrew Syntax*, §430a.

d. Though the logic of the narrative would appear to make the nuance of the *waw* consequential (Chisholm, *Exegesis*, 132; *GBHS* §3.5.1.b) the flow makes it sequential (*GBHS* §3.5.1.a).

e. Sequential *waw*. *GBHS* §3.5.1.a.

f. It is understood that though the logic of the narrative would seem to make the nuance of the *waw* consequential (Chisholm, *Exegesis*, 132; *GBHS* §3.5.1.b), the flow itself makes it sequential (*GBHS* §3.5.1.a). For more information on the verbal form here, see GKC §72aa.

g. The prohibition particle indicates the "subject . . . is prohibited from doing the action (or being in the state) described by the verb." Williams, *Hebrew Syntax*, §396.

h. The article has a "generic function, indicating the class, i.e., "humankind." Williams, *Hebrew Syntax*, §92. The same rule applies to each of the other instances of the article in this pericope.

i. Causal preposition. *GBHS* §4.1.5.f.

j. Synchronic *waw*. Chisholm, *Exegesis*, 126.

k. The context makes clear that (by metonymy) this stands for the time when seeds are planted. See the NET Bible.

l. This coordinative *waw* joins opposites as do each of the *waws* immediately following it. Williams, *Hebrew Syntax*, §430a and §431. For further information on the "strong vocalization" of the *waws* that follow this *waw* here, see Joüon §104d.

m. Though generally translated as "in his heart" in many EVV, this term refers to "the center of one's being, an image for a person's thought life, reflections, and will. The story of the 'heart' reveals a person's commitment and direction in life." VanGemeren, "The Heart," 1019. See also *DCH* 4:506–9; Luc, *NIDOTTE* 2:752; Bowling, *TWOT* 1:466–67; *HALOT* 1:513–15; von Rad, *Genesis*, 117; *IBHS* §11.2.5.f.

n. The idea is that "so long as the earth exists," or "while there are yet all the days of the earth." See Wenham, *Genesis 1–15*, 191.

Extended Analysis

On leaving the ark, Noah built an "altar" (מזבח).[60] Noah sacrificed to the LORD (Gen 8:20). The text does not make the reason for the sacrifice explicit. It may be presumed, however, the offering is in response to Noah's gratitude for his deliverance.[61] While sacrifice had already been made prior to this point in Genesis (Gen 4:3–5), this is the first mention of an "altar" (מזבח) being made (Gen 8:20).[62] While "Noah's altar is not described, the first audience would have assumed it conformed to the Mosaic legislation requiring all temporary altars be constructed of 'earth' or 'unhewn stones' (e.g., Exod 20:24–26; Deut 27:5–6)."[63] The text mentions Noah "took of every clean animal and of every clean bird" (Gen 8:20). According to Leviticus 1:

> The whole burnt offering . . . represented the worshiper's complete surrender and dedication to the LORD. After the flood Noah could see that GOD was not only a GOD of wrath, but a GOD of redemption and restoration. The one who escaped the catastrophe could best express his gratitude and submission through sacrificial worship, acknowledging GOD as the sovereign of the universe.[64]

Following Noah's sacrifice it is written "the LORD smelled the pleasing odor" (Gen 8:21a). The language shows GOD's pleasure towards both the

---

60. See *HALOT* 1:564; Averbeck, *NIDOTTE* 2:888–908.
61. Mathews, *Genesis 1—11:26*, 391–92. Cf. Walton, *Genesis*, 315.
62. Wenham, *Genesis 1–15*, 189.
63. Mathews, *Genesis 1—11:26*, 391–92.
64. The NET Bible. See also Hartley, *Leviticus*, 17–18.

gift and the giver (e.g., Exod 29:18, Lev 1:9, Num 15:3).[65] A refusal to receive or "smell" the sacrifice depicts God's rejection of the worship act (Lev 26:31, cf. Amos 5:21).[66] Hamilton argues: "since 'ōla, the Hebrew word for '(whole) burnt offering,' is related to 'ālâ, a verb meaning 'to ascend,' it is natural to perceive the smoke of Noah's offering ascending heavenward. Movement up and down as already been made in the Deluge story—rising sin, falling divine forbearance; rising waters falling waters, rising smoke."[67]

There are also several sound plays on the name Noah that are brought together here: "through the 'soothing' offerings (nîḥōaḥ), God is brought to 'rest' (nûaḥ) by 'Noah' (nōaḥ). Thus by 'Noah' (nōaḥ) the divine 'grief/regret' (nḥm) over human creation (6:6) and his decision to 'wipe out' (mḥh; 6:7) all humanity is transformed into his 'compassion' (nḥm) for postdiluvian humanity."[68] The text communicates God's mercy. God will no longer give his fallen creatures their "just desserts. The punishable will not be punished."[69]

It is significant God's promise to never again destroy the earth via the Flood is repeated. First, God states he will "never again curse the ground anymore, due to humanity" (Gen 8:21a).[70] Following this, Yahweh affirms he will never again anymore destroy all life as he had just done (Gen 8:21b). The Flood is an unrepeatable event—a type of salvation (1 Pet 3:21).[71]

The poem which follows further underscores Yahweh's promise (Gen 8:22). God will preserve the earth and its "ecology" until the final judgment (1 Peter 3:20-21; 2: Peter 2:5-12).[72] Sarna puts it well: "the ordered processes of nature will never again be interrupted. The rhythm of

65. Mathews, *Genesis 1—11:26*, 392. Cf. Kidner, *Genesis*, 93.

66. Mathews, *Genesis 1-11:26*, 392.

67. Hamilton, *Genesis 1-17*, 308.

68. Mathews, *Genesis 1—11:26*, 393. See also van Wolde, *Words Become Worlds*, 82-83.

69. Hamilton, *Genesis 1-17*, 310.

70. Hamilton asserts God self-deliberated due to the potential of magic being involved. Hamilton, *Genesis 1-17*, 309. For more details on magic in the ANE see Oswalt, *Bible Among the Myths*, 54-55, 75-76. For details on curses and blessings in Gen 1-11, see Patty, "Curse and the Power of Blessings." Cf. Sollereder, *Animal Suffering*, 28-29.

71. Longman, *Genesis*, 124-25. For details on typology and Noah's Flood, see Yoshikawa, "Noachic Flood," 443-90.

72. Waltke and Fredricks, *Genesis*, 143. Cf. Fisher, "Gilgamesh and Genesis," 401.

life" is "reflected in the rhythmic quality of the language."[73] In sum, "God pledges to allow time, and the liturgical cycle, to continue."[74] The text communicates God's long-suffering.

The poem is comprised of four couplets or pairs of merisms: (1) seedtime and harvest, (2) cold and heat, (3) summer and winter, and (4) day and night.[75] These describe "environmental phenomena: agricultural, climatic, and temporal."[76] Walton maintains these denote "food, weather, and time," respectively, the three staple things required to sustain life on the earth.[77] The text explicates the assurance of God's promise to form a new creation—a cosmos renewed.

STEP FOUR: DETERMINING THE RHETORICAL EFFECTIVENESS

Having outlined the rhetorical units of Gen 8:1–22 (step one of the rhetorical-critical method), delineated the entextualized rhetorical situation/showcased its exigences (step two), and provided a commentary on the various rhetorical strategies employed in the text (step three), the final step of the rhetorical-critical method involves determining the rhetorical effectiveness (step four).

Concerning the massive amount of water involved in the Flood, this tension is altogether eliminated for the Flood itself has been fully reckoned with. Not only have the waters ceased their raging and are now calm; they have also dissipated and the land has become dry, bearing vegetation (Gen 8:13–14). Full and complete closure to this matter is also underscored by God's declaration that he will never again send a Flood such as this one ever again (Gen 8:21–22).

With respect to the exigence involving God, Noah, and the covenant, it is clear Noah remains fully obedient to God. The one who heeded the Creator's imperative to build, stock, and enter the ark (Gen 6:14–22; 7:1–5, 7–9, 13–16) also obeyed the command to exit the ark

---

73. Sarna, *Genesis*, 59.

74. Cotter, *Genesis*, 59.

75. Hamilton, *Genesis 1–17*, 310. For details on merisms, a poetic device which functions to convey the idea of completeness or totality, see Watson, *Classical Hebrew Poetry*, 31.

76. Sarna, *Genesis*, 59.

77. Walton, *Ancient Cosmology*, 170.

(Gen 8:15–19). Though silent, Noah's actions speak volumes (see too Gen 6:22; 7:5, 7, 9, 13–16).

Yahweh may also be said to have fulfilled his covenant obligations to Noah. First, GOD promised Noah he would establish his covenant with him (Gen 6:18). Then, after Noah entered the ark (Gen 7:5, 7, 13, 15), Yahweh's hand of protection rested on all those aboard the ark (see Gen 7:16). Thus, Noah's life was spared (Gen 7:23). Next, GOD remembered Noah and all those on the ark and began to reverse the Flood waters (Gen 8:1). Following this, once the earth was dry, GOD commanded Noah and company to leave the ark (Gen 8:15). Yahweh then promised to never again destroy all life again through the same type of cataclysmic Deluge (Gen 8:21–22).

The primary exigence concerning humanity and "violence" (חמס) remains unresolved. If GOD is no longer able to send a Flood to check the problem of humanity's hell-bent tendencies, what *will* he do in order to help curb humanity's self-destructive potential? This issue will be addressed in the next chapter which seeks to bring resolution to this problem.

How might the people in an exilic/post exilic Israelite context have considered this text? McKeown states the Noachian deluge narrative would be "particularly relevant to early Israelite readers who were longing to return to their homeland after a period of enforced exile with hopes of a new beginning."[78] As it is written:

> "For a little while I forsook you,
> But with vast love I will bring you back.
> In slight anger, for a moment,
> I hid My face from you;
> But with kindness everlasting
> I will take you back in love
>   —said the LORD your Redeemer.
> For this to Me is like the waters of Noah:
> As I swore that the waters of Noah
> Nevermore would flood the earth,
> So I swear that I will not
> Be angry with you or rebuke you.
> For the mountains may move
> And the hills be shaken,
> But my loyalty shall never move from you,
> Nor My covenant of friendship be shaken
>   —said the LORD, who takes you back in love."
> (Isa 54:7–10 JPS)

---

78. McKeown, *Genesis*, 63.

McKeown further asserts, "This passages shows ... in spite of the long delay GOD did permit a new beginning ... the message of the flood story is that after even the most severe judgment comes mercy ... a new beginning would bring encouragement and hope to the exiles and be an antidote to despair."[79] GOD's commitment to Noah's seed is just as true for the Hebrew exiles.[80]

CONCLUSION

This chapter analyzed the text of Gen 8:1–22 by means of the rhetorical-critical method outlined in chapter 2. It started (step one) by determining the rhetorical units of the passage. It was demonstrated the text was constructed of several main rhetorical subunits, namely "The Flood Waters Abate" (Gen 8:1–5), "After the Rain" (Gen 8:6–14), "Disembarking the Ark" (Gen 8:15–19), and, lastly, "Noah's Sacrifice and GOD's Promise" (Gen 8:20–22). The analysis also determined that each of these main subsections consisted of numerous other subunits.

Following this, in step two, determining the rhetorical situation, it was re-asserted that the secondary exigence pertaining to the potential risk of covenant infidelity on the part of GOD and Noah was fully resolved. The secondary exigence concerning the delicate balance between destruction and deliverance with respect to the Flood water was also fully resolved. The primary exigence concerning humanity's "violence" (חמס), however, remains unresolved. How GOD will mitigate their self-destructive habits once humanity starts to multiply after the Flood?

Concerning step three, determining the rhetorical strategy, the text's aesthetic appeal and rhetorical efficacy in communicating GOD's salvific nature and his judgment were duly noted (see below). With respect to step four, determining the rhetorical effectiveness, it is clear that while the text's secondary exigencies have been resolved, the primary exigence remains at large. This section also noted the marked effect this text would have on an exilic/post-exilic Israel.

Concerning universalistic language, the Hebrew term "all" (כל) occurs fourteen times in total within this pericope (Gen 8:1–22). Only once (roughly 7 percent of all of the occurrences here) does the sense relate to

---

79. McKeown, *Genesis*, 63.

80. Mathews, *Genesis 1—11:26*, 393. See too Dumbrell, "Covenant with Noah," 7–8.

judgment (Gen 8:9). To be clear, once Noah released the dove from the ark she was unable to find rest because water covered all the surface of the earth (Gen 8:9).

The Hebrew term "all" (כל) thus occurs thirteen times (roughly 93 percent) with the sense relating to salvation (Gen 8:1x2; 17x3, 19x4, 20x2, 21x2). Many of these occurrences pertain to all of the animals which God either: (a) remembered (see Gen 8:1x2) or (b) commanded to leave the ark (see Gen 8:17x3, 19x4). Of course, one also notes Noah took from all of the clean animals and all of the clean birds and sacrificed them to the LORD (Gen 8:20x2). The most important, climatic usages of the Hebrew term "all" (כל) with respect to salvation, however, pertain to God's promise that: (1) he would never again destroy all life as he had just done with the Flood (Gen 8:21) and (2) as long as the earth endures, i.e. "all the days of the earth," i.e., the cycles of nature and ecology, will continue (Gen 8:22).

In addition, while the text notes some challenges involved with the Flood water (Gen 8:6–9) and humanity's thoroughly self-destructive propensities (see Gen 8:21), the vast majority of verses in this pericope (Gen 8:1–22), i.e., eighteen verses (roughly 82 percent) relate to a hope-filled, new creation (Gen 8:1–5, 10–22). To be clear, I count only four verses in total (roughly 18 percent) as directly pertaining to judgment. Though portions of Gen 8:21 do relate to humanity's incorrigible propensity to evil, the overarching sense of the verse remains quite positive.

Concluding, this book contends the text of the Noachian deluge narrative categorically underscores all God did to preserve life in spite of the disaster. Despite the picture of devastation that the narrative depicts, the prominent emphasis of the text is on deliverance and redemption i.e., salvation, not judgment. The focus of the Genesis Flood is acutely bent towards God's salvific rather than punitive purposes.

The arc of salvation within the Flood narrative can be broken down into two main ideas. First, God's intention for creation is not thwarted and, secondly, God commits himself to his intentions of creation. His intention for creation can be stated as thus: the establishment of order via covenant showing the sanctity of human life and the upholding of all life.

The text of Gen 8:1–22 markedly bolsters this assertion as demonstrated through the universalistic language summation and the preceding analysis.

6

The Covenant
Conditions and Assurance (Genesis 9:1–17)

INTRODUCTION

PRIOR TO EXPOUNDING ON the passage at hand, it is prudent to offer a brief summary of the plot of the Noachian deluge narrative thus far. Despite GOD instituting an epic Flood of cataclysmic proportions so as to obliterate all life on earth (Gen 6:5–7), Noah found favor with GOD (Gen 6:8). As such, GOD commanded Noah to build a colossal, salvific, nautical vehicle—the ark—so as to ensure his and his immediate family's survival as well as the survival of all the different kinds of creatures GOD created on earth (Gen 6:9–21). In full obedience to GOD, Noah built, victualed, and entered the ark, along with Shem, Ham, Japheth, Noah's wife, the three wives of his sons, and select representatives from each of the different kinds of animals—then the LORD shut them in (Gen 6:22—7:16). All life outside the ark died as the waters prevailed on the earth for one hundred and fifty days (Gen 7:17–24).

At the most turbulent time of the Flood, however, GOD remembered Noah and everyone else on board the ark (Gen 8:1a). GOD caused the Flood waters to begin to recede and stopped the machinations of the Flood (Gen 8:1b–3). The ark came to rest among the mountains of Ararat and Noah proceeded to discern the habitability of life on the earth through the raven and a dove (Gen 8:4–12). In the process of time, the ground dried and GOD commanded Noah and company to exit the ark (Gen 8:13–17). Noah obeyed as did all those aboard the ark (Gen 8:18–19). Noah built an altar to the LORD and sacrificed an offering to GOD (Gen 8:20). Yahweh received Noah's sacrifice and promised to never again send a Flood such as that ever again and that he would never again destroy every living thing as he had just done with the Flood (Gen 8:21–22).

This chapter's analysis will offer clear resolution to the main exigence of the rhetorical situation, namely humanity's "violence" (חמס). To be clear, "GOD will seek every conceivable means to keep the [covenant] relationship intact; throughout history the salvific will of GOD for the people remains constant . . . Through it all, GOD's faithfulness and gracious purposes remain constant and undiminished."[1] Humanity now has the privileged responsibility to mitigate blood-thirst through a special provision that empowers mortals to act for GOD—as his image—to the extent of even being able to take human life (Gen 9:1–7).

The remainder of the narrative reveals GOD's blessing(s). By means of several speeches, GOD shares the promise of good news with Noah, his sons, and all living things (Gen 9:1–7, 9–11, 12–16). He also provides a signifier of this positive turn of events, the bow, which functions as the sign of the covenant GOD made with all creation (Gen 9:12–16, 17. Cf. Gen 6:18).

STEP ONE: DETERMINING THE RHETORICAL UNITS

This section will follow the same procedure and definitions as in each of the previous chapters. The first main subunit is entitled "Be Fruitful and Multiply!" (Gen 9:1–7).[2] It hangs together by virtue of it being a divine speech. As such, the introductory formula, "thus he said to them," Gen 9:1, is the surest indicator of this being a unit.[3] The referential, situational, relational, and structural coherence of this unit is also demonstrated through there being correspondence of: (a) time and place, i.e., the unit covers a single conversation (Gen 9:1–7, cf. 9:8–11), (b) primary

---

1. Fretheim, *Suffering of God*, 111.

2. The demarcation of Gen 9:1–7 being a unit is generally uncontested. See Mathews, *Genesis 1—11:26*, 399; Waltke and Fredricks, *Genesis*, 143; Kidner, *Genesis*, 100; Hamilton, *Genesis 1–17*, 311, 316, 319; McKeown, *Genesis*, 63–64. Some, however, extends the unit to Gen 9:18. See Wenham, *Genesis 1–15*, 191–92. Still, others extend it all the way to Gen 9:19. See Sailhamer, *Pentateuch*, 128–29.

3. See Dorsey, *Literary Structure*, 23. Cf. Meier, *Speaking*, 59; Miller, *Speech*, 400.

participants, namely GOD (Gen 9:1, 4, 5, 6), Noah (Gen 9:1–7), and his sons (Gen 9:1–7), and (c) topic, theme, and mood, namely the nature of relationships under GOD's authority (Gen 9:1–7).

This may be compared to the shift that transpires in the following divine speech, which focuses on the covenant GOD makes with all of creation and the promise there will never again be another Flood like the one in Genesis so as to destroy and ruin all of the earth (Gen 9:8–11).

Each of the rhetorical units of this portion of text are depicted below:

The Covenant: Conditions and Assurance (Gen 9:1–17)

I. Be Fruitful and Multiply! (Gen 9:1–7)
   1. GOD's initial proclamation of blessing (Gen 9:1)
      i. summative statement of GOD's blessings (Gen 9:1a)
      ii. formulaic introduction to the divine speech (Gen 9:1b)
      iii. particulars of the blessings (Gen 9:1c)
   2. dominion of humanity over the animal kingdom (Gen 9:2)
      i. initial comments concerning relationships to animals (Gen 9:2a–d)
      ii. acknowledgement of humanity's sovereignty over animals (Gen 9:2e)
   3. matters concerning food (Gen 9:3–4)
      i. meat and green plants (Gen 9:3)
      ii. prohibition of blood (Gen 9:4)
   4. human death and the image of GOD (Gen 9:5–6)
      i. death of a human being by an animal (Gen 9:5a–b)
      ii. death of a human being by another human being (Gen 9:5c–9:6)
   5. reiteration of GOD's blessings (Gen 9:7)

The next main subunit is entitled "The Covenant Promise: Never Again!" (Gen 9:8–11).[4] It is another divine speech. As such, the introductory for-

---

4. The demarcation of Gen 9:8–11 being a unit is not uncommon. See Wenham, *Genesis 1–15*, 194; Mathews, *Genesis 1—11:26*, 408. Some scholars, however, do not

mula, "Then GOD said to Noah, and to his sons with him," see Gen 9:8, is the clearest indicator of this portion of text being a distinct unit.[5] Aside from this, the referential, situational, and structural (relational) coherence of this unit is also demonstrated through there being sameness of: (a) time and place, that is, the unit covers a single conversation in a single location (Gen 9:8–11, cf. 9:12–16), (b) primary participants, namely GOD (Gen 9:1, 11), Noah (Gen 9:9, 11), Noah's descendants (Gen 9:9), and every living creature of the earth (Gen 9:10–11), and (c) sameness of mood, topic, and theme, namely the covenant of creation (Gen 9:9–11). The section which follows focuses more particularly on the sign of the covenant, namely the bow (Gen 9:12–16).

Each of the main rhetorical units of this portion of text are depicted below:

The Covenant: Conditions and Assurance (Gen 9:1–17)

  II. "The Covenant Promise: Never Again!" (Gen 9:8–11)

    1. GOD spoke to Noah (Gen 9:8)

      i. formulaic introduction (Gen 9:8a)

      ii. GOD spoke to Noah (Gen 9:8a)

      iii. GOD spoke to Noah's sons with him (Gen 9:8b)

    2. GOD's covenant with humanity (Gen 9:9)

      i. Noah and his sons (Gen 9:9a)

      ii. the descendants of Noah and his sons (Gen 9:9b)

      iii. acknowledgement of humanity's sovereignty over animals (Gen 9:9e)

    3. GOD's covenant with animals (Gen 9:10)

      i. iteration of covenant with everything on the ark (Gen 9:10a)

      ii. covenant with birds/domesticated animals (Gen 9:10b–c)

---

differentiate these units. See Hamilton, *Genesis 1–17*, 316; Sailhamer, *Pentateuch*, 126–27. Others, though, extend the unit (Gen 9:8–17). See Kidner, *Genesis*, 101; McKeown, *Genesis*, 64; Waltke and Fredricks, *Genesis*, 140–41. One notes that this fails to differentiate the divine speeches.

5. See Dorsey, *Literary Structure*, 23. Cf. Meier, *Speaking*, 59; Miller, *Speech*, 400.

       iii. reiteration of covenant with everything on the ark (Gen 9:10d)

       iv. covenant with every beast of the earth (Gen 9:10e)

   4. reiteration of the restoration of peace and order (Gen 9:11)

       i. re-affirmation of the covenant (Gen 9:11a)

       ii. re-affirmation that there will never again be a Flood (Gen 9:11b–c)

The next main subunit is entitled "The Covenant Sign: The Rainbow" (Gen 9:12–16).[6] It hangs together by virtue of it being a divine speech. The introductory formula, "GOD said" (Gen 9:12) marks this as a unit.[7] The referential, situational, and structural (relational) coherence of this unit (Gen 9:12–16), is also demonstrated through there being: (a) sameness of time and place, that is, the unit covers a single conversation occurring in the same location (cf. Gen 9:17), (b) sameness of participants, namely GOD (Gen 9:12–16), and every living creature on earth (Gen 9:12–16), and (c) sameness of topic, theme, and mood, i.e., the covenant and the bow (Gen 9:12–16). Although this is the same topic and theme as Gen 9:17, that verse has an introductory formula which marks it as a new conversation and thus makes it an independent unit of text.

Each of the rhetorical units of this portion of text are depicted below:

The Covenant: Conditions and Assurance (Gen 9:1–17)

   III. "The Covenant Sign: The Bow" (Gen 9:12–16)

      1. initial comments concerning the sign of the covenant (Gen 9:12)

         i. formulaic introduction (Gen 9:12a)

         ii. initial comments about the covenant (Gen 9:12b–e)

           a. the sign of the covenant (Gen 9:12b)

---

6. Gen 9:12–16 being a unit is not generally contested. See Waltke and Fredricks, *Genesis*, 145. Cf. Wenham, *Genesis 1–15*, 195 who extends the unit (Gen 9:12–17).

7. The demarcation of Gen 9:8–11 being a unit is not unknown within scholarship. See Wenham, *Genesis 1–15*, 194, Mathews, *Genesis 1—11:26*, 408. Cf. Hamilton, *Genesis 1–17*, 316; Sailhamer, *Pentateuch*, 126–27. See also Kidner, *Genesis*, 101; McKeown, *Genesis*, 64; Waltke and Fredricks, *Genesis*, 140–41 who extend the unit (Gen 9:8–17). This scheme fails to differentiate the divine speeches as distinct units.

The Covenant   193

   b. affirmation of the covenant for humans (Gen 9:12c)
   c. affirmation of the covenant for animals (Gen 9:12d)
   d. affirmation of the effectiveness of the covenant (Gen 9:12e)
 2. particulars concerning the bow (Gen 9:13–15)
    i. initial comments concerning the bow and covenant (Gen 9:13)
       a. GOD will set the bow in the clouds (Gen 9:13a)
       b. the bow will be the sign of the covenant (Gen 9:13b)
    ii. affirmation with respect to the bow and the Flood (Gen 9:14–15)
       a. further comments concerning the bow (Gen 9:14)
       b. further comments concerning the covenant (Gen 9:15)
 3. re-affirmation of GOD's faithfulness (Gen 9:16)
    i. matters pertaining to the bow (Gen 9:16a–b)
    ii. matters pertaining to the covenant (Gen 9:16c–e)

The final main unit is entitled "Reiteration of the Covenant Sign of the Rainbow" (Gen 9:17).[8] It is the last divine speech that occurs in the Noachian deluge narrative. The introductory formula, "then GOD said to Noah" (Gen 9:17) is the clearest indicator of this text forming a unit. Aside from this, however, the coherence of this specific unit (Gen 9:17), is also demonstrated through there being: (a) sameness of time and place, that is, the unit covers a single conversation in the same location (Gen 9:17), (b) sameness of the primary participants, namely GOD (Gen 9:17), Noah (Gen 9:17), and every living creature on the earth (Gen 9:17), and (c) sameness of topic, theme, and mood, namely GOD's covenant with creation (Gen 9:17).

Each of the rhetorical units of this portion of text are depicted below:

---

8. Though some scholars place Gen 9:17 with Gen 9:8–16 together, this ignores the procedures for determining the primary apertures and closings of speech. Cf. Mathews, *Genesis 1—11:26*, 407; Waltke and Fredricks, *Genesis*, 145.

The Covenant: Conditions and Assurance (Gen 9:1–17)

    IV. Reiteration of the Covenant Sign of the Rainbow (Gen 9:17)

        1. formulaic introduction (Gen 9:17a)

        2. reiteration of the covenant sign of the bow (Gen 9:17b–c)

At this time it is required to offer rationale as to why Gen 9:1–17 is comprised as a unit, in and of itself, and why it is best to end one's analysis of the Noachian deluge narrative at this point, given that the *toledoth* of Shem, Ham, and Japheth begins at Gen 10:1 and Noah's *toledoth* continues until Gen 9:29. To begin, a brief synopsis of the following passage (Gen 9:18–29) is in order. The narrative opens (Gen 9:18–19) by noting Shem, Ham, and Japheth were the sons of Noah who came out of the ark and that from them the whole earth was populated. The narrative turns to Noah planting a vineyard, imbibing of the wine he had made, and becoming naked inside his tent (Gen 9:20–21). After this, Ham saw his father's nakedness (Gen 9:22–23). The details of this immoral deed need not detain us.[9] Shem and Japheth safeguard their father and honor him by covering his nakedness (Gen 9:23). The story concludes with "patriarchal curse and blessing."[10] Ham, i.e., Canaan, is cursed (Gen 9:25). Shem and Japheth are blessed (Gen 9:26–27).

Literary speaking, there is a clear shift that takes place in the narrative. Aside from the brief comments concerning the ark and the repopulation of the earth (an indicator of the judgment of the Flood) the text bears very little resemblance to the rest of the Flood account.[11] In this way, Gen 9:18–20 forms both the conclusion of the Noachian deluge narrative and an introduction to the episode of Noah's nakedness. As one scholar explains:

> These verses are a good example of the author's style of composition throughout Genesis. By means of these short transitional units the author ties together individual, self-contained narratives into a larger line of stories. In this . . . unit one should not

---

9. Aside from the commentaries, see Embry, "Reassessing Voyeurism," 417–33; Bassett, "Noah's Nakedness," 232–37; Bergsma, "Noah's Nakedness," 25–40.

10. Sailhamer, *Narrative*, 129. See too Mathews, *Genesis 1:1—11:26*, 412.

11. Keiser, *Genesis 1–11*, 139–40. The demarcation of Gen 9:18–29 is generally uncontested. See Collins, *Reading Genesis Well*, 192; Waltke and Fredricks, *Genesis*, 147; Mathews, *Genesis 1—11:26*, 412; Hamilton, *Genesis 1–17*, 319; Sailhamer, *Genesis*, 132; McKeown, *Genesis*, 65; Kidner, *Genesis*, 102.

overlook the identification of Canaan as one of the sons of Ham (9:18). That bit of information is crucial to the meaning of the narrative to follow (cf. 9:22, 25).[12]

Collins summarizes:

> Noah's behavior shows that, for all his goodness (6:9), it is as true for him as it is for all the rest of humankind that the evil inclination of his heart remains. GOD's project of restoring Adamic innocence will take some more doing, and Israel must see themselves as a further step toward finishing that project.[13]

Finally, it is interesting to note that Noah lived another 350 years after the Flood (Gen 9:28). Altogether Noah lived 950 years and then he died (Gen 9:29). After the Flood, many children were born to Shem, Ham, and Japheth, the three sons of Noah (Gen 10:1). All the nations of the earth descended from Noah's sons and their decent lines were traced after the Flood (Gen 10:32).

STEP TWO: DETERMINING THE RHETORICAL SITUATION

Multiple exigences exist in the Noachian deluge narrative. A secondary tension concerns GOD and the Flood. Another secondary tension concerns the covenant between GOD, Noah, his descendants, and all of creation. As noted above, though, the primary exigence pertains to "violence" (חמס) and how GOD and humanity should respond in an effective fashion to this sin.

Concerning the exigence of the Flood, not only has all the water dried up (Gen 8:13–14) but GOD has also provided ample reassurance that never again will all life be cut off by the water of the Flood and never again shall there be a Flood to destroy all life on earth (Gen 9:11, 15). GOD marks this promise with a bow—a sign of peace and hope for all of creation (Gen 9:12–16, 17). The threat of such a calamity ever happening again is gone completely now and for all time.

Concerning the faithfulness of the two covenant parties (GOD and Noah), it has already been noted that Noah has fulfilled all of his

---

12. Sailhamer, *Narrative*, 129. See too Mathews, *Genesis 1:1—11:26*, 412.
13. Collins, *Reading Genesis Well*, 192. See too Wenham, *Rethinking Genesis*, 46. Cf. Halton, ed., *Genesis*, 110-39; Steinmetz, "Vineyard, Farm, and Garden," 193-207.

covenant stipulations. Nothing more can be done. Through building an altar and sacrificing, Noah has proven himself immeasurably faithful for he went above the stipulations GOD had commanded him. GOD too was immeasurably faithful to the covenant he made with Noah (Gen 6:18). He preserved Noah's life and the life of his immediate kin through the Flood (Gen 7:23), remembered him and all those aboard the ark (Gen 8:1), caused the Flood to stop (Gen 8:1b–3), enabled the ark to come to rest safely without incident (Gen 8:4), and honored the sacrifice Noah made (Gen 8:21–22). GOD even gave "a bow in the sky."[14] This bow serves as a reminder: "Despite the fact that the world deserves judgment, GOD will show restraint and mercy."[15] Another scholar states, "The sign is a self-maledictory oath. In essence, GOD is saying, 'if I break this promise, may I die.'"[16]

With respect to the primary exigence of the narrative, namely humanity's "violence" (חמס), despite the universal nature of the covenant and the language of perpetuity involved with respect to it (see Gen 9:9–17), there remains a high level of human responsibility to mitigate blood lust (Gen 9:1–7).[17] Life and death are now given primarily into human hands (Gen 9:5–6). Through this provision, the exigence of the account for the Flood may be considered resolved since a way is made for humanity to be fruitful, multiply, and refresh the earth (Gen 9:7).

With respect to audience, the text communicates the necessity of GOD-ordained societal order. Measures must be taken in order to "restore humanity to its intended position of blessing and representation."[18] Sarna notes: "the destruction of the old world calls for the repopulation of the earth and the remedying of the ills that brought on the Flood. Society must henceforth rest on more secure moral foundations."[19] Pointedly, Arnold opines, "Those who try to apply this to capital punishment in contemporary societies miss the subtle ambiguities of 9:6 due to the

---

14. Hamilton, *Genesis 1–17*, 316.

15. Hamilton, *Genesis 1–17*, 316. See too Batto, *Slaying the Dragon*, 88.

16. Longman, *Genesis*, 122. Longman credits Kline with this comment but no references are provided. Elsewhere, Kline maintains: "the rainbow in the clouds (v. 13) pictures GOD's battle-bow, used in the flood-storm to shoot his shafts of wrath on the earth, now suspended in a condition of peace, a sign that the divine warrior is governing rebellious mankind with forbearance for a season." Kline, *Genesis*, 42.

17. Cf. Westmoreland and Stassen, "Biblical Perspectives," 127.

18. Keiser, *Genesis 1–11*, 135.

19. Sarna, *Genesis*, 60.

concise poetry, fail to understand the inappropriateness of modern nation states to execute this principle, and miss the thrust of the *imago dei* statement of 9:6b."[20]

That being said, "in light of the unrestrained violence before the flood and the coming promise of safety, GOD reminds all people that even though the whole earth remains safe from destruction [by means of a cataclysmic, universal Flood], there will still be consequences for sin, especially sin which disrupts the divine plan to fill the earth with his image."[21]

STEP THREE: DETERMINING THE RHETORICAL STRATEGY

The focus of this step is on delineating and assessing the rhetorical strategies the text employs to make its persuasive appeal. As in each of the previous chapters, the analysis will begin with a fresh, English translation along with a commentary of certain grammatical/syntactical features (including text criticism issues). The analysis will be divided according to the main subunits noted above in step one of the analysis, namely: (I) "Be Fruitful and Multiply!" (Gen 9:1–7), (II), "The Covenant Promise: Never Again!" (Gen 9:8–11), (III), "The Covenant Sign: The Bow" (Gen 9:12–16), and (IV) "Reiteration of the Covenant Sign of the Bow" (Gen 9:17).

The Covenant: Conditions and Assurance (Gen 9:1–17)

I. *Be Fruitful and Multiply! (Gen 9:1–7)*

[a]ויברך אלהים את נח [b]ואת בניו [c]ויאמר להם

פרו [d]ורבו ומלאו [e]את הארץ

ומוראכם וחתכם יהיה על כל חית [f]הארץ ועל כל עוף השמים

בכל אשר תרמש האדמה [g]ובכל דגי הים בידכם [h]נתנו

---

20. Arnold, *Genesis*, 110. Cf. Middleton, *Liberating Image*, 221.
21. I am indebted to Jacob Burnette for this insight (private communiqué).

כל רמש אשר הוא חי לכם יהיה לאכלה כירק עשב נתתי לכם את כל

[i]אך בשר [j]בנפשו דמו [k]לא תאכלו [l]ואך את דמכם לנפשתיכם [m]אדרש

[n]מיד כל חיה אדרשנו [o]ומיד [p]האדם מיד איש אחיו אדרש את נפש האדם

[q]שפך דם האדם [r]באדם דמו ישפך [s]כי [t]בצלם אלהים עשה את האדם

[u]ואתם פרו [v]ורבו [w]שרצו בארץ ורבו [x]בה

Then GOD blessed Noah and his sons.
Thus he said to them:
Be fruitful! Multiply! Fill the earth!
The fear of you and the dread of you[y] shall be upon all the wild animals of the earth, and upon all the birds of the heavens, on everything that creeps on the ground, and on every fish of the sea—into your power they are delivered. Every moving thing that lives for you will be for food; as the green plants, I now give you everything.
Only flesh with its life in it (that is, its blood) you must not eat.[z]
Surely your blood-life, I will require a reckoning.
    From the hand of every beast I will require it.
    And from the hand of human beings,
        from the hand of every man's brother,
    I will require the life of a human being.
    Whoever sheds the blood of a human being,
        by a human being his blood shall be shed.
    For in the image of GOD he made humanity.
But you, fruitfully multiply! Bring forth abundantly on the earth! Multiply!

---

a. Sequential *waw*. *GBHS* §3.5.1.a.
b. Coordinative/conjunctive *waw*. Williams, *Hebrew Syntax*, §430a.
c. Synchronic waw (displaying simultaneous action). Chisholm, *Exegesis*, 126, *GBHS* §3.5.4.b.
d. This *waw* and the following ones (unless indicated otherwise) are each synchronic. Chisholm, *Exegesis*, 126.
e. Note: LXX adds "and subdue it," thus bringing Gen 9:1 into conformity with Gen 1:28. See Wenham, *Genesis 1–15*, 154.

The Covenant

f. Note: LXX adds "and over all domesticated animals." Wenham, *Genesis 1–15*, 154.

g. Coordinative/conjunctive *waw*. Williams, *Hebrew Syntax*, §430a. The preposition is spatial in relationship (metaphorically). *GBHS* §4.1.5.a.

h. Note: Both the SamPent and the LXX read "I have given it." Wenham, *Genesis 1–15*, 154.

i. Restrictive adverb. Williams, *Hebrew Syntax*, §388; Wenham, *Genesis 1–15*, 154.

j. The preposition communicates the idea of "proximity," "vicinity near," and "association with something." See GKC §119n. The rendering may also be "with." See Wenham, *Genesis 1–15*, 154.

k. Categorical prohibition. Williams, *Hebrew Syntax*, §396; Hamilton, *Genesis 1–17*, 314.

l. This disjunctive *waw* is dramatic or contrastive. Chisholm, *Exegesis*, 126.

m. The word order (object preceding the verb) places emphasis on the verb. *GBHS* §5.1.2.b.2.

n. Though the Hebrew reads "hand," it is symbol for strength, power, and authority. Ryken et al. eds., *DBI*, 360–62.

o. Sequential *waw*. See *GBHS* §3.5.1.a; Chisholm, *Exegesis*, 120.

p. The article has a "generic function, indicating the class, i.e., "humankind." Williams, *Hebrew Syntax*, §92. The same rule applies to each of the other instances within this pericope.

q. The Qal participle stands at the beginning of the sentence as a "*causus pendens* (or as the subject of a *compound noun-clause* . . .) to indicate a condition, the contingent occurrence of which involves a further consequence." GKC §116w. Italics original.

r. The preposition could be understood as a "*bet pretii*," yielding the translation "*for* a human will that person's blood be shed," thus leaving the "executor of justice undefined" (cf. LXX) and allowing the possibility that "only God may seek vengeance." See Wilson, "Blood," 269. A thorough defense, however, of the rendering "*by* a human" (so NRSV, NIV 1984/2011, NASB, NJPS, KJV, NKJV ESV, NLT), i.e., a "*beth instrumenti*," may be found in *BHRG* §39.6.3.a; *GBHS* §4.1.5.c; GKC §121f. See too Hamilton, *Genesis 1–17*, 315. Cf. Harland, *Human Life*, 161. Waltke and Fredricks make clear: "the preposition could be read 'in exchange for.' Most English versions rightly understand the preposition to indicate agency. This is its normal meaning with Niphal (*IBHS* §23.2.2f); it avoids a tautology with 9:5 and lays a solid foundation for capital punishment as exacted later in the Mosaic law (cf. Ex. 31:12–14; Num. 35:16–32; Deut. 17:6–7; 19:15)." Waltke and Fredricks, *Genesis*, 145.

s. Evidential conjunction. See *GBHS* §4.3.4.b.

t. Essence preposition. *GBHS* §4.1.5.h.

u. Concluding (disjunctive) *waw*. Chisholm, *Exegesis*, 127.

v. Coordinate *waw*. See *GBHS* §4.3.3.g.

w. Note: SamPent, LXX, and Vg "insert 'and' unnecessarily." Wenham, *Genesis 1–15*, 155.

x. Spatial preposition. See *GBHS* §4.1.5.a.

y. Hamilton (*Genesis 1–17*, 311) renders this as "dread fear." Cf. EVV.

z. For a defense of this rendering, see GKC §131k, 138b; Wenham, *Genesis 1–15*, 154.

Extended Analysis

This section underscores "divine blessing."[22] This is the third time humanity has been told to "multiply" (רבה) by God (Gen 1:28; 8:17; 9:1) and the third time they have been "blessed" (ברך) by him (Gen 1:28; 5:2; 9:1).[23] "The 'blessing' of procreation and dominion conferred upon the postdiluvian world is a restatement of God's creation promise for the human family and the creatures . . . but now its provisions are modified in light of encroaching societal wickedness."[24]

Since humanity's inability to effectively relate to God and one another was the primary factor of his decision to send the Flood (see Gen 6:5–7, 11–13) and since humanity shows no signs of improving in the post-Flood world (see Gen 8:21), the Creator now implements certain regulations so as to "insure the continuation of the earth until its final, future redemption."[25]

The text communicates God's wisdom in making provision to safeguard and protect human life. This involves empowering humanity to mediate justice via *lex talionis*. Wilson states: "God here *delegates* to humanity the power to punish . . . Humans . . . are to enact their role as God's image by *imitating* God and punishing murderers by taking their life."[26]

Many questions, however, remain unanswered. Though the text communicates the human responsibility to de-escalate "violence" (חמס) by virtue of sanctioned blood-shedding, it does not provide enough particulars to determine all of the nuances which are involved: "Who, precisely, is able to authorize the death penalty and why them, specifically?"

22. Waltke and Fredricks, *Genesis*, 143.
23. Wenham, *Genesis 1–15*, 192.
24. Mathews, *Genesis 1—11:26*, 398.
25. Mathews, *Genesis 1—11:26*, 398.
26. Wilson, "Blood," 269. All emphases original. Cf. Middleton, *Liberating Image*, 294–95.

"If any nondescript person can wield such power, would not the world be back to where it was before the Flood?" "In what way and under what circumstances does this 'delegation' of GOD apply?" "What exactly does the narrator imply in saying that being made in the image of GOD grants one the authority to take human life?" In general terms:

> The 'violence' advocated in this text is not to be equated with bloodlust, and in many ways the principle of *lex talionis* (blood-for-blood) in Gen 9:6 functions to prevent the escalation of aggression that could expand to include a murderer's relatives. But while this verse may limit violence, it certainly does not eradicate it; and in this text the reader is far removed from the pacifistic ethic of nonviolence that others have identified as the primary meaning of the *imago Dei*.[27]

With the above in mind, whatever authority GOD gave humanity to take away life, it must also be understood within the context and constraints of creatureliness and underscored by an acute awareness of GOD's character and nature who is both just *and* merciful (Exod 34:6–7). As one scholar adeptly puts it, humans are to be "life producers, not life takers."[28]

Despite the echoes of creation, there are also discontinuities. In contrast to the tranquility and vegetarian diet of the Garden of Eden, the presence of humans now brings terror to animals and people are allowed to eat them but are not permitted to consume blood (Gen 9:2–3. Cf. Gen 1:29. See too Lev 17:10–14; Acts 15:20, 29; 21:25).[29]

II. *The Covenant Promise: Never Again! (Gen 9:8–11)*

[a]ויאמר אלהים אל נח [b]ואל בניו אתו לאמר

[c]ואני [d]הנני מקים את בריתי אתכם [e]ואת זרעכם אחריכם

ואת כל נפש החיה אשר אתכם

---

27. Wilson, "Blood," 271–72. See too Dumbrell, "Covenant With Noah," 9.

28. Hamilton, *Genesis 1–17*, 316.

29. "The fact that Israel's neighbors possessed no parallel law indicates that the prohibition cannot be a vestige of primitive taboo, but the result of a deliberate, reasoned enactment." Milgrom, "Blood," *EncJud* 4:1115. For further details on certain aspects of the meaning and significance of the relevance of this prohibition for Acts (aside from the commentaries), see Dawson, *Message of the Jerusalem Council*.

בעוף בבהמה ובכל חית הארץ אתכם ᶠמכל יצאי התבה לכל חית הארץ

ᵍוהקמתי את בריתי אתכם

ʰולא יכרת כל בשר עוד ⁱממי המבול

ʲולא יהיה עוד מבול לשחת הארץ

Then GOD said to Noah, and to his sons with him:
"I will establish my covenant with you, along with your descendants after
    you and with every living creature that is with you: among birds, among
    domesticated animals, and among every beast with you—namely
    everything that came out of the ark—to every beast of the earth!
I will establish my covenant with you. All life will not be cut off again by the
waters of the Flood, nor shall there be a Flood to destroy the earth."

---

a. Sequential *waw*. See *GBHS* §3.5.1.a, and Chisholm, *Exegesis*, 120.
b. Coordinative *waw*. Williams, *Hebrew Syntax*, §430a.
c. Dramatic *waw*. Chisholm, *Exegesis*, 126. The additional pronoun serves to give "strong emphasis." See GKC §135.d.
d. The function is to point an addressee to something in the speech situation that is newsworthy and is often used for dramatic effect. See *BHRG* §40.22.4; Chisholm, *Exegesis*, 126.
e. This *waw* (and the ones that follow unless indicated otherwise) are accompaniment *waw*s. Williams, *Hebrew Syntax*, §436.
f. Explicative (or, perhaps, emphatic) preposition. Williams, *Hebrew Syntax*, §326/325.
g. Resumptive *waw*. Chisholm, *Exegesis*, 121.
h. Summarizing or concluding (disjunctive) *waw*. Chisholm, *Exegesis*, 123. There is "an element of emphasis" in the use of the negation. See Joüon §160b.
i. "Unusually ... 'from' expresses the agent of the passive (GKC, 121f)." Wenham, *Genesis 1–15*, 155. It is possible that the more common *beth* preposition is avoided here so as to avoid the ambiguity "in/by the waters." See Wenham, *Genesis 1–15*, 155; Joüon §132d.
j. Summarizing or concluding (disjunctive) *waw*. Chisholm, *Exegesis*, 123.

Extended Analysis

God assures once more that the Flood was a one-time event (Gen 9:11). Though the "possibility of future judgment is not eliminated . . . that judgment will not be manifested as a flood."[30] While humanity's sin caused unspeakable damage to all life, destroying the earth (Gen 6:13; 9:11; 2 Pet 2:5, 3:6), God's covenant makes clear that never again will "all life" (כל בשר) be "cut off" (כרת) from the "Flood" (מבול) and never again shall there be a "Flood" (מבול) so as to "destroy" (שחת) the earth (Gen 9:11, 15).[31] The Creator's commitment is "irreversible . . . Noah's covenant is continually presented as universal and inclusive, involving all the animal life that emerged from the ark."[32] The text communicates God's steadfastness and the wonders of his love.

Humanity now bears a great responsibility. If Gen 9:5–6 is ignored or if the proscription is abused, the result seems to be that the world would once again descend into "violence" (חמס). Though the covenant provides assurance for the continuation of all life on earth, the quality of life remains contingent upon humanity's willingness to submit to God's order and structure for society and to manifest his values as bearers of the divine image (Gen 9:6).[33]

---

30. Hamilton, *Genesis 1–17*, 316.

31. Pointedly, one scholar observes, "If the Noahic Flood were anything less than a global event, then the Noahic Covenant—and as such, the *divine oath*—would be abrogated and thus rendered meaningless" (Stallings, *Genesis Cataclysm*, 33; italics original). Another individual asserts, "God makes a covenant with the earth and with all flesh, swearing to never again do what He had just done. Is His covenant only with the people and animals of a particular region, while people and animals who now happen to live in other regions of the world are out of luck? Maybe. Again, there is subjectivity here, but to me, this story does not read like a local flood. On this score, I am in agreement with Answers in Genesis, on whose behalf Andrew Snelling and Ken Ham write, 'So frequent is this use of universal terms, and so powerful are the points of comparisons ('high hills,' 'whole heaven,' and 'mountains'), that it is extremely difficult to imagine what more could have been written under the direction of the Holy Spirit to express the concept of a global Flood!'" (Griffin, *Creation and the Flood*, 160). For more details on the universal scope of the Noahic covenant, see Williamson, "Covenant," 141.

32. Mathews, *Genesis 1–11:26*, 408–9.

33. Greenberger goes too far when he states: "God promises not to bring destruction on the world because it will not be necessary, as man [sic] will become accountable and prevent the moral deterioration which would necessitate such an action. God puts his faith in man [sic]." Greenberger, "Noah," 31. Cf. Moberly, *Genesis*, 110; Schreiner, *Covenant*, 38. See too Hodge, *Days of Genesis*, 138.

Every animal (even birds) are included with Noah in God's covenant (Gen 9:9–10). Animals thus play an "honorable role in the biblical economy," for not only does God hold them responsible for "crimes of brutality" (see Gen 9:5) but he "enters into promissory arrangements with them."[34] Wilson states:

> The account of Noah and the flood serves as a reminder not only to people of the monotheistic faiths . . . but also to everyone that we must be stewards of the earth in an environmentally responsible way. The plants, animals, birds, and fish, as creations of God, are to be a blessing to humanity both to use and to enjoy.[35]

Ronald A. Simkins uses the rubric of "harmony with nature," "mastery over nature," and "subjugation to nature" to describe the ways humanity can choose to conduct their life; Simkins, of course, advocates for "harmony" with nature and one another.[36] The implications of this with respect to ecological stewardship, animal husbandry, nature conservation, and such are far reaching.[37] Alexander C. Stewart states:

> By combining ecological virtue ethics with biblical theology, we can attend to the suffering of creation in the Scriptures and in our present contexts, in order to cultivate empathetic sensitivity that benefits our Christian character and our communities.[38]

In point of fact, a "growing theological movement, called 'creation care,' seeks to emphasize and inculcate the Christian responsibility to steward God's creation."[39] In the conclusion of this book, it is advocated that future study of the Noachian deluge narrative should extend this idea.

---

34. Hamilton, *Genesis 1–17*, 316.

35. Wilson, "Noah," 12. See too Simkins, *Creation*, 256–66. Cf. Peterson, *Genesis*, 70.

36. Simkins, *Creation*, 171. Cf. Mbuvi, *Belonging in Genesis*, 109–47.

37. See Simkins, *Creation*, 256–66.

38. Stewart, "Ecological Suffering," 19.

39. Davidson and Turner, *Manifold Beauty*, 46. Other examples may be found in the conclusion of this book.

III. The Covenant Sign: The Rainbow (Gen 9:12–16)

ויאמר אלהיםa

זאת אות הברית אשר אני נתן bביני וביניכם ובין כל נפש חיה אשר אתכם לדרת עולם

את cקשתי נתתי בענן dקשתי נתתי בענן eובין הארץ

fוהיה בענני ענן על הארץ gונראתה הקשת בענן

hוזכרתי את בריתי אשר ביני iוביניכם ובין כל נפש חיה בכל בשר

jולא יהיה עוד המים למבול לשחת כל בשר

kוהיתה הקשת בענן

lוראיתיה לזכר ברית עולם בין אלהים

mובין כל נפש חיה בכל בשר אשר על הארץ

Then GOD said:
"This is the sign of the covenant I am making between me and between you and between every living creature with you for all future generations:
    I will set my bow in the clouds.
    Thus it shall be a sign of the covenant between me and the earth.
    Then, whenever I bring clouds over the earth, and the bow is seen in the clouds, I shall thus call to mind the covenant that is between me and you and between every living creature from among all life.
    Never again will the waters become a Flood to destroy all life.
    (For when the bow is in the clouds, then I will look so as to remember the long-lasting[n] covenant between GOD (myself) and between every living thing among all life that is on the earth)."

---

a. Sequential *waw*. See *GBHS* §3.5.1.a and Chisholm, *Exegesis*, 120.

b. This *waw* and the next one are both accompaniments. Williams, *Hebrew Syntax*, §436.

c. The placing of the object first emphasizes it. See Wenham, *Genesis 1–15*, 155.

d. Sequential *waw*. See *GBHS* §3.5.1.a; Chisholm, *Exegesis*, 120.

e. Consequential *waw*. Chisholm, *Exegesis*, 120.

f. Supplemental or parenthetical *waw*. Chisholm, *Exegesis*, 122.

g. Accompaniment *waw*. Williams, *Hebrew Syntax*, §436.

h. Consequential *waw*. Chisholm, *Exegesis*, 120.

i. This *waw* and the next one are both accompaniment *waws*. Williams, *Hebrew Syntax*, §436.

j. Climatic (disjunctive) *waw*. Chisholm, *Exegesis*, 132. There is "an element of emphasis" in the use of the negation. See Joüon §160b. For more details on the form, see GKC §72w.

k. Supplemental or parenthetical *waw*. Chisholm, *Exegesis*, 122.

l. Sequential *waw*. See *GBHS* §3.5.1.a, and Chisholm, *Exegesis*, 120.

m. Accompaniment *waw*. Williams, *Hebrew Syntax*, §436.

n. On this translation, see Niehaus, *Biblical Theology*, 210–14; Longman, *Genesis*, 122.

Extended Analysis

The "long-standing" or "everlasting" (עוֹלָם) nature of the Noachic covenant is emphasized in this speech.[40] Notably, this is also the first occurrence in the Bible of the term "sign" (אוֹת), the other main instances of a covenant sign being circumcision and the Sabbath day (see, for example, Gen 17:11 and Exod 31:16–17).[41] Here, "the giving of the 'sign' guarantees the parties of its perpetual validity."[42] The term "bow" (קשתי) is usually used in reference to a projectile-type weapon.[43] As such, many propose GOD means to intimate he is hanging up his "battle bow at the end of the flood, indicating he is now at peace with humankind."[44] One scholar states: "GOD has holstered his weapon."[45] There are also many ANE motifs involved. Bernard F. Batto asserts:

> After his victory over Tiamat and her allies, Marduk . . . "hung up" his bow. The bow, undrawn, is placed in the heavens to

---

40. This term conveys the sense of a "long time . . . usually eternal . . . but not in a philosophical sense." *HALOT* 1:798. For more details, see Mason, *Covenant*, 43–44; Walton, *Covenant*, 131–32.

41. Mathews, *Genesis 1—11:26*, 409. See also Helfmeyer, *TDOT* 1:170–71.

42. Mathews, *Genesis 1—11:26*, 408–9.

43. See *DCH* 7:339–40; Younger, *NIDOTTE* 3:1004–6.

44. The NET Bible. See also Waltke and Fredricks, *Genesis*, 146.

45. Wilson, "Rainbow," 32. Cf. Speiser, *Genesis*, 59; Boyd, *Crucifixion*, 1132.

shine as the bowstar. One will not be far off the mark in interpreting this bowstar both as a sign of the definitiveness of Marduk's victory over the rebellious forces of chaos (in that he can afford to lay it aside) and as a guarantee that good order reigns within the cosmos.[46]

Extending this idea further, Batto states:

> The flood is an extension of *Chaoskampf*. Through human violence (*ḥāmās*, Gen 6:11–13), chaos (*těhôm*) had reentered the cosmos and threatened to undo GOD's initial victory of chaos (cf. Gen 1:2 and 7:11). Thus we are justified in appealing to the parallel in *Enuma Elish* and in interpreting the rainbow as a sign that GOD's victory is total and that GOD has indeed hung up his bow used to subdue the enemy. With the reestablishment of divine rule, a new and more perfect order has been achieved. Humankind . . . acknowledges its proper position before GOD. GOD binds himself to an everlasting covenant of peace with all creation. The rainbow now appears in the heavens to signal forevermore the advent of a new era of peace and harmony between GOD and the cosmos.[47]

Irrespective of any ANE connections and/or nuances with respect to the bow imagery itself, within the Noachian deluge narrative, specifically, it is clear that the bow functions as a token of GOD "invisible word of grace."[48] Ephraim E. Speiser states things quite beautifully: "the rainbow is introduced as a bright and comforting reminder that the race shall ensure, however transient the individual."[49] The term "bow" (קשתי) occurs three times within just as many verses (Gen 9:13, 14, 16).[50] As another scholar eloquently opines: "[s]treched between heaven and earth, it is a bond of peace between both, and, spanning the horizon, it points to the all-embracing universality of the Divine mercy."[51] The text communicates there is a blessed assurance for all the inhabitants of the earth—both human and non-human alike—forevermore. Whenever GOD sees the bow, the Creator will "call to mind" his covenant (see NJB). "The harmony of

---

46. Batto, *In the Beginning*, 183.
47. Batto, *In the Beginning*, 183. See too Batto, *Slaying the Dragon*, 87–88.
48. Mathews, *Genesis 1—11:26*, 409. See too Schreiner, *Covenant*, 34–39.
49. Speiser, *Genesis*, 59. See too Wilson, "Rainbow," 32.
50. It is uncertain, however, what significance, if any, its thrice-time pairing with "clouds" has.
51. Delitzsch, *A New Commentary on Genesis*, 290.

the entire created order is guaranteed by this confirmation."⁵² The text communicates how the preservation of humanity in the postdiluvian world "is founded on GOD's justice and mercy, and the reliability of the created world."⁵³ As R. W. L. Moberly asserts:

> [The bow] is one of the most . . . beautiful, and moving of all recurrent natural phenomena. Its symbolic resonances are many, and one can imagine it variously . . . It usually appears after a time of heavy rain when the sun comes out and shine [sic] again but while dark clouds are still in the sky; and often the dark clouds are a backdrop for the many colours of the rainbow. Thus, when the rainbow is viewed in the light of the preceding Flood narrative, its appearance at the very moment when one can see both darkness and light in the sky comes to symbolize GOD's commitment to light over darkness, to beauty over chaos, to life over death.⁵⁴

The text communicates GOD's purpose of salvation and blessing for creation.⁵⁵

IV. *Reiteration of the Covenant Sign of the Rainbow (Gen 9:17)*

ויאמר אלהים ᵇאל נחᵃ

זאת אות הברית אשר הקמתי ביני ᶜובין כל בשר אשר ᵈעל הארץ

Then GOD said to Noah:
"This is the sign of the covenant that I established between me and between everything which is upon the earth."

---

a. Sequential *waw*. See *GBHS* §3.5.1.a and Chisholm, *Exegesis*, 120.
b. The preposition is declarative (marking the recipient of a verb of speech). *GBHS* §4.1.2.c.
c. Coordinative *waw*. Williams, *Hebrew Syntax*, §430a.
d. The preposition is spatial/locative in a vertical relationship. *GBHS* §4.1.16.a.i.

52. Dumbrell, "Covenant with Noah," 6. See too Walton, "Flood," 323.
53. Clifford, *Creation Accounts*, 149.
54. Moberly, *Genesis*, 110–11. See too Mason, *Covenant*, 83–85.
55. See Gilbert, *God Never Meant for Us to Die*, xvii.

Extended Analysis

The emphasis here is not on the covenant *per se* but rather the sign, i.e., the bow.[56] The bow is a sign for humanity to reaffirm their humility, accept their creatureliness before GOD, and "show gratitude for being GOD's partner in a covenant that allows him [sic] to continue to flourish within his [sic] imperfection."[57] GOD reiterates the "formal establishment of the agreement . . . 'I have established,' echoing the divine initiation and completion of the covenant; and 'all flesh,' showing the inclusive character of the agreement."[58] Though the Noachic covenant does not, in itself, provide redemption, "the preservation of creation is the context in which redemption will be realized."[59] The text communicates GOD's desire to provide salvation and blessing to all life.

STEP FOUR: DETERMINING THE RHETORICAL EFFECTIVENESS

As noted above in step two (determining the rhetorical situation), both of the secondary exigences of the Flood, as well as the primary exigence, are completely resolved. Not only did GOD repeat that he will never again send a Flood (Gen 9:11, 15) he also instituted a covenant—complete with the bow as its sign—to provide complete assurance that the Flood will never happen ever again (Gen 9:12–17). In sum, the exigence between GOD and the Flood is gone.

Concerning the role the covenant parties play, it was noted above that though Noah and GOD have both fulfilled the stipulations of the covenant agreement there remains the new conditions of Gen 9:1–6 to reckon with. This ties directly to the exigence of humanity's "violence" (חמס). While GOD has made a way for humanity to move forward without the threat of another Flood, the future of humanity remains at risk. Without a judicious exercising of GOD's gift of "new-creation" by means of stewarding one's relationships with one another and all of creation, humanity runs the risk of falling into the same depraved spiral of sin, death, and destruction. Humanity requires wisdom, discernment, and understanding

---

56. Hamilton, *Genesis 1–17*, 318.
57. Greenberger, "Noah," 32.
58. Mathews, *Genesis 1—11:26*, 412.
59. Schreiner, *Covenant*, 39.

in order to know how best to execute their authority and responsibility to execute the *lex talionis* principle. Most of all, it is required of human beings to recognize and respect their creatureliness before GOD. Without cognizance of one's position under GOD's umbrella of authority, it is impossible to walk in harmony with one another relationally or to exercise a circumspect form of ecology. The text is persuasive in communicating the truth that humanity will win or lose by the way they choose.

With respect to those persons within the exilic/postexilic Israelite period (Gen 9:8–17), it is clear the promises of GOD within the Genesis Flood text were not given solely to Shem alone or to any other specific people group but rather to all of creation and all life on earth (see Gen 9:8–9, 12, 15, 16, 17). All people, everywhere, for all time are entitled to the benefits of GOD's "eternal covenant."[60] As Steven D. Mason asserts: "there is a robust message here of GOD's intention for the preservation of Israel's international enemies."[61] The question is not just "what does it mean to live faithfully when somebody else is in charge?"[62] The true import of the passage manifests itself best in what the prophet Jeremiah (Jer 29:7) admonished Israel to do when "the captives faced the challenge of living as political outsiders."[63]

The "missional responsibilities" of Israel in Exile are understood to be predicated upon GOD's promises to all of creation (Gen 9:8–17).[64] One can either stand in judgment against GOD, denouncing his acts and questioning his standards, or accept that GOD's promises were extended freely to all persons for all time.[65] The text communicates that one ought to be at peace with their neighbor and seek to achieve harmony with all of creation, resting in the knowledge that "GOD is the LORD of history and that . . . blessing and prosperity . . . are under his righteous control."[66]

With respect to universalistic language, the Hebrew term "all" (כל) occurs nineteen times in total within this pericope (Gen 9:1–17). Seven times (roughly 37 percent of all of the occurrences here) the sense relates to non-salvific components (Gen 9:2x4, 3x2, 5). Four times it refers to

60. See Mason, *Covenant*, 82.
61. See Mason, *Covenant*, 82.
62. See Cochran and Van Drunen, eds., *Law and the Bible*, 76.
63. Cochran and Van Drunen, eds., *Law and the Bible*, 76.
64. Brueggemann, *Jeremiah*, 257–58.
65. As one scholar states: "GOD blesses all; he calls an individual [sic—Canaan] cursed." Vermeulen, "Blessing and Cursing," 127.
66. Cochran and Van Drunen, eds., *Law and the Bible*, 76.

the fear that humanity will bring to animals, i.e., the beasts of the earth, the birds of the air, every creature moving along the ground, and all the fish (Gen 9:2x4). Twice the term pertains to people's diet, i.e., how humans are now permitted to eat everything that lives and moves and are not restricted to plants and fruit (Gen 9:3x2). Once the term pertains to blood-shed (Gen 9:5).

The Hebrew term "all" (כל) also occurs twelve times (roughly 63 percent of all occurrences here) with the sense relating to salvation (Gen 9:10x4, 11, 12, 15x3, 16x2, 17; cf. Gen 9:19, 29). Four times the reference pertains to the animals which came off the ark (Gen 9:10x4). Eight times it pertains to GOD's covenant with all life on earth (Gen 9:11, 12, 15x3, 16x2, 17).

Alongside this, while a number of verses underscore the fear of humans that animals will have after the Flood (see Gen 9:2), or highlight the severe nature of the *lex talionis* principle (Gen 9:5–6), every other verse in this portion of text (Gen 9:1–17) relates either to humanity's diet (Gen 9:3–4) or carries an overtly positive, salvific component (Gen 9:1, 7–17). That is, of the seventeen verses in this pericope (Gen 9:1–17), only five verses in total (roughly 29 percent) do not relate to salvation while twelve verses (roughly 71 percent) pertain directly to salvific components.

To conclude, this book contends the text of the Noachian deluge narrative categorically underscores all GOD did to preserve life in spite of the disaster. Despite the picture of devastation that the Genesis Flood narrative depicts, the prominent emphasis of the text is on deliverance and redemption i.e., salvation, not judgment. The focus of the Flood is distinctly and acutely bent towards GOD's salvific rather than punitive purposes.

The arc of salvation within the Flood narrative can be broken down into two main ideas. First, GOD's intention for creation is not thwarted and, secondly, GOD commits himself to his intentions of creation. His intention for creation can be stated as thus: the establishment of order via covenant showing the sanctity of human life and the upholding of all life. This involves, in particular, humanity as his image bearers, including the *lex talionis* (life for life) principle.

The text of Gen 9:1–17 clearly and significantly bolsters this assertion as demonstrated through the universalistic language summation and the preceding analysis.

7

Conclusion

INTRODUCTION

ONE ASPECT OF THIS study was to showcase and demonstrate the usefulness of rhetorical-critical (rhetoric as persuasion) methods for the study of Hebrew narrative texts. Through investigating the specific rhetorical strategies the text employs to construct its argument(s), I have considered the persuasive nature of the Genesis Flood. This book contends the text of the Noachian deluge narrative categorically underscores all GOD did to preserve life in spite of the disaster. Despite the picture of devastation that the narrative depicts, the prominent emphasis of the text is on deliverance and redemption i.e., salvation, not judgment. The focus of the Genesis Flood is acutely bent towards GOD's salvific rather than punitive purposes.

The arc of salvation within the Flood narrative can be broken down into two main ideas. First, GOD's intention for creation is not thwarted and, secondly, GOD commits himself to his intentions of creation. His intention for creation can be stated as thus: the establishment of order via covenant showing the sanctity of human life and the upholding of all life. This involves, in particular, humanity as his image bearers, including the *lex talionis* (life for life) principle.

This study is sensitive to the broader context of scholarship concerning the Noachian deluge narrative, including diachronic (source-critical) and synchronic (literary-critical) analyses. It reflects on the long-standing debate over the Flood narrative's composition and lends support to theories of the rhetorical cohesion of the text. In this way, this study supplements the work of other scholars as the rhetorical-critical (rhetoric as persuasion) model "fills the void" between diachronic and synchronic approaches (such as form, source, literary, and narrative criticisms).[1] Although the Flood account intersects with the rest of the book of Genesis and, by extension, the Pentateuch, the rest of the Deuteronomistic history, notwithstanding the entire HB/OT, and the canon, in general, it is a distinct literary and rhetorical unit in its own and was analyzed as such.

THE RHETORICAL-CRITICAL MODEL

The refinement and development of the Kennedy rhetorical-critical model, supplemented by the works of Möller, Shaw, Barker, and Ahn, in particular, is also important to this study. Each of the aforementioned practitioners of this model, including some others, use similar approaches to delimit rhetorical units and consider the rhetorical strategies revealed through the text's literary devices and structural arrangements.[2] This study supplements many of the steps of the model.

With respect to step one, this study leverages a particularly nuanced approach to determining the rhetorical units by means of a close examination of: (1) persons of verbs, (2) the uses of *waw*, (3) and verbal forms. This study's approach to determining rhetorical situation (step two) and determining the rhetorical effectiveness (step four), also nuances the work of other HB/OT scholars. An entextualized rhetorical situation attempts to push rhetorical effectiveness in the direction of the implied audience that is constructed in the text and other audiences.

This is often required of different canonical texts since it cannot generally be determined how the primary audience responded to them in their initial setting and environment, aside from the fact that the texts are well-preserved and included in the collection of writings which eventually came to be known as Scripture. As such, discussion of rhetorical effectiveness aligned with the hermeneutics of affirmation, i.e., reading

---

1. Kennedy, *New Testament Interpretation*, 3–4. Cf. Barker, *From the Depths of Despair*, 32, 37.

2. I am indebted to Barker for much of the wording of this sentence. See Barker, *From the Depths of Despair*, 262.

the text in such a way that the interpreter can experience the text's persuasive authority.³ There are, however, clear signals in the final form of the Pentateuch for an exilic/postexilic audience. As such, some time was spent discussing how those people at that time might have identified with the message of the Flood text as a whole.

With respect to step three, determining the rhetorical species (or genre) of the text, this study also supplements the aforementioned rhetorical-critical works. Rather than subordinating this discussion to the rhetorical strategies the text employs in order to make its persuasive appeal, it has been suggested this step should be entirely re-thought. In brief, belaboring the nuances of *judicial*, *epideictic*, and *deliberative* rhetoric potentially places an "Occidental paradigm on an Oriental work."⁴ Instead, this study argues that one should re-classify the canonical text as being intellectual, worldview formative rhetoric. Once this is achieved, one may abandon any further delineation of the species entirely, thus eliminating step three of the model altogether.

In sum, each of the steps of the Kennedy model have been carefully nuanced.

ELEMENTS OF PERSUASION IN THE NOACHIAN DELUGE NARRATIVE

Throughout this study I analyzed the Noachian deluge narrative by the four-step model of rhetorical criticism offered above. I noted the text's rhetoric persuasively communicated certain things concerning Noah, the Flood, humanity, and Yahweh.

Concerning Noah, the text's rhetoric communicated Noah was a figure of no small import. Noah was an upstanding patriarch of his family who had a distinguished lineage. After the Flood, Noah's descendants would repopulate the earth. Shem, one of Noah's sons, would ultimately be connected with the esteemed patriarch, Abraham, from whom Jacob and the sons of Israel came. Noah was an exemplary individual and a model of faithful obedience to God. In addition to this, Noah practiced and modeled wisdom, foresight, intelligence, and gratitude.

With respect to the Flood and humanity, the text's rhetoric communicated the "moral malaise of humanity was a chronic condition and not

---

3. See Barker, *From the Depths of Despair*, 262–63.
4. Hwang, *Rhetoric of Remembrance*, 10.

Conclusion

just a spasmodic lapse."[5] GOD's judgment was thus absolutely necessary. Despite the pervasiveness of sin, though, both before and after the Flood, humanity remained blessed of GOD for they alone bear his image within the created order.

Concerning Yahweh, the Genesis Flood communicated GOD's desire for life to prevail over death and for a "renewal of the kinship relationship" between humanity and himself.[6] By means of the covenant GOD implemented with Noah, his sons, and all of creation, including representatives of the entire animal kingdom within their kinds, the text communicates how all life is precious to GOD. Though judgment for sin is certain and the penalty for disobedience is grave, whatever befalls the earth, it will always teem with life for GOD is gracious and merciful.

SUMMARY OF RESULTS: UNIVERSALISTIC LANGUAGE (JUDGMENT AND SALVATION)

The Hebrew term "all" (כל) occurs sixty seven times in total within the portion of text this book analyzed (Gen 6:5—9:17). Twenty four times (roughly 36 percent) the sense relates to judgment.

In Gen 6:5-22 the specific verse references are Gen 6:5x2, 12, 13, and 17x2. Within Gen 7:1-24 the verse references are Gen 7:4, 11, 19x2, 21x3, 22x2, and 23. In Gen 8:1-22 the only reference to judgment is Gen 8:9. In Gen 9:1-17 the specific verse references are Gen 9:2x4, 3x2, and 9:5.

Alongside this, of the eighty one verses analyzed within this study, thirty verses in total (roughly 37 percent), do not refer to salvific components. In Gen 6:5-22 the specific verse references are Gen 6:5, 6, 7, 11, 12, 13, and 17. In Gen 7:1-24 the verse references are Gen 7:4, 6, 7, 10, 11, 12, 17, 18, 19, 20, 21, 22, 23, and 24. In Gen 8:1-22 the references pertinent to judgment are Gen 8:6, 7, 8, and 9. NB: as noted above, though portions of Gen 8:21 do relate to judgment, it is not counted within this particular analysis since the overarching sense of the verse is positive. In Gen 9:1-17 the specific verse references that do not relate to salvation are Gen 9:2, 3, 4, 5, and 6.

On the flip side, the Hebrew term "all" (כל) relating to salvation within Gen 6:5—9:17 occurs forty three times in total (roughly 64 percent). In Gen 6:5-22 the specific verse references are Gen 6:19x2, 20, 21,

---

5. Hamilton, *Genesis 1–17*, 273.
6. Boda, *Heartbeat of Old Testament Theology*, 100.

and 22. Within Gen 7:1–24 the verse references are Gen 7:1, 2, 3, 5, 8, 14x6, 15, and 16 (cf. portions of Gen 7:23 which is not counted here). In Gen 8:1–22 the explicitly salvific references are Gen 8:1, 2, 3, 4, 5, 10, 11, 12, 13, 14, 15, 16, 17, 18, 19, 20, 21, and 22. In Gen 9:1–17 the specific verse references are Gen 9:10x4, 11, 12, 15x3, 16x2, 17 (cf. Gen 9:19, 29).

Alongside this, of the eighty one verses analyzed within this study, more than half, i.e., fifty one verses in total (roughly 63 percent), refer to salvific components. In Gen 6:5–22 the specific verses are Gen 6:8, 9, 10, 14, 15, 16, 18, 19, 20, 21, and 22. Within Gen 7:1–24 the verse references are Gen 7:1, 2, 3, 7, 8, 9, 13, 14, 15, 16. NB: as noted above, though portions of Gen 7:23 relate to salvation it is not counted within this particular analysis. In Gen 8:1–22 the references pertinent to salvation are Gen 8:1, 2, 3, 4, 5, 10, 11, 12, 13, 14, 15, 16, 17, 18, 19, 20, 21, and 22. In Gen 9:1–17 the specific verse references are Gen 9:1, 7, 8, 9, 10, 11, 12, 13, 14, 15, 16, and 17.

In sum, the statistics provided above concerning Gen 6:5—9:17 markedly bolsters the argument that the text of the Genesis Flood categorically underscores all GOD did to preserve life in spite of the disaster. Despite the picture of devastation the narrative depicts, the prominent emphasis of the text is on deliverance and redemption i.e., salvation, not judgment. The focus of the text of Noah's Flood is acutely bent towards GOD's salvific rather than punitive purposes.

FURTHER WORK

Further work on the Noachic Flood could involve increased inter-textual analysis. Boda notes:

> The Noachic covenant plays many functions within the OT. While it shows the creational and universal implications of the redemptive agreements established within Israel, it also provides hope that those redemptive agreements will endure and reach their fullest potential (Jer. 30–31). At times it is used to comfort (Isa. 54–55) and even to announce judgment in the present (Nah. 1:8) as well as the future (Isa. 24; Zeph 1–2). It can prompt praise (Ps. 29:10) but also be used in lament (Ps. 89).[7]

---

7. Boda, *Heartbeat of Old Testament Theology*, 100.

A thorough, methodologically rigorous, description of the Flood and these aspects (including their import in the NT) would prove beneficial and enlighten different aspects of this study.[8]

The Noachian deluge narrative also stimulates necessary discussions about nature conservation, ecological stewardship, animal husbandry, and the like. These matters were only briefly touched on in this book. More focused study would elucidate other relevant implications.[9]

Lastly, a concerted focus relating to civil and national politics, government affairs, and other aspects of social discourse, especially concerning the *lex talionis* principle, could also be done.[10]

---

8. Cf. Schnittjer, *Old Testament Use of Old Testament*.

9. Some examples within evangelicalism include, Bouma-Prediger, *For the Beauty of the Earth*; Moo and Moo, *Creation Care*, Sleeth, *Serve God, Save the Plant*; Wirzba, *From Nature to Creation*. These examples were provided courtesy of Davidson and Turner, *Manifold Beauty*, 46.

10. The most recent study by an HB/OT scholar that I am aware of on this topic is Longman, *The Bible and Ballot*.

Bibliography

Aaron, David H. "Early Rabbinic Exegesis on Noah's Son Ham and the So-Called 'Hamitic Myth.'" *Journal of the American Academy of Religion* 63 (1995) 721–59.
———. *Genesis Ideology: Essays on the Uses and Meaning of Stories.* Eugene, OR: Cascade Books, 2017.
Ahn, Suk-il. *The Persuasive Portrayal of David and Solomon in Chronicles: A Rhetorical Analysis of the Speeches and Prayers in the David-Solomon Narrative.* McMaster Biblical Studies Series 3. Hamilton, ON: McMaster Divinity College Press, 2018.
Alexander, T. Desmond. *From Paradise to Promised Land: An Introduction to the Pentateuch.* 4th ed. Grand Rapids: Baker Academic, 2022.
Alexiou, Evangelos. *Greek Rhetoric of the 4th Century BC: The Elixir of Democracy and Individuality.* Translated by Daniel Webber. Berlin: de Gruyter, 2020.
Alter, Robert. *The Art of Biblical Narrative.* Rev. and updated ed. New York: Basic Books, 2011.
Anderson, Bernhard W. "From Analysis to Synthesis: The Interpretation of Genesis 1–11." *JBL* 97 (1978) 23–29.
———. *From Creation to New Creation: Old Testament Perspectives.* OBT. Minneapolis: Fortress, 1994.
———. "The New Frontier of Rhetorical Criticism: A Tribute to James Muilenburg." In *Rhetorical Criticism: Essays in Honor of James Muilenburg*, edited by Jared J. Jackson and Martin Kessler, ix–xviii. Pittsburgh Theological Monograph Series 1. Pittsburgh: Pickwick Publications, 1974.
Anderson, Francis I. *The Sentence in Biblical Hebrew.* Janua Linguarum: Series Practica 231. The Hauge: Mouton, 1974.
Aristotle. *Rhetoric.* Dover Thrift Editions. Translated by W. Rhys Roberts. Mineola, NY: Dover, 2004.
Armstrong, James Franklin. "Short Notes: A Critical Note on Genesis VIaα." *VT* 10 (1960) 328–33.

Arnold, Bill T. *Genesis.* New Cambridge Bible Commentary. New York: Cambridge University Press, 2009.

Arnold, Bill T., and John H. Choi. *A Guide to Biblical Hebrew Syntax.* 2nd ed. New York: Cambridge University Press, 2018.

Arnold, Carroll C. "Oral Rhetoric, Rhetoric, and Literature." *Philosophy & Rhetoric* 40 (2007) 170–87.

Baden, Joel S. *The Composition of the Pentateuch: Renewing the Documentary Hypothesis.* New York: Yale University Press, 2012.

Bailey, Lloyd R. *Noah: The Person and the Story in History and Tradition.* Columbia: University of South Carolina Press, 1989.

Baker, David W. "Source Criticism." In *Dictionary of the Old Testament: Pentateuch,* edited by Alexander, T. Desmond and David W. Baker, 798–805. Downers Grove, IL: InterVarsity, 2003.

Baker, L. S., Jr. et al., eds. *Exploring the Composition of the Pentateuch.* BBRS 27. University Park, PA: Pennsylvania State University Press, 2020.

Bandstra, Barry. *Genesis 1–11: A Handbook on the Hebrew Text.* Baylor Handbook on the Hebrew Bible. Waco, TX: Baylor University Press, 2008.

Bar-Efrat, Shimeon. *Narrative Art in the Bible.* New York: T. & T. Clark, 2004.

———. "Some Observations on the Analysis of Structure in Biblical Narrative." *VT* 30 (1980) 154–73.

Barker, Joel. "From the Depths of Despair to the Promise of Presence: A Rhetorical Reading of the Book of Joel." PhD diss., McMaster Divinity College, 2009.

———. *From the Depths of Despair to the Promise of Presence: A Rhetorical Reading of the Book of Joel.* Siphrut 11. Winona Lake, IN: Eisenbrauns, 2014.

———. "Rhetorical Criticism." In *Dictionary of the Old Testament: Prophets,* edited by Mark J. Boda and J. Gordon McConville, 676–84. Downers Grove, IL: IVP Academic, 2012.

Barker, John Robert. "Disputed Temple A Rhetorical Analysis of the Book of Haggai." PhD diss., Boston College, 2016.

———. *Disputed Temple A Rhetorical Analysis of the Book of Haggai.* Minneapolis: Fortress, 2017.

Barré, L. M. "The Riddle of the Flood Chronology." *JSOT* 41 (1988) 3–20.

Bartholomew, Craig G. *Introducing Biblical Hermeneutics: A Comprehensive Framework for Hearing God in Scripture.* Grand Rapids: Baker Academic, 2015.

Bartholomew, Craig G., and Michael W. Goheen. *Living at the Crossroads: An Introduction to Christian Worldview.* Grand Rapids: Baker Academic, 2008.

Bartoletti, Susan Campbell. *Naamah and the Ark at Night.* Somerville, MA: Candlewick, 2011.

Barton, John. *Reading the Old Testament: Method in Biblical Study.* Rev. ed. Louisville: Westminster John Knox, 1996.

———. "Reflections on Literary Criticism." In *Method Matters: Essays on the Interpretation of the Hebrew Bible in Honor of David L. Peterson,* edited by Joel M. Lemon and Kent Harold Richards, 523–40. Resources for Biblical Study 56. Atlanta: SBL, 2009.

Bassett, Frederick W. "Noah's Nakedness and the Curse of Canaan: a Case of Incest?" *VT* 21 (1971) 232–37.

Batto, Bernard F. *In the Beginning: Essays on Creation Motifs in the Ancient Near East and the Bible.* Siphrut 9. Winona Lake, IN: Eisenbrauns, 2013.

———. *Slaying the Dragon: Mythmaking in the Biblical Tradition.* Louisville: Westminster John Knox, 1992.

Bauks, Michaela. "Intratextual Exegesis in the Primeval History: The Literary Function of the Genealogies in View of the Formation of Gen1–11." *ZAW* 131 (2019) 177–93.

Beal, T. K. et al. "Literary Theory, Literary Criticism, and the Bible." In *Methods of Biblical Interpretation: Excerpted from the "Dictionary of Biblical Interpretation,"* edited by John H. Hayes, 159–67. 2004. Reprint, Eugene, OR: Wipf & Stock, 2004.

Bebbington, David W. *The Evangelical Quadrilateral: Characterizing the British Gospel Movement.* 2 vols. Waco, TX: Baylor University Press, 2021.

———. *Evangelicalism in Modern Britain: A History from the 1730s to the 1980s.* London: Allen & Unwin, 1989.

Beckerleg, Catherine Leigh. "The 'Image of God' in Eden: The Creation of Mankind in Genesis 2:5—3:24 in Light of the *mīs pî pīt pî* and *wpt-r* Rituals of Mesopotamia and Ancient Egypt." PhD diss., Harvard University, 2009.

Bediako, Daniel. "A Note on *Rûaḥ* 'Spirit/Wind' in Genesis 1:2." *Valley View University Journal of Theology* 4 (2017) 78–84.

Beekman, John et al. *The Semantic Structure of Written Communication.* Dallas: SIL, 2017.

Bergsma, John Sietze, and Scott Walker Hahn. "Noah's Nakedness and the Curse on Canaan (Genesis 9:20–27)." *JBL* 124 (2005) 25–40.

Berlin, Adele. *Poetics and Interpretation of Biblical Narrative.* 5th ed. Bible and Literature Series 9. Winona Lake, IN: Eisenbrauns, 1983.

Best, Robert M. *Noah's Ark and the Ziusudra Epic: Sumerian Origins of the Flood Myth.* Fort Myers, FL: Enlil, 1999.

Beyer, Brian E. *Encountering the Book of Isaiah: A Historical and Theological Survey.* Encountering Biblical Studies. Grand Rapids: Baker Academic, 2007.

Bitzer, Lloyd F. "Functional Communication: A Situational Perspective." In *Rhetoric in Transition: Studies in the Nature and Uses of Rhetoric*, edited by Eugene E. White, 21–38. University Park: Pennsylvania State University Press, 1980.

———. "The Rhetorical Situation." *Philosophy and Rhetoric* 1 (1968) 1–14.

Black, C. Clifton. "Rhetorical Criticism." In *Hearing the New Testament: Strategies for Interpretation*, edited by Joel B. Green, 167–88. 2nd ed. Grand Rapids: Eerdmans, 2010.

———. "Rhetorical Criticism and Biblical Interpretation." *Expository Times* 100 (1989) 252–58.

———. "Rhetorical Criticism and the New Testament." *Proceedings* 8 (1988) 77–92.

Blenkinsopp, Joseph. *Creation, Un-creation, Re-Creation: A Discursive Commentary on Genesis 1–11.* New York: T. & T. Clark, 2011.

———. "P and J in Genesis 1:1—11:26: An Alternative Hypothesis." In *Fortunate the Eyes That See: Essays in Honor of David Noel Freedman in Celebration of His Seventieth Birthday*, edited by Astrid B. Beck et al., 1–15. Grand Rapids: Eerdmans, 1995.

———. *The Pentateuch: An Introduction to the First Five Books of the Bible.* Anchor Yale Bible Reference Library. New Haven: Yale University Press, 2000.

Block, Daniel I. *The Book of Ezekiel: Chapters 1–24.* NICOT. Grand Rapids: Eerdmans, 1997.

———. *Covenant: The Framework of God's Great Plan for Redemption.* Grand Rapids: Baker Academic, 2021.

Boadt, Lawrence et al. *Reading the Old Testament: An Introduction.* Rev. ed. Mahwah, NJ: Paulist, 2012.

Boda, Mark J. "Chiasmus in Ubiquity: Symmetrical Mirages in Nehemiah 9." *JSOT* 71 (1996) 55–70.

———. *The Heartbeat of Old Testament Theology: Three Creedal Expressions*. Acadia Studies in Bible and Theology. Grand Rapids: Baker Academic, 2017.

———. "Old Testament Foundations of Christian Spirituality." In *Dictionary of Christian Spirituality*, edited by Glen G. Scorgie, 40–45. Grand Rapids: Zondervan, 2011.

———. "Prayer as Rhetoric in the Book of Nehemiah." In *A New Perspective on Ezra-Nehemiah: Story and History, Literature and Interpretation*, edited by Isaac Kalimi, 279–96. Winona Lake, IN: Eisenbrauns, 2007.

———. *A Severe Mercy: Sin and Its Remedy in the Old Testament*. Siphrut 1. Winona Lake, IN: Eisenbrauns, 2009.

Bodi, Daniel. "Mesopotamia and Anatolian Iconography." In *Behind the Scenes of the Old Testament: Cultural, Social, and Historical Contexts*, edited by Jonathan S. Greer et al., 165–71. Grand Rapids: Baker Academic, 2018.

Boomershine, Thomas E. "The Structure of Narrative Rhetoric in Genesis 2–3." *Semeia* 18 (1980) 113–29.

Booth, Wayne C. *The Rhetoric of Fiction*. 2nd ed. Chicago: University of Chicago Press, 1983.

Borgman, Paul. *Genesis: The Story We Haven't Heard*. Downers Grove, IL: InterVarsity, 2001.

Bouma-Prediger, Steven. *For the Beauty of the Earth: A Christian Vision for Creation Care*. 2nd ed. Grand Rapids: Baker Academic, 2010.

Bovard, Matthew. "Reexamining Amos' Use of Rhetorical Questions in Hebrew Prophetic Rhetoric." MA thesis, Liberty University School of Divinity, 2019.

Boyd, Steven W., and Andrew A. Snelling, eds. *Grappling with the Chronology of the Genesis Flood: Navigating the Flow of Time in Biblical Narrative*. Green Forest, AR: Master, 2014.

Boyd, Gregory A. *The Crucifixion of the Warrior God: Interpreting the Old Testament's Violent Portraits of God in Light of the Cross*. Vol. 2, *The Cruciform Thesis*. Minneapolis: Fortress, 2017.

Brandt, William J. *The Rhetoric of Argumentation*. New York: Bobbs-Merrill, 1970.

Branson, Robert. "Shifting Paradigms for Interpreting Genesis 1–11." *Wesleyan Theological Journal* 44 (2009) 141–56.

Brasnett, Bertrand. *The Suffering of the Impassible God*. London: Macmillan, 1928.

Brinton, Alan. "Situation in the Theory of Rhetoric." *Philosophy and Rhetoric* 14 (1981) 234–48.

Brodie, Thomas L. *Genesis as Dialogue: A Literary, Historical, and Theological Commentary*. Oxford: Oxford University Press, 2006.

Brown, William P. *Character and Scripture: Moral Formation, Community, and Biblical Interpretation*. Grand Rapids: Eerdmans, 2002.

———. *The Ethos of the Cosmos: The Genesis of Moral Imagination in the Bible*. Grand Rapids: Eerdmans, 1999.

Brueggemann, Walter. *A Commentary on Jeremiah: Exile and Homecoming*. Grand Rapids: Eerdmans, 1998.

———. *Genesis*. Interpretation. Louisville: John Knox, 1982.

———. *Theology of the Old Testament: Testimony, Dispute, Advocacy*. Minneapolis: Fortress, 1997.

Buchanan, Paul. "Literary Devices." In *Dictionary of Biblical Criticism and Interpretation*, edited by Stanley E. Porter, 202–4. New York: Routledge, 2009.

Burgers, Christian et al. "HIP: A Method for Linguistic Hyperbole Identification in Discourse." *Metaphor and Symbol* 31 (2016) 163–78.

Burke, Kenneth. *A Rhetoric of Motives*. Berkeley: University of California Press, 1969.

Burlet, Dustin G. "Choose Your Own Adventure! Heutagogy and Teaching Genesis 1–11." *Didakitos* 4 (2021) 30–33.

———. "Cosmos to Chaos—Chaos to Covenant: A Rhetorical-Critical Reading of the Noachic Deluge Narrative." PhD diss., McMaster Divinity College, 2019.

———. "Impassible Yet Impassioned: The Doctrine of Divine Impassibility in Conversation with the Noachian Deluge of Genesis." *Didaskalia* 28 (2017) 96–128.

———. Review of *The Lost World of the Flood: Mythology, Theology, and the Deluge Debate*, by Tremper Longman III and John H. Walton. *McMaster Journal of Theology and Ministry* 19 (2017–2018) R67–R72.

———. Review of *Reading Genesis Well: Navigating History, Poetry, Science, and Truth in Genesis 1–11*, by C. John Collins. *Canadian American Theological Review* 8 (2019) 140–44.

Buth, R. "Methodological Collision Between Source Criticism and Discourse Analysis: The Problem of 'Unmarked Temporal Overlay' and the Pluperfect/Nonsequential *wayyiqtol*." In *Biblical Hebrew and Discourse Linguistics*, edited by Robert D. Bergen, 138–54. Winona Lake, IN: Eisenbrauns, 1994.

Callow, John. "Units and Flow in the Song of Songs 1:1—2:6." In *Biblical Hebrew and Discourse Linguistics*, edited by Robert D. Bergen, 462–88. Winona Lake, IN: Eisenbrauns, 1994.

Campbell, Antony F., and Mark A. O'Brien. *Rethinking the Pentateuch: Prolegomena to the Theology of Ancient Israel*. Louisville: Westminster John Knox, 2005.

———. *Sources of the Pentateuch: Texts, Introductions, Annotations*. Minneapolis: Fortress, 1993.

Carasik, Michael. *Theologies of the Mind in Biblical Israel*. Studies in Biblical Literature 85. New York: Lang, 2006.

Carlson, Richard F., and Tremper Longman III. *Science, Creation and the Bible: Reconciling Rival Theories of Origins*. Downers Grove, IL: IVP Academic, 2010.

Carr, David M. *Reading the Fractures of Genesis: Historical and Literary Approaches*. Louisville: Westminster John Knox, 1996.

Carroll, M. Daniel R., and J. Wilgus, eds. *Wrestling with the Violence of God: Soundings in the Old Testament*. BBRSup 10. Winona Lake, IN: Eisenbrauns, 2015.

Carson, D. A. "Adam in the Epistles of Paul." In *In the Beginning . . . A Symposium on the Bible and Creation*, edited by N. M. de S. Cameron, 28–43. Glasgow: Biblical Creation Society, 1980.

———. "Genesis 1–3: Not Maximalist, But Seminal." *Trinity Journal* 39 (2018) 143–63.

Cartledge, Tony W. Review of *Reading Genesis Well: Navigating History, Poetry, Science, and Truth in Genesis 1–11*, by C. John Collins. *Review & Expositor* 116 (2019) 370–72.

Casson, Lionel. *Ships and Seafaring in Ancient Times*. London: British Museum, 1994.

Cassuto, U. *A Commentary on the Book of Genesis*. Vol. 1. Translated by Israel Abrahams. Jerusalem: Magnes, 1964.

Chaffey, Tim, and Jason Lisle. *Old Earth Creationism on Trial*. Green Forest, AR: Master, 2008.

Chatman, Seymour. *Story and Discourse: Narrative Structure in Fiction and Film*. Ithaca, NY: Cornell University Press, 1978.

Chen, Y. S. *The Primeval Flood Catastrophe: Origins and Early Development in Mesopotamia Traditions*. Oxford Oriental Monographs. Oxford: Oxford University Press, 2013.

Childs, Brevard S. *Memory and Tradition in Israel*. Studies in Biblical Theology 1/37. London: SCM, 1962.

Chisholm, Robert B. Jr. *A Commentary on Judges and Ruth*. Kregel Exegetical Library. Grand Rapids: Kregel, 2013.

———. "The 'Everlasting Covenant' and the 'City of Chaos': Intentional Ambiguity and Irony in Isaiah 24." *Criswell Theological Review* 6 (1993) 237–53.

———. *From Exegesis to Exposition: A Practical Guide to Using Biblical Hebrew*. Grand Rapids: Baker, 1998.

———. "History or Story? The Literary Dimension in Narrative Texts." In *Giving the Sense: Understanding and Using Old Testament Historical Texts*, edited by David M. Howard Jr. and Michael A. Grisanti, 54–73. Grand Rapids: Kregel Academic, 2004.

———. "Old Testament Source Criticism: Some Methodological Miscues." In *Do Historical Matters Matter to Faith? A Critical Appraisal of Modern and Postmodern Approaches to Scripture*, edited by James K. Hoffmeier and Dennis R. Magary, 181–200. Wheaton, IL: Crossway, 2012.

———. *A Workbook for Intermediate Hebrew: Grammar, Exegesis, and Commentary on Jonah and Ruth*. Grand Rapids: Kregel, 2006.

Christian, James L. *Philosophy: An Introduction to the Art of Reading*. 6th ed. Boston: Harcourt, 1994.

Clark, W. Malcolm. "The Flood and the Structure of the Pre-Patriarchal History." *ZAW* 83 (1971) 184–211.

———. "The Righteousness of Noah." 21 *VT* (1971) 261–80.

Clifford, Richard J. *Creation Accounts in the Ancient Near East and in the Bible*. The Catholic Biblical Quarterly Monograph Series 26. Washington, DC: The Catholic Biblical Association of America, 1994.

———. "Inundation or Interpretation." *America* 188 (2003) 25.

Clines, David J. A. "The Many Voices of Isaiah 40." In *Let Us Go up to Zion: Essays in Honour of H. G. M. Williamson on the Occasion of His Sixty-Fifth Birthday*, edited by Iain Provan and Mark J. Boda, 113–26. VTSup 153. Leiden: Brill, 2012.

———. "Noah's Flood I: The Theology of the Flood Narrative." *Faith and Thought* 100 (1972) 128–42.

———. "The Significance of the 'Sons of God' Episode (Genes 6:1–4) in the Context of the 'Primeval History' (Genesis 1–11)." *JSOT* 13 (1979) 33–46.

———. *The Theme of the Pentateuch*. 2nd ed. JSOTSup 10. London: Continuum, 1997.

Clines, David J. A et al., eds. *Art and Meaning: Rhetoric in Biblical Literature*. JSOTSup 19. Sheffield: Dept. of Biblical Studies, Sheffield University, 1982.

Cochran, Robert F. Jr., and David Van Drunen, eds. *Law and the Bible: Justice, Mercy, and Legal Institutions*. Downers Grove, IL: IVP Academic, 2013.

Cohen, H. R. *Biblical Hapax Legomena in the Light of Akkadian and Ugaritic*. SBLDS 37. Missoula, MT: Scholars, 1978.

Cohn, Norman. *Noah's Flood: The Genesis Story in Western Thought*. New Haven: Yale University Press, 1996.

Collins, C. John. *Reading Genesis Well: Navigating History, Poetry, Science, and Truth in Genesis 1–11*. Grand Rapids: Zondervan, 2018.

———. "The Wayyiqtol as 'Pluperfect': When and Why." *Tyndale Bulletin* 46 (1995) 117–40.
Combrink, Bernard H. J. "The Rhetoric of Sacred Scripture." In *Rhetoric, Scripture, and Theology: Essays from the 1994 Pretoria Conference*, JSNTSup131, edited by Stanley E. Porter and Thomas H. Olbricht, 102–23. England: Sheffield Academic, 1996.
Consigny, Scott. "Rhetoric and Its Situations." *Philosophy and Rhetoric* 7 (1974) 175–86.
Cooper, Alan, and Bernard R. Goldstein. "The Development of the Priestly Calendars (I): The Daily Sacrifice and the Sabbath." *HUCA* 74 (2003) 1–20.
Copan, Paul, and Douglas Jacob. *Origins: The Ancient Impact and Modern Implications of Genesis 1–11*. Nashville: Morgan James, 2019.
Copan, Paul et al., eds. *Dictionary of Christianity and Science: The Definitive Reference for the Intersection of Christian Faith and Contemporary Science*. Grand Rapids: Zondervan, 2017.
Cotter, David W. *Genesis*. Berit Olam. Collegeville, MN: Liturgical, 2003.
Cotterell, Peter, and Max Turner. *Linguistics and Biblical Interpretation*. Downers Grove, IL: IVP Academic, 1989.
Crawford, Cory D. "Noah's Architecture: The Role of Sacred Space in Ancient Near Eastern Flood Myths." In *Constructions of Space IV: Further Developments in Examining Ancient Israel's Social Space*, edited by Mark K. George, 1–22. LHBOTS 569. London: Bloomsbury, 2013.
Cruise, Charles E. "A Methodology for Detecting and Mitigating Hyperbole in Matthew 5:38–42." *JETS* 61 (2018) 83–103.
Dalton, Russell W. *Children's Bibles in America: A Reception History of the Story of Noah's Ark in US Children's Bibles*. Scriptural Traces Critical Perspectives on the Reception and Influence of the Bible. LHBOTS 614. New York: Bloomsbury T. & T. Clark, 2016.
Davids, Peter H. *The Letters of 2 Peter and Jude*. Pillar New Testament Commentary. Grand Rapids: Eerdmans, 2006.
Davidson, Gregg, and Kenneth J. Turner. *The Manifold Beauty of Genesis One: A Multi-Layered Approach*. Grand Rapids: Kregel, 2021.
Davidson, Jo Ann. "'Even if Noah, Daniel, and Job' (Ezekiel 14:14, 20): Why These Three?" *Journal of the Adventist Theological Society* 12 (2001) 132–44.
Dawson, Zachary K. *The Message of the Jerusalem Council in the Acts of the Apostles: A Linguistic Stylistic Analysis*. Linguistic Biblical Studies 22. Leiden: Brill, 2022.
Day, John. *From Creation to Babel: Studies in Genesis 1–11*. New York: Bloomsbury T. & T. Clark, 2013.
———. *God's Conflict with the Dragon and the Sea: Echoes of a Canaanite Myth in the Old Testament*. University of Cambridge Oriental Publication 35. Cambridge: Cambridge University Press, 1985.
Dearman, Andrew J. *The Book of Hosea*. NICOT. Grand Rapids: Eerdmans, 2010.
Delitzsch Franz. *A New Commentary on Genesis*. Vol. 1. 5th ed. Edinburgh: T. & T. Clark, 1888.
Dershowitz, Idan. "Man of the Land: Unearthing the Original Noah." *ZAW* 128 (2016) 357–73.
Dillow, Joseph C. *The Waters Above: Earth's Pre-Flood Vapor Canopy*. Chicago, IL: Moody, 1981.
Donaldson, David C. "New Rhetoric." In *Dictionary of Biblical Criticism and Interpretation*, edited by Stanley E. Porter, 245–47. New York: Routledge, 2009.

Dorsey, David. *The Literary Structure of the Old Testament: A Commentary on Genesis–Malachi*. Grand Rapids: Baker Academic, 1999.

Dozeman, Thomas B. "Old Testament Rhetorical Criticism." In *ABD*, 5:712–15.

———. *The Pentateuch: Introducing the Torah*. Introducing Israel's Scriptures. Minneapolis: Fortress, 2017.

Dozeman, Thomas B. et al., eds. *The Pentateuch: International Perspectives on Current Research*. Tübingen: Mohr Siebeck, 2011.

Dozeman, Thomas B., and Konard Schmid, eds. *Farewell to the Yahwist? The Composition of the Pentateuch in Recent European Interpretation*. Society of Biblical Literature Symposium Series 34. Atlanta: SBL, 2006.

Driver, Samuel Rolles. *The Book of Genesis: with introduction and notes*. 3rd ed. Westminster Commentaries. New York: Methuen, 1905.

———. *A Treatise on the Use of Tenses in Hebrew and Some Other Syntactical Questions*. 4th ed. The Biblical Resource Series. Grand Rapids: Eerdmans, 1998.

Duguid, Iain M. *Ezekiel*. The NIV Application Commentary. Grand Rapids: Zondervan, 1999.

Duke, Rodney K. *The Persuasive Appeal of the Chronicler: A Rhetorical Analysis*. JSOTSup 88. Sheffield: Sheffield Academic, 1990.

Dumbrell, William J. *Covenant and Creation: A Theology of Old Testament Covenants*. Grand Rapids: Baker, 1984.

———. "The Covenant with Noah." *Reformed Theological Review* 38 (1979) 1–9.

Dundes, Alan, ed. *The Flood Myth*. Berkeley: University of California Press, 1988.

Eagleton, Terry. *Literary Theory: An Introduction*. 2nd ed. Minneapolis: University of Minnesota Press, 1996.

Embry, Brad. "The 'Naked Narrative' from Noah to Leviticus: Reassessing Voyeurism in the Account of Noah's Nakedness in Genesis 9.22–24." *JSOT* 35 (2011) 417–33.

Enns, Peter. *Inspiration and Incarnation: Evangelicals and the Problem of the Old Testament*. 2nd ed. Grand Rapids: Baker Academic, 2005.

———. "Reflections (Personal and Otherwise) on Protestantism's Uneasy and Diverse Response to Higher Criticism." *Studies in the Bible and Antiquity* 8 (2016) 45–63.

Etshalom, Yitzchak. *Between the Lines of the Bible. Genesis: Recapturing the Full Meaning of the Biblical Text*. Revised and Expanded. Jerusalem: Orthodox Union and Urim, 2015.

Evans, Craig A. et al., eds. *The Book of Genesis: Composition, Reception, and Interpretation*. VTSup 152. Leiden: Brill, 2012.

Evans, John F. *A Guide to Biblical Commentaries and Reference Works*. 10th ed. Grand Rapids: Zondervan, 2016.

Evans, Paul S. *The Invasion of Sennacherib in the Book of Kings: A Source-Critical and Rhetorical Study of 2 Kings 18–19*. VTSup 125. Leiden: Brill, 2009.

Faulkner, Danny R. *The Expanse of Heaven: Where Creation & Astronomy Intersect*. Green Forest, AR: Master, 2017.

———. *Falling Flat: A Refutation of Flat Earth Claims*. Green Forest, AR: Master, 2019.

Faro, Ingrid. *Evil in Genesis: A Contextual Analysis of Hebrew Lexemes for Evil in the Book of Genesis*. Studies in Scripture and Biblical Theology. Bellingham, WA: Lexham, 2020.

Fee, Gordon D. *New Testament Exegesis: A Handbook for Students and Pastors*. 3rd ed. Louisville: Westminster John Knox, 2002.

Feinman, Peter Douglas. "Sons of God (Genesis 6:1–14): Power Politics In Ancient Israel." *Conversations with the Biblical World* 34 (2014) 73–100.

Filby, Frederick A. *The Flood Reconsidered: A Review of the Evidences of Geology, Archeology, Ancient Literature, and the Bible*. London: Pickering & Inglis, 1970.

Finkel, Irving. *The Ark Before Noah: Decoding the Story of the Flood*. London: Hodder & Stoughton, 2014.

Fishbane, Michael. *Text and Texture*. New York: Schocken, 1979.

Fisher, Eugene. J. "Gilgamesh and Genesis: The Flood Story in Context." *CBQ* 32 (1970) 392–403.

Fitzgerald, C. "A Rhetorical Analysis of Isaiah 56–66." PhD diss., Dallas Theological Seminary, 2003.

Fokkelman, J. P. *Reading Biblical Narrative: An Introductory Guide*. Louisville: Westminster John Knox, 1999.

Fox, Michael V. "The Rhetoric of Ezekiel's Vision of the Valley of the Bones." *HUCA* 51 (1980) 1–15.

France, R. T. *The Gospel of Matthew*. New International Commentary on the New Testament. Grand Rapids: Eerdmans, 2007.

Fretheim, Terence E. *Creation, Fall, and Flood: Studies in Genesis 1–11*. Minneapolis: Augsburg, 1969.

———. *Creation Untamed: The Bible, God, and Natural Disasters*. Theological Explorations for the Church Catholic. Grand Rapids: Baker Academic, 2010.

———. "God and Violence in the Old Testament." *Word & World* 24 (2004) 18–28.

———. *God and World in the Old Testament: A Relational Theology of Creation*. Nashville: Abingdon, 2005.

———. *The Pentateuch*. Interpreting Biblical Texts. Nashville: Abingdon, 1996.

———. *The Suffering of God: An Old Testament Perspective*. OBT 14. Philadelphia: Fortress, 1984.

———. "Theological Reflections on the Wrath of God in the Old Testament." *Horizons in Biblical Theology* 24 (2002) 14–17

Friedman, Richard Elliot. *The Bible With Sources Revealed: A New View Into the Five Books of Moses*. New York: HarperCollins, 2003.

Frymer-Kensky, Tikva S. "The Atrahasis Epic and Its Significance for Our Understanding of Genesis 1–9." *Biblical Archeologist* 40 (1977) 147–55.

———. "Pollution, Purification, and Purgation in Biblical Israel." In *The Word of the Lord Shall Go Forth: Essays in Honor of David Noel Freedman in Celebration of His Sixtieth Birthday*, edited by Carol L. Meyers and M. O'Connor, 399–414. American Schools of Oriental Research Special Volume. Winona Lake: IN: Eisenbrauns, 1983.

Fuller, David J. *A Discourse Analysis of Habakkuk*. Studia Semitica Neerlandica 79. Leiden: Brill, 2019.

Galambush, Julie. *Reading Genesis: A Literary and Theological Commentary*. Macon, GA: Smyth & Helwys, 2018.

Garret, Mary, and Xiaosui Xiao. "The Rhetorical Situation Revisited." *Rhetoric Society Quarterly* 23 (1993) 30–40.

Garrett, Duane A. *Rethinking Genesis: The Sources and Authorship of the First Book of the Pentateuch*. Grand Rapids: Baker, 1991.

———. "The Undead Hypothesis: Why the Documentary Hypothesis Is the Frankenstein of Biblical Studies." *Southern Baptist Journal of Theology* 5 (2001) 28–41.

Genette, Gérard. *Narrative Discourse: An Essay in Method*. Translated by Jane E. Lewin. Ithaca: Cornell University Press, 1983.

———. *Narrative Discourse Revisited*. Translated by Jane E. Lewin. Ithaca: Cornell University Press, 1998.

Gentry, Peter J., and Stephen J. Wellum. *Kingdom through Covenant: A Biblical-Theological Understanding of the Covenants*. 2nd ed. Wheaton, IL: Crossway, 2018.

George, Andrew. *The Babylonian Gilgamesh Epic*. Oxford: Oxford University Press, 2003.

———. *The Epic of Gilgamesh*. New York: Barnes & Noble, 1996.

———. "The Tower of Babel: Archeology, History and Cuneiform Texts." *Archiv für Orientforschung* 51 (2005) 75–95.

Gertz, Jan Christian. "Source Criticism in the Primeval History of Genesis: An Outdated Paradigm for the Study of the Pentateuch?" In *The Pentateuch: International Perspectives on Current Research*, edited by Thomas B. Dozeman et al., 169–80. Tübingen: Mohr Siebeck, 2011.

Gevaryahu, Gilad J. "What did the Dove Bring to Noah?" *JBQ* 43 (2015) 172–75.

Gilbert, Pierre. *God Never Meant for Us to Die: The Emergence of Evil in the Light of the Genesis Creation Account*. Eugene, OR: Wipf & Stock, 2020.

Gitay, Yehoshua. "The Projection of the Prophet: A Rhetorical Presentation of the Prophet Jeremiah." In *Prophecy and Prophets: The Diversity of Contemporary Issues in Scholarship*, edited by Yehoshua Gitay, 41–55. Semeia Studies 33. Atlanta: Scholars, 1997.

———. "Rhetorical Criticism." In *To Each Its Own Meaning: An Introduction to Biblical Criticisms and Their Application*, edited by Steven L. McKenzie and Stephen R. Haynes, 135–49. Louisville: Westminster John Knox, 1993.

Glover, Gordon J. *Beyond the Firmament: Understanding Science and the Theology of Creation*. Chesapeake, VA: Watertree, 2007.

Gmirkin, Russell B. *Brossus and Genesis, Manetho and Exodus: Hellenistic Histories and the Date of the Pentateuch*. New York: T. & T. Clark, 2006.

Goldingay, John. *Genesis*. Baker Commentary on the Old Testament: Pentateuch. Grand Rapids: Baker Academic, 2020.

———. *Old Testament Theology: Volume One: Israel's Gospel*. Downers Grove, IL: IVP Academic, 2003.

Gorman, Michael J. *Elements of Biblical Exegesis: A Basic Guide for Students and Ministers*. 3rd ed. Grand Rapids: Baker Academic, 2020.

Gorrell, Donna. "The Rhetorical Situation Again: Linked Components in a Venn Diagram." *Philosophy and Rhetoric* 30 (1997) 395–412.

Gravett, Sandra L. et al. *An Introduction to the Hebrew Bible: A Thematic Approach*. Louisville: Westminster John Knox, 2008.

Greenberger, Chaya. "Noah's Survival and Enduring Legacy." *JBQ* 45 (2017) 27–33.

Greenspahn, Frederick E. Review of *The Persuasive Appeal of the Chronicler: A Rhetorical Analysis*, by Rodney K. Duke. *Association Jewish Studies* 18 (1993) 108–10.

Greenway, William. *For the Love of All Creatures: The Story of Grace in Genesis*. Grand Rapids: Eerdmans, 2015.

Greenwood, Kyle. *Scripture and Cosmology: Reading the Bible Between the Ancient World and Modern Science*. Downers Grove, IL: IVP Academic, 2015.

Greer, Jonathan S. et al., eds. *Behind the Scenes of the Old Testament: Cultural, Social, and Historical Contexts*. Grand Rapids: Baker Academic, 2018.

Griffin, John K. *Creation and the Flood: A Journey of Scripture, Science and Faith*. Potomac, MD: Proclamation, 2020.

Griffith, Tim, and Natali Miller trans. *Johannes Buteo's The Shape and Capacity of Noah's Ark*. Center for Origins Research Issues in Creation 2. Eugene, OR: Wipf & Stock, 2008.

Gunkel, Hermann. "The Legends of Genesis." In *Genesis: Translated and Interpreted by Hermann Gunkel*. Macon GA: Mercer University Press, 1997.

Gunn, David M. "Deutero-Isaiah and the Flood." *JBL* 94 (1975) 493–508.

Gupta, Nijay K. *Prepare, Succeed, Advance: A Guidebook for Getting a PhD in Biblical Studies and Beyond*. 2nd ed. Eugene, OR: Cascade Books, 2019.

Habel, Norman C. "The Two Flood Stories in Genesis." In *The Flood Myth*, edited by Alan Dundes, 13–28. Berkeley: University of California Press, 1988.

Habel, Norman C., and Peter Trudinger eds. *Exploring Ecological Hermeneutics*. SBLSymS 46. Atlanta: SBL, 2008.

Halley, Keaton. Review of *The Lost World of the Flood: Mythology, Theology, and the Deluge Debate*, by Tremper Longman III and John H. Walton. *Journal of Creation* 32 (2018) 36–39.

Hallo, William W. "Introduction: Ancient Near Eastern Texts and their Relevance for Biblical Exegesis." In *The Context of Scripture*. Vol. 1, *Canonical Compositions from the Biblical World*, edited by William W. Hallo et al., xxiii–xxviii. Leiden: Brill, 2003.

Halpern, Baruch. "What They Don't Know Won't Hurt Them: Genesis 6–9." In *Fortunate the Eyes That See: Essays in Honor of David Noel Freedman in Celebration of his Seventieth Birthday*, edited by Astrid B. Beck et al., 16–34. Grand Rapids: Eerdmans, 1995.

Halton, Charles, ed. *Genesis: History, Fiction, or Neither? Three Views on The Bible's Earliest Chapters*. Counterpoints: Bible and Theology. Grand Rapids: Zondervan, 2015.

Hamilton, Victor P. *The Book of Genesis: Chapters 1–17*. NICOT. Grand Rapids: Eerdmans, 1990.

Harland, P. J. *The Value of Human Life: A Study of the Story of the Flood (Genesis 6–9)*. VTSup 64. Leiden: Brill, 1996.

Harper, Elizabeth. "It's All in the Name: Reading the Noah Cycle in the Light of its Plot Markers." In *Opening Heaven's Floodgates: The Genesis Flood Narrative, Its Context, and Reception*, edited by Jason M. Silverman, 31–55. Biblical Intersections 12. Piscataway, NJ: Gorgias, 2013.

Harrison, R. K. *Introduction to the Old Testament*. Grand Rapids: Eerdmans, 1969.

Hartley, John E. *Genesis*. Understanding the Bible Commentary Series. Grand Rapids: Baker, 1995.

———. *Leviticus*. Word Biblical Commentary 3. Nashville: Nelson, 1992.

Hasel, Gerald F. "The Fountains of the Great Deep." *Origins* 1 (1974) 67–72.

———. "The Semantic Values of Derivatives of the Hebrew Root Š'R." *Andrews University Seminary Studies* 11 (1973) 152–69.

Hatch, Nathan O. "Christian Thinking in a Time of Academic Turmoil." In *Faithful Learning and the Christian Scholarly Vocation*, edited by Douglas V. Henry and Bob R. Agee, 87–100. Grand Rapids: Eerdmans, 2003.

Hawk, L. Daniel. "Literary/Narrative Criticism." In *Dictionary of the Old Testament: Pentateuch*, edited by T. Desmond Alexander and David W. Baker, 536–44. Downers Grove, IL: InterVarsity, 2003.

———. *The Violence of the Biblical God: Canonical Narrative and Christian Faith*. Grand Rapids: Eerdmans, 2019.

Hawking, Stephen. *A Brief History of Time: From the Big Bang to Black Holes*. New York: Bantam, 1990.

Hays, Christopher B. *Hidden Riches: A Sourcebook for the Comparative Study of the Hebrew Bible and Ancient Near East*. Louisville: Westminster John Knox, 2014.

Heidel, Alexander. *The Babylonian Genesis: A Complete Translation of All the Published Cuneiform Tablets of the Various Babylonian Creation Stories*. 2nd ed. Chicago: University of Chicago Press, 1951.

Heller, Roy L. *Narrative Structure and Discourse Constellations: An Analysis of Clause Functions in Biblical Hebrew Prose*. Harvard Semitic Studies 55. Winona Lake, IN: Eisenbrauns, 2004.

Hendel, Ronald S. "Of Demigods and the Deluge: Towards an Interpretation of Genesis 6:1–4." *JBL* 106 (1987) 13–26.

———. "The Shape of Utnapishtim's Ark." *ZAW* 107 (1995) 128–29.

———. *The Text of Genesis 1–11: Textual Studies and Critical Edition*. Oxford: Oxford University Press, 1998.

———. "When the Sons of God Consorted with the Daughters of Men." *Bible Review* 3 (1987) 8–13, 37.

Hendel, Ronald S., and Jan Joosten. *How Old Is the Hebrew Bible? A Linguistic, Textual, and Historical Study*. The Anchor Bible Yale Reference Library. New Haven: Yale University Press, 2018.

Heras, Henry. "'The Crow' of Noe." *CBQ* 10 (1948) 131–39.

Herrick, James. *The History and Theory of Rhetoric: An Introduction*. 6th ed. New York: Routledge, 2018.

Hess, Richard S. "The Genealogies of Genesis 1–11 and Comparative Literature." In *"I Studied Inscriptions before the Flood": Ancient Near Eastern, Literary, and Linguistic Approaches to Genesis 1–11*, edited by Richard S. Hess and David T. Tsumura, 58–72. Sources for Biblical and Theological Study 4. Winona Lake, IN: Eisenbrauns, 1994.

———. *The Old Testament: A Historical, Theological, and Critical Introduction*. Grand Rapids: Baker Academic, 2016.

Hester, James D. "Kennedy and the Reading of Paul: The Energy of Communication." In *Words Well Spoken: George Kennedy's Rhetoric of the New Testament*, edited by C. Clifton Black and Duane F. Watson, 139–62. Waco, TX: Baylor University Press, 2008.

———. "Re-discovering and Re-inventing Rhetoric." *Scriptura* 50 (1994) 1–22.

———. "Speaker, Audience, and Situations: A Modified Interactional Model." *Neotestamentica* 32 (1998) 75–94.

Hiebert, Theodore. *The Yahwist's Landscape: Nature and Religion in Early Israel*. New York: Oxford University Press, 1996.

Hilber, John W. *Old Testament Cosmology and Divine Accommodation: A Relevance-Theory Approach*. Eugene, OR: Cascade Books, 2020.

Hill, Andrew E. "Genealogy." In *Dictionary for Theological Interpretation of the Bible*, edited by Kevin J. Vanhoozer, 243–46. Grand Rapids: Baker Academic, 2005.

Hill, Andrew E., and John H. Walton. *A Survey of the Old Testament*. 3rd ed. Grand Rapids: Zondervan Academic, 2009.

Hill, Carol A. "Making Sense of the Numbers of Genesis." *Perspectives on Science and Christian Faith* 55 (2003) 329–51.

———. "The Noachian Flood: Universal or Local?" *Perspectives on Science and Christian Faith* 54 (2002) 170–83.

———. "A Third Alternative to Concordism and Divine Accommodation: The Worldview Approach." *Perspectives on Science and Christian Faith* 59 (2007) 129–34.

———. *A Worldview Approach to Science and Scripture*. Grand Rapids: Kregel, 2019.

Hill, Carol A. et al., eds. *The Grand Canyon, Monument to an Ancient Earth: Can Noah's Flood Explain the Grand Canyon?* Grand Rapids: Kregel, 2016.

Hiltz, Patrick L. Review of *The Lost World of the Flood: Mythology, Theology, and the Deluge Debate*, by Tremper Longman III and John H. Walton. *Review & Expositor* 115 (2018) 616–17.

Hodge, B. C. *Revisiting the Days of Genesis: A Study of the Use of Time in Genesis 1–11 in Light of Its Ancient Near Eastern and Literary Context*. 1990. Reprint, Eugene, OR: Wipf & Stock, 2011.

Hoffmeier, James K. "Genesis 1–11 As History and Theology." In *Genesis: History, Fiction, or Neither? Three Views on The Bible's Earliest Chapters*, edited by Charles Halton, 23–58. Counterpoints: Bible and Theology. Grand Rapids: Zondervan, 2015.

Holloway, Steven W. "What Ship Goes There: The Flood Narrative in the Gilgamesh Epic and Genesis Considered in Light of Ancient Near Eastern Temple Ideology." *ZAW* 103 (1991) 328–55.

Hordes, Ami. "Why Doesn't Noah Have More Children After the Flood?" *JBQ* 44 (2016) 211–20.

Horowitz, Wayne. "The Isles of the Nations: Genesis x and Babylonian Geography." In *Studies in the Pentateuch*, edited by J. A. Emerton, 35–43. VTSup XLI. Leiden: Brill, 1990.

———. *Mesopotamian Cosmic Geography*. 2nd ed. Mesopotamia Civilizations 8. Winona Lake, IN: Eisenbrauns, 2011.

House, Paul R., and Eric Mitchell. *Old Testament*. 2nd ed. Nashville: B. & H., 2007.

Howard, David M. "Rhetorical Criticism in Old Testament Studies." *BBR* 4 (1994) 87–104.

Huey, F. B. Jr. "Are the 'Sons of God' in Genesis 6 Angels? Yes." In *The Genesis Debate: Persistent Questions about Creation and the Flood*, edited by Ronald Youngblood, 184–209. 1990. Reprint, Eugene, OR: Wipf & Stock, 1999.

Humphreys, W. Lee. *The Character of God in the Book of Genesis: A Narrative Appraisal*. Louisville: Westminster John Knox, 2011.

Hunsaker, David M., and Craig R. Smith. "The Nature of Issues: A Constructive Approach to Situational Rhetoric." *Western Speech Communication* 41 (1976) 144–56.

Hwang, Jerry. *The Rhetoric of Remembrance: An Investigation of the "Fathers" in Deuteronomy*. Siphrut 8. Winona Lake, IN: Eisenbrauns, 2012.

Iser, W. *The Implied Reader*. Baltimore: Johns Hopkins University Press, 1974.

———. "The Reading Process: A Phenomenological Approach." *New Literary History* 3 (1972) 279–99.

Jacobsen, T. "The Eridu Genesis." *JBL* 100 (1981) 513–29.

Jacobus, Helen R. "Flood Calendars and Birds of the Ark in the Dead Sea Scrolls (4Q252 and 4Q254a), Septuagint, and Ancient Near East Texts." In *Opening Heaven's Floodgates: The Genesis Flood Narrative, its Context, and Reception*, edited by Jason M. Silverman, 85–112. Biblical Intersections 12. Piscataway, NJ: Gorgias, 2013.

Janssen, Luke Jeffrey. *Soul-Searching: The Evolution of Judeo-Christian Thinking on the Soul and the Afterlife*. Eugene, OR: Wipf & Stock, 2019.

Johnson, Marshall. *The Purpose of Biblical Genealogies: with special reference to the setting of the genealogies of Jesus*. 2nd ed. New York: Cambridge University Press, 1988.
Jones, Barry A. Review of *From the Depths of Despair to the Promise of Presence: A Rhetorical Reading of the Book of Joel*, by Joel Barker. *Journal for the Evangelical Study of the Old Testament* 4 (2015) 92–94.
Joüon, Paul, and Takamitsu Muraoka. *A Grammar of Biblical Hebrew*. Rev. ed. Subsidia Biblica 27. Rome: Pontifical Biblical Institute, 2006.
Jungels, Cameron. Review of *From the Depths of Despair to the Promise of Presence: A Rhetorical Reading of the Book of Joel*, by Joel Barker. *BBR* 24 (2014) 566–68.
Kaminski, Carol M. "Beautiful Women or 'False Judgment'? Interpreting Genesis 6.2 in the Context of the Primaeval History." *JSOT* 32 (2008) 457–73.
———. *From Noah to Israel: Realization of the Primaeval Blessing After the Flood*. New York: T. & T. Clark, 2004.
———. *Was Noah Good? Finding Favour in the Flood Narrative*. New York: Bloomsbury T. & T. Clark, 2014.
Kaminsky, Joel S. "The Theology of Genesis." In *The Book of Genesis: Composition, Reception, and Interpretation*, by Craig A. Evans et al., eds., 635–56. VTSUP 152. Leiden: Brill, 2012.
———. *Yet I Loved Jacob: Reclaiming the Biblical Concept of Election*. Nashville: Abingdon, 2007.
Kawashima, Robert S. "Sources and Redaction." In *Reading Genesis: Ten Methods*, edited by Ronald Hendel, 47–70. New York: Cambridge University Press, 2010.
Keegan, Terence J. *Interpreting the Bible: A Popular Introduction to Biblical Hermeneutics*. Mahwah, NJ: Paulist. 1985.
Keel, Othmar. "Das sogenannte altorientalische Weltbild." *Biki* 40 (1985) 157–61.
Keel, Othmar, and Silvia Schroer. *Creation: Biblical Theologies in the Context of the Ancient Near East*. Translated by Peter T. Daniels. Winona Lake, IN: Eisenbrauns, 2015.
Keil, C. F., and F. Delitzsch. *Commentary on the Old Testament: The Pentateuch, vol I*. Translated by J. Martin. Reprint, Grand Rapids: Eerdmans, n.d. [1866].
Keiser, Thomas A. "Divine Sovereignty Vs. Human Responsibility: Nuancing Kaminski's *Was Noah Good?*" *WTJ* (2019) 195–204.
———. *Genesis 1–11: Its Literary Coherence and Theological Message*. Eugene, OR: Wipf & Stock, 2013.
———. "The 'Sons of God' in Genesis 6:1–4: A Rhetorical Characterization." *WTJ* 80 (2018) 103–20.
Keiter, Sheila Turner. "Noah and the Dove: the integral connection between Noah and Jonah." *JBQ* 40 (2012) 261–64.
Kelle, Brad E. Review of *From the Depths of Despair to the Promise of Presence: A Rhetorical Reading of the Book of Joel*, by Joel Barker. *Religious Studies Review* 41 (2015) 188.
Kempf, S. W. "A Discourse Analysis of Genesis 2:25—3:24 with Implications for Interpretation and Bible Translation." PhD diss., University Laval, 1995.
Kennedy, George A. *Comparative Rhetoric: An Historical and Cross-Cultural Introduction*. New York: Oxford University Press, 1998.
———. *New Testament Interpretation through Rhetorical Criticism*. Chapel Hill: University of North Carolina Press, 1984.
Kidner, Derek. *Genesis: An Introduction and Commentary*. Tyndale Old Testament Commentaries. Downers Grove, IL: Inter-Varsity, 1967.

Kikawada, Isaac M., and Arthur Quinn. *Before Abraham Was: The Unity of Genesis 1–11*. Nashville: Abingdon, 1985.
Kissileff, Beth, ed. *Reading Genesis: Beginnings*. New York: Bloomsbury T. & T. Clark, 2016.
Kitchen, K. A. *On The Reliability of the Old Testament*. Grand Rapids: Eerdmans, 2006.
Kline, Meredith G. *Genesis: A New Commentary*. Peabody. MA: Hendrickson, 2016.
Kloppenborg, John S. "Source Criticism." In *Dictionary of Biblical Criticism and Interpretation*, edited by Stanley E. Porter, 340–44. New York: Routledge, 2009.
Knafl, Anne K. *Forming God: Divine Anthropomorphism in the Pentateuch*. Siphrut 12. Winona Lake, IN: Eisenbrauns, 2014.
Knight, G. M. Review of *From the Depths of Despair to the Promise of Presence: A Rhetorical Reading of the Book of Joel*, by Joel Barker. *JSOT* 39 (2015) 74.
Konkel, August H. "In Defense of Human Values: The Good Life under Divine Covenant." *Didaskalia* 24 (2015) 25–39.
———. *Promise and Covenant*. Otterburne, MB: Providence Theological Seminary Bookstore, 2010.
Korpel, Marjo C. A., and Joseph M. Oesch, eds. *Delimitation Criticism: A New Tool in Biblical Scholarship*. Pericope 1. Assen: Van Gorcum, 2000.
Kotter, John P. *Leading Change*. Brighton, MA: Harvard Business School, 1996.
Kruger, Mike. "Genesis 6–9: Does 'All' Always Mean All?" *Creation Ex Nihilo Technical Journal* 10 (1996) 214–18.
Kvanig, Helge S. *Primeval History: Babylonian, Biblical, and Enochic: An Intertextual Reading*. Supplements to the Journal for the Study of Judaism 149. Leiden: Brill, 2011.
LaHaye, Tim, and John Morris. *The Ark on Ararat*. Nashville: Nelson, 1976.
Lamb, David T. *God Behaving Badly. Is the God of the Old Testament Angry, Sexist, and Racist?* Downers Grove, IL: IVP Academic, 2011.
Lambert, W. G. *Babylonian Creation Myths*. Winona Lake, IN: Eisenbrauns, 2013.
Lambert, W. G., and A. R. Millard. *Atra-Ḫasīs: The Babylonian Story of the Flood*. Winona Lake, IN: Eisenbrauns, 1999.
Lambdin, Thomas O. *Introduction to Biblical Hebrew*. London: Darton, Longman & Todd, 1973.
Lamoureux, Denis O. *The Bible & Ancient Science: Principles of Interpretation*. Tullahoma, TN: McGahan, 2020.
———. *Evolutionary Creation: A Christian Approach to Evolution*. Eugene, OR: Wipf & Stock, 2008.
———. "No Historical Adam: Evolutionary Creation View." In *Four Views on the Historical Adam*, edited by Matthew Barrett and Ardel B. Caneday, 37–88. Counterpoints. Grand Rapids: Zondervan, 2013.
Lapointe, Roger. "Divine Monologue as a Channel of Revelation." *CBQ* 32 (1970) 161–81.
Larsson, Gerhard. "Remarks Concerning the Noah-Flood Complex." *ZAW* 112 (2000) 75–77.
Lee, Jae Hyun. *Paul's Gospel in Romans: A Discourse Analysis of Rom. 1:16—8:39*. Linguistic Biblical Studies 3. Leiden: Brill, 2010.
Lee, John A. *The Greek of the Pentateuch*. Grinfield Lectures on the Septuagint 2011–2012. New York: Oxford University Press, 2018.
Lenchak, T. A. *Choose Life! A Rhetorical-Critical Investigation of Deuteronomy 28:69—30:20*. Analecta Biblica 129. Rome: Pontifical Biblical Institute, 1993.

Lennox, John C. *Seven Days that Divide the World: The Beginning According to Genesis and Science.* 10th Anniversary Edition. Grand Rapids: Zondervan, 2021.

Levin, Yigal. "Understanding Biblical Genealogies." *Currents in Biblical Research* 9 (2001) 11–46.

Lewis, C. S. *A Preface to Paradise Lost.* Oxford: Oxford University Press, 1942.

Licht, Jacob. *Storytelling in the Bible.* 2nd ed. Jerusalem: Magnes, 1978.

Linville, J. "Bugs Through the Looking Glass: The Infestation of Meaning in Joel." In *Reflection and Refraction: Studies in Biblical Historiography in Honour of A. Graeme Auld,* edited by R. Rezetko et al., 283–98. Cambridge: Cambridge University Press, 2006.

Linzey, Andrew and Dan Cohn-Sherbok. *After Noah: Animals and the Liberation of Theology.* Herndon, VA: Mowbray, 1997.

Long, Philips V. *The Art of Biblical History.* In *Foundations of Contemporary Interpretation: Six Volumes in One,* edited by Moisés Silva, 281–429. Grand Rapids: Zondervan, 1996.

———. *The Reign and Rejection of King Saul: A Case for Literary and Theological Coherence.* SBLDS 118. Atlanta: Scholars, 1989.

Longacre, Robert E. "Discourse Structure, Verb Forms, and Archaism in Psalm 18." *Journal of Translation and Textlinguistics* 15 (2003) 35–55.

———. "The Discourse Structure of the Flood Narrative." *Journal of the American Academy of Religion* XLVII (1979) 89–133.

———. *The Grammar of Discourse.* 2nd ed. Topics in Language and Linguistics. New York: Plenum, 1996.

Longman, Tremper, III. "Avoid Theological Tribalism: Read Broadly." *Didaktikos* 4 (2020) 42.

———. *The Bible and the Ballot: Using Scripture in Political Decisions.* Grand Rapids: Eerdmans, 2020.

———. *Genesis.* The Story of God Bible Commentary. Grand Rapids: Zondervan, 2016.

———. *How to Read the Psalms.* Downers Grove, IL: InterVarsity, 1988.

———. *Literary Approaches to Biblical Interpretation.* In *Foundations of Contemporary Interpretation: Six Volumes in One,* edited by Moisés Silva, 91–192. Grand Rapids: Zondervan, 1996.

———. "Rhetoric." In *The Baker Illustrated Bible Dictionary,* edited by Tremper Longman III, 1427–28. Grand Rapids: Baker, 2013.

———. "What I Mean by Historical-Grammatical Exegesis: Why I am Not A Literalist." *Grace Theological Journal* 11 (1990) 137–55.

Longman, Tremper III., and John H. Walton. *The Lost World of the Flood: Mythology, Theology, and the Deluge Debate.* Downers Grove, IL: IVP Academic, 2018.

Longman, Tremper III., and Raymond B. Dillard. *An Introduction to the Old Testament.* 2nd ed. Grand Rapids: Zondervan, 2006.

Lovett, Ken. Review of *The Lost World of the Flood: Mythology, Theology, and the Deluge Debate,* by Tremper Longman III and John H. Walton. *Journal of Biblical and Theological Studies* 4 (2019) 149–51.

Lovett, Tim. *Noah's Ark: Thinking Outside the Box.* Green Forest, AR: Master, 2008.

Lowery, Daniel D. *Towards a Poetics of Genesis 1–11: Reading Genesis 4:17–22 in Its Near Eastern Context.* BBRSup 7. Winona Lake, IN: Eisenbrauns, 2013.

Lundbom, Jack R. *Jeremiah: A Study in Ancient Hebrew Rhetoric.* 2nd ed. Winona Lake, IN: Eisenbrauns, 1997.

Lyon, Ashley E. *Reassessing Selah*. Athens, GA: College & Clayton, 2021.
Lyon, Jeremy D. *Qumran Interpretation of the Genesis Flood*. Eugene, OR: Pickwick Publications, 2015.
Mack, Burton L. *Rhetoric and the New Testament*. Guides to Biblical Scholarship: New Testament Series. Minneapolis: Fortress, 1990.
Maier, Walter A., III, "Does God 'Repent' or Change His Mind?" *Concordia Theological Quarterly* 68 (2004) 127–43.
Mann, Thomas W. *The Book of the Torah*. 2nd ed. Eugene, OR: Cascade Books, 2013.
Marcus, David. "The Mission of The Raven (Gen. 8:7)." *Journal of Ancient Near Eastern Studies* 29 (2002) 71–80.
Markos, Louis. Review of *Reading Genesis Well: Navigating History, Poetry, Science, and Truth in Genesis 1–11*, by C. John Collins. *Themelios* 44 (2019) 129–31.
Marrs, Rick "The Sons of God (Genesis 6:1–4)." *Restoration Quarterly* 23 (1980) 218–24.
Martin, Ernest L. *Solving the Riddle of Noah's Flood*. N.p.: A S K, 1988.
Mason, Steven D. "Another Flood: Genesis 9 and Isaiah's Broken Eternal Covenant." *JSOT* 32 (2007) 177–98.
———. *"Eternal Covenant" In the Pentateuch: The Contours of an Elusive Phrase*. New York: T. & T. Clark, 2008.
Mathews, Kenneth A. *Genesis 1—11:26*. New American Commentary. Nashville: B. & H., 1996.
———. "Genesis." In *New Dictionary of Biblical Theology: Exploring the Unity and Diversity of Scripture*, edited by T. Desmond Alexander et al., 140–46. Downers Grove, IL: IVP Academic, 2000.
Matz, Robert J., and A. Chadwick Thornhill, eds. *Divine Impassibility: Four Views of God's Emotions and Suffering*. Downers Grove, IL: IVP Academic, 2019.
Mbuvi, Amanda Beckenstein. *Belonging in Israel: Biblical Israel and the Politics of Identity Formation*. Waco: TX, Baylor University Press, 2016.
McCann, Jason Micahel. "'Woven of Reeds': Genesi 6:14b as Evidence for the Preservation of the Reed-Hut *Urheiligtum* in the Biblical Flood Narrative." In *Opening Heaven's Floodgates: The Genesis Flood Narrative, Its Context, and Reception*, edited by Jason M. Silverman, 113–39. Biblical Intersections 12. Piscataway, NJ: Gorgias, 2013.
McCarthy, D. J. "The Uses of $w^ehinnēh$ in Biblical Hebrew." *Biblica* 61 (1980) 330–42.
McComiskey, Thomas E. *The Covenants of Promise: A Theology of the Old Testament Covenants*. Eugene, OR: Wipf and Stock, 2019.
McDougall, Colin S. *Models for Disciple-Makers*. Robbinsville, NC: Eternal Truth Ministries. 2002.
McDowell, Catherine L. *The Image of God in the Garden of Eden: The Creation of Humankind in Genesis 2:5—3:24 in Light of the mīs pî, pīt pî, and wpt-r Rituals of Mesopotamia and Ancient Egypt*. Siphrut 15. Winona Lake, IN: Eisenbrauns, 2015.
McKeown, James. *Genesis*. Two Horizons Old Testament Commentary. Grand Rapids: Eerdmans, 2008.
McLean, G. S. et al. *The Evidence for Creation: Examining the Origin of Planet Earth*. 3rd ed. Santa Ana, CA: Understand the Times, 1995.
Meek, T. J. "Old Testament Notes." *JBL* 67 (1948) 236–38.
Meier, Samuel A. *Speaking of Speaking: Marking Direct Discourse in the Hebrew Bible*. VTSup 46. Leiden: Brill, 1992.
Meiring, Jacob. "Shem, Ham, Japheth and Zuma: Genesis 9:25–27 and Masculinities in South Africa." *Stellenbosch Theological Journal* 2 (2016) 223–40.

Mettinger, Tyggve N. D. *The Eden Narrative: A Literary and Religio-Historical Study of Genesis 2–3*. Winona Lake, IN: Eisenbrauns, 2007.

Middleton, J. Richard. *The Liberating Image: The Imago Dei in Genesis 1*. Grand Rapids: Brazos, 2005.

Miglio, Adam E. et al., eds. *For Us, but Not to Us: Essays on Creation, Covenant, and Content in Honor of John H Walton*. Eugene, OR: Pickwick Publications, 2020.

Miller, Arthur B. "Rhetorical Exigence." *Philosophy & Rhetoric* 5 (1972) 111–18.

Miller, Cynthia L. *The Representation of Speech in Biblical Hebrew Narrative: A Linguistic Analysis*. HSM 55. Atlanta: Scholars, 1996.

Miller, Johnny V., and John M. Soden. *In the Beginning . . . We Misunderstood: Interpreting Genesis 1 in Its Original Context*. Grand Rapids: Kregel, 2012.

Miller, Stephen M. *The Complete Guide to the Bible*. Uhrichsville, OH: Barbour, 2007.

Mitchell, Margaret M. "Rhetorical and New Literary Criticism." In *The Oxford Handbook of Biblical Studies*, edited by J. W. Rogerson and Judith M. Lieu, 614–33. Oxford Handbooks. New York: Oxford University Press, 2008.

Moberly, R. W. L. *Old Testament Theology: Reading the Hebrew Bible as Christian Scripture*. Grand Rapids: Baker, 2015.

———. *The Theology of the Book of Genesis*. Old Testament Theology. Cambridge: Cambridge University Press, 2009.

———. "Why Did Noah Send Out a Raven?" *VT* 50 (2000) 346–56.

Möller, Karl. *A Prophet in Debate: The Rhetoric of Persuasion in the Book of Amos*. JSOTSup 372. Sheffield, England: Sheffield Academic, 2003.

———. "Rhetorical Criticism." In *Dictionary of Theological Interpretation of the Bible*, edited by Kevin J. Vanhoozer, 689–92. Grand Rapids: Baker Academic, 2005.

Moo, Douglas J., and Jonathan A. Moo. *Creation Care: A Biblical Theology of the Natural World*. Biblical Theology for Life. Grand Rapids: Zondervan, 2018.

Moore, Michael. Review of *Reading Genesis Well: Navigating History, Poetry, Science, and Truth in Genesis 1–11*, by C. John Collins. *CBQ* 82 (2020) 114–15.

Moore, Robert A. "The Impossible Voyage of Noah's Ark." *Creation/Evolution Journal* 4 (2008) 1–39.

Morris, John D. *Noah's Ark: Adventures on Ararat*. Dallas: Institute for Creation Research, 2014.

Mortenson, Terry "The Firmament: What Did God Create on Day 2?" *Answers Research Journal* 13 (2020) 113–33.

Muilenburg, James. "Form Criticism and Beyond." *JBL* 88 (1969) 1–18.

———. "The Linguistics and Rhetorical Usages of the Particle kî in the Old Testament." *HUCA* 32 (1961) 136–60.

Muraoka, Takamitsu. *Emphatic Words and Structures in Biblical Hebrew*. Jerusalem: Magnes, 1997.

Naudé, Jacobus A. "The Interpretation and Translation of the Biblical Hebrew Quantifier KOL." *Journal for Semitics* 22 (2011) 408–21.

Nelles, William. "Historical and Implied Authors and Readers." *Comparative Literature* 45 (1993) 22–46.

Neufeld, Waldie N. *Teaching Stones to Love: Jesus' Model of Disciple-Making*. Independently published. 2020.

Niehaus, Jeffrey J. *Ancient Near Eastern Themes in Biblical Theology*. Grand Rapids: Kregel, 2008.

Noll, Mark A. *The Scandal of the Evangelical Mind*. Grand Rapids: Eerdmans, 1994.

Noonan, Benjamin J. *Advances in the Study of Biblical Hebrew and Aramaic: New Insights for Reading the Old Testament.* Grand Rapids: Zondervan, 2020.

———. Review of *Reading Genesis Well: Navigating History, Poetry, Science, and Truth in Genesis 1–11*, by C. John Collins. BBR 29 (2019) 551–53.

Noort, Ed. "Stories of the Great Flood." In *Interpretations of the Flood*, edited by Florentino García Martínez, and Gerard P. Luttikhuizen, 1–38. Themes in Biblical Narrative: Jewish and Christian Traditions 1. Leiden: Brill, 2008.

Oates, G. W. "The Curse in God's Blessing." In *Die Botschaft und die Boten: Festschrift für Hans Walter Wolff zum 70. Geburtstag*, edited by Jörg Jeremías and Lothar Perlitt, 32–33. Neukirchen-Vluyn: Neukirchener, 1981.

O'Connor, Kathleen M. *Genesis 1–25A*. Smyth & Helwys Bible Commentary 1A. Macon, GA: Smyth & Helwys, 2018.

Okoye, James Chukwuma. *Genesis 1–11: A Narrative-Theological Commentary.* Eugene, OR: Cascade Books, 2018.

Olbricht, Thomas H. "Rhetorical Criticism." In *Dictionary of Biblical Criticism and Interpretation*, edited by Stanley E. Porter, 325–27. New York: Routledge, 2009.

———. "Delivery and Memory." In *Handbook of Classical Rhetoric in the Hellenistic Period:330 B.C.–A.D. 400*, edited by Stanley E. Porter, 159–70. Leiden, Brill, 1997.

Osborne, Grant R. *The Hermeneutical Spiral: A Comprehensive Introduction to Biblical Interpretation. Revised and Expanded.* Downers Grove, IL: IVP Academic, 2006.

Oswalt, John N. *The Bible among the Myths: Unique Revelation or Just Ancient Literature?* Grand Rapids: Zondervan, 2009.

———. *The Book of Isaiah: Chapters 1–39*. NICOT. Grand Rapids: Eerdmans, 1986.

———. *The Book of Isaiah: Chapters 40–66*. NICOT. Grand Rapids: Eerdmans, 1998.

Pao, David W., and Eckhard J. Schnabel. "Luke." In *Commentary on the New Testament Use of the Old Testament*, edited by G. K. Beale and D. A Carson, 251–414. Grand Rapids: Baker Academic, 2007.

Patai, Raphael. *The Children of Noah: Jewish Seafaring in Ancient Times.* Princeton: Princeton University Press, 1998.

Patrick, Dale. *The Rhetoric of Revelation in the Hebrew Bible.* OBT. Minneapolis: Fortress, 1999.

Patrick, Dale, and Allen Scult. *Rhetoric and Biblical Interpretation.* LHBOTS 26. Sheffield: Almond, 1990.

———. "Rhetoric and Ideology: A Debate within Biblical Scholarship over the Import of Persuasion." In *The Rhetorical Interpretation of Scripture: Essays from the 1996 Malibu Conference*, edited by Stanley E. Porter and Dennis L. Stamps, 63–83. JSNTSup 180. Sheffieldm England: Sheffield Academic, 1999.

Patterson, Todd L. *The Plot-structure of Genesis: 'Will the Righteous Seed Survive?' in the Muthos-logical Movement from Complication to Dénouement.* Biblical Interpretation Series 160. Leiden: Brill, 2018.

Patty, Tyler J. "Curse and the Power of Blessing: A Linguistic Study of Genesis 1–11." MA thesis, Trinity Evangelical Divinity School, 2016.

———. "Narrative Technique in Genesis 4: Syntax, Linguistics, Poetics." Unpublished paper. 1–33.

Perelman, C., and L. Olbrechts-Tyteca. *The New Rhetoric: A Treatise on Argumentation.* Translated by J. Wilkinson and P. Weaver. Notre Dame, IN: University of Notre Dame Press, 1969.

Peters, Dorothy M. *Noah Traditions in the Dead Sea Scrolls: Conversation and Controversies of Antiquity*. Early Judaism and Its Literature 26. Atlanta: Society of Biblical Literature, 2008.

Peterson, Brian Neil. *Genesis as Torah: Reading Narrative as Legal Instruction*. Eugene, OR: Cascade Books, 2018.

Peterson, Eugene. *Working the Angles: The Shape of Pastoral Integrity*. Grand Rapids: Eerdmans, 1989.

Phelan, James. *Somebody Telling Somebody Else: A Rhetorical Poetics of Narrative*. Columbus: Ohio State University Press, 2017.

Pickering, Wilbur N. *A Framework for Discourse Analysis*. Arlington: University of Texas Press, 1980.

Pinkney, Jerry. *Noah's Ark*. New York: SeaStar, 2002.

Porter, Stanley E. "Ben Witherington on Rhetoric One Last Time (I Hope)." *BBR* 26 (2016) 551–52.

———. "C. S. Lewis's Worldview and His Literary Criticism." *McMaster Journal of Theology and Ministry* 16 (2014–2015) 3–50.

———. *Inking the Deal: A Guide for Successful Academic Publishing*. Waco, TX: Baylor University Press, 2010.

———. "Pericope Markers and Paragraph: Textual and Linguistic Implications." In *The Impact of Unit Delimitation on Exegesis*, edited by Raymond De Hoop et al., 175–95. Pericope 7. Leiden: Brill, 2009.

———. "'When It Was Clear That We Could Not Persuade Him, We Gave Him Up and Said, "The Lord's Will Be Done"' (Acts 21:14): Good Reasons to Stop Making Unproven Claims for Rhetorical Criticism." *BBR* 26 (2016) 533–45.

Porter, Stanley E., ed. *Handbook of Classical Rhetoric in the Hellenistic Period: 330 B.C.–A.D. 400*. Leiden, Brill, 1997.

Porter, Stanley E., and Bryan R. Dyer. "Oral Texts? A Reassessment of the Oral and Rhetorical Nature of Paul's Letters in Light of Recent Studies." *JETS* 55 (2012) 323–41.

Porter, Stanley E., and Dennis L. Stamps, eds. "Introduction: Rhetorical Criticism and the Florence Conference." In *Rhetorical Criticism and the Bible*, edited by Stanley E. Porter and Dennis L. Stamps, 17–23. JSNTSup 195. Sheffield: Sheffield Academic, 2002.

Porter, Stanley E., and Thomas H. Olbricht, eds. *Rhetoric and the New Testament: Essays from the 1992 Heidelberg Conference*. JSNTSup 90. Sheffield: Sheffield Academic, 1993.

———. *Rhetoric, Scripture, and Theology: Essays from the 1994 Pretoria Conference*. JSNTSup 131. Sheffield: Sheffield Academic, 1996.

———. *The Rhetorical Analysis of Scripture: Essays from the 1995 London Conference*. JSNTSup 146. Sheffield: Sheffield Academic, 1997.

Powell, Mark Allan. *What Is Narrative Criticism?* Guides to Biblical Scholarship: New Testament Series. Minneapolis: Fortress, 1990.

Powell, Mark, and Angie Powell. "Noah's Ark as Mosaic Tabernacle." Unpublished paper. 1–27.

Prescott, Deborah Lee. *Imagery from Genesis in Holocaust Memoirs: A Critical Study*. Jefferson, NC: McFarland, 2010.

Presutta, David. *The Biblical Cosmos versus Modern Cosmology: Why the Bible Is not the Word of God*. Coral Springs, FL: Llumina, 2007.

Provan, Iain. *Discovering Genesis: Content, Interpretation, Reception*. Discovering Biblical Text. Grand Rapids: Eerdmans, 2015.

Provan, Iain, et. al. *A Biblical History of Israel*. 2nd ed. Louisville: Westminster John Knox, 2015.

Purcell, Richard Anthony. Review of *From the Depths of Despair to the Promise of Presence: A Rhetorical Reading of the Book of Joel*, by Joel Barker. *Review & Expositor* 113 (2016) 114–16.

Quine, Cat. Review of *The Persuasive Portrayal of David and Solomon in Chronicles: A Rhetorical Analysis of the Speeches and Prayers in the David-Solomon Narrative*, by Suk-il Ahn. *JSOT* 43 (2019) 102–3.

Rad, Gerhard von. *Genesis: A Commentary*. Rev. ed. Translated by John H. Marks. Old Testament Library. Philadelphia: Westminster, 1972.

———. *Old Testament Theology*. Vol. 1, *The Theology of Israel's Historical Traditions*. Translated by D. M. G. Stalker. Reprint. Peabody, MA: Prince, 2005.

Ramm, Bernard. *The Christian View of Science and Scripture*. Grand Rapids: Eerdmans, 1968.

Ray, Janet Kellogg. *Baby Dinosaurs on the Ark? The Bible and Modern Science and the Trouble of Making it All Fit*. Grand Rapids: Eerdmans, 2021.

Rawson, K. J., and E. C. Tupper. *Basic Ship Theory*. Vol. 1. 5th ed. Woburn, MA: Butterworth-Heinemann, 2001.

Reed, Jeffrey T. *A Discourse Analysis of Philippians: Method and Rhetoric in the Debate Over Literary Integrity*. JSNTSup 136. Sheffield: Sheffield Academic, 1997.

Rendtorff, Rolf. "Gen 8:21 und die Urgeschichte des Jahwisten." *Kerygma und Dogma* (1961) 69–78.

Reno, R. R. *Genesis*. Brazos Theological Commentary on the Bible. Grand Rapids: Brazos, 2017.

Renz, Thomas. *The Rhetorical Function of the Book of Ezekiel*. VTSup 76. Leiden: Brill, 2009.

Richter, Sandra L. *The Epic of Eden: A Christian Entry into the Old Testament*. Downers Grove, IL: IVP Academic, 2008.

Rimmon-Kenan, Shlomith. *Narrative Fiction*. 2nd ed. London: Routledge, 2002.

Roaf, Michael. "Palaces and Temples in Ancient Mesopotamia," in *Civilizations of the Ancient Near East*, 423–41, edited by Jack M. Sasson. New York: Charles Scribner's Sons, 1995.

Robertson, O. Palmer. *The Christ of the Covenants*. Phillipsburg, NJ: P. & R., 1987.

Robinson, J. C. "Narrative." In *Dictionary of Biblical Criticism and Interpretation*, edited by Stanley E. Porter, 236–37. New York: Routledge, 2009.

Rogers, Lynden J. ed. *The Biblical Flood: The Context and History of Seventh-day Adventist Understanding*. 2nd ed. Cooranbong, Australia: Avondale Academic, 2020.

Ron, Zvi. "The Book of Jubilees and the Midrash: Part 2—Noah and the Flood." *JBQ* 42 (2014) 103–13.

Rooker, Mark F. "The Genesis Flood." *Southern Baptist Journal of Theology* 5 (2001) 58–74.

Ross, Hugh. *Hidden Treasures in the Book of Job: How the Oldest Book in the Bible Answers Today's Scientific Questions*. Grand Rapids: Baker, 2011.

———. *Navigating Genesis: A Scientist's Journey through Genesis 1–11*. Covina, CA: Reasons to Believe, 2014.

Routledge, Robin. *Old Testament Theology: A Thematic Approach*. Downers Grove, IL: IVP Academic, 2012.

Ryken, Leland. *How to Read the Bible as Literature . . . and Get More Out of It*. Grand Rapids: Zondervan, 1984.

———. *Words of Delight: A Literary Introduction to the Bible*. 2nd ed. Grand Rapids: Baker, 1993.

Sailhamer, John. "Creation, Genesis 1–11, and the Canon." *BBR* 10 (2000) 89–106.

———. "Genesis." In *A Complete Literary Guide to the Bible*, edited by Leland Ryken and Tremper Longman III, 108–20. Grand Rapids: Zondervan, 1993.

———. *Genesis*. In *The Expositor's Bible Commentary: Revised Edition*, edited by Tremper Longman III and David Garland, 21–331. Grand Rapids: Zondervan, 2008.

———. *Genesis Unbound: A Provocative New Look at the Creation Account*. 2nd ed. Colorado Springs: Dawson, 2011.

———. *The Meaning of the Pentateuch: Revelation, Composition, and Interpretation*. Downers Grove, IL: IVP Academic, 2009.

———. *The Pentateuch as Narrative: A Biblical-Theological Commentary*. Library of Biblical Intersection. Grand Rapids: Zondervan, 1992.

Sandy, D. B. *Plowshares and Pruning Hooks: Rethinking the Language of Biblical Prophecy and Apocalyptic*. Downers Grove, IL: InterVarsity, 2002.

Sarfati, Jonathan. *The Genesis Account: A Theological, Historical, and Scientific Commentary on Genesis 1–11*. Powder Springs, GA: Creation, 2015.

Sargent, Andrew Dean. "Wind, Water, and Battle Imagery in Genesis 8:1–3." PhD diss., Trinity International University, 2010.

Sarna, Nahum M. *Genesis*. JPS Torah Commentary. Philadelphia: Jewish Publication Society, 1989.

———. *Understanding Genesis: The World of the Bible in the Light of History*. Melton Research Center Series 1. New York: Melton Research Center, 1966.

Sasson, Jack M. "Word-Play in Gen 6:8, 9." *CBQ* 37 (1975) 165–66.

Schmid, Wolf. *Narratology: An Introduction*. New York: de Gruyter, 2010.

Schmidt, Peter. "Translating *Kōl*: When 'All' Does Not Mean 'All.'" *Bible Translator* 71 (2020) 179–91.

Schneider, Tammi J. "In the Beginning and Still Today: Recent Publications on Genesis." *Currents in Biblical Research* 18 (2020) 142–59.

Schnittjer, Gary Edward. *Old Testament Use of Old Testament: A Book-by-Book Guide*. Grand Rapids: Zondervan, 2021.

Schreiner, Thomas R. *Covenant: God's Purpose for the World*. Short Studies in Biblical Theology. Wheaton, IL: Crossway, 2017.

———. *The King in His Beauty: A Biblical Theology of the Old and New Testaments*. Grand Rapids: Baker Academic, 2013.

Scott, Eugenie C. *Evolution vs. Creationism: An Introduction*. 2nd ed. Westport, CT: University of California Press, 2009.

Scult, Michael Allen. "The Rhetoric of the Pentateuch: An Analysis of the Argument for the Hebrew Concept of God." PhD diss., University of Wisconsin, 1975.

Seely, Paul H. "The Firmament and the Water Above: Part 1: The Meaning of *raqiaʿ* in Gen 1:6–8." *WTJ* 53 (1991) 227–40.

———. "The Firmament and the Water Above: Part II: The Meaning of "The Water above the Firmament" in Gen 1:6–8." *WTJ* 54 (1992) 47–63.

———. "The Geographical Meaning of 'Earth' and 'Seas' in Genesis 1:10." *WTJ* 59 (1997) 231–55.

———. "Noah's Flood: Its Date, Extent, and Divine Accommodation." *WTJ* 66 (2004) 291–311.

Sexton Jeremy. "Andrew E. Steinmann's Search for Chronological Gaps in Genesis 5 and 11: A Rejoinder." *JETS* 62 (2018) 39–45.

———. "Evangelicalism's Search for Chronological Gaps in Genesis 5 and 11: A Historical, Hermeneutical, and Linguistic Critique." *JETS* 62 (2018) 5–25.

Shaviv, Shemuel. "The Polytheistic Origins of the Biblical Flood Narrative." *VT* 54 (2004) 527–48.

Shaw, Charles S. *The Speeches of Micah: A Rhetorical-Historical Analysis*. JSTOTSup 145. Sheffield: Sheffield Academic, 1993.

Shemesh, Abraham Ofir. "Religious Literature, The Realistic, and the Fantastic: Mythological Creatures in Midrashic Interpretations of the Story of the Flood and Noah's Ark." *Estudos de Religião* 33 (2019) 235–55.

Shen, Dan. "What is the Implied Author?" *Style* 45 (2011) 80–98.

Siegert, Folker. "Homily and Panegyrical Sermon." In *Handbook of Classical Rhetoric in the Hellenistic Period: 330 B.C.–A.D. 400*, edited by Stanley E. Porter, 421–43. Leiden, Brill, 1997.

Sigler, Charles. "Faith Seeking Understanding. The Not-So Global Flood: Part Two." 10/9/18. http://faith-seeking-understanding.org/tag/genesis-flood-hyperbole/.

Silverman, Jason S. "Yes We Can (Hyperbolize)! Ideals, Rhetoric, and Tradition Transmission." *Journal of the Bible and Its Reception* 1 (2014) 263–84.

Simkins, Ronald A. *Creator and Creation: Nature in the Worldview of Ancient Israel*. Peabody, MA: Hendrickson, 1994.

Sire, James W. *Naming the Elephant: Worldview as a Concept*. 2nd ed. Downers Grove, IL: IVP Academic, 2015.

———. *The Universe Next Door: A Basic Worldview Catalog*. 6th ed. Downers Grove, IL: IVP Academic, 2020.

Ska, Jean-Louise. *Introduction to Reading the Pentateuch*. Translated by Pascale Dominique. Winona Lake, IN: Eisenbrauns, 2006.

Skinner, John. *A Critical and Exegetical Commentary on Genesis*. 2nd ed. International Critical Commentary. Edinburg: T. & T. Clark, 1930.

Sleeth, Matthew J. *Serve God, Save the Planet: A Christian Call to Action*. Grand Rapids: Zondervan, 2007.

Smith, A. R. *The Babylonian Gilgamesh Epic: Introduction, Critical Edition, and Cuneiform Texts*. Volume I. Oxford: Oxford University Press, 2003.

Smith, Douglas K. "Whom, Where, or What Could 'All the Earth' Mean? A Case Study in the Implications of Context and Intertextuality for Translating and Interpreting Kol Ha-Aretz (כל הארץ) in the Pentateuch." *Interdisciplinary Journal on Biblical Authority* 1/2 (2020) 135–53.

Smith, Gary V. *Isaiah 40—66*. The New American Commentary. Nashville: B. & H., 2009.

Smith, Mark S. *The Priestly Vision of Genesis 1*. Minneapolis: Fortress, 2010.

Snelling, Andrew A. *Earth's Catastrophic Past: Geology, Creation, and the Flood*. 2 vols. Dallas: Institute for Creation Research, 2009.

Soden, John M. "Cosmology, Biblical." In *Dictionary of Christianity and Science: The Definitive Reference for the Intersection of Christian Faith and Contemporary Science*, edited by Paul Copan et al., 120–24. Grand Rapids: Zondervan, 2017.

Sollereder, Bethany N. *God, Evolution, and Animal Suffering: Theodicy without a Fall.* Routledge Science and Religion Series. New York: Routledge, 2019.

Sonnet, J. P. Review of *Choose Life! A Rhetorical-Critical Investigation of Deuteronomy 28:69—30:20*, by T. C. Lenchak. *Biblica* 76 (1995) 93–98.

Soulen, Richard N., and R. Kendall Soulen. *Handbook of Biblical Criticism.* 4th ed. Louisville: Westminster John Knox, 2011.

Sparks, Kenton L. *God's Word in Human Words: An Evangelical Appropriation of Critical Biblical Scholarship.* Grand Rapids: Baker Academic, 2008.

———. *The Pentateuch: An Annotated Bibliography.* 2000. Reprint, Eugene, OR: Wipf & Stock, 2019.

Speiser, E. A. "The Biblical Idea of History in Its Common Near Eastern Setting." In *The Jewish Expression*, edited by Judah Goldin, 1–17. New Haven: Yale University Press, 1976.

———. *Genesis.* Anchor Bible 1. Garden City, NY: Doubleday, 1964.

Spero, Shubert. "Sons of God, Daughters of Men?" *Jewish Bible Quarterly* 40 (2012) 15–18.

Stallings, Joseph W. *The Genesis Cataclysm: Proposing a Noahic Global Flood within an Old-Earth Scriptural Paradigm.* Eugene, OR: Resource Publications, 2020.

Stamps, Dennis L. "Rethinking Rhetorical Situation: The Entextualization of the Situation in New Testament Epistles." In *Rhetoric and the New Testament: Essays from the 1992 Heidelberg Conference*, edited by Stanley E. Porter and Thomas H. Olbricht, 193–210. JSNTSup 90. Sheffield: Sheffield Academic, 1993.

———. "Rhetoric." In *Dictionary of New Testament Background*, edited by Craig A. Evans and Stanley E. Porter, 953–59. Downers Grove, IL: InterVarsity, 2000.

———. "Rhetorical and Narratological Criticism." In *A Handbook to the Exegesis of the New Testament*, edited by Stanley E. Porter, 219–40. New Testament Tools and Studies 25. Leiden: Brill, 1997.

Stamps, Dennis L. "The Use of the Old Testament in the New Testament as a Rhetorical Device: A Methodological Proposal." In *Hearing the Old Testament in the New Testament*, edited by Stanley E. Porter, 9–37. McMaster New Testament Studies. Grand Rapids: Eerdmans, 2006.

Stanhope, Ben. *(Mis)interpreting Genesis: how the Creation Museum Misunderstands the Ancient Near Eastern Context of the Bible.* Louisville, KY: Scarab, 2020.

Stefanescu, Maria. "Revisiting the Implied Author Yet Again: Why (Still) Bother?" *Style* (2011) 48–66.

Stein, Stephen K, ed. *The Sea in World History: Exploration, Travel, and Trade.* Vol. 1, *Ancient Egypt through the First Global Age.* 2 vols. Santa Barbara, CA: ABC–CLIO, 2017.

Steinberg, Naomi A. "The World of the Family in Genesis." In *The Book of Genesis: Composition, Reception, and Interpretation*, by Craig A. Evans et al., eds., 279–300. VTSup 152. Leiden: Brill, 2012.

Steiner, Richard C. "'He Said, He Said': Repetition of the Quotation Formula in the Joseph Story and Other Biblical Narratives." *JBL* 138 (2019) 473–95.

Steiner, V. J. "Literary Structure of the Old Testament." In *Dictionary of the Old Testament: Pentateuch*, edited by Alexander, T. Desmond and David W. Baker, 544–56. Downers Grove, IL: IVP Academic, 2003.

Steinmann, Andrew. *Genesis.* Tyndale Old Testament Commentaries. Downers Grove, IL: IVP Academic, 2019.

———. "A Reply to Jeremy Sexton Regarding the Genealogies in Genesis." *JETS* 62 (2018) 27–37.

Steinmetz, Devora. "Vineyard, Farm, and Garden: The Drunkenness of Noah in the Context of Primeval History." *JBL* 113 (1994) 193–207.
Sternberg, Meir. "The Genealogical Framework of the Family Stories in Genesis." *Semeia* 46 (1989) 41–50.
———. *The Poetics of Biblical Narrative: Ideological Literature and the Drama of Reading*. Indiana Studies in Biblical Literature. Bloomington: Indiana University Press, 1987.
Stewart, Alexander Coe. "The Ethos of the Cosmos in Amos: Creation Rhetoric and Character Formation in Old Testament Ethics." PhD diss., McMaster Divinity College, 2019.
———. "Heaven Has No Sorrow that Earth Cannot Feel: The Ethics of Empathy and Ecological Suffering in the Old Testament." *Canadian Theological Review* 4 (2015) 19–34.
Streett, Daniel R. "As it was in the Day's of Noah: The Prophets' Typological Interpretation of Noah's Flood." *Criswell Theological Review* 5 (2007) 33–51.
Stuart, Douglas. *Hosea–Jonah*. Word Biblical Commentary 31. Waco, TX: Nelson, 1987.
Stuckenbruck, Loren T. *The Myth of the Rebellious Angels: Studies in Second Temple Judaism and New Testament Texts*. Wissenschaftliche Untersuchungen zum Neuen Testament 335. Tübingen: Mohr Siebeck, 2014.
Swart, I. "In Search of the Meaning of *hamas*: Studying an Old Testament Word in Context." *Journal for Semitics* 3 (1991) 156–66.
Teeple, Howard M. *The Noah's Ark Nonsense*. Truth in Religion 1. Evanston, IL: Religion and Ethics Institute, 1978.
Thomas, Huw. *In the Way of the Story: Reading Biblical Narrative*. Eugene, OR: Wipf & Stock, 2021.
Thomas, Matthew A. *These Are the Generations: Identity, Covenant, and the 'Toledot' Formula*. LHBOTS 551. New York: T. & T. Clark, 2011.
Throntveit, Mark A. Review of *The Persuasive Appeal of the Chronicler: A Rhetorical Analysis*, by Rodney K. Duke. *Interpretation* 46 (1992) 312–14.
Thurén, Lauri. *Argument and Theology in 1 Peter: The Origins of Christian Paraenesis*. JSNTSup 114. New York: Bloomsbury T. & T. Clark, 1995.
———. *The Rhetorical Strategy of 1 Peter, with Special Regard to Ambiguous Expressions*. Abo, Finland: Abo Academy Press, 1990.
Trible, Phyllis. *Rhetorical Criticism: Context, Method, and the Book of Jonah*. OBT. Minneapolis: Fortress, 1994.
Tov, Emmanuel. *Scribal Practices and Approaches Reflected in the Texts Found in the Judean Desert*. Studies on the Texts of the Desert of Judah 54. Atlanta: SBL, 2004.
Turner, L. A. *Announcements of Plot in Genesis*. JSOTSup 96. Sheffield: JSOT Press, 1990.
———. "The Rainbow as the Sign of the Covenant in Genesis IX 11–13." *VT* 43 (1993) 119–24.
Tsumara, David Toshio. *Creation and Destruction: A Reappraisal of the Chaoskampf Theory in the Old Testament*. Winona Lake, IN: Eisenbrauns, 2005.
———. "Genesis and Ancient Near Eastern Stories of Creation and Flood: An Introduction." In *"I Studied Inscriptions before the Flood": Ancient Near Eastern, Literary, and Linguistic Approaches to Genesis 1–11*, edited by Richard S. Hess and David T. Tsumura, 27–57. Sources for Biblical and Theological Study 4. Winona Lake, IN: Eisenbrauns, 1994.

Tverbg, Lois. "The Flood's Deeper Message of Mercy." June 17, 2019. No pages. https://engediresourcecenter.com/2019/06/17/the-floods-deeper-message-of-mercy/.

Unger, Richard W. *The Art of Medieval Technology: Images of Noah the Shipbuilder*. New Brunswick, NJ: Rutgers University Press, 1991.

VanGemeren, Willem A. "The Heart." In *NLT Study Bible*, edited by Sean A. Harrison, 1019. Carol Stream, IL: Tyndale, 2008.

———. "The Sons of God in Genesis 6:1–4 (An Example of Evangelical Demythologization)." *WTJ* 43 (1981) 320–48.

Vanhoozer, Kevin J. "Exegesis and Hermeneutics." In *New Dictionary Biblical Theology*, edited by T. Desmond Alexander et al., 52–64. Downers Grove, IL: IVP Academic, 2000.

———. *First Theology: God, Scripture & Hermeneutics*. Downers Grove, IL: IVP Academic, 2002.

———. *Remythologizing Theology: Divine Action, Passion, and Authorship*. Cambridge Studies in Christian Doctrine. Cambridge: Cambridge University Press, 2010.

VanOsdel, Jessica Lee. "The Rhetorical Situation: its historical situation and its current limitations." MA thesis, Iowa State University, 2005.

Van Pelt, Miles V., ed. *Basics of Hebrew Discourse: A Guide to Working With Hebrew Prose and Poetry*. Zondervan Language Basics. Grand Rapids: Zondervan, 2019.

Van Seters, John. *The Yahwist: A Historian of Israelite Origins*. Winona Lake, IN: Eisenbrauns, 2013.

Vatz, Richard E. "The Myth of the Rhetorical Situation." *Philosophy and Rhetoric* 6 (1974) 154–61.

Vaux, Roland de. *Ancient Israel: Its Life and Institutions*. Translated by John McHugh. 1961. Reprint, Biblical Resource Series. Grand Rapids: Eerdmans, 1997.

Vermeulen, Karolien. "The Art of Blessing and Cursing in Genesis 1–11." In *Doubling and Duplicating in the Book of Genesis: Literary and Stylistic Approaches to the Text*, edited by Elizabeth R. Hayes, and Karolien Vermeulen, 113–28. Winona Lake: IN, Eisenbrauns, 2016.

Vogt, Peter T. *Interpreting the Pentateuch: An Exegetical Handbook*. Handbooks for Old Testament Exegesis. Grand Rapids: Kregel, 2009.

Wachsmann, Shelley. *Seagoing Ships and Seamanship in the Bronze Age Levant*. London: Chatman, 1998.

Walker, Jeffrey. *Rhetoric and Poetics in Antiquity*. New York: Oxford University Press, 2000.

Walsh, Brian J., and J. Richard Middleton, *The Transforming Vision: Shaping a Christian Worldview*. Downers Grove, IL: IVP, 1984.

Walsh, Jerome T. *Old Testament Narrative: A Guide to Interpretation*. Louisville: Westminster John Knox, 2009.

Waltke, Bruce K. "The Phenomenon of Conditionality within Unconditional Covenants." In *Israel's Apostasy and Restoration: Essays in Honor of Roland K. Harrison*, edited by Avraham Gileadi, 123–39. Grand Rapids: Baker, 1988.

Waltke, Bruce K., and Cathi J. Fredricks. *Genesis: A Commentary*. Grand Rapids: Zondervan, 2001.

Waltke, Bruce K., and Charles Yu. *An Old Testament Theology: An Exegetical, Canonical, and Thematic Approach*. Grand Rapids: Zondervan, 2007.

Walton, John H. *Ancient Near Eastern Thought and the Old Testament: Introducing the Conceptual World of the Hebrew Bible*. 2nd ed. Grand Rapids: Baker, 2018.

———. "Are the 'Sons of God' in Genesis 6 Angels? No." In *The Genesis Debate: Persistent Questions about Creation and the Flood*, edited by Ronald Youngblood, 184–209. 1990. Reprint, Eugene, OR: Wipf & Stock, 1999.

———. "Cosmology, Ancient." In *Dictionary of Christianity and Science: The Definitive Reference for the Intersection of Christian Faith and Contemporary Science*, edited by Paul Copan et al., 116–20. Grand Rapids: Zondervan, 2017.

———. *Covenant: God's Purpose, God's Plan*. Grand Rapids: Zondervan, 1994.

———. "Flood." In *Dictionary of the Old Testament: Pentateuch*, edited by Alexander, T. Desmond and David W. Baker, 315–26. Downers Grove, IL: InterVarsity, 2003.

———. *Genesis*. The NIV Application Commentary. Grand Rapids: Zondervan, 2001.

———. *Genesis 1 as Ancient Cosmology*. Winona Lake, IN: Eisenbrauns, 2011.

———. "Interactions in the Ancient Cognitive Environment." In *Behind the Scenes of the Old Testament: Cultural, Social, and Historical Contexts*, edited by Jonathan S. Greer et al., 333–39. Grand Rapids: Baker Academic, 2018.

———. "Interpreting the Bible as an Ancient Near East Document." In *Israel: Ancient Kingdom or Late Invention?*, edited by Daniel I. Block, 298–327. Nashville: B. & H., 2008.

———. *Job*. NIV Application Commentary. Grand Rapids: Zondervan, 2012.

———. *Old Testament Theology for Christians: From Ancient Context to Enduring Belief*. Downers Grove, IL: IVP Academic, 2017.

———. "Sons of God, Daughters of Man." In *Dictionary of the Old Testament: Pentateuch*, edited by Alexander, T. Desmond and David W. Baker, 793–98. Downers Grove, IL: InterVarsity, 2003.

Walton, John H. et al., eds. *The IVP Bible Background Commentary: Old Testament*. Downers Grove, IL: InterVarsity, 2000.

Walton, Steve. "Rhetorical Criticism." *Themelios* 21 (1996) 4–9.

Watson, Duane F., and Alan J. Hauser. *Rhetorical Criticism of the Bible: A Comprehensive Bibliography with Notes on History and Method*. Biblical Interpretation Series 4. Leiden: Brill, 1994.

Watson, Wilfred G. E. *Classical Hebrew Poetry: A Guide to Its Techniques*. JSOTSup 26. Sheffield: JSOT Press, 1986.

Weaver, J. Denny. *The Nonviolent God*. Grand Rapids: Eerdmans, 2013.

Webb, Robert L. "The Petrine Epistles: Recent Developments and Trends," in *The Face of New Testament Studies: A Survey of Recent Research*, edited by Scot McKnight and Grant R. Osborne, 373–90. Grand Rapids: Baker Academic, 2004.

Weeks, Noel K. *Sources and Authors: Assumptions in the Study of Hebrew Bible Narrative*. Perspectives on Hebrew Scriptures and Its Contexts 12. Piscataway, NJ: Gorgias, 2011.

Welch, Laura ed. *Inside Noah's Ark: Why it Worked*. Green Forest, AR: Master, 2016.

Wendland, Ernst R. *The Discourse Analysis of Hebrew Prophetic Literature: Determining the Larger Textual Units of Hosea and Joel*. Mellen Biblical Press Series 40. Lewiston, NY: Mellen, 1995.

Wenham, Gordon J. *Exploring the Old Testament: A Guide to the Pentateuch*. Downers Grove, IL: InterVarsity, 2003.

———. *Genesis 1–15*. Word Biblical Commentary 1A. Waco, TX: Nelson, 1987.

———. "Genesis, Book of." In *Dictionary for Theological Interpretation of the Bible*, edited by Kevin J. Vanhoozer, 246–52. Grand Rapids: Baker Academic, 2005.

———. "Method in Pentateuchal Source Criticism." *VT* 41 (1991) 84–109.

———. "Pondering the Pentateuch: The Search for a New Paradigm." In *The Face of Old Testament Studies: A Survey of Contemporary Approaches*, edited by David W. Baker and Bill T. Arnold, 116–44. Grand Rapids: Baker Academic, 1999.

———. *Rethinking Genesis 1–11: Gateway to the Bible*. Didsbury Lectures 2013. Eugene, OR: Cascade Books, 2015.

———. Review of *Was Noah Good?* by Carol C. Kaminski. *Journal of Theological Studies* 67 (2016) 172–73.

———. *Story as Torah: Reading the Old Testament Ethically*. London Bloomsbury, 2004.

Westermann, Claus. *Genesis 1–11*. Translated by John J. Scullion. Continental Commentary. Minneapolis: Augsburg, 1984.

———. *Genesis: An Introduction*. Minneapolis: Augsburg, 1992.

Westfall, Cynthia, L. *A Discourse Analysis of the Letter to the Hebrews: The Relationship between Form and Meaning*. LNTS 297. London: T. & T. Clark, 2005.

———. "Narrative Criticism." In *Dictionary of Biblical Criticism and Interpretation*, edited by Stanley E. Porter, 237–39. New York: Routledge, 2009.

———. "The Relationship between the Resurrection, The Proclamation to the Spirits in Prison, and Baptismal Regeneration: 1 Peter 3:19–22." In *Resurrection*, edited by Stanley E. Porter et. al., 106–35. Sheffield: Sheffield Academic, 1999.

Wevers, William John. *Notes on the Greek Text of Genesis*. Society of Biblical Literature Septuagint and Cognate Studies Series 35. Atlanta: Scholars, 1993.

Whedbee, William J. *The Bible and the Comic Vision*. 1998. Reprint, Minneapolis: Fortress, 2002.

White-Westmoreland, Michael L., and Glen S. Stassen. "Biblical Perspectives on the Death Penalty." In *Religion and the Death Penalty: A Call for Reckoning*, edited by Erick C. Owens et al., 123–38. The Eerdmans Religion, Ethics, and Public Life Series. Grand Rapids: Eerdmans, 2004.

Wiesel, Elie. "Noah's Warning." *Religion & Literature* 16 (1984) 3–20.

Wilgus, Blair J., and M. Daniel Carroll R. *Wrestling with the Violence of God: Soundings in the Old Testament*. BBRSup 10. Winona Lake, IN: Eisenbrauns, 2015.

Williams, Ronald J. *Williams' Hebrew Syntax*. 3rd ed. Revised and Expanded by John C. Beckman. Toronto: University of Toronto Press, 2007.

Williamson, Paul R. "Covenant." In *Dictionary of the Old Testament: Pentateuch*, edited by Alexander, T. Desmond and David W. Baker, 139–55. Downers Grove, IL: InterVarsity, 2003.

———. *Sealed With an Oath: Covenant in God's Unfolding Purpose: New Studies in Biblical Theology*. Downers Grove, IL: IVP Academic, 2007.

Wilson, Andrew. "The Rainbow Connections." *Christianity Today* October (2018) 32.

Wilson, Mark. "Noah, the Ark, and the Flood in Early Christian Literature." *Scriptura* (2014) 1–12.

Wilson, Robert R. *Genealogy and History in the Biblical World*. Yale Near Eastern Researches 7. New Haven: Yale University Press, 1977.

Wilson, Stephen M. "Blood Vengeance and the *Imago Dei* in the Flood Narrative (Genesis 9:6)." *Interpretation* 71 (2017) 263–73.

Witherington, Ben, III. "'Almost thou persuadest me . . .': The Importance of Greco-Roman Rhetoric for the Understanding of the Text and Context of the NT." *JETS* 58 (2015) 63–88.

Witherington, Ben, III, and Jason A. Myers. "Response to Stanley Porter." *BBR* 26 (2016) 547–49.

Wirzba, Norman. *From Nature to Creation: A Christian Vision for Understanding and Loving Our World*. The Church and Postmodern Culture. Grand Rapids: Baker Academic, 2015.

Wolde, Ellen van. "'Creation Out of Nothing' and the Hebrew Bible. In *Creation Stories in Dialogue: The Bible, Science, and Folk Traditions*, edited by R. Alan Culpepper and Jan G. van der Watt, 157–76. Biblical Interpretation Series 139. Leiden: Brill, 2016.

———. *Words Become Worlds: Semantic Studies of Genesis 1–11*. Biblical Interpretation Series 6. Leiden: Brill, 1994.

Wolters, Albert M. *Creation Regained: Biblical Basics for a Reformational Worldview*. 2nd ed. Grand Rapids: Eerdmans, 2005.

Wood, Todd Charles, and Megan J. Murray. *Understanding the Pattern of Life: Origins and Organization of the Species*. Nashville: B. & H., 2003.

Woodmorappe, John. *Noah's Ark: A Feasibility Study*. Dallas: Institute for Creation Research, 1996.

Wright, Archie. T. *The Origin of Evil Spirits. The Reception of Genesis 6:1–4 in Early Jewish Literature*. Rev. ed. Minneapolis: Fortress, 2015.

Wright, J. W. "Genealogies." In *Dictionary of the Old Testament: Pentateuch*, edited by Alexander, T. Desmond and David W. Baker, 345–50. Downers Grove, IL: InterVarsity, 2003.

Wuellner, Wilhelm H. "Arrangement." In *The Rhetorical Analysis of Scripture: Essays from the 1995 London Conference*, edited by Stanley E. Porter and Thomas H. Olbricht, 51–87. JSNTSup 146. Sheffield: Sheffield Academic, 1997.

———. The Rhetorical Genre of Jesus' Sermon in Luke 12:1—13:9." In *Persuasive Artistry: Studies in New Testament Rhetoric in Honor of George A. Kennedy*, edited by Duane F. Watson, 93–118. JSNTSup 50 Sheffield: Sheffield Academic, 1991.

———. "Where Is Rhetorical Criticism Taking Us?" *CBQ* 49 (1987) 448–63.

Yamauchi, Edwin M. *Foes from the Northern Frontier: Invading Hordes from the Russian Steppes*. 1982. Reprint, Eugene, OR: Wipf & Stock, 2003.

Yoshikawa, Scott T. "The Prototypical Use of the Noahic Flood in the New Testament." PhD diss., Trinity Evangelical Divinity School, 2004.

Young, Davis A., and Ralph F. Stearley. *The Bible, Rocks and Time: Geological Evidence for the Age of the Earth*. Downers Grove, IL: IVP Academic, 2008.

Young, Marilyn J. "Lloyd F. Bitzer: Rhetorical Situation, Public Knowledge, and Audience Dynamics." In *Twentieth Century Roots of Rhetorical Criticism*, edited by Jim A. Kuypers and Andrew King, 275–301. Westport, CT: Praeger, 2001.

Youngblood, Ronald, ed. *The Genesis Debate: Persistent Questions about Creation and the Flood*. 1986. Reprint, Eugene, OR: Wipf & Stock, 1999.

Subject Index

Adam (*'adam*), xviii, 5, 6, 28, 93, 101, 137, 167
Akkadian (Sumerian), 16, 112, 147, 171
altar, 11, 181, 182, 196
ancient Near Eastern background (ANE), xvii, 2, 16, 17, 18, 25, 75, 77, 114, 140, 150, 153, 175, 183, 206, 207
anger (God), 3, 12, 17, 18, 84, 125, 182, 185, 196
anthropomorphism (God), 22
anthropopathism (God), 11, 12, 19, 20, 96, 97, 98, 99
ark, 84, 93, 110–24, 138–50
Atrahasis, 16, 112, 117
audience (*see also* rhetorical situation), 46–55
authorship and date (Genesis), 80–81

blessing, 3, 4, 5–6, 189, 196, 200, 208
blood (*see also lex talionis*), 6, 189, 196, 198, 200, 201
bow (rainbow), 165, 189, 196, 205–9

capital punishment, 196–97, 217
chaos (*Chaoskampf*), xviii, 11, 148, 154, 159, 166, 207, 208

chiasm, 12, 25, 41
cosmology, xvii, 68, 69, 147
constraints (*see also* rhetorical situation), 55–56
covenant, 4, 5, 6, 21, 24, 80, 93, 107, 121, 137, 140, 150, 165, 185, 189, 190, 196, 202, 203–10, 216
curse, 159, 181–83, 194, 210
creation care, 204, 217

Deuteronomist (D source, *see* Documentary Hypothesis—JEDP)
Documentary Hypothesis (JEDP), 21–25, 140

election, 3, 14, 99, 100, 103, 104
Elohist (E source, see documentary hypothesis—JEDP)
Enuma Elish, 147, 207
exigence (*see also* rhetorical situation alongside step(s) two and four within the table of contents), 45, 46, 47, 48, 49, 55, 57, 58, 79, 83, 93, 94, 95, 125, 126, 135, 136, 137, 155, 156, 157, 165, 166, 184, 185, 186, 189, 195, 196, 209

Subject Index

flood (universal/global), xxvii, 2, 23, 120, 136, 142, 157, 203, 216
flood (geology), 78, 79, 203

hyperbole, 9, 77, 78, 79, 115, 117, 118

justice (God), 12, 84, 199, 208

Kennedy style of rhetorical criticism, 36–83

image of God (*imago dei*), 99, 197, 201

lex talionis, xxviii, 4, 6, 200, 201, 210, 211, 212, 217
linguistics, 30, 42–43, 65
literary criticism, 8, 25–29

mercy (God), 13, 14, 15, 24, 128, 154, 155, 170, 183, 186, 196, 207, 208

narrative (story arc/plot), 26, 74, 84, 93, 94, 128, 137, 152, 159, 188
Noah's son (Shem, Ham, Japheth), 6, 28, 101, 102, 104, 105, 122, 141, 148, 194, 195
Noah's wife (Naamah), 90, 122, 141, 144, 148, 149, 185
narrator, 51, 52, 53, 54, 55, 73, 74

oath, 196, 203
obedience, 18, 95, 103, 137, 141, 143, 149, 180, 214

palistrophe (*see* chiasm)
Priestly (P source, see JEDP)

rhetoric (definition), 7, 31, 32, 65
rhetoric (as persuasion), 7, 8, 33–35, 212, 213, 214

rhetoric (as story, Hebrew Bible), 36, 65–70
rhetoric (worldview), 8, 10, 64–69, 81, 82, 214
rhetorical effectiveness (*see also* step four in the table of contents), 79–82
rhetorical situation (exigence, constraints, audience, see also step two in the table of contents), 43–55, 56–58, 58–62
rhetorical species (judicial, deliberative, demonstrative), 35, 62–65, 214
rhetorical strategy (see also step three in the table of contents), 70–79
rhetorical units (*see waw* and step one in the table of contents), 38–43

sacrifice, 13, 15, 16, 17, 18, 24, 142, 163, 165, 179, 180, 182, 183, 186, 189, 196
Sitz im Leben, 32, 44, 45

toledoth, 2, 27, 28, 100, 101, 104, 194

universalistic language, 77, 95, 99, 106, 121, 126, 157, 186, 210, 215
Utnapishtim, 16, 112, 113, 117

violence (*hamas*), xxvii, 3, 7, 23, 84, 93, 94, 106, 109, 125, 135, 155, 157, 185, 186, 189, 195, 196, 197, 200, 201, 203, 207, 209

waw (*see also* rhetorical units), 41–43
wrath (*see* anger)

Yahwist (J source, see documentary hypothesis—JEDP)

Ziusudra, 16, 147, 171

Author Index

Aaron, David H., 66, 105
Ahn, Suk-il, 8, 30, 32, 33, 34, 37, 38, 39, 40, 46, 47, 49, 50, 51, 52, 53, 54, 55, 62, 63, 66, 71, 72, 73, 75, 79, 80, 125
Alexander, Desmond T., 19, 21, 80, 101
Alexiou, Evangelos, 65
Alter, Robert, 75, 102
Anderson, Bernhard W., 27, 30, 59, 68, 80
ANET, 171
Aristotle, 50
Armstrong, James Franklin, 112, 113
Arnold, Bill T. (see also *GBHS*), 80, 103, 141, 142, 148, 153, 176, 197
Arnold, Carroll C., 48

Baden, Joel S., 21
Bailey, Lloyd R., 111, 114, 117
Baker, David W., 21
Baker L. S., Jr., 21
Bandstra, Barry, 139
Bar-Efrat, Shimeon, 40, 75
Barker, Joel, 7, 8, 30, 31, 32, 33, 34, 35, 36, 37, 38, 39, 42, 44, 45, 46, 47, 48, 49, 50, 56, 57, 58, 59, 60, 61, 62, 63, 64, 69, 70, 71, 79, 80, 81, 93, 95, 213, 214
Barker, John Robert, 7, 8
Barré, L. M., 147
Bartholomew, Craig G., 67
Bartoletti, Susan Campbell, 149
Barton, John, 8, 26, 82
Bassett, Frederick W, 194
Batto, Bernard F., 25, 196, 207
Bauks, Michaela, 2
BDB, 102, 111, 144, 174
Beal, T. K., 26
Bebbington, David W., xxiii
Beckerleg, Catherine Leigh, 86
Bediako, Daniel, 170
Beekman, John, 40
Bergsma, John Sietze, 194
Berlin, Adele, 32, 40, 76, 77
Best, Robert M., 16, 115
Beyer, Brian E., 125
BHRG, 15, 42, 78, 97, 98, 99, 102, 103, 105, 106, 107, 108, 110, 111, 123, 139, 143, 169, 199, 202
BHQ, 111, 119, 139, 144, 146, 169
Bitzer, Lloyd F., 44, 45, 46, 47, 55, 56, 60, 75, 95
Black, C. Clifton, 30, 37, 38, 62

Blenkinsopp, Joseph, 21, 114, 117, 135, 142, 149, 170
Block, Daniel I., 6, 20, 84, 103
Boadt, Lawrence, 22, 24, 82
Boda, Mark J., 2, 4, 6, 7, 12, 14, 20, 21, 26, 27, 28, 29, 75, 215, 216
Bodi, Daniel, 77
Boomershine, Thomas E., 74
Booth, Wayne C., 48, 51, 53, 54
Borgman, Paul, 20
Bouma-Prediger, Steven, 217
Bovard, Matthew, 38, 96
Boyd, Gregory A., 4, 14, 206
Boyd, Steven W., 147, 154
Brandt, William J., 71
Branson, Robert, 10
Brasnett, Bertrand, 12
Brinton, Alan, 58
Brodie, Thomas L., 27
Brown, William P., 19, 68
Brueggemann, Walter, 14, 97, 166, 167, 210
Buchanan, Paul, 73, 84
Burgers, Christian, 78
Burke, Kenneth, 46
Burlet, Dustin G., 1, 9, 10, 12, 46, 60, 64, 79, 114
Buth, R., 25

Callow, John, 39
Campbell, Antony F., 21, 22, 23, 24, 27
Carasik, Michael, 75
Carlson, Richard F., 69, 70
Carr, David M., 21
Carroll, M. Daniel R., 12
Carson, D. A., 69, 167
Cartledge, Tony W., 10
Casson, Lionel, 114, 115
Cassuto, U., 153
Chaffey, Tim, 120
Chatman, Seymour, 51, 52
Chen, Y. S., 1
Childs, Brevard S., 170
Chisholm, Robert B., Jr. (see also *Exegesis [to Exposition]*), 22, 25, 42, 67
Choi, John H. (see *GBHS*)
Christian, James L., 68

Clark, Warren. Malcolm, 2, 103
Clifford, Richard. J., 22, 208
Clines, David J. A. (see also *DCH*), 2, 3, 7, 11, 14, 27, 33, 53, 102
Cochran, Robert F. Jr., 210
Cohen, H. R., 112
Cohn, Norman, 1, 113
Cohn-Sherbok, Dan, 170
Collins, C. John, 3, 5, 9, 10, 23, 31, 62, 66, 67, 68, 69, 72, 73, 77, 81, 93, 96, 101, 137, 142, 147, 152, 165, 169, 194, 195
Combrink, Bernard H. J., 68
Consigny, Scott, 44, 57
Cooper, Alan, 176
Copan, Paul, 1, 68, 76, 80, 81
COS, 16
Cotter, David W., 55, 184
Cotterell, Peter, 42
Crawford, Cory D., 114, 117
Cruise, Charles E., 78

Dalton, Russell W., 15, 149, 156
Davids, Peter H., 2, 68
Davidson, Gregg, 1, 5, 29, 67, 147, 204, 217
Davidson, Jo Ann, 103
Dawson, Zachary K., 201
Day, John, 2, 112, 118
DBI, 72, 74, 75, 117, 142, 199
DCH, 3, 78, 97, 98, 99, 102, 105, 106, 107, 111, 112, 120, 140, 141, 143, 147, 177, 182, 206
Dearman, Andrew J., 25
Delitzsch Franz, 4, 207
Dershowitz, Idan, 94
De Vaux, Roland, 176
DG, 99, 100, 124, 141, 174
Dillard, Raymond B., 51, 74, 80
Dillow, Joseph C., 68
Donaldson, David C., 8, 30, 34
Dorsey, David, 39, 40, 86, 89, 163, 189, 191
Dozeman, Thomas B., 21, 22, 32, 80
Driver, Samuel Rolles, 22, 25, 112, 178
Dyer, Bryan R., 38
Duguid, Iain M., 75
Duke, Rodney K., 64, 71

Author Index

Dumbrell, William J., 25, 186, 201, 208
Dundes, Alan, 3, 8

Eagleton, Terry, 46, 65
Embry, Brad, 194
EncJud, 201
Enns, Peter, xxiii, 67, 68
Etshalom, Yitzchak, 175, 176
Evans, John F., 8, 22
Evans, Paul S., 7, 31, 32
Exegesis [to Exposition], 42, 96, 97, 98, 99, 105, 108, 110, 111, 119, 121, 122, 123, 139, 143, 144, 146, 149, 151, 152, 168, 169, 173, 174, 179, 181, 198, 199, 202, 205, 206, 208

Faulkner, Danny R., 68
Faro, Ingrid, 3, 64, 75, 108
Fee, Gordon D., 34, 38
Feinman, Peter Douglas, 2
Filby, Frederick A., 113
Finkel, Irving, 118
Fishbane, Michael, 71
Fisher, Eugene. J., 183
Fitzgerald, C., 31, 32, 40
Fokkelman, J. P., 40
Fox, Michael V., 29
France, R. T., 2
Fredricks, Cathi J., 32, 78, 84, 85, 86, 87, 88, 89, 93, 94, 101, 103, 104, 106, 113, 119, 124, 129, 130, 131, 132, 133, 136, 137, 142, 152, 160, 161, 163, 170, 175, 180, 183, 189, 191, 192, 193, 194, 199, 200, 206
Fretheim, Terence E., 3, 4, 12, 20, 26, 66, 69, 80, 81, 97, 189
Friedman, Richard Elliot, 140
Frymer-Kensky, Tikva S., 23
Fuller, David J., 42

Galambush, Julie, 22
Garret, Mary, 48
Garrett, Duane A. 21
GBHS, 42, 96, 97, 98, 105, 106, 108, 110, 111, 119, 121, 122, 139, 144, 146, 149, 151, 152, 168, 169, 173, 174, 178, 179, 181, 198, 199, 200, 202, 205, 206, 208
Genette, Gérard, 101
Gentry, Peter J., 2, 4, 5, 6, 18
George, Andrew, 16, 76, 150
Gertz, Jan Christian, 25
Gevaryahu, Gilad J., 177
Gilbert, Pierre, 100, 208
Gitay, Yehoshua, 50, 60
GKC, 96, 99, 109, 110, 119, 121, 139, 144, 145, 146, 148, 149, 151, 168, 169, 173, 174, 175, 176, 179, 181, 199, 200, 202, 206
Glover, Gordon J., 68
Gmirkin, Russell B., 21
Goldingay, John, 1, 4, 12, 15, 16, 18, 97, 99, 103, 108, 109, 113, 120, 142, 143, 145, 174, 175, 179
Goldstein, Bernard R., 176
Goheen, Michael W., 67
Gorman, Michael J., 12, 30, 40, 44, 74
Gorrell, Donna, 57
Gravett, Sandra L., 101
Greenberger, Chaya, 13, 94, 203, 209
Greenspahn, Frederick E., 64
Greenway, William, 4
Greenwood, Kyle, 67, 68
Greer, Jonathan S., 76
Griffin, John K., 9, 10, 79, 113, 118, 119, 203
Griffith, Tim, 113
Gunkel, Hermann, 22, 69
Gunn, David M., 25
Gupta, Nijay K., xxii

Habel, Norman C., 22, 107
Halley, Keaton, 9
Hallo, William W. (see also *COS*), 16
HALOT 3, 78, 97, 98, 99, 102, 106, 111, 112, 120, 140, 141, 147, 175, 177, 182, 206
Halpern, Baruch, 25
Halton, Charles, xxix, 28, 195
Hamilton, Victor P., 15, 16, 18, 22, 27, 28, 85, 86, 88, 89, 90, 97, 99, 102, 103, 107, 108, 109, 110, 112, 113, 129, 132, 133, 140, 142, 143, 145, 146, 149, 153, 154,

160, 161, 170, 171, 172, 174, 175, 176, 177, 178, 179, 180, 183, 184, 189, 191, 192, 194, 196, 199, 200, 201, 203, 204, 209, 215
Harland, P. J., 103, 199
Harper, Elizabeth, 8, 42, 140, 141
Harrison, R. K., 27
Hartley, John E., 17, 18, 142, 182
Hasel, Gerald F., 147, 154
Hatch, Nathan O., xxiii
Hauser, Alan J., 32, 36, 70
Hawk, L. Daniel, 18, 26
Hawking, Stephen, xix
Hays, Christopher B., 16
Heidel, Alexander, 147
Heller, Roy L., 39, 43
Hendel, Ronald S., 3, 80, 114, 117
Heras, Henry, 175
Herrick, James, 31
Hess, Richard S., 80, 101
Hester, James D., 39, 49, 63, 70
Hiebert, Theodore, 2
Hilber, John W., 16, 68
Hill, Andrew E., 68, 101
Hill, Carol A., 66, 68, 142, 147, 153
Hiltz, Patrick L., 9
Hodge, B. C., 75, 142, 167, 180, 203
Hoffmeier, James K., 17
Holloway, Steven W., 114, 117
Hordes, Ami, 122
Horowitz, Wayne, 68, 105
House, Paul R., 68
Howard, David M., 34, 69, 70
Huey, F. B. Jr., 2
Humphreys, W. Lee, 4, 16, 19, 20, 55, 94, 106
Hunsaker, David M., 50
Huw, Thomas, 73
Hwang, Jerry, 31, 33, 34, 38, 214

IBHS, 42, 43, 100, 103, 106, 108, 109, 119, 122, 139, 145, 151, 168, 169, 174, 182, 199
Iser, W., 51

Jacob, Douglas, 1, 68, 76, 80, 81
Jacobsen, T., 12

Jacobus, Helen R., 175
Janssen, Luke Jeffrey, 1
JM (see *Joüon*)
Johnson, Marshall, 28
Jones, Barry A., 61
Joosten, Jan, 80
Joüon, Paul, 42, 109, 119, 122, 139, 141, 144, 146, 148, 151, 168, 169, 173, 174, 182, 202, 206
Jungels, Cameron, 61

Kaminski, Carol M., 2, 3, 4, 13, 21, 22, 25, 26, 27, 103
Kaminsky, Joel S., 104
Kawashima, Robert S., 22, 23, 24, 26, 80
Keegan, Terence J., 52
Keel, Othmar, 68, 76
Keil, C. F., 4
Keiser, Thomas A., 2, 3, 4, 29, 103, 129, 130, 132, 133, 152, 194, 196
Keiter, Sheila Turner, 94, 175
Kelle, Brad E., 61
Kempf, S. W., 86
Kennedy, George A., 8, 34, 37, 38, 44, 47, 49, 58, 62, 63, 72, 79, 213
Kidner, Derek, 1, 15, 97, 103, 160, 163, 177, 178, 183, 189, 191, 192, 194
Kikawada, Isaac M., 22, 111
Kissileff, Beth, 12
Kitchen, K. A., 66
Kline, Meredith G., 196
Kloppenborg, John S., 22
Knafl, Anne K., 94, 105
Knight, G. M., 61
Konkel, August H., 3, 4
Korpel, Marjo C. A., 40
Köstenberger, Andreas J., xxiv
Kotter, John P., 48
Kruger, Mike, 78
Kvanig, Helge S., 2

LaHaye, Tim, 122
Lamb, David T., 12
Lambert, W. G., xvii, 16
Lambdin, Thomas O. (*Introduction to Biblical Hebrew*), 42, 106, 108, 119, 174
Lamoureux, Dennis O., 16, 67, 68

Lapointe, Roger, 108
Larsson, Gerhard, 176
Lee, Jae Hyun, 42
Lee, John A., 174
Lenchak, T. A., 71
Levin, Yigal, 101
Lewis, C. S., 72
Licht, Jacob, 152
Linville, J., 59
Linzey, Andrew, 170
Lisle, Jason, 120
Long, Philips V., 73, 74, 76, 102
Longacre, Robert E., 40, 84, 140
Longman, Tremper, III, xxiv, 3, 9, 17,
    19, 26, 51, 65, 66, 69, 70, 73, 74,
    76, 77, 80, 84, 86, 100, 101, 103,
    111, 112, 113, 114, 117, 118,
    180, 183, 196, 206, 217
Lovett, Ken, 9
Lovett, Tim, 113
Lowery, Daniel D., 33, 70
Lundbom, Jack R., 30, 31, 71
Lyon, Ashley E., 40
Lyon, Jeremy D., 152, 171

Mack, Burton L., 36, 65, 66
Maier, Walter A., III, 19
Mann, Thomas W., 20, 22, 97
Marcus, David, 175
Markos, Louis, 10
Marrs, Rick, 2
Martin, Ernest L., 172
Mason, Steven D., 6, 206, 208, 210
Mathews, Kenneth A., 17, 21, 84, 85, 86,
    87, 88, 89, 92, 99, 101, 102, 103,
    104, 105, 106, 109, 112, 113,
    114, 120, 122, 129, 130, 133,
    135, 141, 142, 144, 145, 152,
    153, 154, 160, 161, 163, 165,
    169, 170, 171, 177, 178, 180,
    182, 183, 189, 190, 192, 193,
    194, 195, 200, 203, 206, 207, 209
Matz, Robert J., 20
Mbuvi, Amanda Beckenstein, 204
McCann, Jason Michael, 112
McCarthy, D. J., 106, 108, 119
McComiskey, 107
McDougall, Catherine M., 86

McDougall, Colin S., 95
McKeown, James, 85, 87, 88, 89, 93, 103,
    111, 123, 129, 133, 136, 137,
    141, 142, 156, 160, 185, 186,
    189, 191, 192, 194
McLean, G. S., xxii
Meek, T. J., 174
Meier, Samuel A., 86, 89, 163, 189, 191
Meiring, Jacob, 105
Mettinger, Tyggve N. D., 11
Middleton, J. Richard, 27, 67, 197, 200
Miglio, Adam E., 16
Millard, A. R., 16
Miller, Arthur B., 46, 50
Miller, Cynthia L., 74, 75, 85, 89, 163,
    189, 191
Miller, Johnny V., 28, 68
Miller, Natali, 113
Miller, Stephen M., 147
Mitchell, Eric, 68
Mitchell, Margaret M., 38
Moberly, R. W. L., 175, 203, 208
Möller, Karl, 32, 33, 34, 36, 38, 44, 45,
    46, 59, 62, 63, 71, 72, 79, 125
Moo, Douglas J., 217
Moo, Jonathan A., 217
Moore, Michael, 10
Moore, Robert A., 114, 115
Morris, John D., 111, 122
Mortenson, Terry, 67, 68
Muilenburg, James, 30, 31, 32, 40, 44
Muraoka, Takamitsu (see also Joüon,
    Paul), 119
Murray, Megan J., 142
Myers, Jason A., 38

Naudé, Jacobus A., 78
Nelles, William, 50, 51
Neufeld, Waldie, 95
Niehaus, Jeffrey J., 206
NIDDOTE 3, 5, 42, 78, 97, 98, 99, 102,
    105, 106, 107, 111, 112, 120,
    140, 141, 143, 147, 172, 175,
    177, 182, 206
Noll, Mark A., xxiii
Noonan, Benjamin J., 10, 42
Noort, Ed., 11, 175

Oates, G. W., 13
O'Brien, Mark A., 21, 22, 23, 24, 27
O'Connor, Katheleen, 20
O'Connor, Michael Patrick (see *IBHS*)
Oesch, Joseph M., 40
Olbricht, Thomas H., 64, 71
Olbrechts-Tyteca, L., 33, 36, 46, 48, 49, 50, 63, 66, 70
Okoye, James Chukwuma, 3, 17, 68, 96, 106, 121, 123, 150, 153, 165, 170
Osborne, Grant R., 33, 42
Oswalt, John N., 5, 16, 125, 183

Pao, David W., 2
Patai, Raphael, 111, 113, 114, 115, 116, 118
Patrick, Dale, 65
Patterson, Todd L., 25
Patty, Tyler J., 42, 43, 183
Perelman, C., 33, 46, 48, 49, 63, 65, 70
Peters, Dorothy M., 13
Peterson, Brian Neil, 17, 29, 125, 204
Peterson, Eugene, 68
Phelan, James, 51, 74
Pickering, Wilbur N., 40
Pinkney, Jerry, 15
Porter, Stanley E., xxv, 31, 34, 38, 40, 67
Powell, Angie, 178
Powell, Mark Allan, 50
Powell, Mark, 178
Prescott, Deborah Lee, 18
Presutta, David, 68
Provan, Iain, 9, 16, 76, 80, 81
Purcell, Richard Anthony, 61

Quine, Cat, 64
Quinn, Arthur, 22

Ramm, Bernard, 113, 153
Rawson, K. J., 115
Ray, Kellogg Janet, xii
Reed, Jeffrey T., 42
Rendtorff, Rolf, 2
Reno, R. R., 26
Renz, Thomas, 63
Richter, Sandra L., 6
Rimmon–Kenan, Shlomith, 52
Roaf, Michael, 153

Robertson, O. Palmer, 19
Robinson, J. C., 66
Rogers, Lynden J., 10, 79
Ron, Zvi, 104, 105
Rooker, Mark F., 26
Ross, Hugh, 68, 111, 113
Routledge, Robin, 68
Ryken, Leland (see too *DBI*), 66, 73, 74, 78, 84, 102, 106, 109

Sailhamer, John, 51, 52, 80, 81, 85, 87, 89, 103, 129, 133, 136, 137, 149, 153, 160, 161, 163, 170, 172, 180, 189, 191, 192, 194, 195
Sandy, D. B., 48
Sarfati, Jonathan, 111
Sargent, Andrew Dean, 150, 152, 155, 170, 171
Sarna, Nahum M., 17, 68, 104, 109, 111, 113, 115, 120, 123, 142, 147, 154, 170, 171, 172, 174, 177, 180, 184, 196
Sasson, Jack M., 103
Schmid, Wolf, 55
Schmidt, Peter, 78
Schnabel, Eckhard J., 2
Schneider, Tammi J., 8
Schnittjer, Gary Edward, 8, 75, 217
Schreiner, Thomas R., 6, 102, 106, 203, 207, 209
Schroer, Silvia, 68, 76
Scott, Eugenie C., 68
Scult, Allen, 50, 65, 70
Scult, Michael Allen, 8
Seely, Paul H., 101
Sexton Jeremy, 101
Shaviv, Shemuel, 4, 16, 140
Shaw, Charles S., 59, 96
Shemesh, Abraham Ofir, 152
Shen, Dan, 52
Siegert, Folker, 62
Sigler, Charles, 118
Silverman, Jason S., 78
Simkins, Ronald A., 16, 67, 70, 204
Sire, James W., 67
Ska, Jean-Louise, 2
Skinner, John, 22, 109, 141
Sleeth, Matthew J., 217

Author Index

Smith, A. R., 142, 175
Smith, Craig R., 50
Smith, Douglas K., 78
Smith, Gary V., 125
Smith, Mark S., 23
Snelling, Andrew A., 79, 147, 154
Soden, John M., 28, 67, 68
Sollereder, Bethany N., 13, 183
Sonnet, J. P., 34
Soulen, Kendall R., 30
Soulen, Richard N., 30
Sparks, Kenton L., xxiii, 8
Speiser, E. A., xviii, 22, 94, 109, 206
Spero, Shubert, 2
Stallings, Joseph W., 1, 10, 79, 118, 120, 153, 203
Stamps, Dennis L., 31, 34, 38, 56, 59, 61, 65
Stanhope, Ben, 68
Stassen, Glen S., 196
Stearley, Ralph F., 67
Stefanescu, Maria, 52
Stein, Stephen K., 114
Steinberg, Naomi A., 2, 104, 141
Steiner, Richard C., 75
Steinmann, Andrew, 16, 22, 101, 140, 154
Steinmetz, Devora, 195
Sternberg, Meir, 2, 32, 75, 124
Stewart, Alexander Coe, 7, 63, 65, 96, 204
Streett, Daniel R., 25
Stuart, Douglas, 25
Stuckenbruck, Loren T., 3
Swart, I., 109

TDOT, 3, 78, 93, 97, 99, 120, 206
Teeple, Howard M., 111
Thurén, Lauri, 31, 45, 60, 65
Thomas, Matthew A., 28, 74, 101, 102
Thornhill, A. Chadwick, 20
Throntveit, Mark A., 64
TLOT, 3, 78, 102, 106
Trible, Phyllis, 7, 30, 31, 32, 33, 34, 71
Tov, Emmanuel, 40
Tupper, E. C., 115
Trudinger, Peter, 107

Turner, Kenneth J., 1, 5, 17, 29, 67, 147, 204, 217
Turner, L. A., 27, 153
Turner, Max, 42
Tsumara, David Toshio, 16, 147
Tverbg, Lois, 12
TWOT, 78, 140, 172, 182

Unger, Richard W., 115

Van Drunen, David, 210
Van Seters, John, 21, 23
Van Wolde, Ellen, 147, 183
VanGemeren, Willem A. (see also *NIDOTTE*), 3, 184
Vanhoozer, Kevin J., xxiii, 20, 66
VanOsdel, Jessica Lee, 44
Van Pelt, Miles V., 42, 43, 75, 160
Vatz, Richard E., 56
Vermeulen, Karolien, 210
Vogt, Peter T., 66, 74, 75
Von Rad, Gerhard., 2, 7, 22, 25, 120, 182

Wachsmann, Shelley, 175
Walker, Jeffrey, 31
Walsh, Brian J., 67
Walsh, Jerome T., 7, 37, 51, 52, 53, 54
Waltke, Bruce K. (see also *IBHS*), 3, 4, 7, 14, 18, 19, 25, 28, 29, 32, 73, 84, 86, 87, 88, 89, 93, 94, 101, 103, 104, 106, 113, 119, 124, 129, 130, 131, 132, 133, 136, 137, 142, 152, 160, 161, 163, 165, 170, 175, 180, 183, 189, 191, 192, 193, 194, 199, 200, 206
Walton, John H., xviv, 2, 3, 4, 16, 17, 20, 21, 26, 28, 66, 67, 68, 76, 77, 101, 104, 111, 112, 113, 114, 117, 118, 120, 142, 154, 169, 172, 182, 184, 206, 208
Walton, Steve, 38, 63
Watson, Duane F., 32, 36, 70
Watson, Wilfred G. E., 12, 77, 78, 99, 121, 184
Weaver, Denny J., 19
Webb, Robert L., 72
Weeks, Noel K., 26
Welch, Laura, 113, 115

Wellum, Stephen J., 2, 4, 5, 6, 18
Wendland, Ernst R., 39
Wenham, Gordon J., 7, 12, 17, 21, 66, 80, 84, 85, 86, 87, 89, 92, 103, 104, 106, 108, 109, 110, 112, 113, 114, 117, 120, 121, 122, 129, 133, 139, 140, 143, 145, 147, 149, 150, 151, 152, 153, 154, 160, 161, 163, 169, 171, 172, 174, 175, 177, 178, 179, 182, 189, 190, 192, 195, 198, 199, 200, 202, 205
Westfall, Cynthia, L., 42, 53, 65
Westermann, Claus, 22, 23, 24
Wevers, William John, 13, 108, 139, 144, 152, 170
Whedbee, William J., 17
White-Westmoreland, Michael L., 196
Wiesel, Elie, 12, 18
Wilgus, Blair J., 12
Williams, Ronald J. (*Hebrew Syntax*), 97, 98, 102, 105, 108, 110, 111, 119, 121, 122, 139, 144, 146, 149, 151, 152, 168, 169, 174, 178, 179, 181, 182, 198, 199, 202, 203, 205, 206, 208
Williamson, Paul R., 5, 203
Wilson, Andrew, 206, 207
Wilson, Mark, 204
Wilson, Robert R, 104, 122, 200, 201
Wilson, Stephen M., 199
Wirzba, Norman, 217
Witherington, Ben, III, 38
Wolters, Albert M., 67
Wood, Todd Charles, 142
Woodmorappe, John, 113
Wright, Archie. T., 2
Wright, J. W., 101
Wuellner, Wilhelm H., 32, 34, 39, 45, 60, 65, 71, 72

Xiao, Xiaosui, 48, 50

Yamauchi, Edwin M., 171
Yoshikawa, Scott T., 2, 183
Young, Davis A., 67
Young, Marilyn J., 57, 58
Youngblood, Ronald, 165
Yu, Charles, 3, 4, 7, 14, 18, 19, 28, 29

Ancient Document Index

ANCIENT NEAR EASTERN DOCUMENTS

Atrahasis
3.2.51 — 112

Gilgamesh
11.44, [65], 66 — 112

OLD TESTAMENT/ HEBREW BIBLE

Genesis
1—11	xxviii, 2, 14, 17, 183
1:1—11:26	2
1—9	2
1:1—2:3	28, 153
1	123, 170
1:2	180, 207
1:6–7	148, 153
1:11–12	177
1:20–22	145
1:21	179
1:24–30	145
1:26–31	3
1:28	198, 200
1:29	141, 201
1:30	177
1:31	xxvii, 3
2	120
2:4—4:26	28, 101
2:7	97, 99, 153
2:19	97
3	6
3:16	xviii
3:17	xviii
3:19	99
4:1–7	165
4:3–5	182
4:24	xviii
5:1—6:8	28, 101
5:1–3	6
5:2	167, 200
5:22	103
5:24	103
5:29	xviii
5:32	122
6	5
6:1–4	2
6:3	94
6:5—9:17	xxviii, 215, 216

Ancient Document Index

Genesis (*cont.*)

6:5–22	94, 215, 216
6:5–12	85
6:5–10	86
6:5–8	22, 84, 86, 94, 96, 125, 126, 127, 128, 159
6:5–7	xxviii, 3, 11, 12, 15, 17, 18, 21, 95, 100, 109, 124, 127, 188, 200
6:5–6	xxvii, 3, 7, 85, 86, 94, 96, 126
6:5	xviii, 12, 21, 23, 24, 85, 93, 97, 126, 215
6:5a	85
6:5b	13, 85
6:6–7	23
6:6	85, 95, 101, 183, 215
6:6a	12
6:6b	12
6:7	xxvii, 3, 85, 86, 92, 94, 96, 98, 99, 108, 126, 140, 153, 166, 183, 215
6:7a	12, 86
6:7b	12, 86
6:7c	86
6:8–9	95
6:8	xxvii, 3, 12, 23, 85, 86, 95, 96, 99, 100, 120, 124, 126, 127, 183, 216
6:9—9:29	2, 27, 28, 87, 100, 101
6:9–22	22, 84, 87, 88, 90, 92, 94, 96, 100, 125, 126, 127, 128, 135, 159
6:9–21	188
6:9–10	86, 88, 124, 127
6:9	2, 23, 86, 87, 103, 124, 165, 167, 170, 195, 216
6:9a	86, 87, 96, 100, 104, 126
6:9b–12	87
6:9b–10	64, 87, 96, 102, 126
6:9b–21	87
6:9b–c	87
6:9b	87, 88
6:9c	88
6:10	87, 88, 104, 216
6:10a	88
6:10b	88
6:11–13	xxvii, 3, 7, 23, 88, 109, 124, 127, 200, 207
6:11–12	88, 96, 105, 126
6:11	88, 93, 101, 106, 109, 127, 215
6:11a	88
6:11b	88
6:12	xxvii, 2, 88, 106, 126, 127, 215
6:12a	88
6:12b	89
6:12c	89
6:13–21	64, 89, 90, 92, 94, 96, 108, 119, 126, 129, 140, 141, 143, 163, 179
6:13	86, 88, 89, 90, 92, 93, 107, 108, 109, 126, 127, 135, 140, 159, 166, 203, 215
6:13a	90
6:13b–d	90
6:13b	90, 109
6:13c	90
6:13d	90
6:14–22	184
6:14–21	169
6:14–16	89, 90, 110, 111, 119, 120, 123, 124, 127, 159
6:14	95, 120, 123, 166, 216
6:14a	90
6:14b–16d	90
6:14b	90
6:14c	90
6:15	90, 123, 216
6:15a	90

6:15b–d	90	7:1–24	92, 128, 129, 131, 132, 133, 135, 154, 155, 156, 158, 215, 216
6:16	112, 123, 177, 216		
6:16a	91		
6:16b	91		
6:16c	91	7:1–5	22, 166, 184
6:16d	91	7:1–4	64, 89, 92, 94, 108, 129, 136, 138, 140, 141, 143, 155, 156, 163, 169, 172
6:17	xxvii, 3, 89, 91, 92, 107, 119, 120, 124, 126, 127, 135, 153, 159, 166, 215		
		7:1–3	xxvii, 3, 92, 128, 129, 136, 158
6:17a–b	91		
6:17a	91	7:1–2	129
6:17b	91	7:1	64, 86, 93, 104, 129, 131, 140, 141, 145, 155, 157, 167, 170, 216
6:17c	91		
6:18–22	64		
6:18–21	xxvii, 3, 90, 91, 121, 127, 128, 159, 166		
		7:1a	129, 140
		7:1b–3	129
6:18–20	91, 140	7:1b–c	129
6:18	4, 5, 93, 95, 104, 122, 123, 124, 141, 149, 159, 165, 170, 185, 189, 196, 216	7:1b	129, 130
		7:1c	130
		7:2–4	129
		7:2–3	130, 141
		7:2	157, 216
6:18a	91	7:2a	130
6:18b	91	7:2b	130
6:18c	91	7:3	145, 157, 216
6:19–21	123, 124	7:3a	130
6:19–20	91, 123, 142	7:3b	130
6:19	107, 123, 127, 215, 216	7:4	xxvii, 3, 92, 130, 132, 136, 145, 154, 155, 157, 158, 166, 215
6:19a	91		
6:19b	91		
6:19c	91		
6:19d	91	7:4a	130, 155
6:19e	91	7:4b	130
6:19f	91	7:4c	130
6:20	127, 215, 216	7:5–16	129
6:21	90, 91, 120, 123, 127, 215, 216	7:5–10	129
		7:5	64, 89, 92, 124, 129, 130, 136, 137, 138, 143, 145, 156, 157, 163, 165, 170, 179, 185, 216
6:21a	91		
6:21b	91		
6:21c	91		
6:22—7:16	188		
6:22	89, 92, 94, 95, 96, 123, 124, 126, 127, 129, 137, 143, 159, 163, 165, 170, 179, 185, 216	7:6	22, 92, 122, 129, 130, 131, 136, 146, 155, 158, 215
		7:6–10	130

Ancient Document Index

Genesis (*cont.*)

7:6–9	130, 131, 132, 138, 144, 145, 155, 156
7:7–10	22
7:7–9	xxvii, 3, 64, 92, 128, 130, 131, 136, 137, 145, 149, 158, 166, 169, 184
7:7–8	145
7:7	92, 104, 122, 130, 131, 141, 149, 158, 165, 185, 215, 216
7:7a	131
7:7b	131
7:8–9	130, 131
7:8–9b	131
7:8	131, 157, 215, 216
7:9	130, 145, 185, 216
7:9b	131
7:10–12	64, 130, 131, 138, 146, 154, 155, 156
7:10	92, 129, 130, 131, 132, 136, 158, 166, 215
7:10a	132
7:10b	132
7:11–16	131
7:11–12	131
7:11	22, 92, 97, 130, 131, 132, 136, 146, 148, 154, 157, 158, 166, 176, 207, 215
7:11a	132
7:11b	132
7:12	22, 92, 130, 132, 136, 154, 158, 215
7:12a	132
7:12b	132
7:13–16	xxvii, 3, 92, 128, 130, 131, 132, 133, 136, 138, 148, 155, 156, 158, 166, 169, 184, 185
7:13–16a	22
7:13–14	137
7:13	92, 104, 122, 130, 131, 132, 141, 149, 165, 185, 216
7:13a	133
7:13b	133
7:14	132, 157, 216
7:14–16a	133
7:14–16b	133
7:15–16	107, 137
7:15	132, 142, 157, 158, 165, 185, 216
7:16	128, 154, 155, 156, 158, 159, 185, 216
7:16b	22, 133
7:16c	133
7:17–24	64, 92, 128, 133, 134, 136, 138, 150, 152, 154, 155, 156, 157, 158, 159, 160, 161, 164, 166, 188
7:17–22	132
7:17–20	133
7:17	136, 152, 215
7:17a	22, 134
7:17b	22
7:17b–c	134
7:17–18	134
7:18–21	22
7:18–20	136
7:18	92, 133, 136, 152, 215
7:18a–b	134
7:18c	134
7:19–20	135
7:19	133, 152, 157, 215
7:19a	135
7:19b–20	135
7:20	133, 152, 215
7:21–23	xxvii, 3, 133, 135, 136
7:21–23e	135
7:21	107, 153, 157, 215
7:21a	134
7:21b–d	134
7:22–23	22
7:22	153, 157, 215
7:22a–b	134
7:23	64, 92, 128, 133, 136, 140, 153, 155, 156, 157, 158, 159, 161, 165, 166, 169, 185, 196, 215, 216

Ancient Document Index

7:23a–b	134	8:6–14	160, 161, 162, 167, 172, 186
7:23b	137	8:6–13	162, 165
7:23c–d	134	8:6–12	22, 64
7:23e	134	8:6–9	187
7:23f–g	135	8:6–7	162
7:24	22, 132, 133, 135, 136, 152, 159, 161, 215	8:6	111, 160, 162, 175, 215
7:24a	135	8:6a	162
7:24b	135	8:6b	162
8:1–22	135, 154, 159, 160, 161, 162, 163, 164, 184, 186, 187, 215, 216	8:7–8	175
		8:7	162, 173, 174, 215
		8:8–12	162
		8:8–11	179
8:1–14	160	8:8–9	162
8:1–5	160, 161, 167, 186, 187	8:8	162, 174, 215
		8:9–12	162
8:1–4	159	8:9	187, 215
8:1–3	161	8:9a	162
8:1–2a	22	8:9b	162
8:1	135, 159, 160, 161, 164, 166, 167, 169, 170, 187, 196, 216	8:9c	162
		8:10–22	187
		8:10–11	162
8:1a	160, 161, 188	8:10	162, 216
8:1b–3	188, 196	8:10a	162
8:1b	161	8:10b	162
8:1c	161	8:11	216
8:1d	161	8:11a	162
8:2–5	164	8:11b	162
8:2	166, 216	8:12	163, 216
8:2a	161	8:12a	163
8:2b–3a	22	8:12b	163
8:2b	161	8:13–17	189
8:2c	161	8:13–14	184, 195
8:3–5	171	8:13	64, 162, 165, 177, 216
8:3–4	154		
8:3	160, 161, 166, 216	8:13a	22
8:3b–5	22	8:13b	22
8:4–12	188	8:14–19	22
8:4a–5a	161	8:14	146, 162, 165, 176, 177, 216
8:4	154, 160, 161, 162, 171, 172, 192, 196, 216	8:15–19	163, 167, 178, 185, 186
		8:15–17	94, 108, 179
8:5	160, 161, 165, 166, 172, 216	8:15	86, 162, 163, 185, 216
8:5a	160	8:16–22	xxvii, 3, 163
8:5b	160	8:16–19	166

Genesis (*cont.*)

8:16-17	163
8:16	104, 122, 141, 149, 163, 180, 216
8:17	107, 163, 178, 180, 187, 200, 216
8:18-20	163
8:18-19	163, 179, 189
8:18	104, 122, 141, 149, 165, 180, 216
8:19	165, 180, 187, 216
8:20—9:17	123, 163
8:20-22	xxviii, 11, 13, 15, 17, 18, 22, 24, 155, 163, 164, 167, 180, 186
8:20	18, 164, 182, 187, 189, 216
8:21-22	3, 18, 64, 93, 108, 159, 163, 164, 166, 167, 184, 185, 186, 189, 192, 196
8:21	xviii, 3, 17, 19, 21, 22, 86, 163, 165, 166, 187, 200, 215, 216
8:21 (LXX)	13
8:21a	182, 183
8:21b-22	24
8:21b	13, 15, 183
8:22	24, 164, 183, 187, 216
9	5
9:1-17	xxvii, 3, 22, 24, 78, 155, 163, 188, 190, 191, 192, 194, 197, 210, 211, 215, 216
9:1-7	64, 93, 94, 108, 163, 166, 179, 189, 190, 196, 197, 216
9:1-6	209
9:1	86, 164, 190, 191, 198, 200, 211, 216
9:1a	190
9:1b	190
9:1c	190
9:2	64, 190, 210, 211, 215
9:2a-d	190
9:2e	190
9:3-4	190, 211
9:3	190, 210, 211, 215
9:4-6	6, 64
9:4	141, 190, 215
9:5-6	190, 196, 203, 211
9:5	190, 199, 204, 210, 211, 215
9:5a-b	190
9:5c-9:6	190
9:6	24, 190, 196, 215
9:6b	197
9:7-17	211
9:7	190, 196, 216
9:8-17	192, 210
9:8-16	193
9:8-11	94, 108, 189, 190, 191, 192, 197, 201
9:8-9	210
9:8	86, 104, 191, 216
9:8a	191
9:8b	191
9:9-17	170, 196
9:9-11	64, 189, 191
9:9-10	204
9:9	4, 5, 191, 216
9:9a	191
9:9b	191
9:10-11	191
9:10	191, 211, 216
9:10a	191
9:10b-c	191
9:10d	192
9:10e	192
9:11-16	3
9:11	4, 5, 107, 191, 192, 195, 203, 209, 211, 216
9:11a	192
9:11b-c	192
9:12-17	94, 209
9:12-16	64, 108, 189, 191, 192, 195, 197, 205
9:12	4, 5, 86, 192, 210, 211, 216
9:12a	192
9:12b-e	192

9:12b	192	10:32	28, 195
9:12c	193	11	6
9:12d	193	11:1–9	20
9:12e	193	11:10—26	28, 101
9:13–15	193	11:20–26	2
9:13	193, 196, 207, 216	11:27—50:26	2
9:13a	193	11:27—25:11	28
9:13b	193	15:18	5
9:14–15	165, 193	17:1	103
9:14	193, 207, 216	17:7	5
9:15–17	107	17:9	5
9:15	193, 195, 203, 209, 210, 211, 216	17:11	206
		17:21	5
9:16	4, 21, 193, 207, 210, 211, 216	18—19	104
		18:16–33	94
9:16a–b	193	18:17	86
9:16c–e	193	24:40	103
9:17	4, 5, 86, 108, 189, 192, 193, 194, 195, 197, 208, 210, 211, 216	25:8	120
		25:12—18	28
		25:17	120
		25:19—35:29	28
9:17a	194	25:20	142
9:17b–c	194	26:34	142
9:18–29	194	35:39	120
9:18–27	104	36:1—37:1	28
9:18–20	194	36:9	28
9:18–19	6, 194	36:21	81
9:18	104, 189, 195	37:2—50:26	28
9:19	189, 216	48:15	103
9:20–27	21		
9:20–21	194	**Exodus**	
9:22–23	194	6:16	2
9:22	195	6:19	2
9:23	194	20:8	165
9:25–27	108	20:24–26	182
9:25	195	21:12–36	7
9:26	105	24:18	142
9:27	105	26:14	177
9:28	195	28:10	2
9:29	2, 153, 194, 195, 216	29:18	183
		31:12–14	199
10:1—11:9	28, 101	31:16–17	206
10	6	34:6–7	20, 201
10:1–31	104	35:11	177
10:1–32	6	36:19	177
10:1	87, 104, 194, 195		
10:21–31	105		

Leviticus

1	182
1:9	183
2:13	110
14:34	81
17:10–14	201
25:11	146
26:31	183
26:27–44	80

Numbers

1:20–42	2
3:15	177
13:25	142
15:3	183
20:29	120
3:1	2, 28
34:2	81
35:16–32	199

Deuteronomy

1:2	80
1:7	80
2:10–12	81
2:20–23	81
2:34	81
3:4–7	81
3:9	81
3:11	81
3:13–14	81
3:16–17	81
4:9	81
4:20	81
4:23	81
4:25–31	80
4:44–49	81
8:18	165
8:19–20	80
11:6	140
11:30	81
17:6–7	199
18:9	81
19:1	81
19:15	199
26:1	81
27:2	81
27:5–6	182
28:36–37	80
28:45–68	80
29:20–28	80
30:1–20	80
30:1	81
31:1–9	81
31:6–8	81
34:3	81
34:10–12	81

Joshua

2:12–13	104
20:1–6	7

Ruth

4:18	2

1 Samuel

17:16	142
26:19	15

1 Kings

8:46–53	80
9:6–9	80
19:8	142

2 Kings

21:8–15	80

1 Chronicles

1:4	104
1:29	2
5:7	2
7:2	2
7:4	2
7:9	2
8:28	2
9:9	2
9:34	2
26:31	2

Job

31:7	

Psalms

1:1	107
1:6	107
8:1–9	11
16:16	ix
19:1–6	11
29:10	x, 166, 216
30:5	20
32:8	107
89	216
103:18	165
139:1–18	11
143:8	107
146:9	107

Proverbs

4:19	107
14:2	107
15:9	107
16:25	107

Song of Songs

8:7	4

Isaiah

24	216
30:21	107
40:22	166
48:17	107
54—55	216
54:7–10	185
54:9	11, 125

Jeremiah

12:1	107
29:7	210
30—31	216
42:3	107

Ezekiel

4:6	142
14:14	103, 141
14:20	103, 141
16:47	2
18:20	154
18:23	20
33:11	20

Amos

5:21	183

Jonah

3:4	142
4:11	123, 170

Micah

6:8	103

Nahum

1:8	216

Zephaniah

1—2	216

Malachi

2:6	103
2:8	107

NEW TESTAMENT

Matthew

4:2	142
24:36–44	xxviii, 2

Luke

1:72	165
17:26–27	xxviii, 2

Acts

1:3	142
15:20	201
15:29	201
21:25	201

Romans

5:21–21	167
6:23	154

1 Corinthians

15:20–27	167
15:44–49	167

Colossians

1:20	15

1 Timothy

2:4	20

Hebrews

11:7	xxviii, 2

1 Peter

3:20–21	xxviii, 2, 183
3:21	183

2 Peter

2:5–12	183
2:5	xxviii, 2, 203
3:6	xxviii, 2, 203
3:8–10	20

APOCRYPHA

Sirach

16:7	152
44:17–18	4

Wisdom of Solomon

14:6–7	152

3 Maccabees

2:4	152

PSEUDEPIGRAPHA

1 Enoch

89:5–6	152

Jubilees

5:28	171
7:1	171

DEAD SEA SCROLLS

1QapGen	171
4Q370	152

GRECO-ROMAN WRITINGS

Aristotle, *Rhetoric* 1.9.1257b	50

www.ingramcontent.com/pod-product-compliance
Lightning Source LLC
Chambersburg PA
CBHW061431300426
44114CB00014B/1637